THE DEVELOPMENT OF THE ITALIAN
SCHOOLS OF PAINTING

MADONNA AND CHILD
Detail of Giovanni Bellini's triptych of 1488 in the Frari church in Venice.

Photo Böhm.

THE DEVELOPMENT

OF THE

Italian Schools
of Painting

BY

RAIMOND VAN MARLE

Doctor of the Faculty of Letters of the University of Paris

———————

VOLUME XVII

With 8 collotype plates and 309 illustrations

HACKER ART BOOKS

NEW YORK

1970

First published by Martinus Nijhoff
The Hague 1935
Reprinted by Hacker Art Books
New York 1970

Library of Congress Catalog Card Number—70-116366
SBN: 0-8717-048-0

TABLE OF CONTENTS

The Venetian Schools   I

Chapter   I: Giovanni d'Alemagna and Antonio Vivarini,
                Quirizio da Murano and Antonio da Negro-
                ponte   3

Chapter   II: Jacopo Bellini 56

Chapter   III: Gentile Bellini and Mansueti 132

Chapter   IV: Giovanni Bellini 201

Chapter   V: The Workshop and Pupils of Giovanni Bellini 359

Chapter   VI: Cima da Conegliano 392

Chapter   VII: Marco Basaiti 482

Additions 516

Indices 519

N.B. The terms "right" and "left" are used from the standpoint of the spectator unless the contrary be stated.

THE VENETIAN SCHOOL

THE VENETIAN SCHOOL [1]

If the early Venetian school played but a small part in the history of painting prior to the Renaissance, a change which was hardly expected took place in the 15th century.

[1] B. *Berenson*, V. Painting chiefly before Titian, The Study and Criticism of Italian Art, I, London, 1912, p. 90. *The Same*, V. Painting in America, London, 1916. *T. Borenius*, La mostra di dipinti v. primitivi al Burlington Fine Arts Club, Rassegna d'Arte, 1912, p. 88. *M. Boschini*, Le minere della pittura, Venice, 1664. *Burlington Fine Arts Club*, Early Venetian Pictures (Catalogue of the exhibition, 1912), London, 1912. *Exhibition* of Venetian Art, New Gallery, 1895 (catalogue). *G. Fiocco*, L'esposizione d'arte al Burlington Arts Club di Londra, L'Arte, 1914, p. 382. *The Same*, Le propaggini dell' arte di Alb. Dürer nel Veneto, Atti del X congresso intern. di stor. dell' arte, Rome, 1922, p. 219. *The Same*, L'arte di A. Mantegna, Bologna, 1927. *G. Fiocco e R. Longhi*, Lettere pittoriche, Vita Artistica, Nov.-Dec. 1926, pp. 127, 144. *P. Flat*, Les premiers Vénetiens, Paris, 1899. *G. Fogolari*, La pittura v. in America, Rassegna d'Arte, 1920. *M. Grünewald*, Das Kolorit in der v. Malerei, Nuov. Arch. Venet., XXXIII, 1912. *D. von Hadeln*, V. Zeichungen des Quattrocento, Berlin, 1925. *R. Longhi*, Piero dei Franceschi e lo sviluppo della pittura v., L'Arte, 1914, pp. 198, 241. *G. Lorenzetti*, Venezia e il suo estuario, Venice, Milan, etc. (1926). *G. Ludwig*, Arhival Beitrage zu Gesch. der v. Malerei, Jahrb. der K. Preus. Kunstsamml., 1903. *The Same*, Archival. Beiträge zu Gesch. der v. Kunst, Berlin, 1911. *E. March Phillipps*, The V. School of Painting, London, 1912. *Michiel* (l'Anonimo Morelliano), Notizie d'opere di disegno. *Molmenti*, Le origini della pittura v., Venice, 1890. *The Same*, I primi pittori v., Rassegna d'Arte, 1903, p. 129. *Monticolo*, Il capitolare delle arti dei pittori a V., Nuovo Archiv. Veneto, II, 1891, p. 321. *G. Moschini*, Guida per la città di V., 2 vols. Venice, 1815. *P. Paoletti*, La scuola grande di S. Marco, Venice, 1929. *P. Paoletti e G. Ludwig*, Neue archivalische Beiträge zur Geschichte der venezianischen Malerei, Repert. f. Kunstwiss., XXII, 1899; XXIII, 1900. *The Same*, Raccolti di documenti inediti per servire alla stor. della pitt. v. nel sec. XV e XVI, Padua, 1894. *P. Pinton*, Nuov. Arch. Venet., I, 1891. *C. Ridolfi*, La maraviglia dell'arte 1648, ed. von Hadeln, 2 vols., Berlin, 1914. *M. Salmi*, La pittura v. in Puglia, Rassegna d'Arte, 1920, p. 209. *Sansovino*, V. città nobilissima, Venice, 1591. *E. Schaeffer*, Die Frau in der v. Malerei, Munich, 1899. *G. Soràvia*, Le chiese di V., 3 vols., Venice, 1822—24. *E. Tea*, La mostra

In previous volumes, I have pointed out that, with the exception of the mosaics in S. Marco, the very conservative Venetian primitives were of but minor interest. The Byzantine domination lasted until the end of the 14th century and although there were one or two more outstanding artists such as the fairly skilful "Trecentisti" Maestro Paolo and Lorenzo Veneziano and the charming exponent of the late Gothic current, Giambono, generally speaking there was little above mediocrity until the period of the transition from the calligraphic international Gothic style, so brilliantly represented in Venice by foreigners like Gentile da Fabriano and Pisanello, to the Renaissance of the Quattrocento.

This transition was upheld in Venice by Antonio Vivarini and Jacopo Bellini.

Other influences contributed to making the school of Venice, until now of so little importance, the second in all Italy and the rival of that of Florence which, besides, it greatly surpassed in the following century.

However such geniuses as Giorgione and Titian descend directly from the great Venetian masters of the 15th century.

d'arte antica a V., Rassegna d'Arte, 1920, p. 296. *L. Testi*, Storia della pittura v., 2 vols., Bergamo, 1909. *G. de la Tourelle*, L'Orient et les peintres de V., Paris, 1924. *L. Venturi*, Le origini della pittura v., Venice, 1907. *A. M. Zanetti*, Della pittura v., Venice, 1771. *F. Zanotto*, Storia della pittura v., Venice, 1837. *The Same*, Pinacoteca Veneta, 2 vols., Venice, 1858—60. *E. Zimmermann*, Die Landschaftmalerei in der v. Malerei, Leipzig, 1893.

CHAPTER I

GIOVANNI D'ALEMAGNA AND ANTONIO VIVARINI (¹), QUIRIZIO DA MURANO AND ANTONIO DA NEGROPONTE.

On account of their close collaboration in the creation of many paintings, the identification of the two artistic personalities Giovanni d'Alemagna and Antonio Vivarini, is rather difficult.

We have a certain number of documents and a still greater number of dated works signed by them together, but we possess no authentic painting by Giovanni alone.

We know nothing regarding the origin of Giovanni d'Alemagna and we are not even certain that he was German by birth. I think that his name has contributed very much to the suggestion

---

(¹) *F. Babudri*, Il polittico di A. da M. a Parenzo, Pagine Striane, Nos. 6—9 (1910). *B. Berenson*, G. and A. da M., Venetian Painting in America, London, 1916, p. 5. *Brandolese*, Dubbi sull' esistenza del pittore Giovanni Vivarini da M. etc., Padua, 1807. *Cagnola*, Un opera inedita della scuola di Murano, Rassegna d'Arte, III, 1903, p. 166. *G. Fogolari*, G. d'A. Thieme-Becker, Künstlerlexikon, I, p. 165. *V. Lazzarini, C. Gebhardt*. G. d. A. Zeitschr. f. Kunstwiss., V, 1912 p. 395. Rassegna d'Arte, VI, 1906, Sept. issue, on cover (documents) *G. Lorenzetti*, Un nuovo documento su G. d'A.(?), L'Arte, XIII, 1910, p. 285. *G.Ludwig*, Jahrb. der K. Preus. Kunstsamml., XXVI, 1905, Beiheft, p. 13. *G. Milanesi*, Commentario alla vita di Vittore Carpaccio: Vasari ed. Milanesi, III, p. 666. *Paoletti u. Ludwig*, Neue Archivalische Beiträge etc., Repert. f. Kunstwiss., XXII, p. 427. *F. M. Perkins*, Un polittico di A. V., Rassegna d'Arte, 1909, p. 88. *The Same*, A Painting by A. V., Art in America, XXII. p. 12. *L. Planiscig*, Un polittico sconosciuto di A. V. e di G. d'A, Bollettino d'Arte del Minist. della Pubbl. Istr., March 1922, p. 427. *The Same*, La pala di San Gerolamo gia a S. Stefano a Venezia opera di A. V., idem, March 1923, p. 405. *G. Sinigaglia*, De' Vivarini pittori da Murano, Bergamo, 1905. *A. Venturi*, Un opera di A. e Bartolomeo Vivarini nell'Isola d'Arbe, L'Arte, XXII, 1919, p. 226.

that we should look for obviously Northern elements in his art, the actual presence of which several critics believe they detect. According to Professor Moschetti, he might have been born in Padua and was perhaps the son of Giovanni di Niccolò d'Alle-magne who lived there before 1423 ([1]), but this hypothesis has been abandoned ([2]). In 1417 a painter of the same name received the citizen-ship of Venice which necessitated a domicile of fifteen years in the town ([3]), but we are in no way sure that this is the same person. It is somewhat strange that in his earlier works Giovanni signs himself as "from Murano" and only after 1445 does he make any reference to his German origin. In a document he is described as "theuthonicus", consequently "d'Alemagna" was not only a name but a denomination given him on account of his birth place.

Our first certain knowledge of Giovanni d'Alemagna ([4]) is the appearance of his name united with that of Antonio Vivarini on two altar-pieces in the church of S. Stefano, one of which was dedicated to St. Monica and is mentioned by both Sansovino and Ridolfi ([5]); the former speaks of the ancient dresses of the Vene-tians depicted in this work while the latter refers to the small scenes from the life of the saint.

Further, we find his name, chiefly his signature in connexion with paintings executed between 1441 and 1446 in Venice and between 1447 and 1450 in Padua where he and Antonio were inscribed in the roll of painters and where he died before the 9th of June 1450. He appears constantly associated with Antonio Vivarini whose sister he married.

As to Antonio Vivarini he descends from a Paduan family which however had been settled in Murano for three generations. His father's name was Michele and that of his grandfather, An-tonio. His younger brother was the equally well known painter, Bartolomeo. We do not know when Antonio was born; it might

([1]) *A. Moschetti*, Nuovo Archivio Veneto, N.S., No. 29, p. 147.

([2]) *C. Gebhardt*, Monatsh. f. Kunstwiss., V, p. 395.

([3]) *Lorenzetti*, op. cit.

([4]) For Giovanni d'Alemagna v. specially *Testi*, op. cit., p. 304.

([5]) *Ridolfi*, ed. von Hadeln, II, p. 37. His account of Antonio and Giovanni d'Alemagna, whom he calls Giovanni Vivarini, is particularly short and inaccurate.

have been around 1415 as Testi, for not very obvious reasons, supposes, but his decline which becomes evident as early as 1464 and alarming in 1467, leads us to believe that the date of his birth must have been earlier. From 1441 onward we find him working in collaboration with Giovanni d'Alemagna.

In 1446 he marries, at least a document informs us of the fact that he makes a settlement in favour of his wife. At this time he is living at Sta. Maria Formosa and he is still there in 1461. In 1446 his son Alvise (or Luigi) is born; he too is to become a famous painter; later on another son and a daughter are born. Apart from the signatures on his paintings his name appears as witness in 1453, as bridegroom for the second time in 1461 and as heir to the widow Simeone di Ludovico in 1465 and 1466. From the will of his second wife, which dates from the 24th April 1484, it is evident that Antonio is deceased, while the text of the inscription of his son, Alvise, when he entered the school of Sta. Maria della Carità in 1476, leads us to believe that Antonio was still alive at this date. This, however, is not quite certain. Nor can we have absolute faith in Sansovino's vague statement that "in S. Apollinare Antonio Vivarini del 1470 lasciò diverse opere" etc.; he does not even mention the subjects of these works although he tells us that they were damaged by age. Consequently, the last reliable date we have concerning Antonio is that of 1466 in connexion with the will of the widow Simeone although it is, as we shall see, just possible that he signed a picture in Andria in 1467. But as the regular stream of dated references abruptly stops here I think it suggests that Antonio's career ended around 1470 and possibly even before ([1]).

There are two works which we know Antonio executed alone; at least his is the only name in the signature and there are so many instances when he has added the name either of Giovanni d'Alemagna or of his brother Bartolomeo when they collaborated

---

([1]) As *Testi*, op. cit., p. 320, observes, there is not sufficient reason to identify a "Magister Antonius pictor di Muriano" mentioned in 1472 with our artist; it might refer sooner to a painter of that name living in the S. Cassiano quarter. The inscription with the date 1467 on the panels from Andria, now in the museum of Bari, is a recent addition (v. *Castelfranco*, Bollettino d'Arte. Dec. 1927, p. 294) and not, as *Testi*, op. cit., p. 320 and note 6, affirms, an authentic signature.

with him, that we can assume that he worked alone when no other name is inscribed in the signature. It is for this reason, then, that we can consider as entirely from his hand the polyptych of 1443 or 1445 at Parenzo and the triptych of 1464 in the Vatican Gallery; the obvious difference in style can be explained by the evolution which occurred in his art during the lapse of over twenty years which separates these productions. When we compare these two works with those which Antonio signed together with Giovanni d'Alemagna we are somewhat perplexed; certainly their close collaboration resulted in an almost perfect harmony and similarity. None the less, in most cases it is not impossible to differentiate the two hands. Antonio is smoother in technique, more flowing in line and more regular in the treatment of the rather rotund features of his subjects. At the same time he is the more purely Italian of the two and he comes nearer to such fellow countrymen as Gentile da Fabriano, Giambono and other Venetians than Giovanni d'Alemagna. However, it is easier to recognize Antonio's share in the polyptych at Bologna which is a production of his collaboration with his brother Bartolomeo.

One of the two altar-pieces which, according to Sansovino and Ridolfi, were executed in 1441 in the church of S. Stefano in Venice, has been recognized recently by Dr. Planiscig as that in the "Estensische Sammlung" in Vienna now in the gallery (fig. 1) [1]. Only the former of these two ancient authors furnishes us with the date but both are very precise in affirming that Antonio and Giovanni together executed this work. Sansovino adds that Gaspare Moranzone carried out the sculpture of the "altare" which no doubt means the frame.

The difference between the various panels is so slight that Dr. Planiscig cannot bring himself to admit that more than one painter took part in the execution and he gives the entire work to Antonio. We might all, in fact, be tempted to do likewise but once we have an indication to look for two different hands I think we can find them. The three half-length figures — the Madonna (fig. 2) between SS. John the Baptist and Antony of Padua — in the upper part of the polyptych are smoother,

---

[1] *Planiscig*, op. cit., Bollettino, 1923.

Fig. 1. Antonio Vivarini and Giovanni d'Alemagna, Madonna and Saints.
Museum, Vienna.   Museum Photo.

Fig. 2. Detail of fig 1.   Museum Photo.

Fig. 3. Antonio Vivarini, Madonna and Saints. Cathedral, Parenzo.

Photo Alinari.

sweeter and of more fluent line than the St. Jerome between the
two other standing saints — perhaps SS. Mark and Ambrose —
who occupy the principal panels and who in appearance are more
monumental with better plastic effects but at the same time are
less graceful and somewhat lifeless. It is all the more necessary to
admit that the slight differences we discover in this case constitute two distinct individualities because it is an extremely ardu-
ous task to differentiate the two hands in the other pictures
which we know to be the outcome of their combined labours.

It is just possible that also a fragment of the second altar-piece
from S. Stefano — that dedicated to St. Monica — still exists. In
the Accademia of Venice there is a predella panel (50) on which
a 17th century inscription informs us that it represents the
marriage of St. Monica, so that not only the subject corresponds
but we find as well some examples of ancient Venetian costumes
which seem to have impressed Sansovino. This small panel, which

has greatly suffered, has been so much restored that no serious attribution to either of the artists is any longer possible.

I imagine that among the earliest works of Antonio Vivarini we should include the charming little panel of the Nativity of the Virgin in the collection of Viscount Lee of Fareham, Richmond[1]; in this simple scene we meet with the same stylistic peculiarities which strike us in his panels in the gallery of Vienna. I feel somehow that this is a very early production and was executed probably even prior to the polyptych in the cathedral of Parenzo, the date of which is not quite certain because the last figure has practically disappeared; it has been read sometimes as 1443 and sometimes as 1445 (fig. 3) [2] but the name is quite distinct. The inscription runs: "*144 .... Anthonis de Murano pinxit hoc o ....*". Below, in the centre the Virgin is seated holding the nude Child standing on her knee; to the sides SS. Nicholas of Bari, a prophet, St. Francis and St. James each occupy a panel. Above, the half-length figure of Christ half-arisen from His tomb forms the centre, while to the sides are those of SS. Mary Magdalene, Christopher, Antony Abbot and Catherine. The figures are still less animated than those of the Viennese altar-piece and in this they closely resemble the parts which, I decided, were by Giovanni d'Alemagna, whereas the full soft features and anatomy of Christ as well as the Gothic element in the drapery seem to confirm my opinion with regard to Antonio's authorship of the three panels in Vienna.

Bearing a strong resemblance to the lateral saints at Parenzo are four polyptych panels in the F. L. Bacon collection, New York [3], formerly in the Nevin collection, Rome [4]; although here the figures are shown in full-length there is even a decided correspondence in the choice of the saints; they are SS. Christhopher, Nicholas of Bari, James and Antony Abbot.

---

[1] *T. Borenius*, A Catalogue of the Pictures etc. collected by Viscount, and Viscountess Lee of Fareham, II, 1926, No. 74, attributed it to Masolino. *Longhi*, Vita Artistica, Nov. 1926, p. 128, recognized its true author. v. Vol. IX, p. 302, note 2.

[2] *Testi*, op. cit., p. 332, gives a facsimile of the signature.

[3] *Perkins*, op. cit., Rassegna d'Arte, 1909.

[4] No. 38 of the catalogue of the sale of the Nevin collection, Rome April 1907.

I am of opinion that all these paintings are of an earlier date than the group of works which Antonio Vivarini and Giovanni d'Alemagna executed between 1443 and 1444 for the church of S. Zaccaria and more particularly for the chapel of S. Tarasio which has since become an independent church. The inscription on the principal altar-piece was restored in 1839 but no doubt the original wording has been more or less faithfully repeated. It gives the name of the prioress, Helena Foscari and of the abbess Marina Donato as those who ordered the picture; it mentions a Lodovicus de For. . . . . as the sculptor while the signature of the two painters runs: "*Johannes et Anthonius de Mur. pinxerunt, MCCCCXLIII*". We gather that neither the figures of the date nor all these words were clearly legible prior to the restoration but the copier cannot have mistaken the date by more than a year because Cicogna has found evidence that the chapel was decorated in 1444. In this particular work the sculptor had much more to do than the painter. The enormous tabernacle, full of decorations and terminals and containing many figures of saints, frames but one Madonna and four panels of painted figures. As a matter of fact this imposing retable is representative of the transition from the sculptured reredos, usual in Venice, to the painted altar-pieces. The Madonna is of a curious appearance and of the same type as that shown in the works of Lorenzo Veneziano; in fact, Testi and other critics believe that it is by this master of the previous generation. However, although the type of the Virgin is that of an earlier period, her general appearance is very different and here we should remember, as is not often done, that Cicogna informs us that the Madonna and the saint to either side — SS. Martin and Blaise — were entirely repainted in the restoration of 1839 (¹) and we have no difficulty in believing this statement. Consequently there remain only the two out-side figures — SS. Mark and Elizabeth — to be taken into consideration and they correspond sooner to those parts which, in the Viennese polyptych, I was inclined to ascribe to Giovanni d'Alemagna.

The back of the altar-piece is adorned with a great number of painted panels arranged in four rows (fig. 4) the lowest of which is a predella with scenes from the legend of a saint; the other

(¹) *Cicogna*, Iscrizioni Veneziane, IV, p. 692; II, p. 144.

Fig. 4.   School of Antonio Vivarini and Giovanni d'Alemagna, polyptych.
S. Zaccaria, Venice.   Photo Alinari.

Fig. 5. Antonio Vivarini and Giovanni d'Alemagna, triptych. S. Zaccaria, Venice.   Photo Anderson.

panels show figures of God the Father, of Christ, from Whose wounds the blood flows into chalices held by angels, of many saints and of some angels. Old-time authors, as for example Moschini and Cicogna, misread under two of the panels the word "inocentes" for the name "Joanes", consequently their attribution of all these panels to Giovanni d'Alemagna which was based on this mistake is without any value. It is a school work, inferior to the productions of either of the masters, and not all by one hand ([1]).

The inscription on the second retable which mentions Margherita Donata, a nun in the convent of S. Zaccaria as donor, begins with the words: "*Johanes et Antonius De Murano pinxerunt 1443 M. October hoc opus*" (fig. 5). The letters seem to have been repainted over the original inscription; Cicogna insists that the date is correct and that others, who gave it as 1445, were mistaken. The central figure below is St. Sabina holding a palm leaf and standing on a round pedestal; four little angels hover around her and flowers are seen growing in the background. Platforms and flowers are also depicted in the lateral panels which are occupied by SS. Jerome and Achilles. Above we see the half-length figures of SS. Margaret and Catherine while in the centre an angel holds the inscription: "*Hic est sanguinis Xpi*". Although the frame is richly carved, the pictorial part is more important here than in the previous case.

For our knowledge of the art of the two brothers-in-law these paintings are not of great importance as they have lost much of their original character; no doubt this happened when they were restored in 1839. This too, is the case for the third altar-piece in which again the sculptor has had the lion's share. The inscription, in as far as the painters are concerned, is the same as in the previous retable; Agnesina Justiano is cited as the donor. The painted figures are Pope St. Caius with St. George and St. Achilles with Nero. The three young saints were attired as elegant noblemen of the painters' day but their appearance now is more or less early Victorian. The Resurrection and the dead Christ are sculptured in wood, as are also the other figures in the terminals of the rich frame.

Scarcely less repainted is the large picture of the Coronation of

[1] *Testi*, op. cit., p. 345.

Fig. 6. Antonio Vivarini and Giovanni d'Alemagna, Coronation of the
Virgin. S. Pantaleone, Venice.   Photo Anderson.

the Virgin in S. Pantaleone, which in 1444 the two painters,
together with the sculptor Cristoforo da Ferrara who made the
now lost frame, signed: "*Xpofol de Ferara i(n)taia. Zuane e Antonio de Murane p(i)nse 1444*" (fig. 6). However, when Giambono
was commissioned more or less to copy this panel (his work is

now in the gallery of Venice v. Vol. VII, fig. 247) there is question only of "Johannes theothonicus" as its author ([1]).

The Coronation of the Virgin was a favourite subject in the Venetian school from the 14th century onward but not often is it shown in such an elaborate composition; even Giambono has considerably reduced it in his copy. Yet as precedent to an almost equally grandiose conception might be cited either the fresco by Guariento or the painting of 1432 by Jacobello del Fiore in the gallery of Venice (v. Vol. VII, fig. 234).

However, there is a considerable difference between the picture by Giovanni and Antonio and the compositions of the older masters, and our artists reveal to us that they were not lacking in originality. The eight rows of angels and saints form, as it were, a vault around the very high throne on which God the Father is seated, His hands resting on the shoulder of Christ and of the Virgin. The space under the throne is occupied by numerous putti some of whom carry the instruments of the Passion. In as far as the actual condition of the work allows us to judge, I should say that Antonio Vivarini executed the principal group and probably also the four Church Fathers and Evangelists who are seated below.

In the gallery of Venice (625) we find the enormous canvas of the Madonna enthroned with angels and saints, which originates from the Scuola Grande della Carità; it is signed: "*M 446 Johanes Alamanus*: *Antonius D. Muriano* p. . . . ." ((figs. 7, 8). Although it is generally admitted, we cannot be certain that this is the same picture which the ancient writers — Michiel, Sansovino, Ridolfi, Boschini and Zanetti — mention as in the "Albergo" of this Scuola ([2]). Michiel calls it a panel and says that there is one saint to either side; instead it is a canvas and there are two saints on each side. The others, with the exception of Sansovino, ascribe the painting they saw in the "Albergo" to Jacobello del Fiore, whereas the picture now in the gallery is very clearly signed by Giovanni and Antonio. Perhaps there was another picture in the same albergo by Jacobello. Or did Ridolfi make a mistake when taking his information, as he often did, from Sansovino who just two lines above in his closely printed volume (ed. 1581, fol. 99

([1]) *Testi*, op. cit., p. 15.
([2]) *Testi*, op. cit., p. 356.

Fig. 7.   Antonio Vivarini, Madonna and Saints. Accademia, Venice.

Photo Alinari.

verso) happens to mention a picture by Jacobello? Boschini and
Zanetti repeat the statement which they may have copied from
the older author. All this is possible but it does not change in
any way the picture now in the gallery of Venice, on which we
find the authentic signature and date.

XVII.

It is of an elaborate composition; a fancy wall of Gothic design forms an enclosure; above, and through the openings of it we see trees and shrubs. The throne on which the Madonna is seated is very ornate and the nude Child Who stands on His Mother's knee, holds a pomegranate. Four small angels support the pillars of the baldaquin. To the left are depicted SS. Jerome and Gregory and to the right, SS. Ambrose and Augustine.

A difference of technique is noticeable, particularly in the treatment of the faces; those of the central group are smoother, more conventional in the regularity of the oval shape and much less modelled than the features of the lateral saints, in which the relief effects are more pronounced and which are more individual and less conventional.

If my first supposition is right then here we have to attribute the central part to Antonio and the lateral figures to Giovanni d'Alemagna. Although of course considerably evolved, the painters still clearly reveal in this work their attachment to the dying Gothic tradition and this is evident not only in such features as the wall, its decoration, the strangely ornate throne, the outline of the platform, on which all the figures are placed, and its open-work ornamentation, but also in the obvious taste for detail in dress, in the ornaments worn by the different persons and in the minuteness with which the vegetation is treated.

Continuing our examination of the signed and dated works, we now come to the polyptych which, up to the end of the 18th century, existed in the third chapel to the left in the church of S. Francesco, Padua. It was seen there by Michiel and is described in detail in several old guide books of Padua. After it had been lost for over a century, Dr. Planiscig fortunately discovered it in the chapel of the castle of Konopischt in Czecho-Slovakia (¹). The signature which is inscribed at the foot of the central panel runs: *"MCCCCXLVII Christoph. D Ferara itaia Antonio Da Mra e Johae Alaman p."*. The principal scene is that of the Madonna adoring the Child in front of an open shelter near which Joseph is shown in meditation; the shepherds receiving the glad tidings are shown in the background. SS. Francis, Bartholomew, Vincent Ferrer(?) (²) and Antony of Padua are depicted on the narrow

(¹) *Planiscig*, op. cit., Bollettino d'Arte, 1922.
(²) *Planiscig*, op. cit., identifies this saint as St. Bernardine but, for

Fig. 8. Detail of fig. 7. Photo Anderson.

lateral panels. As Dr. Planiscig observes, the picture is far from
being well preserved and as I know this work only from the

chronological reasons, this is hardly possible because the holy preacher
of Siena was not canonized till 1455. Besides, the figure here seems to
hold a radiating sun, the emblem of St. Vincent Ferrer and St. Thomas
Aquinas.

reproductions published by Dr. Planiscig, and these are not very clear, I shall abstain from attempting to differentiate the two hands. Dr. Planiscig is of the opinion that the centre is by Giovanni d'Alemagna and the lateral saints by Antonio Vivarini.

Antonio Ovetari, who died probably at the beginning of 1448, left a testamentary disposition that his chapel in the Eremitani church must be decorated with frescoes ([1]), and for this purpose the executors engaged in May of this year the up till now almost inseparable Giovanni and Antonio along with Nicolò Pizolo and Mantegna. Our two painters undertook the decoration of the ceiling, illustrations of the Passion over the entrance and medallions in the arch, but Giovanni died long before the ceiling was finished, the work having progressed very slowly probably owing to the latter's ill-health. Judging from the sum which Antonio was to receive if he finished the vault, apparently the greater part of the decoration had still to be carried out. Certainly by Giovanni and Antonio is the leaf ornamentation which frames the four triangles and which corresponds to the decoration in the canvas of 1446 in the gallery of Venice. Perhaps also by them are the eight angelic figures which we see in the angles but not the medallions with the Evangelists, that of St. Luke painting, which is the best preserved, being, I think, more Paduan in appearance ([2]).

No sooner had Giovanni died — which he did in 1450 — than Antonio finds a new partner, this time it is his younger brother Bartolomeo with whom he executes the same year, 1450, the polyptych now in the gallery of Bologna. But here we enter on the second phase of Antonio's career and before discussing this period I should like to mention a few more paintings which were executed during the years he was associated with Giovanni d'Alemagna.

The earliest of these works, which is very similar to the polyptych of Parenzo, is a triptych in a private collection. It shows three half-length figures — the Madonna with the Child in benediction in her arms and two female martyrs, one holding a book,

---

([1]) *Testi*, op. cit., p. 360, gives the reference to the documents.

([2]) Mr. Berenson is of opinion that only the ornaments and foliage are by Giovanni and Antonio.

Fig. 9. Antonio Vivarini, Madonna and two Saints. Private Collection.

the other a vase of flowers, probably St. Dorothy (fig. 9). The forms are very simple and the soberness of the drapery reminds us to a certain extent of that of the previous century. The plastic effects recall the artist whom I suppose to be Giovanni d'Alemagna but the smoothness of the faces and the flowery contours seem to make the attribution to Antonio more acceptable.

A delightful picture in the P. Strauss, collection, New York, formerly in that of the Earl of Northesk, is the Madonna depicted in full-face wearing a dress of a large flowered pattern and adoring the Child Who lies on her knee (fig. 10). The throne is of a pronounced Gothic design and is mounted on that curious open-work

Fig. 10. Antonio Vivarini, Madonna. P. Strauss Collection,
New York.   Photo Offner.

Fig. 11. Antonio Vivarini, Madonna. Pinacoteca, Città di
Castello   Photo Minist. Ed. Naz.

platform, an example of which we have already found in Antonio's works. The Gothic elements, as well as the type of the
Virgin clearly indicate that this painting belongs to Antonio's
early phase and not, as Mr. Perkins assumes, to his "ripest
period" (¹).

Very much less charming is the enthroned Madonna in the
gallery of Città di Castello (fig. 11). Here the Virgin is represented
in three-quarter left profile with the podgy and fully dressed
Child standing on her knee (²). Much attention has been paid to
the decorative element as for example the crown which is in
relief, the abundant ornamentation of the throne and the material
of the Virgin's dress which is of a flowered design with circular
inscriptions in Gothic letters. Mr. Berenson supposes that this
panel was executed in collaboration with Giovanni d'Alemagna.
The figure of the Virgin recalls that which forms the centre of
the large canvas of 1446 and the work may very well have been
executed around this date.

Two half-length figures of holy bishops — one of whom is
St. Nicholas — which have been cut into ovals, hang in the
sacristy of Sta. Maria delle Salute in Venice and show in execution and in type considerable resemblance to the lateral figures
of the same canvas which I believe to be by Giovanni d'Alemagna,
consequently these two holy bishops might also be by this master.

A particularly fine work is the triptych which is now divided
between the Poldi Pezzoli Gallery where we find the central
Madonna (589) (fig. 12) and the National Gallery, London, which
possesses the two lateral panels (768, 1284), on which are depicted
St. Jerome with St. Peter (fig. 13) and St. Francis with St. Mark.
This altar-piece was described in detail by Boschini in his "Minere
della pittura", (p. 104), who tells us that it was on an altar to
the left in the church of S. Mosè. Cavalcaselle saw the picture
still complete in the Molteni collection, Milan, and leaves us in
no doubt as to the identification of the lateral panels one of
which (768) passed through the Zambeccari collection, Bologna
and the Eastlake collection, London, before entering the National
Gallery, while the other was acquired from Dr. G. P. Richter.
The resemblance to the central figure of the canvas of 1446 is

(¹) *Perkins*, op. cit., Art in America, 1927.
(²) *Toesca*, L'Arte, VI, 1903, p. 248.

Fig. 12. Antonio Vivarini, Madonna and Angels. Poldi Pezzoli
Gallery, Milan.

Fig. 13. Giovanni d'Alemagna, two Saints. National Gallery, London.

Photo National Gallery.

again very evident. The nude Child stands however on the other knee of the Virgin, the positions are slightly different, the form of the ornate throne has changed and here two angels look over the sides but the types, draping and open-work platform are very similar. Flowers in the background and ornate Gothic platforms of a considerable height are seen in the two panels in the National Gallery. The SS. Peter and Jerome might be by Giovanni d'Alemagna but the SS. Francis and Mark bear a striking resemblance to the half-length figures of the polyptych of 1441 in Vienna; we observe the same curiously low-shaped heads and the same peculiar features and expression.

There is a certain connexion between the Madonna of Città di Castello and a triptych which shows in the centre the standing figures of St. Ursula and some of her companions and in the wings SS. Peter and Paul. This work is pre-served in the seminary of S. Angelo in Brescia. The robe of St. Ursula is decorated in the same manner as that of the Virgin at Città di Castello. It has been supposed that this triptych is a very early work of Antonio or else an outcome

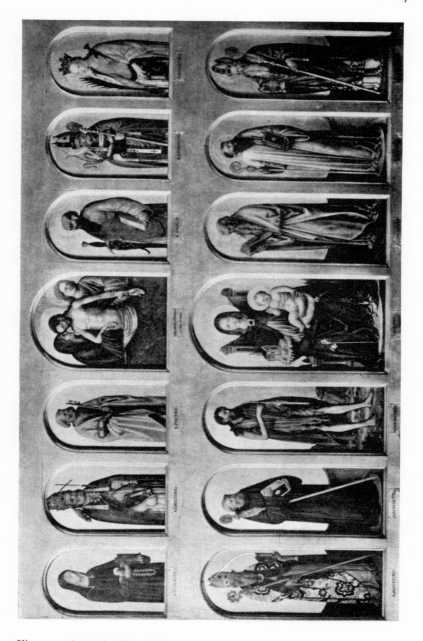

Fig. 14.   Antonio Vivarini and Giovanni d'Alemagna, Madonna and
Saints. Brera Gallery, Milan.   Photo Alinari.

of the combined efforts of Antonio and Giovanni d'Alemagna or Antonio and Bartolomeo ([1]). I do not think that any of these opinions is correct. The principal artist is certainly Antonio Vivarini but I cannot say who collaborated with him. It might have been the anonymous artist who painted probably alone the triptych of the Annunciation with SS. Francis and Michael in the church of S. Giobbe, Venice, which work, however, Mr. Berenson believes to be by Antonio and Giovanni.

There are two paintings which no doubt were executed during the Paduan period because one of them, a polyptych now in the Brera Gallery, Milan, originates from the abbey of Praglia, near Padua (fig. 14), while the other, a Madonna, is still to be found in the oratory of S. Filippo of this town. The latter is of the same type as the central figure of the canvas of 1446, of the Virgin of Città di Castello and of that in the Brera; the elaborate Gothic throne with its high pedestal and curved leaf decoration reminds us most of the first of these works, whereas the positions recall chiefly those of the Brera Madonna. The picture is attributed by Mr. Berenson to the two brothers-in-law and by Signor Testi partly to Giovanni d'Alemagna. Personally I think it more likely that at least the figures of the Madonna and Child are by Antonio. Moreover, when we take into consideration the fact that during the two years which Giovanni d'Alemagna spent in Padua he seems to have been so ill that even with Antonio's help he did not finish the decoration of the vault of the Eremitani chapel, we somehow get the impression that he would hardly have undertaken other works, especially not such a large enterprise as the polyptych from Praglia, the greater part of which Signor Testi ascribes to him. However, I do not think that Testi's division is correct. I am of the opinion that Antonio's manner can be recognized in the enthroned Madonna holding the model of the abbey and the small prior kneeling at her feet, in the Pietà and in the half-length figures of SS. Scolastica and Giustina, although something seems to have happened to the faces of these two saints. The four other half-length figures of SS. Gregory, Peter, Paul and Ambrose and the standing figures of SS. Augustine, Benedict, John the Baptist, Jerome, Bruno and Prodocimo are obviously homogeneous and if Giovanni had any share in the

([1]) For the different opinions v. *Testi*, op. cit., p. 333.

Fig. 15. Antonio Vivarini and Giovanni d'Alemagna, Adoration of the
Magi. Museum, Berlin.   Museum Photo.

execution we should have to ascribe all these figures to him. But I feel very doubtful whether we should assign this polyptych to the collaboration of these two masters because the entire work has a somewhat peculiar appearance; the Gothic element is less marked in the shape of the throne while the figures are more minute and daintier than usual and the colouring is softer and of finer quality.

We gather the impression that this is the beginning of a new phase in the art of Antonio rather than an unexpected artistic revival on the part of Giovanni who was at death's door.

Before leaving Giovanni d'Alemagna I should like to mention yet one picture which seems to be the outcome of his collaboration with Antonio but in which he seems to have had the greater share especially if, as I suppose is the case, it was the German who had the pronounced taste for an abundance of decorative effects. The picture I mean is the Adoration of the Magi in the gallery of Berlin (fig. 15). The event is shown in a very crowded composition; the Magi who have just arrived are followed by a throng of people marvellously attired and carrying flags and banners; the equipment of the horses is not less magnificent; the procession of knights reaches far into the distance; the sky is covered with angels; the landscape is extensive and a beautifully constructed town is depicted in the background. Much of the ornamentation, including the nimbi of God the Father and the Holy Ghost, are worked in relief. Many details in this painting are borrowed from Gentile's famous picture of this subject which the artist obviously knew. There are as well elements which are markedly reminiscent of Antonio Vivarini but at the same time do not seem to be actually from his hand and I should not be surprised if this somewhat barbaric-looking achievement were the work of Giovanni d'Alemagna when he had been but for a short time an adherent of Italian art.

Giovanni d'Alemagna, however, remains something of a mystery. Which part he really executed of the pictures he signed together with Antonio Vivarini is far from certain. The diversity of manner which can be observed in different parts is sufficiently small to allow us believe that it is only a slight variation in the work of one artist and I do not exclude the possibility that Giovanni was the master who undertook the decorative part

Fig. 16. Antonio and Bartolomeo Vivarini, Madonna and Saints. Gallery, Bologna.   Photo Anderson.

which, in all the works due to the collaboration of the two brothers-in-law, is very important and of real artistic value.

Moreover, we notice the absence of this abundance of decoration in the polyptych of Parenzo, which is signed by Antonio alone, and this element is also absent, or at least almost so, in all the works which Antonio executed after Giovanni's death. At the same time we observe in Antonio's art a diminution in the Gothic effects; this is particularly evident in the shape of the throne which becomes purely Renaissance in style and acquires the character of a real seat with depth, whereas before it produced more the effect of a frame.

The first production of Antonio's collaboration with his younger brother, Bartolomeo, is the polyptych of 1450 which Pope Nicholas V gave to the Certosa of Bologna and which is now in the town gallery (205) (fig. 16). Besides the name of the donor, the inscription at the foot of the central panel mentions very clearly the names of the two painters and the date of execution, it runs: "*Anno domini MCCCCL Hoc op. inceptum fuit et perfectum Venetiis ab Antonio et Bartolomeo Fra. ib (Fratribus) De Murano*" etc.

If we examine with close attention the different parts of this polyptych we notice that in general appearance and in neatness of execution, it shows a marked resemblance to the above mentioned altar-piece in the Brera Gallery and we are led to suppose that around the year 1450, that is to say when Giovanni's death ended the partnership, a new phase seems to have set in in Antonio Vivarini's art. We might have been inclined to look for the influence of the younger brother, Bartolomeo, were it not for the fact that, born in 1431 or 1432, he was only about eighteen years old at this time and his collaboration with Antonio could only have been that of pupil and master. Also in this polyptych it is not easy at first sight to differentiate the two hands. However, a more minute examination reveals to us that one of the four figures standing below, the St. Jerome, is very different in style and psychology from Antonio's art; it is stronger in build, the expression of the third dimension, especially in the formation of the head, is more marked and the plastic elegance is more evident. I think that Bartolomeo should be held responsible also for St. Augustine and probably for the bodies of St. John the Baptist, whose legs are very sinewy, and of St. Nicholas. The heads of the two last saints seem to be by Antonio who executed

Fig. 17.   Antonio and Bartolomeo Vivarini, polyptych.   St. Eufemia
Convent, Island of Arbe.   Photo Minist. Ed. Naz.

the rest of the polyptych: the Madonna enthroned adoring the
Child Who lies sleeping on her knee, the two small angels holding
a crown over her head, the half-length figures of the dead Saviour
and two angels, SS. Peter, Gregory, a holy bishop and St. Paul.
The Gothic effect of the enormous carved tabernacle does not
allow us at a first glance to realize that in the painting itself the
Gothicism is considerably reduced; the throne is purely Renaissance in form but in one of the panels below the Gothic design
is very noticeable.

XVII.

3

Two years later the brothers signed the pictorial part of a triptych in the Cagnola collection, Milan (¹); it comprises the figures of SS. Philip and Augustine on the lateral panels and is signed: "*MCCCCLII Bartholomeus et Antonius Fratres De Murano pinxerunt*". In all probability the more robust St. Philip is by Bartolomeo and the smoother St. Augustine by Antonio; anyhow the head of the latter saint seems to be typical of the elder brother's art. The central part of this work is composed of the figures of the Annunciation in sculpture.

In 1458 Antonio and Bartolomeo together signed a polyptych in the convent of St. Eufemia on the Island of Arbe, off the coast of Dalmatia (²). It is not a very fine production and shows but little inspiration (fig. 17). By Antonio are certainly the central figure of St. Bernardine, the half-length figure of the Virgin above, the SS. Peter and Christopher of the four full-length figures standing below, the head and hand of the female martyr above and the bust of the holy bishop (St. Louis of Toulouse?). The half-length figures of SS. Jerome and John the Baptist, the full-length SS. Francis and Antony of Padua and the body of the female martyr above seem to be by Bartolomeo.

Six polyptych panels, representing the full-length figures of SS. Nicholas, Peter, Paul and George and the busts of SS. Catherine and Mary Magdalene, which are preserved in the Collegiata of SS. Pietro, Paolo and Donato at Pausola in The Marches, have the general appearance of the works of Antonio Vivarini but, as is often the case in paintings destined for small centres, they are of somewhat mediocre quality (³). According to a manuscript description written by a priest of the name of Bartolozzi, the picture once upon a time showed the inscription: "*Hoc opus factum fuit tempore Dni Jacobi Mari de Murano prepositi 1462*"(⁴).

(¹) *Cagnola*, op. cit., Rassegna d'Arte, 1906. *Testi*, op. cit., p. 387. I know this work only from reproduction.

(²) *A. Venturi*, op. cit., L'Arte, XXII, omits to say that the picture is signed and dated.

(³) Attributed to Antonio by *Cavalcaselle e Morelli*, Gallerie Naz. Ital., II, pp. 27 and 43. *Crowe and Cavalcaselle*, op. cit., ed. Borenius, I, p.32, to Antonio and Bartolomeo. *Cagnola*, Rassegna d'Arte, 1903, p. 168, to the manner of Antonio, after having attributed it to Antonio himself.

(⁴) *G. M. Rushfort*, Carlo Crivelli, London, 1900, p. 13. *Astolfi*, L'Arte, V, 1902, p. 193. *Testi*, op. cit., p. 388.

Fig. 18. Antonio Vivarini, polyptych. Gallery, Città del Vaticano.
Photo Anderson.

Very probably it is a work executed by the two brothers; the figure of St. Peter is the most characteristic of Bartolomeo who painted very likely also the St. Nicholas and possibly the St. Paul; the archangel and the two half-length figures are no doubt from the hand of Antonio.

Although we do not find the united signature of Antonio and Bartolomeo on other pictures, I think all the same they collaborated on one or two other occasions. The important polyptych

signed: *"1464 Antonius De Murano pinxit"*, which originates from
the church of the Confraternity of S. Antonio Abate in Pesaro
but is now in the Vatican Gallery, shows in the centre the figure
of St. Antony in sculpture while to the sides we see SS. Sebastian,
Christopher, Venantius and Roch in full-length figure and above,
the half-length figures of the dead Saviour, St. Jerome, St. Peter
and a holy bishop (St. Louis of Toulouse?) (fig. 18). The two
busts of SS. Jerome and Peter seem somewhat different from the
rest of the work and it is just possible that Bartolomeo, notwithstanding the signature, had a small share in the execution of this
altar-piece, in which, however, he adapted himself to Antonio's
manner. Technically speaking, this work has the usual qualities
of accuracy but there is a rigidity in attitude and outline as well
as a lack of charm and life, shortcomings which we notice here
for the first time. They are no doubt the earliest signs of Antonio's
artistic decline although his probable age at this moment would
hardly suggest the possibility.

Admitting this premature decadence, we might believe with
Mr. Berenson that it was Antonio who executed part of the
polyptych in the town hall of Osimo in The Marches but originally
in the Franciscan church of Sma. Annunziata, which, for I know
not what reason, is supposed to have been painted in 1464. The
part in question includes the half-length figures of the dead Christ
and St. Catherine and the entire figures of St. Peter and a Franciscan monk, probably St. Antony. This picture is often attributed
to Bartolomeo and helpers or to the school of Bartolomeo ([1])
but I think that again Mr. Berenson is right in assigning the rest
of it to Bartolomeo himself. If Antonio really executed those
panels for which we have held him responsible, then we are forced
to admit that in his later years he was influenced by the manner
of his younger brother; here in fact there is very little left of the
graceful Gothic line which charmed us in his earlier productions.

With this picture we should associate a panel of the half-length
figure of the dead Saviour -- no doubt a terminal of a polyptych —
in the Platt collection, Englewood, and another of St. Catherine
which in the last few years I have seen in the hands of different dealers. Both paintings are free copies of the corresponding
figures at Osimo.

([1]) *Cavalcaselle e Morelli*, op. cit., p. 249. *Testi*, op. cit., pp. 396, 489.

Fig. 19. Antonio Vivarini, two Saints. Museum, Bari.

Photo Minist. Ed. Naz.

In the later part of his career, certainly after Giovanni d'Alemagna's death in 1450 and probably several years after this date,
should, I think, be placed a half-length figure of the Madonna
with the nude Child seated on her hands in the Fine Arts Museum, Worcester, U.S.A., where it is attributed to Masolino, and
a picture of St. Mary Magdalene borne to heaven by six small
angels with a prioress kneeling in adoration in the rocky landscape
below, which is preserved in the museum of Berlin (1154) ([1]). The
latter originates from Sta Maria delle Verghini, Venice and was
ascribed to Giambono by Sansovino.

The polyptych panels which were transferred from the monastery of the Frati Minori of Andria to the Museum of Bari are of
such inferior quality that Dr. Castelfranco ([2]) denies the authorship of Antonio and assigns them to his workshop. They represent
the dead Saviour in bust length and the entire figures of SS. Francis, John the Baptist (fig. 19), Louis of Toulouse and Antony of
Padua; on the last mentioned panel we read the fairly recent
inscription: *"Ant' de Murano 1467"*. Belonging to the same
altar-piece is also the figure of St. Bernardine in the store-room([3]).
The central figure — perhaps in sculpture — the four lateral
half-length figures and one full-length figure were missing but
recently Dr. Castelfranco discovered three of the half-length
figures of saints — Augustine, Bernardine and Clare — in the
convent from which the other panels originate. The signature
with the date was probably taken from the inscription which, as
usual, must have been shown at the foot of the central panel. If
we have to hold Antonio responsible for even the better parts of
these panels, his decadence has made rapid steps in the three
years which separate these paintings from the none too beautiful
polyptych of 1464 in the Vatican Gallery. The figures of SS. Francis and John the Baptist at Bari and the bust of St. Augustine

---

([1]) According to Mr. Berenson this work was executed in collaboration
with Giovanni d'Alemagna but to me it seems to be of later date. *Testi*,
op. cit., p. 405, thinks it is more likely a school production.

([2]) *G. Frizzoni*, Bollettino d'Arte del Minist. della Pubbl. Istr., VIII,
1914, p. 33. *Castelfranco*, idem, N.S., VII, 1927, p. 294.

([3]) The bust of an adoring nun is a later addition to this panel regarding
which Dr. Castelfranco, I think, makes a mistake in saying that it represents St. Peter. There is a picture of this saint in the store-room but it
is smaller and quite different in appearance.

at Andria are slightly superior in inspiration, in design and in modelling to the wooden and lifeless figures of SS. Louis, Antony and the other saints. But as I said before his decline, which is again evident, must have been very premature if he was really born around the year 1415.

Somewhat superior, but no doubt of the same period, that is to say Antonio's last years which he must have spent in Apulia, is a polyptych in the parish church of Rutigliano (¹). This altar-piece is complete. The centre is occupied by the Madonna enthroned with the nude Child standing on her knee and although of poor quality it has none the less quite the character of a work by Antonio himself. The lateral saints are Francis, Christopher, Bernardine and Antony while above we see Christ resurrected and the half-length figures of SS. Lucy, Margaret, Nicholas and Cosmo.

The better parts of this polyptych, which are more especially the panels of the female saints, are certainly from Antonio's own hand; some of the other figures may have been left to a helper.

Antonio was a very productive artist and still quite a number of other works have been attributed to him (²).

(¹) *Salmi*, L'Arte, XXII, 1919, p. 165: workshop of the Vivarini, possibly with the help of Quirizio da Murano.

(²) **Altenburg,** Gallery, No. 157, Madonna (*Berenson*). **Baltimore,** Jacobs coll., polyptych, St. Michael slaying the dragon, the Madonna and eight saints (reprod. in *Berenson*, Venetian Painting in America, fig. 3, as by Giovanni d'Alemagna and Antonio Vivarini, but it seems to me to be a rather late production of the latter artist); Walters coll., No. 537, Madonna of Humility which I think nearer to Giambono; No. 693, St. Jerome (*Berenson* ascribes it to Giovanni d'Alemagna and A. Vivarini but I am rather doubtful). **Bassano,** Museum, triptych (*Berenson*). **Berlin,** ex-von Kaufmann coll., Madonna (*Testi*, op cit., p. 406). **Chartres,** Museum, No. 56, bust of St. Peter (*Berenson*). **Città del Vaticano,** Gallery, store-room, St. Peter cutting off ear; dead Christ (*Berenson*). **London,** Harewood coll., two monks in a landscape (part of stigmatization of St. Francis?; reprod. in Apollo, Feby. 1925, p. 66 and Oct. 1927, p. 160); for sale 1926, half-length figure of the Madonna, early (Burlington Magazine, June 1926, p. XLV). **Milan.** Brera Gallery, No. 226, two scenes from the life of St. Jerome (*Testi*, op, cit., p. 406); Municipal Museum, head of the Madonna (*Toesca*, L'Arte, VI, 1903, p. 250, says with Giovanni d'Alemagna; *Testi*, op. cit., p. 378, ascribes it to the school of Antonio); Cologna coll., Madonna seated lowly adoring the Child Who sleeps on her knee(?) (*F. Wittgens*, L'Arte, XXXII,

From old descriptions such as those of Sansovino, Boschini, etc., we learn that once upon a time there existed quite a number of other works by Antonio, either alone or in collaboration with Giovanni d'Alemagna or Bartolomeo ([1]).

There are many erroneous attributions to Antonio ([2]) and almost all the work of his school has at one time or another been ascribed to him.

The following works are very near to the master: the triptych with the Annunciation, which I have already mentioned, in the church of S. Giobbe, Venice, which Mr Berenson thinks is due to the collaboration of Antonio and Giovanni d'Alemagna (fig. 20); the triptych of St. Bernardine between SS. Jerome and Louis of Toulouse in the church of S. Francesco della Vigna, Venice, which is rather ordinary to ascribe to Antonio's own hand, more especially as it does not correspond in style to the master's mature manner; and a St. Lawrence in the gallery of Venice (20).

A production of Antonio's workshop is the large polyptych in

1929, p. 213). **Paris,** Louvre, No. 1640, St. Louis of Toulouse (*Toesca* and *Testi*, loc. cit., express same opinion as before); private coll., half-length figures of St. Antony of Padua and a holy bishop. **Philadelphia,** Johnson coll., St. Bernardine (*Berenson*) Catalogue, No. 154). **Rheims,** Museum, SS. James and Petronius (*Berenson*). **Verona,** S. Gerolamo Monastery, St. Christopher (*Berenson*).

([1]) They have already been enumerated by *Testi*, op. cit., pp. 367, 388, 397. *Sansovino*, ed. 1581, pp. 86a and 91a, speaks of pictures "dai Vivarini" without defining which.

([2]) For some of the wrong attributions v. also those which I include in Antonio Vivarini's school; besides these I shall cite: **Bergamo,** Accademia Carrara, St. Jerome and an old saint with a book (*Frizzoni*, op. cit.); it is rather an early work by Bartolomeo Vivarini. **Bologna,** Davia Bargellini Museum, No. 224, Madonna, by Bartolomeo. **Budapest,** Museum, No. 103, Madonna enthroned; *A. Venturi*, op. cit., says by Giovanni d' Alemagna but I think it is by Giambono; Nos. 119, 120, SS. Mary Magdalene and Lucy and their pendants SS. Catherine and Clare which are in the store-room, attributed to Antonio Vivarini in *von Terry's* catalogue; they are fine paintings of the Venetian school of the early 15th century and are near Giambono. **Ravenna,** Accademia di Belle Arti, No. 183, St. John weeping; as *Testi*, op. cit., p. 408, says, it has no connexion with Antonio and perhaps is not even Venetian. **Venice,** Accademia, No. 33, Coronation of the Virgin by Giambono with the false signature of Giovanni and Antonio da Murano, 1440, which has deceived some authors of a previous generation.

Fig. 20.   School of Antonio Vivarini, Annunciation. S. Giobbe, Venice.
Photo Alinari.

the museum of Lecce, which shows the figures of the Madonna,
the Trinity with adorers and twelve saints and in whic h Mr Be-

renson recognizes the combined hands of Antonio and Bartolomeo. Throughout this work we are constantly and strongly
reminded of these two painters but on a close examination there
is not one piece which can actually be considered the work of
either master. Still more mediocre and further removed from
Antonio are twelve panels of saints in the store-room of the museum of Berlin (1548, 1549, 1549a) (¹).

There are two picture which are rather puzzling. One of them
is found in the museum of Berlin (1058) and represents the
following six scenes from the lives of the Virgin and Jesus: the
Presentation of the Virgin in the Temple, the Coronation of the
Virgin, her Nativity, her Marriage, the Adoration of the Magi
and the Circumcision (fig. 21). Testi's attribution to Giambono is
not in my opinion correct; nor does Prof. L. Venturi's to Giovanni
d'Alemagna convince me even though there is an evident connexion with the Adoration of the Magi in the same museum,
which I think might be by this master. Although somewhat
gauche and ungraceful, the artist decidedly belongs to the same
group as Giovanni and Antonio da Murano.

Perhaps by the same hand, though painted in a manner nearer
to Antonio Vivarini's is an oblong panel representing in the centre
the Crucifixion and to the sides twelve scenes from the Passion,
narrating the events from the Last Supper to the Ascension,
which passed from the Corpus Domini Convent to the gallery of
Vienna but which was restored to Italy in 1919 and is now in
the Ca d'Oro, Venice. A great variety of attributions have been
assigned to this picture. They range from "Antonio himself"
(Berenson), to "nothing to do with Antonio" (Testi) while personally I think that this rather mediocre painting is a production
of Antonio's school (²). In the same category might be classified
a fairly large picture of the Madonna enthroned nursing the Child
in the sacristy of S. Lorenzo at Sebenico.

Very closely connected with our master is an enthroned
Madonna which was formerly in the Pálffy collection, Budapest

---

(¹) Attributed to Antonio by *L. Venturi*, Pitt. Venez., p. 116, but this
is contested by *Testi*, op. cit., p. 392.

(²) v. *Fogolari, Nebbia e Moschini*, La R. Galleria G. Franchetti alla
Ca d'Oro, Venice, 1929, p. 87, Antonio Vivarini (?). Here the bibliography
and the opinions of other writers are given.

but is now I believe in the gallery in that town; it was once upon a time ascribed to Antonio's own hand ([1]).

Three panels, illustrating some unidentified legend, in the Walters collection, Baltimore (1462—1464) are still further remote from Antonio. They date from about 1470 and show a profusion of contemporary architecture and costume ([2]). There is in fact very little in these paintings which reminds us of Antonio and I am not even certain that this hybrid work — as cassone panels so often are — was even executed in Venice.

A more evolved painter who still shows some connexion with Antonio Vivarini, especially in his morphological types, executed an important polyptych of the old Venetian form in the church of S. Andrea at Asola.

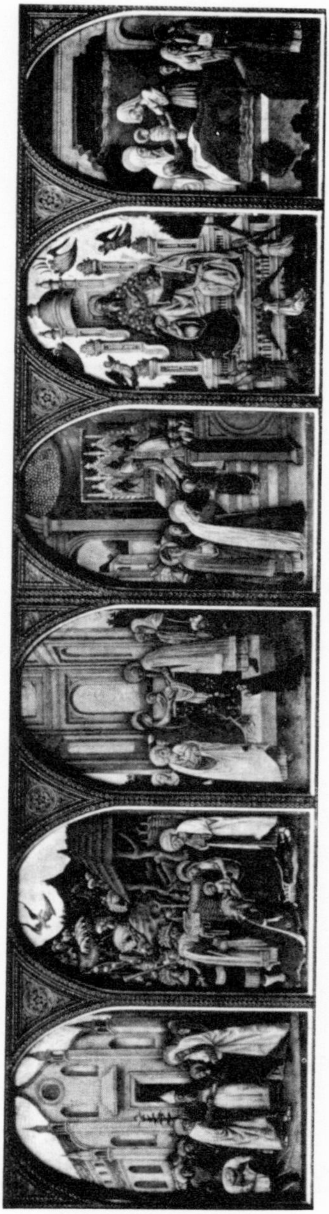

Fig. 21. Workshop of Antonio Vivarini, Scenes from the lives of Christ and the Virgin. Museum, Berlin.   Museum Photo

---

([1]) *A. Colasanti and T. Borenius*, Rassegna d'Arte, XII, 1912, p. 111, which attribution is contested by *Testi*, op. cit., p. 398.

([2]) *Berenson*, Venetian Painting in America, p. 13, states that he does not attribute these paintings to Antonio because he finds the drawing too poor; he goes on to say "and there are such slight divergences in type as one would expect in a work designed by a master and executed by his pupils".

He has since changed his mind because in the last edition of his lists he gives them to Antonio with the mention of "late."

The central figure is that of the Madonna protecting some adorers under her cloak and accompanied by saints; four full-length figures of saints occupy the lateral panels while above we see the Crucifixion and four busts of saints. As Signor Pacchioni observes ([1]), some influence of Mantegna is noticeable in these panels, in which however archaisms intermingle with more evolved forms.

In the museum of Berlin an altar-piece comprising six panels (1143) is classified as a production of the studio of Antonio Vivarini but it is only the upper central part — Christ between two angels — which shows a vague resemblance to Antonio's manner; the rest of the work is by Alvise ([2]).

*
* *

Antonio Vivarini, like Jacopo Bellini, is an artist who marks the transition from the late Gothic style of the early 15th century to that of the Renaissance which was already well established before the end of his career. His inability to follow the new direction was probably the cause of his emigration first to The Marches and finally to the easily satisfied Apulia where he ended his days.

With regard to his artistic entanglement with Giovanni d'Alemagna I have already said enough when dealing with this artist. No attempt to differentiate the two hands in every production we owe to this association is entirely satisfactory.

I do not think that there is in Antonio's art any actual connexion with German painting and more especially with the school of Cologne on which Signor Testi insists so much. Any similarity, if it does exist, is due only to the fact that both belonged to the international late Gothic style of painting, in fact we cannot fail to notice a resemblance in the works of all the painters who belonged to this movement.

([1]) *G. Pacchioni*, Un ignoto Vivarinesco a S. Andrea d'Asola, Bollettino d'Arte del Minist. della Pubbl. Istr., VIII, 1914, p. 399. It has been attributed to Gerolamo da Cremona by *Fogolari*, Dedalo, V, 1924, p. 67, and to Gentile Bellini by *Longhi*, Vita Artistica, 1927, p. 134.

([2]) Of little importance are two small panels in the gallery of Toulouse (451, 452) showing the Baptist with St. Jerome, and St. Louis of Toulouse with St. Clare; other still weaker paintings are the St. Francis with St. Jerome and the Baptist with St. James in the same gallery (449, 450).

It is also for this reason that I do not agree with the hypothesis upheld by Morelli and others that Antonio Vivarini was a pupil of Gentile da Fabriano or Pisanello. The evidence on which this theory is based again derives from the fact that Gentile and Pisanello were the chief Italian exponents of this international tendency to which Antonio Vivarini also belonged. I find a much more direct link between his art and that of Giambono or even that of the rather mediocre Francesco de' Franceschi, whose human types with round bulging eyes Antonio seems to have adopted, or again that of the master of the twelve scenes from the life of the Virgin in the Louvre. Many attributions have been proposed for this work; among them there is that to Antonio Vivarini himself by Mr. Berenson who, however, has now a-bandoned this idea (¹).

Antonio Vivarini was a somewhat second-rate artist and com-pared with his contemporary Jacopo Bellini he was more con-ventional and technically speaking decidedly inferior. His best period was early in his career when he collaborated with Giovannei d'Alemagna who succeeded in giving so much decorative effect to their combined labours. The death of Giovanni broke up this partnership and although immediately after this separation Antonio created some particularly fine paintings, a fact which might even lead us to believe that his talent had been somewhat suppressed by that of his collaborator, nevertheless the loss of Giovanni seems to have been the cause of his premature and rapid decline.

***

Besides his brother Bartolomeo, Antonio Vivarini had two more or less gifted pupils who continued certain late Gothic elements well into the second half of the 15th century although their art really belongs to the Renaissance which at that time was already well established. They are Quirizio da Murano and Antonio da Negroponte.

As to Quirizio (²) we know that he acted as witness in 1461 and 1478 (³) and his signature followed by the date 1462 is found on

---

(¹) For this work and the different attributions v. Vol. VII, p. 396.

(²) *Romualdi*, Rassegna d'Arte, I, 1901, p. 140. *P. della Pergola*, Thieme-Becker, Kunstlerlexikon, XXVII, p. 527.

(³) *Paoletti u. Ludwig*, Repert. f. Kunstwiss., XXII, 1899, p. 441.

Fig. 22.   Quirizio da Murano, St. Lucy and scenes from her legend.
Pinacotęca, Rovigo.   Photo Alinari.

a picture in the gallery of Rovigo. His name appears on one or
two other paintings; they include a Madonna adoring the sleeping
Child and Christ enthroned giving the holy sacrament to a kneeling nun, both in the gallery of Venice (29, 659).

The three signed works show us quite different manners; that
at Rovigo (fig. 22) is the most primitive and bears most connexion with Antonio Vivarini, especially the central figure of
St. Lucy in a marvellous cut velvet robe standing holding a
palm leaf and a chalice while two little angels place a crown on
her head and a nun kneels praying at her feet; to either side
three scenes illustrate the legend of the saint. On a label in the
centre of this rather small panel we read the inscription: *"Opus
Quiricius De Joanes Venecis M4C62"*. In some of the round faces
and linear effects of the features we can discern the influence of
Bartolomeo intermingling with the more dominant one of his
elder brother Antonio. The latter source of inspiration is still
more evident in the half-length figure of the Virgin adoring the
sleeping Child Jesus Who lies on a low wall in front of her, in the

Fig. 23. Quirizio da Murano, the Saviour and a female donor. Accademia
Venice. Photo Anderson.

gallery of Venice (29); it is signed: " . . . . *uiritius De Murano*".
The sleeping Infant is a favourite motif of Bartolomeo but the
presence of this feature need not induce us to assign this painting
to a much later date because it appears in Antonio and Bartolomeo's polyptych as early as 1450.

Regarding the third picture in which the signature, "*Quiricius de Murano F.*" is written on the lower part of the throne, the sweetness of the Saviour's features and the impression of distance in the landscape might lead us to look for the influence of Giovanni Bellini; the marvellous tissue of Christ's robe and the ornaments of the throne are both of an almost over-rich decorative effect (fig. 23).

The difference in manner of Quirizio's three authentic works makes the attribution of other paintings to him rather hazardous but all the more tempting ([1]).

It seems highly likely that Quirizio executed a triptych in the Correr Museum representing the Madonna attired in beautiful velvets adoring the Child Who lies sleeping on her knee; she is seated on a throne of Renaissance style and a drapery hangs down her back. To the sides are the standing figures of St. Jerome carrying the model of a church and St. Augustine in a very fine bishop's cope (fig. 24). Cavalcaselle was perhaps the first to associate this picture with the name of Quirizio.

The attribution to Quirizio of the half-length figure of the suffering Christ with the instruments of the Passion in the background, in the gallery of Venice (30), really leads the way to our including among his works also the Coronation of the Virgin in the Art Gallery of Turin (fig. 25), in which picture the elements borrowed from Antonio and Bartolomeo are so very obvious that it has been attributed to the brothers separately or to their collaboration. The composition of God the Father placing His hands on the shoulder of His son and on that of the Virgin is of an old Venetian tradition. These figures are depicted in the midst of a host of angels. The Gothic line, which is somewhat more marked than usual, might point to an early period in the painter's career.

([1]) The following works which are certainly not by Quirizio have been erroneously ascribed to him: **Budapest,** Gallery, No. 94, Madonna and Child. **Venice,** S. Giobbe, triptych with the Annunciation which I have already ascribed to a pupil of Antonio Vivarini; Ca d'Oro, Crucifixion and twelve scenes from the life of Christ which I have also assigned to a pupil of Antonio; and some other works, v. *Testi*, op. cit., p. 527. I do not know the triptych with the Madonna, Annunciation, Nativity and Pietà which, Cavalcaselle describes as in the collection of Lord Wemyss, Gosford House, near Edinburgh, and attributes to Quirizio.

Fig. 24. Quirizio da Murano, Madonna and Saints. Museo Civico, Venice.
Photo Alinari.

The combined influence of the two Vivarini brothers is manifest also in a triptych showing the half-length figure of the Madonna with the Child and the angel and the Virgin of the Annunciation against landscape backgrounds, preserved in the Correr Museum (50). It may be by Quirizio, whose name might also be associated with a picture of St. Jerome, holding the model of a church, against a background strangely filled with architecture; two repainted busts of angels are depicted above the long description which is inscribed at the foot of the panel. This painting, also in the Correr Museum, shows a connexion in style with the bust of Christ in the Accademia and the Coronation of the Virgin in Turin.

A comparison with the lateral scenes of the signed altar-piece at Rovigo confirms the attribution to Quirizio of a small panel representing a Dominican saint exorcizing an evil spirit out of a woman, which once formed part of the Paolini collection (¹).

(¹) No. 90 of the catalogue of the Paolini sale which took place in New York in Dec. 1924.

XVII.

Fig. 25. Quirizio da Murano, Coronation of the Virgin. Museo Civico, Turin.   Photo Anderson.

Fig. 26. Antonio da Negroponte, Madonna. S. Francesco
della Vigna, Venice.   Photo Alinari.

The general appearance of Quirizio's authentic works and those for which he perhaps may be held responsible, always brings us back to the influence of Antonio and Bartolomeo Vivarini. The fact that elements borrowed from the former are invariably present and that he was never entirely dominated by the younger brother, as well as the general appearance of his work, does not justify in my opinion Signor Testi's hypothesis that the artist worked for quite a long time after the last mention we have of him in 1478. On the whole, however, he was never anything but a mediocre and somewhat provincial painter.

* * *

Antonio da Negroponte [1], whom Sansovino (fol. 15B) and some other ancient authors call by mistake Francesco, is rather a perplexing problem because his charming panel in the church of S. Francesco della Vigna in Venice with the signature, "*Frater Antonius de Negropon pinxit*" to which the words "*ordinis minorum*" have been added at a later date, leads us to believe that he was a painter of some importance (fig. 26). However, not a single record can be found concerning him and not another picture can with any certainty be associated with his name. There is mention, it is true, of a certain "Antonio Falerio pictore habitatore Negroponti" in a document of 1469, in which also Jacopo Bellini figures [2], but it is by no means sure that this is a reference to our painter.

The signed panel is slightly retouched in the flesh parts. It represents the Madonna seated on a very elaborate throne with a very high back which finishes in a garland of flowers (God the Father above is obviously a later addition); a flowering hedge forms the background and several birds are depicted in the foreground; angelic figures not only adorn the throne but also accompany the Virgin; the base of the throne is decorated with heads — which are perhaps meant to be of a classical character but are not — and other ornamental motifs. The Madonna, whose expression is very sweet, and who wears a marvellous robe of velvet with a large flowered pattern, adores the Child Who lies awake on her knee.

---

[1] *Fogolari*, Thieme-Becker, Künstlerlexikon, II, p. 2.
[2] *Paoletti*, Raccolta di documenti inediti, I, 1897, p. 11.

Fig. 27. Antonio da Negroponte(?), St. Michael.
Museum, Berlin.

Museum Photo.

Perhaps a little too much importance has been given to the Paduan character of some of the elements in this picture which, before anything else, is Venetian. The heads in grisaille might contain something humanistic and Paduan but a similar and even more elaborate array of angels is used as a decorative motif in the Coronation of the Virgin by Antonio Vivarini and Giovanni d'Alemagna in the San Pantaleone, Venice. The type of the Virgin and Child, although restoration may have slightly altered it, likewise reminds us of Antonio Vivarini. The abundance of flowers and birds points to a survival of the late Gothic tradition.

It is indeed curious that among all the pictures we know there is not one which seems to be by the same hand. A charming picture of the archangel slaying the dragon in the museum of Berlin ([1]) approaches the signed work in manner and sentiment and we should not exclude the possibility that it might be by the same hand (fig. 27).

Cavalcaselle thought that Antonio da Negroponte might have painted the Madonna in the Oratorio della Disciplina at Legnago and with this opinion Fogolari is inclined to agree.

The art of Antonio da Negroponte shows a connexion with the earliest and most ornate works of Bartolomeo Vivarini when strongly influenced by Mantegna, as for instance the Madonna and angels in a painted frame in the museum of Berlin (27) and the Virgin in a landscape adoring the Child Who lies sleeping on her lap, in the gallery of Padua.

*
* *

From the material with which we have dealt it is evident that Murano possessed a local group of painters if not a real school. The Vivarini brothers came from there; Giovanni d'Alemagna settled in this little town; Quirizio as his surname indicates originated from Murano, as did also Andrea da Murano with whom we shall deal later. In Murano apparently the Gothic tradition lasted somewhat longer than it did in Venice and this may be due to the presence there of a painter from Germany. The painters of this town continued the custom of showing fine contemporary costumes, magnificent tissues, and a profusion of

([1]) At the present moment I believe it is not exhibited: Photo Hanfstaengl 558.

decorative details and ornaments in gold, and these features give the productions of Murano a somewhat archaic appearance and a certain peculiar character. This we noticed was the case in those works which were but distantly connected with Antonio Vivarini's art and which I mentioned among his school productions.

Of Muranese origin also is I think a pleasing panel of a young male saint in elegant contemporary attire, holding the model of a town and a banner, preserved in the museum of Dijon, as well as an enthroned Madonna nursing the Child, formerly in the von Nemes collection, Munich (¹). I do not think, however, that either of these paintings can be associated with any of the identified masters.

(¹) No. 16 of the catalogue of the von Nemes sale which look place in Amsterdam in November 1928.

CHAPTER II

JACOPO BELLINI (¹).

The name of Bellini is recorded in the poor quarter of S. Nicolo

(¹) *F. Aglietti*, Elogio storico di Jac. e. Giovanni Bellini,Venice, 1808-10.
W. Arslan, Un probabile affresco di J. B., Bollettino d'Arte del Minist. della
Pubbl. Istr., 1926, p. 186. *G. Bernasconi*, Cenni intorno la vita e le opere di
J. B., Verona, 1860. *T. Borenius*, J. B., Apollo, Jan. 1926, p. 31. *G. Cagnola*,
Intorno a J. B., Rassegna d'Arte, IV, 1904, p. 117. *The Same*, Un interes-
sante aquisto della fondazione Poldi Pezzoli, Rassegna d'Arte, X, 1910,
p. 65. *G. Cantalamessa*, L'Arte di J. B., Venice, 1896. *The Same*, L'Arte di
J. B., Conferenze d'arte, Rome, 1926, p. 111. *A. Chiapelli*, Per un quadro
di J. B., Corriere della Sera, 27th July 1908 (v. L'Arte, 1908, p. 316).
G. Fiocco, Dante und Petrarca von J. B., Pantheon, Feby. 1932, p. 41.
G. Fogolari, Dipinti ignoti di J. B. a Bassano, Bollet. Mus. Civico di
Bassano, I, 1904, No. 3. *The Same*, La nuova Madonna di J. B. delle
Gallerie di Venezia, Bollettino d'Arte del Minist. Pubbl. Istr., Sept. 1921,
p. 104. *C. Frati*, La leggenda di S. Caterina da Siena con disegni attribuiti
a J. B., La Bibliofilia, XXV, 1923, fasc. 4. *G. Frizzoni*, Il libro di disegni
di J. B. al Louvre, Rassegna d'Arte, IX, 1909, p. 55. *L. Fröhlich-Bum*,
Bemerkungen zu den Zeichnungen des J. B. und zur seiner Kunst, Mit-
theil. der Geselsch. f. vervielfältigende Kunst., Vienna, 1916, p. 41. *R. E.
Fry*, A Note on an early Venetian Picture, Monthly Review, 1901, p. 686.
C. Gamba, Una Madonna di J. B. agli Uffizi, Rassegna d'Arte, VI, 1906,
p. 59. *V. Goloubew*, Les dessins de J. B. au Louvre et au British Museum,
2 vols., Brussels, 1908, 1912. *G. Gronau*, Notes sur J. B. et sa famille,
Chronique des Arts, 1895, p. 267. *The Same*, Ein Madonnenbild des J. B.,
Zeitschr. f. Bild. Kunst, XVII, 1906, p. 266. *The Same*, Die Künstler-
familie Bellini (Künstlermonographie), Bielefeld-Leipzig, 1909. *The Same*,
in Thieme-Becker, Künstlerlexikon, III, p. 252. *F. Malaguzzi Valeri*, Un
nuovo quadro di J. B. aquistato del Museo Poldi Pezzoli, Rassegna d'Arte,
VIII, 1908, p. 166. *C. de Mandach*, Le symbolisme dans les dessins de J. B.,
Gazette des Beaux Arts, July-Aug. 1922. *M. de Mas-Latrie et E. Galichon*,
J., Gentile et Giov. Bellini, Gazette des B. A., 1866, p. 281. *A. L. Mayer*,
Bildnes des J. B., International Studio, December 1930, p. 102. *P. Molmenti*, I pittori Bellini, Arch. Veneto, XXXVI, 1888, p. 225 and Studi e
ricerchi di Stor. ed Arte, Turin, 1892, p. 109. *E. Müntz*, J. B. et la Renais-
sance dans l'Italie Septentrionale, Gazette des B. A., 1884, pp. 346, 434.

dei Mendicoli in Venice as early as 1340 (¹), but it has been impossible to establish any connexion between the persons cited in the documents of this period and Niccolò Bellino, a plumber, the father of Jacopo Bellini, who was born in all probability around the year 1400. His mother was Giovanna, Niccolò's first wife.

We meet with him for the first time in June 1423, if the "Jacobus Pieri pictor de Venetis" mentioned in this document is really the same person as Jacopo Bellini, but this seems somewhat doubtful considering that the father of our Jacopo was not called Piero but Niccolo or rather Nicoletto.

In order to include this record in the life of Jacopo Bellini, various inventions, more or less ingenious, have been made to explain the error in the father's name.

The argument which I think is most convincing is that the painter's name is followed by the description "famuli et discepuli magistri Gentilini pictoris de Fabriano, habitatoris in populo Sancti Marie Virginis Ugonis de Florentia" and, as we shall see later, Jacopo Bellini was without any doubt a pupil of Gentile da Fabriano. As it is very improbable that the latter master had two Venetian pupils of the name of Jacopo, I am inclined

---

C. *Philips*, An unrecognized Portrait by J. B., Burlington Magazine, XVI, 1910, p. 200. L. *Planiscig*, J. u. Gentile Bellini, Jahrb. Kunsthist. Samml. in Wien, N. F., Sonderheft, 12, 1928. C. *Ricci*, Una Madonna di J. B., Rassegna d'Arte, I, 1901, p. 113. *The Same*, Altri due dipinti di J. B., Idem, III, 1903, p. 161. *The Same*, I dipinti di J. B., Emporium, Nov. 1903. *The Same*, J. B. e Leonello d'Este, Emporium, Dec. 1903. *The Same*, Ancora di J. B., Rassegna d'Arte, IV, 1904, p. 12. *The Same*, Una Madonna di J. B., Rivista d'Arte, IV, 1906, p. 22. *The Same*, J. B. e i suoi libri di disegni, 2 vols., Florence, 1908 (L'Arte, XI, 1908, p. 153). *The Same*, Una Madonna di J. B. finora sconosciuta, Boll. Minist. Pubbl. Istr., VI, 1912, fasc. 8. G. M. *Richter*, New light on J. B., The Connaisseur, LXII, March 1922, No. 247. E. *Rigoni*, J. B. a Padova nel 1430, Rivista d'Arte, 1929, p. 261. L. *Simeoni*, La Crocefissione di J. B., Atti dell'Accademia etc. di Verona, serie 4, vol. V, 1904—5, p. 29. L. *Testi*, Pei disegni di J. B., Rassegna d'Arte, IX, 1909, No. 5, p. V. A. *Venturi*, J. B., Pisanello und Mantegna in den Sonetten des Dichters Ulisse, Der Kunstfreund (Berlin), 1885, No. 19. *The Same*, Das Bildnis des Leonello d'Este von J. B., Pantheon, 1929, p. 201. L. *Venturi*, A mythological Picture by J. B., Burlington Magazine, Nov. 1926, p. 205. *The Same*, A J. B., L'Arte, XXXIII, 1930, p. 180.

(¹) *Testi*, op. cit., II, p. 144.

to believe that the document in question refers to Jacopo Bellini,
especially as such errors, as here in the name of the father, are
not rare in notarial acts.

The record ([1]) informs us that Jacopo in a scuffle had wounded
the son of a notary in the arm but, according to Jacopo, it was the
notary's son who had provoked the quarrel by throwing stones
into a courtyard where his master Gentile had placed some
paintings and pieces of sculpture. He was fined a large sum
during his absence and on his return was to have been arrested
but on account of his poverty he was pardoned.

In the incident of 1423 there is a suggestion that Jacopo was
born somewhat later than 1395, the date proposed by Testi,
because we can hardly imagine that a painter of twenty-eight
years old would be sent by his chief to chase away some trouble-
some boys and would finish by having a stand-up fight with them.

The name of Jacopo figures in his father's will of the 11th
April 1424; he evidently had a debt with his parent. His father's
second wife was called Franceschina and he had besides a
daughter named Elena. Jacopo was not married at this time
but in February of 1429 his wife, Anna, had a child who is generally supposed to be Gentile, although this is not at all certain;
perhaps it was his daughter Niccolosa who was born at this time.

Soon afterwards his other son, the famous Giovanni Bellini,
was born. He was very possibly an illigitimate child and, as Testi
observes, the birth at a short interval of two sons by differents
mothers one of whom was not his wife, the debt with his father
and the violent scuffle with blows and wounds, suggest to us
that Jacopo, was hot-tempered and led a rather turbulent life.

Here are some other data that we know concerning him ([2]). In
1430 an estimate was made of the figure of St. Michael which he
had painted in the church dedicated to this saint in Padua. One
of the three judges was the Venetian painter Michele Giambono
and, as Signor Rigoni, who has published this document ([3]),
observes, it seems highly probable that it is the same picture
which Rosetti describes in his guide of 1765 as existing in this

---

([1]) *Milanesi*, note on *Vasari*, III, p. 149; v. Vol. VIII, p. 4. *A. Venturi*,
Gentile da Fabriano e il Pisanello, Florence, 1896, p. 10.

([2]) v. especially *Ricci*, Libri di disegni and *Testi*, op. cit., II, p. 143.

([3]) *Rigoni*, op. cit.

church. According to Rosetti the picture was signed: *"Jacobus de
Neritus discipulus Gentili di Fabriano pinxit"* but Rigoni im-
agines that a mistake was made in the transcription and that the
signature should read *"Jacobus de Venetus"* etc., in other words
Jacopo Bellini. In 1436 he painted a grandiose fresco of the
Crucifixion with many figures, in the chapel of S. Niccolo in the
cathedral of Verona. The work was executed by the order of
Bishop Guido Memmo who, along with other members of the
clergy, figured in the fresco. The taste of a canon for modern art
was the cause of its destruction in 1759. It is often thought that
the Christ on the Cross now on canvas in the museum of Verona
(365) is a fragment of this fresco [1].

The following year Jacopo's name figures among the members
of the confraternity of the Scuola Grande di S. Giovanni Evangelista in Venice where, in 1439, he buys an inlaid panel from the
heritage of Jacobello del Fiore. In 1440 he forms a kind of association with the painter Donato Brigadin but soon afterwards the
idea of this partnership is abandoned.

In 1441 he becomes "decano" of the Scuola Grande di S. Giovanni for the "sestiere" of S. Marco and the same year he goes
to Ferrara where, in competing for the painting of the portrait of
Leonello d'Este, he gains the victory over Pisanello. In the sonnet
which Ulisse de' Aleatti dedicates to this competition he speaks
of Jacopo as "summo pictore novelo fidia al nostro ziecho
mondo". He tells us clearly that it was Leonello's father, Niccolo
III, who decided the victory for Jacopo [2]. From Leonello the
artist received grain to bring back to Venice, no doubt in reward
for the beautiful portrait.

Let us say at once that it seems indeed surprising that these

---

[1] A picture of the Crucifixion in a crowded composition of the school
of Jacopo, once in the Casa Albrizzi in Venice (reprod. in *Crowe and Cavalcaselle*, Painting in North Italy, ed. Borenius, I, p. 110) is supposed to
reproduce Jacopo's fresco in Verona. The same is said of a print which
was made by Paolo Cagliari in 1814 and which corresponds perfectly with
the picture of Casa Albrizzi (reprod. in *Rosini*, The History of Italian
Painting and in *Ludwig e Molmenti*, Carpaccio, p. 9). The composition,
however, does not coincide with the old description of Jacopo's fresco
because for one thing the episcopal donor and his suite are absent.

[2] *A. Venturi*, Gentile, etc., p. 46, with bibliography.

princes, who were such connaisseurs of art, could ever have preferred Jacopo Bellini to Pisanello.

In 1443 Jacopo is mentioned in Venice where, so we are informed, he has had for twelve years his nephew Leonardo di Paolo as helper and pupil.

In 1452 there are three records concerning him. One of these documents tells us that he lived at S. Gimignano in the lagunes. Then he accepts the order for a large panel or processional banner which had to be executed entirely by him, nor was he allowed to leave Venice until he had finished it. He was to be paid 140 ducats but a forfeit was to be made if the work was not carried out within a certain limit of time; on the other hand, if it was delivered before March 1453 he was to receive a gratuity.

In February 1453 his daughter Niccolosa marries Andrea Mantegna and on this occasion Jacopo is given a grant of twenty ducats by the Scuola Grande di S. Giovanni Evangelista.

The following year he is again appointed decano for the "sestiere" of S. Marco in this Scuola Grande and it is in this year that he is remunerated for a figure of Lorenzo Giustiniani which he has executed over this nobleman's tomb in the church of S. Pietro in Castello. For the room of the patriarch in the same church he paints in the following year a canvas representing SS. Peter, Paul and another saint.

In 1457 as well as in 1460, 1466, and 1467 he is called upon as witness. In 1460 he paints, together with his sons, an altar-piece, which they signed and dated, for the Gattamelata chapel in the church of S. Antonio of Padua. In 1465 he had terminated, in collaboration with his sons, eighteen scenes from the lives of Jesus and the Virgin for a hall of the confraternity of the Scuola Grande di S. Marco. A document of 1466 proves that he had finished, and perhaps some time prior to this date, two paintings for the altar of the hall of the same Scuola Grande. Afterwards he is charged to execute two other pictures which he promised to paint with the greatest possible care and the very best pigments. They were to represent a Crucifixion with many figures and "the story of Jerusalem with Christ and the thieves". The Scuola was destroyed by fire in 1485 and the paintings perished on this occasion. Other mentions of Jacopo are made in 1468 and 1469. He was still alive and active at his calling on the

7th January 1470 but from his wife's will of the 25th November 1471 it was evident that Jacopo was then deceased.

The authentic works of Jacopo Bellini are four in number and all four bear the master's signature. They are: the canvas of Christ crucified in the museum of Verona (365), in which on a label at the foot of the cross we read: *"Opus Jacobi Bellini"*; the half-length figure of the Madonna and Child in the Accademia of Venice (582), which is signed: *"Opus Jacobi Bellini Veneti"*; the Madonna from Casalfiumanese now in the Brera Gallery, Milan, which shows the inscription *"1448 Has dedit ingenua — Belinus mente figuras"*; and lastly the Madonna in the Tadini Gallery of Lovere (255) on which we find only the name, *"Jachobus Bellinus"*.

No judgment on Jacopo Bellini's importance and artistic individuality could be more inadequate than that based on the sole knowledge of his pictures. There are in all about twenty, fourteen of which represent the Madonna with the Child, generally in half-length figure. There is little in this group of paintings which might lead us to believe that Jacopo Bellini had a versatile and even somewhat fantastic temperament and that the real tendency of his artistic activity was profane and worldly rather than religious; but it is in this light we learn to know him if we study the two hundred and thirty drawings or more which we have from his hand and which, with but a few rare exceptions, are all united in two albums, one in the Louvre, the other in the British Museum.

The history and detailed list of the contents of these two sketch-books have been published several times [1] and I need not repeat here anything but the more salient facts.

Anna, the widow of Jacopo, mentions in her will of 1471 "libri de dessignis" which are left to her son Gentile and Gentile, as we shall see, speaks on one occasion of the drawings by his father which are in his possession [2]. In his "Notizie" of 1530 Michiel says that in the collection of Gabriel Vendramin "the big book of

---

[1] *Gaye*, op. cit. C. *Ricci*, J. B. e suoi libri di disegni. *Goloubew*, op. cit. *Testi*, Pitt. Venez., II, p. 188. *The Same*, op. cit., L'Arte. *Frizzoni*, op. cit., Rassegna d'Arte.

[2] Arch. Stor. dell'Arte, I, p. 276.

bombassin paper of drawings in lead pencil is from the hand of
Jacomo Bellini" and this is certainly the album which was
bought by the British Museum in 1855, because the drawings in
the other book are executed on vellum.

The drawings in the sketch-book in the British Museum have
all been retraced and, as Goloubew observes, this has been
done probably at two different periods and by two different
hands. The first retouching, which dates from the 16th century, has
re-enforced the outlines and plastic effects, while the second,
which is of the 18th century, has attempted to revive faded lines.

An important indication with regard to the date of the sketch-
book is found in the water-mark of the paper which was not used
prior to 1441. On the first page there is an inscription which runs:
*"De mano De M. S. (Messer) Jacobo Bellino Veneto, 1430, in
Venetia"* but these words are of little value because the appearance of the calligraphy dates the inscription from towards the
end of the 15th century.

As I said before, the great majority of the pages in the
sketchbook acquired by the Louvre in 1884 and before that date
in the castle of the Marquis de Savran Ponterci, near Bordeaux, as well as three sheets which entered the Louvre with the
His de la Salle collection and which might have formed part of
the same album, are of vellum with drawings in pen and ink. I
believe that Mrs Frölich-Bum comes very near the truth when
she states that on the whole these drawings have a more definite
and refined character and are of more finished composition
than the set in the British Museum and I am also of the opinion
that some of the subjects which, in the album in London, are only
roughly and hastily sketched appear in a more finished manner
in the book in the Louvre. I think, however, Mrs Frölich-Bum
goes a little too far in supposing that the connexion between the
two albums is that of preparatory sketches (London) in order to
produce the finished drawings (Paris). The subjects correspond
too rarely; moreover, the London book contains some elaborate
compositions while there are several rough sketches in the one in
Paris. Besides, there remains the important question of what the
drawings in the Louvre originally looked like. Here many are not in
ink, and in those which are, we often discover under the ink traces
of other substances — lead pencil or even sometimes charcoal —

and, as Gentile Bellini frankly confesses that he retraced his father's drawings in pen and ink, I think it highly likely that this is the case in most of the sheets now in the Louvre. We cannot exclude the possibility that in some cases it was Jacopo himself who made the pen drawings, or again that it was some pupil other than Gentile who traced them over, but somehow it seems to me more likely that it was Gentile, especially as the retracing reveals a marked familiarity with Jacopo's style and great respect for the original appearance of the drawings. There are a few subjects treated in colour, as for instance a figure of St. Christopher and an iris; the latter is executed in water-colours and is of a scientific character, resembling in type the illustrations of a book on natural history.

Goloubew is of opinion that this second album was executed around the year 1450 or even later, not only on account of the fact that St. Bernardine (if it is really this saint who is depicted preaching on fol. 73) is represented with a nimbus, which points to a date posterior to his canonisation in 1450, but also because some of the architectural motifs, especially at the beginning of the album, show a neo-classical tendency with which he might have become familiar in Padua, although, as Testi observes, there seems to be no foundation for Goloubew's assertion that Jacopo came in contact with Paduan humanists. Nor do I see which Ferrarese artist Goloubew has in mind when he states that the album in the Louvre reveals less Ferrarese influence than the sketch-book in the British Museum. What painters were there active in Ferrara around the year 1450? Besides, in order to explain the Paduan influence it seems more likely that the second book of drawings — that in the Louvre — did not come into existence before 1460, unless we wish to infer that Jacopo Bellini was a pioneer of the neo-classical style, and we have really no reason to do so. On the contrary we discover in his work, especially in his human figures, a traditionalistic strain which connects his art chiefly with the late Gothic style of the 15th century and most of all with Gentile da Fabriano [1].

---

[1] The nimbus around the head of St. Bernardine of Siena, who was canonized in 1450, has been advanced in favour of the theory of a date posterior to this year. But even if the two drawings of the friar preaching in the London sketch-book really do represent St. Bernardine, and this

We cannot fail to observe that the album in the Louvre can
be differentiated from that in the British Museum by an increase
in the profane elements which, as I have already pointed out, is
one of the characteristics of all Jacopo's drawings. However, even
in the sketches of religious subjects, the worldly settings and
more especially the architectural features gain so much importance
that the theme itself is reduced to practically nothing. Here we
enter into the general survey of Jacopo Bellini's books of drawings,
which will replace the lists and descriptions already published by
others.

There is an obvious analogy between the repertoire of subjects
in the sketch-books of Pisanello and in those of Jacopo Bellini.

The proportions however are quite different and we do not find
in Pisanello's drawings many traces of that keen interest in
architecture which is one of the principal features in Jacopo's art,
while the latter's curiosity does not seem to have been excited by
natural history to the same degree as Pisanello's, because apparently he dedicated only a single sheet to this subject, that on
which is depicted an iris in water-colours, whereas pages of
Pisanello's sketch books are devoted to it. Nor do we find that
Jacopo had that predilection for portraiture, a branch in which
Pisanello excelled. In the entire drawings of the two albums we
find only one portrait but it suffices to reveal to us that Jacopo
had a great gift as a portraitist (fig. 28).

The repertoire of Jacopo as well as that of Pisanello was that
of a court painter whose eye was struck by the beauty, the luxury
of costume and the magnificence of the setting of a princely
existence, but who at the same time was required to collaborate in
its further embellishment. This is the reason why the religious
representations which, especially in Jacopo's art, are so frequent,
lost their importance until gradually even the illustrations
of sacred subjects acquired a profane aspect. It is true that we
do not know much about Jacopo's activity for the Italian princes
but the episode of 1441 at the court of the Este furnishes us with
proof that he was an artist beloved of the lords of Ferrara and

---

is rendered likely by the round object in his hand, which might have
been his sign, I must confess that I do not actually see the nimbus though
this may be due to the actual condition of the drawing. In any case the
nimbi in Jacopo's sketches are often somewhat indistinct.

Fig. 28. Jacopo Bellini, portrait of a man, drawing. Louvre, Paris.

Photo Giraudon.

again a leaf in the sketch-book in the British Museum shows us Leonello on horseback attired for a tourney (fig. 29) and followed by pages. Moreover, many drawings manifest Jacopo's familiarity with palaces, castles and their inhabitants.

XVII.

5

Fig. 29. Jacopo Bellini, nobleman on horseback, drawing. British Museum, London.   Photo Anderson.

I shall not enumerate here every example of this tendency but shall just state that a considerable number of sheets contain images of knights on horseback (fig. 30), often represented as profane-looking St. Georges with the dragon (fig. 31). These knights are sometimes followed by a page, but are also represented on foot, in full armour. Then again they are shown in the company

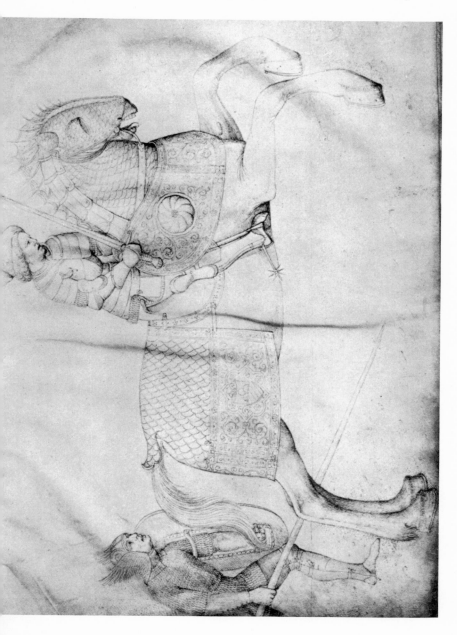

Fig. 30. Jacopo Bellini, knight on horseback and warrior on foot, drawing. Louvre, Paris. Photo Giraudon.

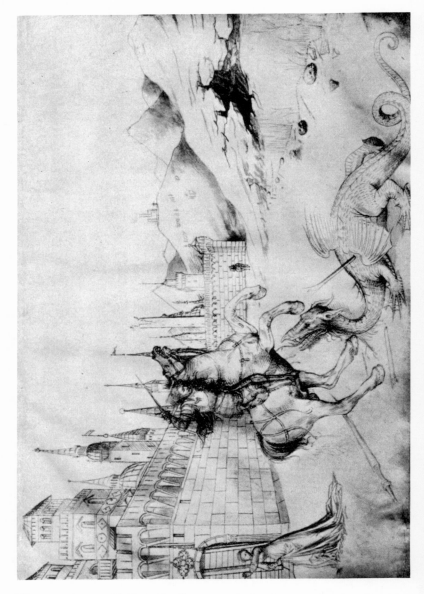

Fig. 31. Jacopo Bellini, St. George and the dragon, drawing. Louvre,
Paris.   Photo Giraudon.

of ladies and jesters or in combat. There are as well fine drawings
of a tourney (fig. 32), a condottiere, gentlemen in magnificent
attire, designs of tissues, two sketches for gold or silver vessels,

Fig. 32. Jacopo Bellini, tourney, drawing. British Museum, London.

Photo Anderson.

an infinity of horses in all sorts of positions (fig. 33) but not the
gruesome sight of dead horses which Pisanello depicts on several
occasions, many dogs and some cheetahs, an animal resembling
the leopard, which, as is well known, was used like the dog for
hunting purposes (¹). There are also several sketches of lions

(¹) *R. van Marle*, Iconographie de l'art profane, I, The Hague, 1931,
p. 211.

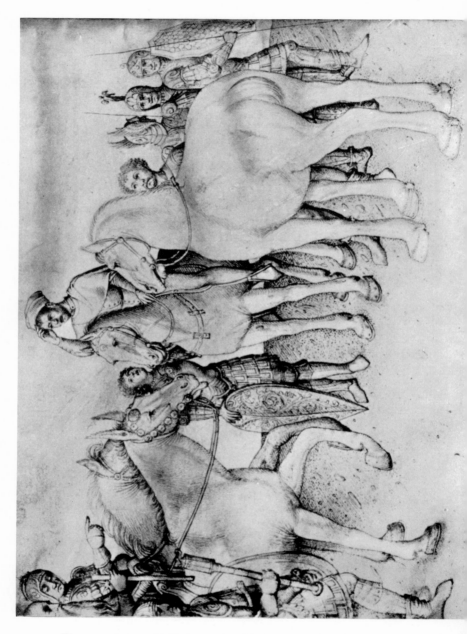

Fig. 33. Jacopo Bellini, people with horses, drawing. Louvre, Paris.

Fig. 34. Jacopo Bellini, drawing. British Museum, London.

Photo Anderson.

(fig. 34) which Jacopo must have seen in the collections of wild animals which at that time were not rare at the Italian courts; some of the drawings even show them behind iron bars.

Other drawings bear reference to the chase; there are a few sketches of deer which appear in several religious scenes where they are quite out of place, as for instance in that of the Lord at the age of twelve teaching in the Temple, the Assumption, the

Fig. 35. Jacopo Bellini, drawing. British Museum, London.

Photo Anderson.

death of St. Isidore and the temptation of St. Antony. There are
many sketches of the Adoration of the Magi in which the holy
travellers have been given the appearance of a cavalcade of
hunters (figs. 35—37) but, as I have said elsewhere ([1]), this is
a peculiarity frequently found in this scene.

Jacopo was impressed more than anything else by the archi-

([1]) *Van Marle*. op. cit., I, p. 226.

Fig. 36. Jacopo Bellini, Adoration of the Magi, drawing. British Museum, London.   Photo Anderson.

tectural grandeur of the princely palaces. Many of his drawings, even those in which we discover, not without difficulty, religious subjects, are really dedicated to the luxurious residences of the local rulers of Northern Italy (figs. 38, 39). He sometimes depicts only the courtyard in which people are moving about, where cheetahs and bears are confined and from which one catches a

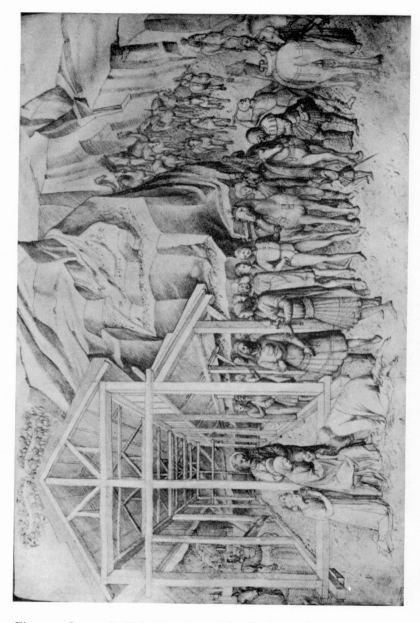

Fig. 37. Jacopo Bellini, Adoration of the Magi, drawing. Louvre, Paris.

Photo Giraudon.

Fig. 38. Jacopo Bellini, allegory, drawing. Louvre, Paris.

Photo Giraudon.

glimpse of the stable beyond. But his imagination at times got the
better of him and some of his architectural designs show a

Fig. 39. Jacopo Bellini, interior of a palace, drawing. Louvre, Paris.
Photo Giraudon.

magnificence and abundance of decorative motifs which certainly never existed.

Jacopo's drawings, however, do not reveal an exclusive interest

Fig. 40.   Jacopo Bellini, peasant on horseback, drawing. British Museum,
London.   Photo Anderson.

in this class of society; on the contrary there are quite a number
of sketches which illustrate the life of the peasant (figs. 40, 41);
we see these country people riding on donkeys, dressed in simple
attire, and carrying grapes in barrels. There is a charming sketch
of the grape harvest in the album in London (fig. 42) and in
the background of the scene of the Calvary we see some shepherds.

Fig. 41. Jacopo Bellini, drawing. British Museum, London.

Photo Anderson.

Then on several occasions he shows us simple soldiers and
warriors: a drawing of the martyrdom of St. Sebastian is chiefly
a study of archers.

Jacopo's interest in architecture is evident in a great number
of drawings in both albums. Whenever the occasion presents
itself he shows us an imposing house. In fact, on quite a number

St. GEORGES SLAYING THE DRAGON

Drawing by Jacopo Bellini, in the British Museum.

Fig. 42. Jacopo Bellini, picking the grapes and pressing the wine,
drawing. British Museum, London.   Photo Anderson.

of the sheets in the London sketch-book the entire left half is
occupied by elaborate drawings of buildings without figures while
on the right half the events are practically lost in the abundance
of architecture. On the other hand some of the pages contain
only a study of woodwork which Jacopo invariably employs for
the shelter in the scenes of the Nativity and Adoration of the Magi.

Fig. 43. Jacopo Bellini, architectural perspective, drawing. British Museum, London.   Photo Anderson.

In some of the sheets we notice that his attention is attracted by the technical side of construction (fig. 43); we see for instance the rough sketch of a balcony, another of the beginning of a brick wall, while in a scene of the Calvary masons are depicted at work.

Jacopo Bellini's sketch-books thus make a considerable contribution to our knowledge of profane architecture of the second half of the 15th century (fig. 44). All the specimens are of northern

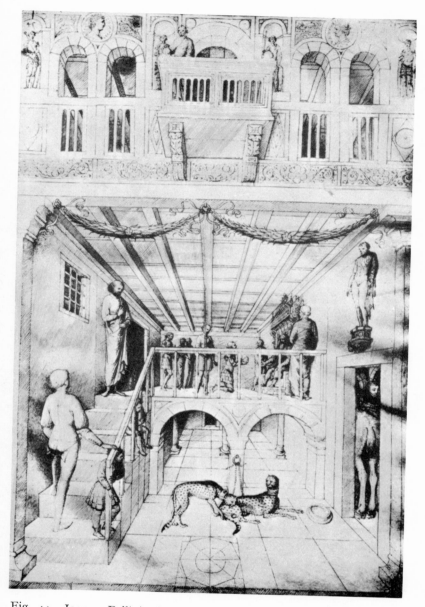

Fig. 44. Jacopo Bellini, the courtyard of a palace, drawing. British Museum, London. Photo Anderson.

appearance and may have existed in the regions of Venice, Padua and Verona, but there are only a few examples of the typical Vene-

XVII.

6

Fig. 45. Jacopo Bellini, Presentation of the Virgin in the Temple, drawing. Louvre, Paris.   Photo Giraudon.

tian palazzi such as were built on the canals of the city. The artist reveals quite a liking for external stair-cases and balconies which are seldom lacking in his architectural designs.

Jacopo's sketches, however, do not give us the impression of any sense of practical utility, and his cartoons were not made with the idea of ever serving as models for real buildings. Jacopo Bellini was certainly not an architect. The houses he depicts, as I said before, have not only frequently something unreal and fantastic in them but even in his day were already old-fashioned and somewhat Gothic, belonging in fact to a previous generation. His drawings of churches are more up to date and several of them seem to belong to the Florentine style of architecture. Probably in his early years he saw in Florence the creations of Brunelleschi and Michelozzo and seems to have been particularly struck by the effect of perspective of their porticoes, which effect he tries to accentuate in his drawings by means of auxiliary lines. On one occasion he shows a fantastic adaptation of a Romanesque building with elements borrowed from the basilica of St. Marco (fig 45). As he could not provide churches with stairways, he often depicts a flight of steps leading up to them. Generally speaking, we obtain from Jacopo's drawings of architecture the idea that he was greatly impressed by the pictorial effect of buildings but did not take into consideration their practical aspect. On one of the last pages in the London sketch-book and on two at the beginning of the Paris album we see architectural arches used as frames around religious scenes.

Jacopo's interest in architecture was not limited to models of churches and houses, for he shows us as well views of entire towns from the outside, and not infrequently in the backgrounds of such religious representations as the Calvary, the nailing of Christ on the Cross, the Crucifixion, and the Funeral of the Virgin, we find city walls sketched in great detail with the houses visible above them (fig. 46). There is also a view of a Venetian canal with a bridge and houses to either side (fig. 47).

In his landscapes Jacopo Bellini remains particularly conventional; he frequently depicts rocks of a peculiar spiral-like effect and a curious sharp-cut shape. They appear in a rather monotonous manner throughout all his work but in certain cases, as in the scene of the stigmatization of St. Francis, they create an

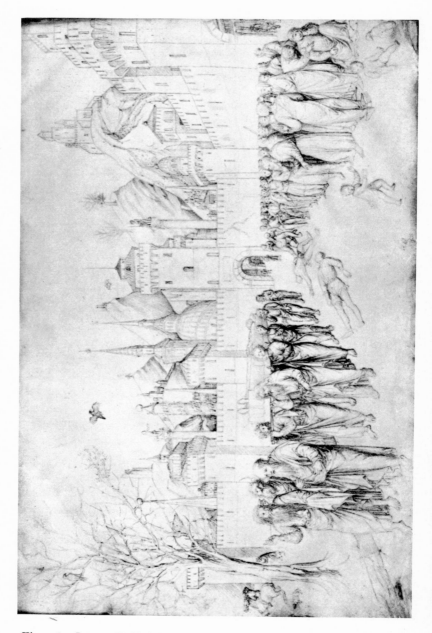

Fig. 46. Jacopo Bellini, Funeral of the Virgin, drawing. Louvre, Paris,
Photo Giraudon.

Fig. 47. Jacopo Bellini, bridge over a canal, drawing. British Museum,
London.   Photo Anderson.

effect of deserted grandiosity or even produce the impression, as
for instance in the scene of Christ in Limbo (fig. 48), of the setting
of an uncanny fairy-tale or the scenery of some Wagnerian opera.

More conventional still are his renderings of forests or other
forms of vegetation. The former invariably look like well-kept
and regularly planted parks, while other botanical manifestations

Fig. 48. Jacopo Bellini, Descent into Limbo, drawing. Louvre, Paris.
Photo Giraudon.

resemble vegetable gardens or flower beds. They remind us a
little of those aspects of nature with which Fra Angelico surrounds his Annunciations.

Jacopo Bellini took a certain interest in classical antiquity.

Fig. 49. Jacopo Bellini, studies of classical sculpture, drawing. Louvre, Paris.

Four sheets show antique monuments and inscriptions (fig. 49) and on some others we see sketches from Roman marble figures, while in a drawing of the Calvary he depicts a sculptor at

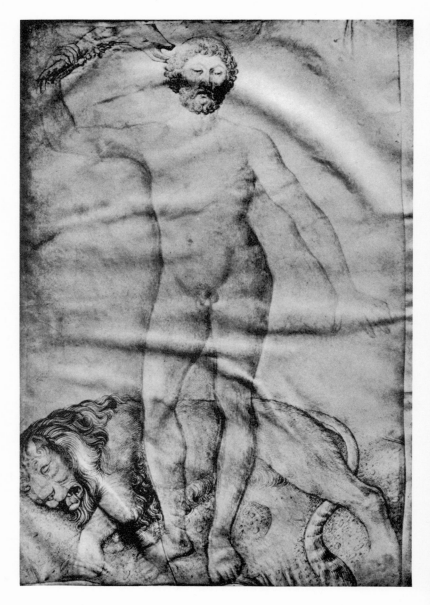

Fig. 50. Jacopo Bellini, Samson, drawing. Louvre, Paris.

Photo Giraudon.

work on the statue of some pagan deity which apparently is to be
placed on the column lying close by, and which in opposition to

Fig. 51. Jacopo Bellini, Silenus on the ass, drawing. British Museum,
London.   Photo Anderson.

Christ carrying the Cross forms a religious allegory, no doubt of
Jacopo's invention. Antique columns stand upright or lie around
in several of Jacopo's compositions of religious subjects, in which
the buildings too are frequently decorated with reliefs of classical
style, illustrating mythological narratives (v. fig. 38). He has
besides a curious habit of placing religious preachers on pedestals
as if they were classical statues. He has also treated other mytho-

Fig. 52. Jacopo Bellini, Combat of Amazons, drawing. British Museum,
London.   Photo Anderson.

logical subjects, such for instance as the triumph of Bacchus and
his chariot, Hercules slaying the lion (fig. 50), the head of Hannibal
presented to Prusias, Silenus on his donkey (fig. 51), a combat
of Amazons (fig. 52), a round temple with an altar, and Eros and
the Faun on Pegasus. In all there are about sixteen drawings
dedicated to classical antiquity; this is not a large proportion and
is certainly not sufficient to give him the reputation of having

Fig. 53. Jacopo Bellini, the Meeting of the Quick and the Dead,
drawing. Louvre, Paris. Photo Giraudon.

been a humanist. On the other hand, the quaint rocky landscapes, the fantastic palaces, the different sketches of dragons and men in combat with them, and the curious atmosphere of such scenes as St. Jerome in the desert reveal to us that Jacopo was not devoid of an imagination of an almost fairy-tale trend.

To the usual profane repertoire belong also the various studies of nudes, of allegories (as for example that of the meeting of the three living and the three dead which Jacopo has treated twice) (fig. 53) and even, as I pointed out elsewhere, Judith with the head of Holofernes [1]. It is quite possible that one of the drawings of nudes on which we see an old haggard woman near a young and handsome one might bear reference to the well known allegory of the different ages.

Six pages show sketches for monuments, one of which is equestrian while three are funereal; in one of the latter Jacopo depicts a half-decomposed body and here we notice a point of contact with Pisanello's sometimes gruesome realism.

In contrast with the profane spirit which Jacopo has often employed in his drawings of religious subjects, there are certain sketches which show him more or less in the light of a mystic. This is noticeable chiefly in compositions of a sad or mournful nature, such as the Crucified alone or accompanied by two figures, the different moments of the Deposition and the Pietàs (fig. 54), in which at a slightly later date the son Giovanni followed his father's example. Not only does a very profound, devout and tragic feeling emanate from these representations, but also, stylistically speaking, they are somewhat different. They reveal a certain traditionalism and a Gothic line and we find that in those compositions in which Jacopo felt a connexion, on account of the subject, with previous generations, he always remained a direct descendant of the late Gothic masters such as Gentile da Fabriano and Giambono; combined with this however we discover a mysticism which he did not borrow from his immediate fore-runners but which seems to originate in the art of the Trecento. We meet with the same Gothic line in a few other drawings of religious subjects, as for example the isolated figures of the Madonna (fig. 55),, of saints especially those of St. Christopher (fig. 56), the Assumption (fig. 57) and God the Father holding

[1] *Van Marle*, op. cit., II, p. 480.

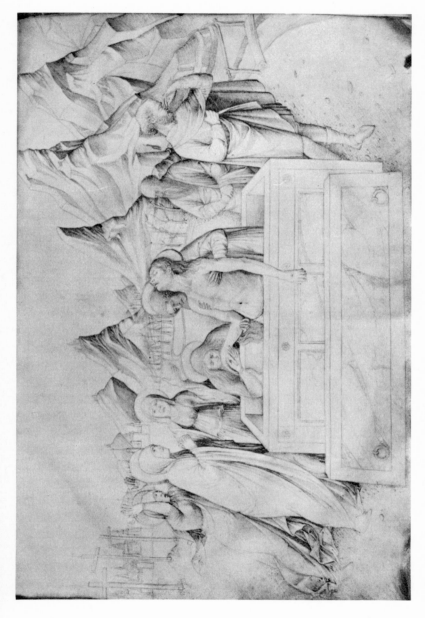

Fig. 54. Jacopo Bellini, Entombment, drawing. Louvre, Paris.

Photo Giraudon.

Fig. 55. Jacopo Bellini, Madonna and Angels, drawing. Louvre, Paris.
Photo Giraudon.

the Cross to which the Saviour is nailed. On the other hand, in
the Crucifixion, which certainly provided him with every oppor-

Fig. 56. Jacopo Bellini, St. Christopher, drawing. British Museum, London. Photo Anderson.

tunity for creating a grandiose composition, the subject is almost lost in a multitude of people and a landscape, or in a view of a city which fills up the background (fig. 58) and the same subject which on one sheet is shown in a mystical dramatic image, in another takes on a thoroughly profane aspect.

Apart from those in the two albums, drawings by Jacopo

Fig. 57. Jacopo Bellini, Madonna in Glory, drawing. British Museum,
London.   Photo Anderson.

Bellini are extremely rare; of these I can cite only the pen and ink
sketch of a grotesque-looking man on horseback in the collection
of the late Mr. Oppenheimer, London, and a very fine St. Christopher in the Albertina in Vienna (¹).

(¹) *A. Stix*, Handzeichnungen aus der Albertina, N. F., II, Vienna,
1925, pl. 11. *A. Stix and L. Fröhlich-Bum*, Beschreib, Katal. der Handzeichn. der Albertina, I, Venez. Schule, Vienna, 1926, No. 16. *Testi*, op.

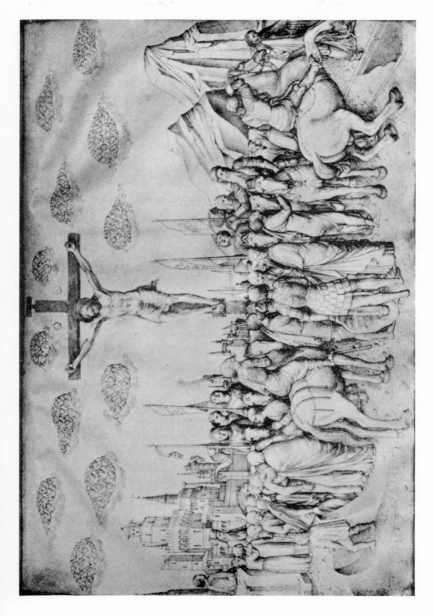

Fig. 58. Jacopo Bellini, Crucifixion, drawing. Louvre, Paris.

Photo Giraudon.

There is not much connexion between the drawings and the paintings by Jacopo Bellini. In the first place the subjects for the greater part are different. In all his sketches there is but one of the Madonna and in that she is depicted in quite another manner than the usual half-length figure which forms the subject of the majority of his paintings.

Although hardly any of Jacopo's drawings have preserved their original appearance, still I think we should be wrong in supposing that they ever possessed very high artistic qualities. Already Testi, with very good reason, has set himself against any comparison in quality with Pisanello's drawings which obviously are the production of an infinitely greater artist and of a much more versatile mentality. Jacopo's forms are elongated and conventional and betray a secretly persisting adherence to the Gothic principles. Jacopo loves height and length, even at the cost of organic construction, as we see in the over-graceful figures, the high rocky peaks, the oft repeated stairway, the flight of steps leading up to buildings and the multi-storeyed houses with tall narrow windows and terraces. On account of this persistent taste for elongated forms, very little in his work is true to nature either in the human proportions or in the architecture. Direct studies of animals, chiefly horses or lions, and of isolated figures of persons are the most realistic, but in larger compositions his taste for conventional forms gets the better of him.

Comparing him with his master Gentile da Fabriano it might almost be said that Jacopo had taken a step backwards where landscapes and perhaps also architecture are concerned. That Gentile was keenly interested in the latter branch of art is obvious from the predella panel of the Presentation in the Temple in the Louvre, in which there is a rich display of contemporary buildings, and although less elaborate than Jacopo's they are certainly of superior execution.

That this example is unique is due in all probability to our incomplete knowledge of Gentile's out-put, because it seems hardly possible that this is the only case in which he depicted buildings; in fact there even exists a tradition that Gentile wrote a treatise on perspective, a science with which Jacopo was not

cit., p. 24. For drawings wrongly attributed to J. B. v. *Testi*, op. cit., pp. 244—247.

very familiar and in the pictorial manifestation of which he made several mistakes.

Also with regard to the landscapes, Gentile was far more accomplished and advanced than Jacopo who compares very unfavourably with him. In one of his drawings Jacopo reproduces Gentile's famous Adoration of the Magi, now in the Uffizi, but the composition lacks elegance and a comparison shows Jacopo as a greatly inferior artist and one altogether unfit to uphold the high level of Gentile's art.

I see no traces of other direct influences on the formation of Jacopo's art. The painters who existed in Ferrara and Padua around the middle of the 15th century are hardly worthy of being taken into consideration. We might think, of course, of a possible knowledge of Donatello's art. There is something in the drawing of the isolated figure of St. John which recalls the type invented by the great Florentine sculptor. Perhaps some points of contact might also be found in his crucifixes and in his taste for perspective in architecture, although the architecture of Donatello's reliefs is very different; but it is chiefly from certain of Jacopo's studies of horses and mounted knights that we are led to believe that he had seen Donatello's Gattamelata. Still, the inference of a knowledge of Donatello's works in Padua would force us to place Jacopo's drawings at a slightly later date because the altar of S. Antonio was inaugurated in 1450 and the equestrian statue in 1453. Personally, I see no difficulty in accepting a somewhat later date for at least a considerable number of the drawings. The different sketches of monuments, which I have already cited, also seem to point to some contact with a sculptor who might have been Donatello.

To give an approximate date to Jacopo's sketch-books still remains a delicate task. We notice such a variety of styles that we can hardly believe that all the works were executed around the same period, but again it might be supposed that the sketches on the same sort of paper were made at a not very great lapse of time from one another. The drawing of Leonello d'Este in tourney attire points to a date approximate to 1441, but many other elements seem to indicate a later period.

Notwithstanding the attractive appearance of Jacopo's drawings, his graceful Gothic lines, the temperament with which he designs the knights in combat, his true portraiture of animals and many other qualities, the albums of London and Paris, when we compare them with those of Pisanello, reveal him as a somewhat second-rate draughtsman.

We may perhaps like him better as a painter; certainly here he shows himself to more advantage. The differentiation between Jacopo as a draughtsman and Jacopo as a painter is very great; as I said before, there is not even much resemblance of subject. A few themes from the albums, however, appear in his late paintings and it may be that very many of his lost paintings were made after these sketches. Still, although some of the subjects naturally coincide, we do not find any striking correspondence between the Christological cycle which Jacopo executed for the Confraternity of S. Giovanni Evangelista, which is minutely enumerated by Ridolfi, and the subjects in the two albums.

**

Of Jacopo Bellini's paintings only one is dated, it is the Madonna originating from Riviera di Casalfiumanese, near Imola, which several years ago was acquired by the Brera Gallery, Milan; the inscription on this picture shows the date 1448. Further, we should in all probability identify the profile portrait of Leonello d'Este in the collection of the late Baron Michele Lazzaroni, Paris, with that which Jacopo executed in 1441 when he competed against Pisanello and won. In the chronological classification of Jacopo's works we should take into consideration also the few vague points of contact with the drawings of his sketch-books; the paintings in which these points of contact exist were executed probably towards 1450 or slightly later, that is to say at a phase which we shall call his middle period. On the other hand those paintings which bear most resemblance to Gentile da Fabriano's art must be his earliest productions.

It is but logical that Jacopo was influenced chiefly by Gentile's last manner, in which the Gothic elements were considerably attenuated.

Probably the earliest work we have from Jacopo's hand which shows the influence of Gentile when this master was still a faithful adherent of the Gothic style, is the enthroned Madonna from the Richter collection, London, now in the Cagnola collection,

Milan. The attribution of this work to Jacopo is not unanimously accepted (¹).

The Madonna seated high and the fully draped Child standing on her knee have a certain connexion with Gentile's picture in the Goldman collection, New York, but in Jacopo's painting there is more severity, less motion and a more marked northern influence in the Gothic style of the throne and calligraphy. In type the Child Jesus betrays a vague resemblance to those depicted by Giambono but there is no trace of a direct influence of this Venetian master.

It is only reasonable that those who ascribe the Madonna in the Cagnola collection to Jacopo hold the same artist responsible for the Annunciation in the church of S. Alessandro at Brescia (fig. 59) (²). A considerable amount of restoration has given a somewhat strange and hard appearance to this panel which none the less seems to me certainly a work by Jacopo Bellini. Inside a room, the perspective of which is augmented by a view of the ceiling, while the back wall is covered with a cloth on the border of which the decoration imitating Kufic letters appears for the first time, we see the Virgin and angel, both attired in magnificent garments, kneeling opposite one another; the Virgin is represented before an inlaid lectern with an oriental rug under her feet.

In the predella there are some elements particularly characteristic of Jacopo's art. His interest in architecture is displayed in the first, second and fourth scenes representing the Nativity of the Virgin, her Presentation in the Temple, where we see a long flight of stairs well in evidence, and the miraculous fall of snow which revealed to Pope Liberius the site of Sta. Maria Maggiore in Rome. In the third scene, the Visitation, and the fifth, the Death of the Virgin, he reproduces those particularly elongated Gothic proportions which we noticed in the drawings of certain religious compositions. In the Visitation we discover that the spiral-shaped rocks of the sketches have been changed into more reasonable but not dissimilar peaked mountains, while in the last scene, the group of the Saviour surrounded by cherubim

---

(¹) *Ricci*, op. cit., Rassegna d'Arte, 1903. *Berenson* and *Gronau* are in favour of this attribution; *Testi* is contrary to this opinion.

(²) Attributed to J. B. by *Berenson*, question-marked by *Gronau* and contradicted by *Testi*.

Fig. 59.   Jacopo Bellini(?), Annunciation, S. Alessandro, Brescia.
Photo Alinari.

carrying the Virgin's soul to heaven bears some connexion with
the Assumption in the London sketch-book. The proportions and
type of the Madonna of the Annunciation remind us of those of
Gentile's middle period.

Under the domination of Gentile's more conservative manner
Jacopo painted also a small panel of the dead Christ, half appearing from His tomb in a rocky landscape, in the gallery of

Fig. 60. Jacopo Bellini, Pietà. Gallery, Verona.   Photo Gracco.

Verona (No. 2148) (fig. 60) and a St. Jerome standing looking at a book and holding a pen while a small lion rubs himself against the saint. This painting, which must have formed part of a polyptych, belonged to the Healy collection, Brooklyn [1] but is now in the Institute of Arts and Sciences of this town.

An influence of the later and somewhat broader manner of Gentile da Fabriano is evident in a half-length figure of the Madonna holding the completely dressed and gesticulating Child on her arm, which was sold with the Paolini collection in New York in December 1924 [2]. The Virgin here is more monumental in appearance but the lines still follow the Gothic formula.

The Madonna in the Poldi Pezzoli Gallery, Milan (fig. 61) [3] shows us a new and more personal type in Jacopo's art. The round oval face, the clear cut features and the high arched eyebrows are decidedly different from the traits we find in the foregoing panels. The calligraphic effect is much less marked in the face of the Virgin and also in the perfectly round head of the

[1] When in this collection it was attributed to Jacopo by *Berenson,* Venetian Painting in America, p. 25.

[2] No. 109 of the sale catalogue in which the attribution to Jacopo is made by von Hadeln.

[3] *Cagnola,* op. cit. *Malaguzzi Valeri,* op. cit.

Fig. 61. Jacopo Bellini, Madonna. Poldi Pezzoli Gallery, Milan.

Photo Anderson.

Infant Christ. Still, the iconographical type of this picture, that
of the Virgin of Humility seated on a cushion on the ground
which is strewn with flowers, is very frequently met with in late
Gothic painting of the early 15th century and, as a matter of
fact, among Gentile's own works. Moreover, the golden hem of
the Madonna's cloak describes a perfectly Gothic line. However,

Fig. 62. Jacopo Bellini, Madonna. J. I. Strauss Collection, New York.

the feeling which emanates from this panel as well as the expression of the Virgin and the Child Jesus is softer and more
human and brings us more closely to the principles of the Renaissance.

Although quite different in appearance, there is an obvious

Fig. 63. Jacopo Bellini (?), portrait. Capitol Museum, Rome. Photo Alinari.

connexion between the above-mentioned Madonna and the half-length figure of the Virgin holding the almost nude Child in her arms, which belongs to Mr. Jesse Isidor Strauss, New York (fig. 62) (¹). At first sight this painting, which is a particularly at-

(¹) *L. Venturi*, op. cit., L'Arte, 1930. *L. Venturi*, Pitture italiane in America, Milan, 1931, pl. 252.

Fig. 64.   Jacopo Bellini (?), Madonna. Louvre, Paris.   Photo Alinari.

tractive production of Jacopo, appears to be of somewhat later
date, but the strong influence of Gentile, very manifest in the
figure of the Child and in the still archaically elongated fingers,
reveals to us that we are dealing with a comparatively early work.

I think we should include among Jacopo Bellini's works a small profile portrait of an aged man with a head-dress hanging down his back, which work is preserved in the Capitol Museum, Rome, where it once bore the name of Giovanni Bellini (fig. 63)(¹). It is certainly Venetian but probably older and is not without a vague connexion with the later manner of Gentile da Fabriano. The attributions to Gentile Bellini and Pisanello, both of which have been proposed by Professor Venturi (¹), seem to me erroneous.

Some resemblance to the art of Gentile da Fabriano is evident in a picture of the Madonna and Child with a tiny adorer in the Louvre (1279) (fig. 64). Many years ago Senator Corrado Ricci and Herr Schubring contradicted the certainly mistaken attribution to Gentile da Fabriano and asserted with conviction that this work was by Jacopo; further, they expressed the opinion that the adoring nobleman was Leonello d'Este (²). Other critics, as for instance Testi, have rejected this attribution but of late Professor Moschetti has pronounced himself in favour of it (³). Personally, although not without some misgiving, I am inclined to include this painting among Jacopo's works. Restoration has somewhat spoiled its original appearance. We discover a certain resemblance to the Madonna in the Cagnola collection but the broader and more mature forms make it obvious that we are dealing with a later production. The landscape is very elaborate and somewhat smoother than that in the predella of the Annunciation at Brescia. The beautiful Gothic letters in the nimbus recall those of the picture in the Cagnola collection. Senator Ricci's affirmation that the kneeling figure is Leonello d'Este and not Sigismondo Malatesta is very convincing; in fact a comparison with Pisanello's medal of circa 1441 (Vol. VIII, fig. 99) leaves no doubt. None the less I do not think that Ricci and Schubring are right in supposing that this is the picture which Jacopo Bellini executed when he competed and won against Pisanello. The subject alone makes it next to impossible, because we can hardly call this panel a portrait of Leonello. There exists, however, a portrait of Leonello

---

(¹) *A. Venturi*, Arch. Stor. dell'Arte, 1889, p. 441. *The Same*, L'Arte, 1918, p. 277.

(²) *Ricci*, op. cit., Rassegna d'Arte, 1904. *Schubring*, Museum, VI, 23.

(³) Dedalo, II³, 1931, p. 602.

Fig. 65. Jacopo Bellini, portrait of Leonello d'Este. Private Collection.

Fig. 66. Jacopo Bellini, Madonna. Brera Gallery, Milan.   Photo Alinari.

which should be taken into consideration. It belonged to the
late Baron Lazzaroni, Paris (¹) and was shown at the exhibition
of ancient Ferrarese art, held in Ferrara in 1933, as a work of
Jacopo Bellini (fig. 65). I feel confident that the attribution is
correct and this might very well be the painting which Leonello's
father preferred to the portrait by Pisanello, now in the gallery
of Bergamo. A fond parent would naturally prefer this painting,
in which the subject has been flattered, as we see if we compare
this likeness with the portrait and medals by Pisanello or even
with the kneeling adorer in the picture in the Louvre.

(¹) *A. Venturi*, op. cit., Pantheon, 1929.

With regard to the next group of works, we have a starting point in the Madonna dated 1448 in the Brera Gallery, Milan, and a drawing in the sketch-book in the Louvre of probably a few years later, which allow us to place the following paintings, all of the Madonna, in the period 1450—1455.

The Madonna in the Brera (fig. 66) is painted on linen stretched on a panel and was discovered in 1912 in the church of the Serviti at Casalfiumanese, near Imola. The picture is polygonal in shape with alternate curves and angles; those to the right are missing so that the words Mater Dei are mutilated. Below, the inscription runs: "*1448 Has dedit ingenua — Belinus mente figuras*" Neither the wording nor the appearance of the letters leads us to believe that the inscription is original. The painting, however, is certainly by Jacopo and as the words of the inscription can be traced a long way back on reliable information, we can only trust that the original date has been repeated. The Virgin is crowned and holds the Child, Who bestows a blessing, carefully in her arms. She has more charm and expression than we have met with up till now and the connexion with Gentile da Fabriano's art has become more distant.

Somewhat broader in conception and in proportions but otherwise not unlike this Madonna is a painting which has belonged to different private collections in Italy. Here the Virgin is depicted in three-quarter length turned towards the Child Jesus Whom she holds with both hands; He is seated on a cushion on a wall in front of her and, looking upwards, blesses.

The type of the Madonna crowned and standing between two angelic musicians with the nude Child in her arms, which forms the subject of one of the drawings in the album in the Louvre, is the same which we find in three half-length figures of the Virgin by Jacopo. They are preserved, one in the Uffizi [1], one at Lovere and one in the Lederer collection, Vienna [2]. In the same group we should include the slightly more than half-length figure of the Virgin in the Brass collection in Venice, even though it is a little different in composition, because here the Madonna is shown

[1] *Ricci*, op. cit., Rivista d'Arte, 1906. *Gamba*, op. cit., *Gronau*, op. cit., Zeitschr. f. Bild. Kunst, 1906. *Giglioli*, Nuovi aquisti della Pall. degli Uffizi, etc. Emporium, XXIII, 1906, p. 231. *Testi*, op. cit., p. 181.

[2] *Planiscig*, op. cit.

Fig. 67. Jacopo Bellini, Madonna. Lederer Collection, Vienna.

Fig. 68. Jacopo Bellini, Madonna. Museum, Lovere.

Photo Minist. Ed. Naz.

seated holding a flower, while the Child Jesus on her knee has a bird in His hand; two cherubim are traced in the background. On the whole this painting seems to be of a somewhat earlier date than the three other works.

The panel in Florence (Plate), on account of its neatness of line, type and attitude, is the one which corresponds most closely with the drawing in the Louvre. The crowned Madonna, of a somewhat Byzantine severity, with down-cast eyes holds the Child, Whose gaze is turned heavenward, tenderly seated on her right palm while she lays her other hand protectingly on His breast. The nimbus and border of her veil are adorned with a design inspired by Kufic writing. This is the finest work we have by Jacopo. The sweet majesty of the Virgin, the superb drawing and the remarkably bright and warm colouring make of this panel a masterpiece, in which charm and technical accomplishments are harmoniously united.

The Madonna in the Lederer collection (fig. 67) is almost a replica of that in the Uffizi. The chief differences are the absence of the crown and the slightly altered inclination of the heads of the Virgin and Child, although the position of the figures is identical. This too is a very fine specimen of Jacopo's brush.

The signed picture in the Tadini Pinacoteca at Lovere (fig. 68) is somewhat different in composition and in type, and corresponds with the Madonna in the Brera rather than with the drawing in the Louvre. Here the Virgin is obviously standing; with both hands she holds the Child Who wears nothing but a coral necklace, and Who bestows a blessing; an open book is placed on the wall on which He stands and close to it there is a label with the signature: "*Jachobus Bellinus*". The nimbus behind the Virgin's crowned head is decorated with an inscription in Gothic letters. The colouring is particularly rich; the cloak of the Madonna is a peculiar shade of green with a gold sheen. The outlines and general appearance are softer and more suave than in the panel in the Uffizi. We discern on the part of the painter a vague evolution towards those handsome human Madonnas, of which the son Giovanni at a slightly later date created such lovely examples.

A few years after this, I think, Jacopo must have executed the rather damaged half-length figure of the Madonna, turned

MADONNA AND CHILD
By Jacopo Bellini, in the Uffizi.

Photo Anderson.

Fig. 69. Jacopo Bellini, Madonna. Accademia, Venice.

towards the right and holding the lively Child Who touches His
Mother's face. This picture, which originates from Legnaro, near
Padua, was acquired by the Accademia of Venice about twelve

years ago (fig. 69). Personally I think that Fogolari (¹) places it at too late a period when he expresses the opinion that it might date from between 1460 and 1470 and that it already betrays an influence of the art of Giovanni. On the contrary, I find that although this fine picture is certainly a production of the Renaissance, it still reveals some reminiscences of the art of Gentile da Fabriano in the type of the Virgin,and that of the Child I should say recalls to a certain extent the works of Giambono.

Several other pictures seem to show some connexion with the drawings in the sketch-books. Two of them are preserved in the museum of Verona; they are the large Crucifixion which is signed and the painting of St. Jerome in the desert. A third work of a mythological subject is found in a private collection.

Of these paintings the Crucifixion is the most important (fig. 70). It is painted on linen and in 1868 was given by Cardinal Luigi di Canossa to the gallery of Verona (365). It has sometimes been supposed that it formed part of the fresco of the Crucifixion which Jacopo painted in 1436 in the cathedral of this town, but this seems impossible; first of all because, in his scenes of the Crucifixion he never leaves so much open space around the central figure as is here the case and secondly, in a fresco he would not have placed his signature at the foot of the cross inscribed on a label, as in this painting: *"Opus Jacobi Bellini"*. Consequently, this picture is not a fragment of a scene of the Crucifixion but a representation of the Crucified. Restoration and repaint have greatly altered the appearance of this painting which originally must have shown considerable analogies with the drawing in the album in the British Museum (fol. 74a); the proportions of the latter, however, are somewhat broader. On another sheet (fol. 55a), although the curve of the body is different, the skull of Adam is depicted at the foot of the cross as it is in the painting at Verona. As has already been observed, it may very well be that Donatello's bronze crucifix in Padua influenced Jacopo when he executed these representations of Christ on the Cross.

The panel of St. Jerome in penitence in the same gallery (306) was ascribed to Jacopo by Senator Ricci (fig. 71). This attribution has been accepted by the majority of art critics but not always without some hesitation, for which I find no reason. Although

---

(¹) *Fogolari*, op. cit.

Fig. 70.   Jacopo Bellini, Crucifixion. Museo Civico, Verona.

Photo Anderson.

Fig. 71. Jacopo Bellini, St. Jerome. Gallery, Verona.   Photo Anderson.

surely his it is not one of Jacopo's finest works. It can be compared with two drawings in the sketch-books, (fol. 17a of London

and fol. 22*b* of Paris). The former sketch shows a greater difference than was perhaps originally the case, because of the fact
that the rocky background has almost entirely disappeared, while
in the latter the figures are much smaller in proportion. None
the less, for the greater part such features as the mountains, the
position of the saint and the animals correspond. However, it is
possible and even seems probable that the painting was executed
some considerable time after the drawings; in fact it may be a
production of Jacopo's late years which would explain the rigidity
and lack of elegance.

The third picture which can be associated with Jacopo's sketch-
books is a mythological scene in a private collection in London. It
represents Hercules shooting his arrow and the rape of the nymph
Deianira by the Centaur [1]. Although this subject does not appear
in the albums, there are drawings of other mythological scenes
with horses and nude figures which in spirit and appearance
are very similar to this rather small panel; it is just possible that
it may have formed part of a cassone.

Lastly, there exists a certain correspondence in composition
between the predella panel of Christ in Limbo in the gallery of
Padua (fig. 72) and two sheets in the sketch-books, one in London
(26*a*), the other in Paris (22*b*). From one or two details, such as
the unusual gesture of Adam kissing the Saviour's hand and the
absence of the door of Hell on which, according to the text and
iconographical tradition, Christ should tread, it is obvious that
the picture follows the drawing in the album in the British Museum; in both points the sketch in the Louvre is different. On
account of the oblong shape of the picture, the mountains are
lower and the composition is continued to the left where several
devils are depicted; one of them evidently replaces the demon
which in both drawings is shown in the right hand corner.
Although numerous elements lead us to ascribe this picture to
Jacopo, it cannot be denied that the work is lacking in style and
it is difficult to believe that a painter to whom we owe such
charming paintings as the Madonnas in the Uffizi and at Lovere
could ever have created such a weak and really rather insipid
work. However, we know nothing of Jacopo's later development

---

[1] *L. Venturi*, op. cit., L'Arte, 1926.

Fig. 72. Jacopo Bellini(?), Descent into Hell. Museum,
Padua   Photo Alinari.

and if his sketchbooks date from around 1450 or slightly later, he lived and worked for almost another twenty years, in fact until he was close on seventy, and the panel in Padua might quite well be a production of his declining years.

It is still more difficult to believe that Jacopo is the author of another predella panel — the Crucifixion in the Correr Museum, Venice, which is still one step further removed from Jacopo as we know him from his authentic works, and even poorer in execution. Many critics reject this attribution and several even doubt that of the foregoing picture. The difference in appearance of the two works seems in part due to their actual condition; both have been restored but that in Venice considerably more so. As the, measurements of these panels correspond, it seems highly likely that originally they belonged to the same altar-piece. In several details this panel shows great similarity with a drawing (37a of the album in the Louvre) where we notice much the same group with the swooning Virgin, the warrior shown from behind holding a shield, though he is in a different place, and the soldier on horseback gesticulating with his right hand. It might be imagined that the last mentioned figure in the panel should represent the converted Centurion, as in fact it does in the drawing, but in the picture a Roman kneeling near the cross obviously is the converted warrior. He appears again in the album in London (86b), along with the soldier seen from behind and a figure of St. John who, to a certain extent, resembles the St. John of the predella panel in Padua. Consequently, it appears likely that the painter was acquainted with both sketches and the presence of two figures which might have been drawn to represent the Centurion indicates that he made a somewhat automatic use of them without any real understanding of their significance. Even if we admit that the Descent into Limbo might be from Jacopo's own hand, I think we are nearer the truth in assigning the Crucifixion panel to his workshop.

An interesting comparison which corroborates the old attribution to Jacopo Bellini of a child's profile portrait formerly in the Dreyfuss collection Paris, now belonging to Duveen Brothers (fig. 73) (¹), is offered to us in the only portrait drawing we possess,

(¹) Once upon a time it was in the O. Mündler collection, Paris, when it was ascribed to Lorenzo di Credi by *S. Reinach*, Tableaux inédits etc.

which is contained in the Paris album (fol. 22a) (fig. 28) (¹); in fact the similarity is such that we might almost admit that the model is the same but, as is often the case when a drawing is used for a painting, the artist would then have slightly corrected the shape of the nose and made the curls descend lower on to the forehead. Besides even if the model is the same, the drawing was obviously made when the subject was of a more mature age and it might be that the person in the sketch is the father of the boy in the picture. The technique is very different from that of the portrait in the Capitol Museum which I imagine to be from the hand of Jacopo; on the other hand it closely resembles that of the painting of Leonello d'Este from the Lazzaroni collection.

Two important Madonnas seem to characterize Jacopo Bellini's later years; they are in any case certainly posterior to those we have dealt with up till now. It cannot be said, however, that the reminiscenes of Gentile da Fabriano's art have completely disappeared; in fact in one of them, that which now forms part of the gallery of Venice (No. 582) (fig. 74), which originates from the Palace of the Doges, the traces of this influence are so manifest that the work is sometimes classified as one of Jacopo's earliest productions. However, if a resemblance in type does exist, there is no longer any trace of the flowery Gothic calligraphic style and this, I think, is a much more significant feature in our determination as to the period in the master's career when this work was executed. The Madonna is shown in half-length figure holding with both hands the Infant Jesus, Who stands on a low wall on which a book is placed. The Child, Who blesses, is fully dressed and holds an apple in His hand. The nimbi and the hem of the young Saviour's robe are decorated with motifs inspired by Kufic characters; a host of cherubim fills up the background, a detail with which we meet in a Crucifixion in the sketch-book in Paris (fol. 55a). The face and hands of the Child have been restored; the construction of the figures, however, is of a monumentality which

---

tirés de collections françaises, Paris, 1900, p. 47. It was claimed to be by Jacopo Bellini in an important article by C. *Philips*, op. cit. This attribution was contested by *Testi*, op. cit., p. 280, but repeated, without mention of Philips' article by L. *Venturi*, op. cit., L'Arte, 1930.

(¹) Reprod. also in Albertina Zeichnungen, No. 1290.

Fig. 73. Jacopo Bellini, portrait of a youth. Duveen Brothers, New York.

is evident for the first time in Jacopo's art. Compared with the
other pictures of the Madonna in which the graceful outline was

Fig. 74. Jacopo Bellini, Madonna. Accademia, Venice.   Photo Anderson.

the dominating factor, here the figure is built up of plastic elements and is three-dimensional, which is typical of the Renaissance. The panel is signed: *"Opus Jacobi Bellini Veneti"*.

The other Madonna belongs to the Burns collection, London ([1]). The composition is very different. The Virgin, depicted in half-length figure, is crowned and Gothic letters adorn her nimbus. Her hands are devoutly crossed on the Child Who lies at her breast, looking round at the spectator; her veil seems to be agitated by the wind. Again cherubim fill up the background and the proportions and plastic effects are very similar to those of the panel in the gallery of Venice; the Gothic calligraphic feature is almost absent and in this picture there is even less which recalls Gentile da Fabriano.

Several critics have attributed to Jacopo an Adoration once in the Vendeghini collection, Ferrara ([2]), but I have never seen this work, while quite recently two busts of Dante and Petrarch have been published as productions of his brush ([3]). Quite a number of other attributions are, I think, inadmissable but most of them have already been contradicted ([4]).

([1]) *Borenius*, op. cit. I have not seen the original.

([2]) *Berenson, Ricci, Testi*, op. cit. with doubt.

([3]) *Fiocco*, op. cit.

([4]) Some of the erroneous attributions are mentioned in *Crowe and Cavalcaselle*, Painting in North Italy, ed. Borenius. I, p. 112 note 2, p. 114, p. 116 note 2. I should like to cite still the following: **Bassano,** Beata Giovanna Church, Madonna and Child (*Fogolari*, op. cit., Boll. Mus. Bassano, also *Ricci*, Disegni, p. 23 and *A. Venturi*, L'Arte, 1905, p. 75; contested by *L. Venturi* and *Testi*); reprod. in my Vol. VII, fig. 246, as by Giambono; Museum, v. school works. **Bergamo,** Gallery, two panels with martyrdom scenes (*Fogolari*, op. cit., *A Venturi* and *L. Venturi*; contested by *C. Ricci* and *Testi*; *Suida*, Monatsh. f. Kunstwiss., 1909, p. 479, judges them to be Lombard); reprod. in my Vol. VII, fig. 260, as possibly by Francesco de' Franceschi; Madonna, generally accepted as a work by Jacopo but seems to me to be without any doubt a production of Gentile da Fabriano and I have reproduced it as such in Vol. VIII, fig. 20. **Berlin,** Kaiser Friedrich Museum, No. 1678, the dead Saviour supported by the weeping Virgin and St. John; the catalogue describes it as possibly a late work by Jacopo, executed under a Paduan influence, and corresponding to a drawing in the Paris sketch-book (fol. 7B); I think it is more likely an early production of Giovanni. **Bologna,** University Library, illustrations in a manuscript of the legend of St. Catherine of Siena, in which I see no connexion whatever with Jacopo Bellini (*Frati*, op. cit.). **London,** ex-Wernher coll., now in Ludlow coll., Annunciation (attributed to J. B. by *Fry*, Monthly Review, 1901, p. 86. *Testi*, judges it to be near Jacopo; ascribed to Gerolamo di Giovanni by *Berenson* and *Ricci* and as such reproduced by me in Vol. XV, fig. 21. **Milan,** Brera Gallery, formerly

The comparatively small number of Jacopo Bellini's extant
paintings is all the more surprising when we learn that many
others seem to have been executed by him. Michiel mentions an

---

No. 485, Madonna and Child originating from Monterubbiano afterwards
at Rovellasca, with the false signature: "*Jacopus Bell . . . . MCCCCLIV*"
v. Le Gallerie italiane, I, pp. 6-7, *Testi*, op. cit., I, p. 224 note 4 and II,
p. 271. It is the centre of a polyptych (now 212) by Pietro Alamanno which
has now been reconstructed; the false signature has been effaced. **New York,**
Metropolitan Museum, Altman coll., profile of a young man, generally
supposed to represent Borso d'Este and attributed to the Ferrarese school
(*Richter* assigns it to Cossa and *Berenson* to Tura but *L. Venturi*, op. cit.,
L'Arte, 1930, who argues that Borso at the age of about twenty, as in this
portrait, could not have been painted by either of these artists, gives it
to Jacopo Bellini; the same argument had already been propounded in the
catalogue of the Altman coll. As I think the painting is a Ferrarese production of the second half of the 15th century and certainly not by Jacopo,
the solution of the problem lies probably in the fact that the subject is not
Borso but some one who bears a strong resemblance to him, possibly one of
his numerous legitimate or illegitimate sons); Chapman coll., Marriage of
the Virgin and Adoration of the Magi (attributed by *Ludwig e Molmenti*,
Carpaccio, pp. 11 and 222, to the bottega of Jacopo and to Jacopo himself. It is hardly likely that they belonged to the decoration of the Scuola
of S. Marco. They should be compared with a Nativity of the Virgin and
an Annunciation in the gallery of Turin (158, 159) v. *Testi*, op. cit., II,
pp. 271 and 282, *L.Venturi*, Pitt. Venez., p. 68 and *Berenson*, Venetian
Painting in America, p. 144. They are weak provincial productions of the
school of Jacopo). **Oxford,** University Gallery, sermon of a Dominican
monk (*Cavalcaselle* and *Ffoulkes*, Arch. Stor. dell' Arte, 1892, p. 70, call it
school of Jacopo; *Testi*, op. cit., II, p. 272, assigns it to the Bolognese
school). **Padua,** S. Clemente, fresco of the Virgin and Child (*W. Arslan*,
op. cit., attributes it to J. B. with a question mark. The work does not
seem to possess the qualities which justify an attribution to Jacopo).
Turin, v. **New York,** Chapman coll. **Venice,** S. Marco, Mascoli Chapel,
the collaboration of Jacopo Bellini with Giambono in the execution of the
mosaic of the Visitation is upheld by *L. Fiocco*, Venezia, Milan-Rome,
1920, p. 229 and *The Same*, Vita Artistica, Dec. 1926, p. 144, who believes,
as before him did also *Thode*, that we owe the architecture to Jacopo. I see
no obvious reasons for this hypothesis; S. Tarasio, the painted decoration
by Andrea del Castagno and Francesco da Faenza (reprod. in my Vol. X,
figs. 206 and 207) were attributed to Jacopo by *Cavalcaselle*, Burckhart
etc.; S. Trovaso, the St. Chrisogonus on horseback for which *Philips*,
Gronau and others hold Jacopo responsible, is by Giambono (reprod. as
such in my Vol. VII, fig. 248); Correr Museum, profile portrait of Doge
Francesco Foscari, sooner by Gentile; No. 62, St. Augustine holding a book;
it shows the false signature "*Jacopo Bellini f. 1430*" and has been made

altar-piece by Jacopo and his two sons in the Gattamelata chapel of S. Antonio in Padua. Polidoro, in his description of this church (1590) gives us the signature as: *"Jacobi Bellini Veneti patris ac Gentilis et Joannis natorum opus MCCCCLX"*. Michiel cites as well a frescoed figure by Jacopo on the first pillar to the left (the text leads us to believe that it was in the Chapter House) in S. Antonio, Padua; a portrait of the father of the philosopher Leonico Tomeo in the same town; a profile portrait of Gentile da Fabriano in the house of Pietro Bembo where there existed another portrait which he believed to be of Bertoldo d'Este. In Venice he refers to the book of drawings on paper — consequently the book now in London — in the house of Gabriel Vendramin.

Vasari speaks of a panel with scenes from the Passion, which Jacopo sent to Verona and in which there was a portrait of the artist, and of a painting of the history of the cross which he believes existed in the Scuola di S. Giovanni Evangelista. He also refers to the fact that the two sons collaborated with their father. Ridolfi seems to know much more about the paintings in this Scuola or Confraternità. He informs us that Vasari is mistaken in stating that Jacopo took any part in the execution of

---

after a drawing in the London sketchbook but it is of later date and is probably a production of the school of Giovanni Bellini.

In his statement that Jacopo Bellini painted the portraits of Giorgio Cornaro and Catherine, Queen of Cyprus, Vasari was possibly mistaken because the latter ascended the throne in 1472, consequently after Jacopo's death (v. *Testi*, op. cit., II, p. 282); however, it might be admitted that Jacopo painted her portrait before she became queen.

With regard to the drawings which seem to be wrongly attributed to Jacopo I shall cite: that of a young man with a bonnet in the Malcolm coll., British Museum (1895-9-15-466); that of a man and two oriental soldiers in the Cocoran Art Gallery, Washington; and that of the head of the Madonna in the Louvre which is reproduced as by Jacopo by *Ricci*, op. cit., Rassegna d'Arte, 1903.

I remain somewhat sceptical about Jacopo's authorship of the grandiose compositions of architecture in chiaroscuro and of the little putto which are preserved in the ex-officina dei Mosaici in S. Marco, where we find as well the inscription *"Maistro Jacopo de la Capela de San Marco"* (v. *Fiocco*, op. cit., in Venezia and in Vita Artistica). The architecture seems to be more evolved in style than that of our artist and I see no reason why the Jacopo mentioned here should be identified with Jacopo Bellini.

the paintings of the miracles of the Cross which are by Gentile
Bellini and others, but from the hand of Jacopo there existed here
a painting of the Saviour — I imagine represented as dead — supported by two angels and scenes from the lives of the Virgin and
St. John which already in Ridolfi's day had fallen into ruin and
had been replaced by more recent compositions of the same scenes.
He gives us a list of the subjects which, according to the document I have already cited, were to be finished by 1465 (¹). Ridolfi
speaks also of many portraits of Venetians, of Jaques Lusignan,
of the King of Cyprus, of some senators, of Petrarch and of a
painting of Laura which once upon a time existed in Treviso (²).

We still know of some other works by Jacopo from their
mention in different records, as for example the fresco of the
Crucifixion of 1436 in Verona, the gonfalon of 1452 in the Scuola
di Sta. Maria della Carità, and the image of Lorenzo Giustiniani
of 1456 over his tomb in S. Pietro in Castello. In 1466 he executed
for the Scuola di S. Marco an altar-piece with the saint and a
cover for it on which the holy patron is again depicted and shortly
after this he painted a Crucifixion with many figures on the
façade and a "telaio dal Chanto sopra la porta de l'albergo" etc.
with the city of Jerusalem, Christ and the two criminals. All this
however was destroyed by fire in 1485 (³). Sansovino (fol. 23
verso) mentions a chapel painted by Jacopo in the church of
SS. Giovanni e Paolo. A picture of a besieged city signed "*Jacopo
Bellini*"(?) was described in 1805 as existing in the Palazzo
Cornaro della Regina, of which we possess a sketch by Cavalcaselle (⁴). We cannot place much confidence in the statements
regarding the existence of an Entry into Jerusalem in the convent
of S. Giorgio Maggiore, Venice, an altar-piece in S. Leonardo,

---

(¹) The Nativity of the Virgin and Joachim writing her name, the
Virgin Mary weaving in the Temple, the Marriage of the Virgin, the
Annunciation, the Visitation, the Nativity under a shelter, the Circumcision, the Flight into Egypt, St. Joseph working at his calling, the return
to Judea, Jesus at the age of twelve teaching in the Temple; the Passion scenes were: the Lord's farewell to His Mother, St. John bringing the
news of Christ's capture to the Virgin, the Calvary, the Crucifixion, the
Resurrection and the Coronation.

(²) *von Hadeln*, note 1 on *Ridolfi*, I, p. 55.

(³) *Testi*, op. cit., p. 255.

(⁴) Idem, p. 257.

Treviso and a picture of Christ in the Accademia of Venice ([1]), all three professedly by Jacopo Bellini. Nor have I any idea of the picture of Venus and Adonis attributed to Jacopo and mentioned by Cavalcaselle as in the collection of Lord Elcho, London ([2]); this critic says that, although similar to, it is more evolved than the panel of the same subject in the Cornaro Palace, Venice, which also is unknown to me.

Works of the school of Jacopo Bellini are rare and generally speaking unimportant ([3]). Obviously, Venetian painting was about to pass into a new phase and this passage was accomplished under the stimulus of Jacopo's most prominent pupils — his own sons. A few drawings of this master's school are found in the well-known Vallardi codex in the Louvre, which contains chiefly drawings by Pisanello.

I find a certain connexion with Jacopo's art in some studies of a horse — a front view, some sketches of legs and another of the head — and still more approximate to the master are: a drawing of a page holding three horses; a sketch of the Centaur carrying away the nymph Deianira — both different from those in

---

([1]) Idem, pp. 257, 258.

([2]) Cited as there by *Testi*. It must be the same work which *Crowe and Cavalcaselle*, Painting in North Italy, ed. Borenius, I, p. 116 note 1, mention as in the collection of Lord Wemyss, Aberlady, near Edinburgh.

([3]) Of the school works I shall cite: **Bassano,** Museum, scenes of the martyrdom of a female saint, attrib. to Jacopo by *Fogolari*, op. cit. and by *A* and *L. Venturi*. This attribution has been quite rightly contested by *Testi*, op. cit., p. 259. *Ricci*, op. cit., is of opinion that it is a school work and this, I think, is the correct classification. It is interesting on account of the architecture and profane dress. **Matelica,** Piersanti Museum, No. 34, 7 small panels with figures of saints showing a certain influence of J. B., as is observed by *Serra*, Rassegna Marchigiana, X, 1932, p. 103 (the second saint is St. Onuphrius and not St. Jerome). These panels have also been attributed to Jacopo himself, to Bartolomeo Vivarini (v. *S. Bigiarette,* Il Museo Piersanti in Matelica, Florence, 1917, p. 26) and by *Serra*, Le Gallerie Comunale delle Marche, Rome (1924), p. 141, to the manner of Jacobello di Bonomo. **Padua,** Gallery, No. 1160, half-length figure of the Madonna giving an apple to the Child; it reveals also some connexion with Giambono. **Venice,** once in Casa Albrizzi, Crucifixion, to which I have already referred as it was supposed to reproduce Jacopo's fresco in Verona; reprod. in *Crowe and Cavalcaselle*, op. cit., I, p. 110. **Verona,** Museum, No. 2139, small Madonna, seated lowly with the Child standing stiffly on her knee.

Jacopo's panel of this subject — and a study of a knight on horseback, of which, however, the front and upper part are missing (¹).

*
* *

One might easily be misled into exaggerating the importance of Jacopo Bellini on account of some of the really fascinating pictures he has created, of which in the first place is the Madonna in the Uffizi. It might also be that a completer knowledge of his paintings than we have nowadays would justify a more general admiration, because his best work leads us to believe that he was gifted with greater talent then he generally displays.

In dealing with Jacopo's drawings I expressed my general opinion concerning his art. However, I should still like to make a few remarks. In the development of Italian painting his place is obviously in the transition from the late Gothic style of the first years of the 15th century to the full-blown Renaissance of which his sons were such important representatives. It appears to me quite evident that he was a greater master as an adherent of the old tradition than as an interpreter of the new manner which, however, was already in full swing before his death in 1470. Besides, even in his late works such as the second Madonna in the gallery of Venice and that in the Burns collection the late Gothic element is not absent.

His principal source of inspiration was Gentile da Fabriano who was also his master, as we gather not only from the documents and from the fact that the elder painter was the god-father of one of his sons but in a still more evident manner from the obvious influence which Gentile exercised on him. However, a local painter also — Giambono — seems at times to have inspired our artist, but more in the choice of his types than in anything else. I have remarked that on certain occasions the appearance of the Child Jesus reminds us of that depicted by Giambono and it was possibly from him that Jacopo took the idea of representing the Madonna with a royal crown, a detail which Gentile never shows but which appears in some of Giambono's paintings as well as in those of his contemporary and fellow-citizen Jacobello del

---

(¹) Les dessins de Pisanello et de son école, publiés par Guiffrey, Paris, 1911, pls. 54, 100, 114, 158.

Fiore, and which might have found its origin in South German or Tyrolese art. The similarity of type explains why Giambono's St. Chrisogonus has been erroneously attributed to Jacopo.

I see really very little of the connexion between Jacopo and Pisanello which Mr. G. F. Hill finds so obvious in some of the sheets in the London sketch-book (¹). I think that any resemblance is probably due to the fact that both artists, especially in their drawings, show, as I said, a tendency towards the same profane repertoire.

Vasari tells us that Jacopo became famous only after the departure of Domenico Veneziano from Venice because after that he had no rival, but this of course is again pure invention on Vasari's part, as is also his affirmation that Jacopo painted on linen because in Venice hardly anyone ever painted on panel.

(¹) G. F. *Hill*, Pisanello, London, 1905, p. 140.

CHAPTER III

GENTILE BELLINI (¹) AND MANSUETI

Concerning Gentile Bellini we have a considerable number of documents(²), from which we learn that he was born in all probability in 1429 and was the son of Jacopo Bellini and his wife Anna who, during her pregnancy, made a will leaving all her belongings

(¹) G. *Biadego*, Variazioni e dinagazioni aproposito di due sonetti di Giorgio Sommariva in onore di Gentile e Giovanni Bellini, Verona, Nozze Gerola-Cena, 1907, L'Arte, 1907, p. 479. *The Same*, Due sonetti di G. Sommariva ne' quali Gentile e Giov. Bellini si dicono a vicende cortesia. *M. A. Chughtai* G. B. and Mehmet II, Burlington Magazine, LXI, 1932, p. 136. *G. Fiocco*, Un nuovo ritratto di G. B., Dedalo, Sept. 1925, p. 205. *Frizzoni*, Bollettino d'Arte, Jany. 1914, *B. Gray*, Two Portraits of Mehmet II, Burlington Magazine, LXI, 1932, p. 4, p. 39. *G. Gronau*, Die Künstler familie Bellini, Bielefeld-Leipzig, 1909, p. 22. *The Same*, A Venetian Senator by G. B., Burlington Magazine, Dec. 1927, p. 264. *D. von Hadeln*, Zur G. B. in der National Gal. in London, Repertorium, XXX, 1907, p. 536. *C. J. Holmes*, in Burlington Magazine, XXXIII, 1918, p. 107. *J. Kurabacek*, Abendländische Künstler zu Konstantinopel, Denkschr. der K. Akad. Vienna, LXII, I, 1918, p. 24. *W. Loftus Hare*, The Portrait of Muhammed II by G. B., Apollo, XX, 1934, p. 249. *A. Luzzio*, Disegni topografici e pitture dei Bellini, Arch. Stor. dell' Arte, I, 1888, p. 276. *F. B. Martin*, A Portrait by G. B. found in Constantinople, Burlington Magazine, IX, 1906, p. 148. *The Same*, New Originals and oriental Copies of G. B. found in the East, Burlington Magazine, XVII, 1910, p. 5. *A. L. Mayer*, Ein Bildnis des G. B., Pantheon, Jany. 1930, p. 17. *F. M. Perkins*, A re-discovered Portrait by G. B., Apollo, March 1927, p. 102. *Ridolfi*, ed. von Hadeln, I, p. 56. *M. Salmi*, L'Arte, XXII, 1919, p. 170. *F. Sarre*, Ein Miniatur G. B.'s gemalt 1479—80 in Konstantinopel, Jahrb. d. K. Preus. Kunstsamml., XXVII, 1906, p. 302. *The Same*, Ein Miniatur G. B.'s, Nachtrag, Jahrb. d. K. Preus. Kunstsamml., XXVIII, 1907, p. 51. *L. Thuasne*, G. B. et Sultan Mohamed II, Paris, Leroux, 1888. *A. Venturi*, Ritratto del Doge Andrea Vendramin per G. B., L'Arte, XXX, Jan.-Feb. 1927, p. 1.

(²) Notes of Milanesi on *Vasari*, III, p. 153. *P. Molmenti*, Studie ricerche di storia e d'arte, Turin, 1892. *Paoletti*, Raccolta di documenti; repeated by *L. Venturi*, op. cit., p. 325.

to the child about to be born, who was no doubt Gentile ([1]).

We know nothing more about him until 1465, the year inscribed on his earliest dated picture; at this time he was thirty-six years old. The following year he is commissioned by the Scuola Grande di San Marco to execute two canvases with scenes of the Exodus of the Jews from Egypt. In 1469 he is knighted and made a Palatine count by the emperor. There are several indications which lead us to suppose that Gentile and Giovanni were very united; even Vasari speaks of this. Very likely they shared a workshop; at least there is a letter of 1471 in which Elisabetta Morosini Frangipane expresses the desire that Gentile and Giovanni should teach the art of drawing to "pre Domenego nostro". In 1474 Gentile receives the charge to repair and keep in order for the rest of his life the ancient paintings in the Sala del Gran Consiglio, which were falling into ruin ([2]). In 1476 Antonio Risso had to execute several low reliefs for the Scuola Grande di San Marco after drawings by Gentile, who was the deacon of this institution.

In 1479 an envoy of Mohammed II, whose portrait had previously been cast by the medallist Matteo de' Pasti, asks the Signoria of Venice for a good portrait-painter willing to go to Constantinople and it was Gentile who went on the 3rd September of this year ([3]). He worked there to the great satisfaction of the sultan and painted erotic scenes in the apartment of the prince; we know of some of the portraits he executed while there. A contemporary, Angiollello, who very probably met Gentile at the court of the sultan, gives us some details about his stay in Constantinople and praises the artist's character; he finds him frank, of an independent spirit, dignified and disinterested ([4]). He was held in such high esteem that on his departure, which took place in November 1480, he was made "bey". According to Vasari the authorities of Venice gave him a pension.

([1]) Testi's objections to this hypothesis have been repeated by *L. Venturi*, loc. cit.

([2]) *Sansovino*, op. cit., fol. 123 verso, also mentions this and speaks of the restorations made in 1474 and 1479 to the ancient paintings by Pisanello and Gentile da Fabriano.

([3]) *Chughtai*, op. cit.

([4]) *Thuasne*, op. cit.

In 1487 Gentile receives payment for the portrait he had made of the late Doge Marco Barbarigo, and two years later he witnesses the testament of the wife of Mansueti. In 1492 he makes an offer to the Scuola Grande di San Marco to replace, with the help of his brother, in a very short time and at a minimum cost, the painted decoration executed by them and their father Jacopo which had been destroyed by fire in 1485; this offer is accepted. The same year we find him acting as an official of the Scuola. Towards the end of 1493 he is charged by Francesco Gonzaga, Marquis of Mantua, to execute a portrait of the Doge Agostino Barbarigo and representations of Cairo and Venice (¹). He requests a recommendation from the marquis in order that the authorities should allow him more time in which he could execute these works. The picture of Cairo was apparently made after a print which the envoy of Gonzaga brought to Venice for the purpose. For the view of Venice he decides to use a sketch made by his father, but as it is old he has to trace it over. I have already referred to this occurrence. The Marquis of Mantua however gets it on loan in order to have it copied by his court painter. In 1497 there is some question of a representation of Genoa which Gentile had to make for Gonzaga.

In 1494 his wife, Caterina Baresina, makes her will and in 1501 Gentile figures in a notarial act in which his titles of knight and palatine count are given in full, with the mention that he received them in 1469 from the Emperor Frederic III (²). In 1502, 1503, 1504, 1505 and 1506 his name appears as witness to various testaments. In 1503 his second wife Maria di Antonio da Gabon from Treviso makes her will which is witnessed by Gerolamo da Santacroce.

In 1504 he decides to make, for a very slight remuneration and chiefly in commemoration of himself, a large picture on canvas for the Scuola Grande di San Marco. The "Guardiano Grande" begs him to execute a second and slightly larger painting for the same sum. His testament, in which he bequeathes almost all his belongings to his wife, contains various items of some interest. He leaves a mosaic of the Madonna to the Scuola Grande di San

---

(¹) *Luzzio*, op. cit.

(²) *Thuasne*, op. cit., p. 49, is mistaken in stating that he got the last-mentioned title from the sultan Mohammed.

Marco and his father's sketch-book to his brother on condition that he finishes the work which Gentile had started for the Scuola; in accordance with this disposition Giovanni makes a contract to finish the Sermon of St. Mark; this picture is now in the Brera Gallery, Milan. Gentile's assistant is bequeathed all his drawings "retracta de Roma" which would lead us to believe that Gentile had been to this city. To the church of S. Giminiano he leaves a large picture of the Madonna. Francesco Gonzaga remained his faithful patron to the end and in 1506 gave an order to Gentile who, however, had to refuse it because he had more work in hand than he could finish. On the 23rd February 1507 Marin Sanudo mentions that Gentile was buried in the church of SS. Giovanni e Paolo, as he had expressed a desire in his will.

Few painters have been made the recipient of such honours as Gentile Bellini — knight, count, bey — and although no one can deny his merits, we are all the same somewhat surprised about these numerous distinctions because Italy can boast of many an artist of equal, and even considerably greater, ability who was not rewarded in this manner.

Further, the master was glorified by poets, particularly by Cillenio and Raffaello Lorenzetti, but he had his opponents as well and among them the most aggressive was the writer Andrea Micheli, known as Strazzola, who speaks of the painter in the most insulting terms and on one occasion, when he was not satisfied with a portrait which Carpaccio had made of him, he scornfully refers to the artist as worthy of being a disciple of Gentile Bellini (¹). Also the manner in which Sansovino speaks of him shows anything but sympathy. In the passage in which he refers to the restoration of the ancient paintings in the Sala del Gran Consiglio, he says that Gentile repainted several of them but he did so out of envy and to conceal the glory of others rather than to improve the old pictures.

The reason why we have no evidence of any form of Gentile's activity prior to the year 1464, that is to say when he was thirty-five years of age, may be due to the fact that up to this date much of his time was spent in collaborating with his father Jacopo. When he started working independently he acquired

---

(¹) *L. Venturi*, op. cit., p. 331.

immediately a valuable artistic personality although it cannot be said that his first dated work — the organ doors in S. Marco — give us a very high opinion of his capabilities. It is just possible that we have an earlier and much superior production of his brush in the profile portrait of the Doge Francesco Foscari in the Correr Museum (Plate). This doge, after a long reign of thirty-four years, died in 1457 and it is hardly likely that this portrait was painted much after his death; in fact the realistic appearance of the picture might lead us to believe that it was executed during his lifetime or perhaps immediately after his decease ([1]).

The attribution of this painting to Gentile is not unanimously accepted but I think all the same it is very likely correct. Although it is decidedly superior to the organ doors of S. Marco, it bears a strong resemblance to the profile portrait of 1465 of St. Lorenzo Giustiniani. In both we notice the same gift for realistic portraiture and the same skilful draughtsmanship. The doge wears his magnificent robes of office and we can easily believe that Gentile's painting of this energetic ruler and shrewd politician is very true to life; the proportions, however, appear to be somewhat heavy.

Another early work is no doubt a panel in the museum of Berlin (1180) representing the Madonna with the Child, Who carries a pomegranate and bestows a blessing on a nobleman and a lady whose busts are depicted below (fig. 75). The signature, *"Opus Gentilis Bellinus"* is inscribed on the frame, but this did not prevent Morelli from contesting Gentile's authorship. Of all Gentile's productions this is the one in which his father's influence is most obvious; this is noticeable particularly in the type of the Madonna and Child. On the whole it is a rather mediocre production.

Concerning the two organ doors of S. Marco, which are now kept in the museum of the church, there exists a tradition that they were painted in 1464 but it is difficult to trace the source of this affirmation. The signature, *"Gentilis Bellini"* is inscribed

---

([1]) *Gronau*, Künstlerfamilie, p. 26, thinks it possible that it might be a later copy of a portrait made during the doge's life time; he finds it too rough to accept as the work of a master but in this I do not agree with him.

THE DOGE FRANCESCO FOSCARI
By Gentile Bellini, in the Correa Museum in Venice.

Photo Anderson.

Fig. 75. Gentile Bellini, Madonna and donors. Museum, Berlin.

Mus. Photo.

Fig. 76. Gentile Bellini, St. Theodore. S. Marco, Venice.

Photo Alinari.

Fig. 77. Gentile Bellini, St. Jerome. Cathedral, Trau.

Photo Minist. Ed. Naz.

Fig. 78. Gentile Bellini, Annunciation. Thyssen-Bornemisza Collection, Lugano.

to the left and right of the two life-sized figures, one of whom is St. Mark, standing reading, while the other is St. Theodore (fig. 76) in the attire of a Roman warrior, holding a broken lance and a shield. Notwithstanding the somewhat Gothic draping of the former we discover in these figures a very obvious influence of Mantegna who, as a matter of fact, had been a co-disciple with Gentile in Jacopo's studio, and who, besides, had been Gentile's brother-in-law for close on ten years. The architectural perspective of the arches which frame the two figures and the garland of fruit seem to have been borrowed from Mantegna's frescoes in the Eremitani chapel, where we find as well Roman soldiers of a similar type and where the figure of St. James might have inspired Gentile when he executed the patron saint of Venice. Further, the figure of St. Theodore bears a considerable resemblance also to Mantegna's St. George in the gallery of Venice, which was finished shortly before 1464. This close connexion with Mantegna's manner is unique in Gentile's work in as far as we know it, although a slight influence is noticeable in other productions. Perhaps Gentile himself realized that he had completely failed in his obvious attempt to imitate Mantegna's grandeur, strength and majesty, and indeed the two saints are heavy and stodgy though it should not be forgotten that they are in a poor state of preservation.

Of greatly inferior technique however are the figures of St. Francis receiving the stigmata and St. Jerome in penitence, more especially the latter; both are painted against a landscape background on the verso of the panels. There can be no doubt that they were left to some assistant.

Rather similar in style are the figures of St. Jerome (fig. 77) and John the Baptist in elaborate landscape backgrounds, which are found in the cathedral of Trau. Mr. Berenson attributes them to Gentile (¹) and this opinion is now generally accepted. The date 1467 which is connected with the building might furnish us with some indication as to the year of the execution of these figures.

An important picture of the Annunciation in the collection of Baron Thyssen-Bornemisza, Lugano (fig. 78) is very likely of earlier date than the two figures in S. Marco (²). The angel is depicted kneeling on the street outside a portico in which the Virgin kneels at a simple lectern. The architecture of the portico is once more obviously inspired by Mantegna's frescoes at Padua, in the backgrounds of which we discover also some buildings resembling those in the side street in this picture. The Madonna is very similar in type to that of the signed painting in Berlin while the angel, though shown in profile, recalls those

---

(¹) G. *Fiocco*, Carpaccio, Rome (1931), pls. 23, 24, ascribes them, however, to Carpaccio.

(²) No. 20 of the catalogue of the exhibition of this collection in the Neue Pinakothek of Munich in 1930. *Burmann*, Cicerone, 1930, p. 368, Pantheon, July 1930, p. 317.

Fig. 79. Gentile Bellini, Beato Lorenzo Giustiniani. Accademia, Venice.
Photo Anderson.

standing to either side of St. Lorenzo Giustiniani of 1465, with
which picture I am about to deal. The signature must have been

Fig. 80. Detail of fig. 79.   Photo Alinari.

inscribed once upon a time on the little label which we see below
but all that remains visible is the word *"opus"*.

The earliest work actually dated by Gentile is the large colourless canvas in the gallery of Venice, representing the first patriarch of Venice, St. Lorenzo Giustiniani, standing in profile and

bestowing a blessing in a landscape background; a cleric kneels to either side; each of them is accompanied by an angel carrying what is obviously meant to be a symbol, to the left it is a long processional cross and to the right a bishop's mitre. Above there was a garland but it is now practically effaced, in fact the entire picture is sadly damaged, apparently by moisture (figs. 79, 80). It originates from the church of the Madonna dell' Orto where Moschini saw it on the first altar to the left. On a label below we read: "*MCCCCLXV opus Gentilis Bellini Veneti*". Although this picture has been very much criticized, I think all the same that the head is a very fine piece of portraiture. It is treated with veracity and soberness but gives the spectator an excellent idea of the individuality of the subject; the expression, which conveys to us that his soul is at perfect peace, is intensified by the position of the body and the movement of the blessing hand. It is just possible that on some other occasion the patriarch, who died in 1455, sat for Gentile. The bodies and draperies are hard and rigid, more especially those of the angels who in type bear a resemblance, perhaps fortuitous, to certain of Piero della Francesco's angelic figures. The two clerics also must have been very realistic portraits; the one to the left, which is better preserved, offers us convincing evidence of the correctness of the attribution to Gentile of the portrait of Francesco Foscari, with which it shows great analogy in style and technique. The composition, however, is poor and as I said before there is an all too evident and reprehensible element of rigidity.

This picture seems to have served as model for the woodcut which illustrates Giustiniano's "Doctrina della vita monastica" which appeared in Venice in 1494; there are besides several more or less free replicas of the bust of this saint, two of which seem to be from Gentile's own hand. One of them is found in the gallery of the seminary of Venice (fig. 81). It is a very fine piece of work. The hand which blesses is visible; the figure is framed by a small arch and short beams of light radiate from his black bonnet. The other, which forms part of a private collection (fig. 82), does not show the hand. Also the nimbus of light is absent and this might be an indication that the picture was painted before the patriarch was beatified. Here the individuality is if anything still more pronounced and the folds, missing in the previous panel, start at

the neck of the robe and follow a straight and rigid line, so characteristic of Gentile. A monochrome copy in the gallery of Bergamo
is very similar to this picture (¹).

Another example exists in the Ecclesiastical Museum of
Breslau while a much later copy, lacking in quality and character,
is preserved in the Johnson collection, Philadelphia (162).

Very close in manner to these small replicas is a portrait, which
I know only from a reproduction, belonging to the de Feltre
family, of an ancestor who was a prelate (²). This again is a sharp
profile full of individuality but here there is less feeling and the
dry lifelessness of old age is more marked. The sitter wears a
bonnet and a white surplice over his ecclesiastical dress.

In all these early portraits Gentile Bellini shows himself to
have been more of a draughtsman than a painter, not only because
these works on the whole are either colourless or lacking in colour,
but also because the entire value of these portraits lies in the
linear drawing which is always conspicuous and skilful, whereas
the plastic effects are neglected. Consequently the connexion with
Mantegna, with whose small portrait in the museum of Naples
a comparison has been made, seems to me very superficial and
does not affect Gentile's technique.

A realistic profile portrait which Professor Planicsig has with
good reason linked with these early examples (³), and which
recalls in particular that of Francesco Foscari, is found on the
painted cover of a Byzantine reliquary of the 14th century which
the Patriarch Gregor Melissenos, who died in 1459, brought to
Rome and left to Cardinal Bessarion. It is now in the gallery of
Venice but for a long time was preserved in the Scuola della
Carità (now the Accademia) to which institution Cardinal Bessarion gave it in 1472 when he went as papal ambassador to
France; his intention had been to let the Scuola della Carità have
it after his death. The fact that, besides the cardinal, two brethren
— probably of the Scuola — are depicted on the cover, might
lead us to suppose that the painting was executed on the occasion
of its presentation to the Scuola, anyhow Bessarion is very aged

---

(¹) *C. Ricci*, Le Gallerie etc. in Bergamo, Bergamo, 1907, reprod. p. 20.
(²) *Fiocco*, op. cit., Dedalo, 1925.
(³) *Planicsig*, Jacopo u. Gent. Bellini.

Fig. 81.   Gentile Bellini, portrait of Beato Lorenzo Giustiniani. Seminary,
Venice.   Photo Böhm.

in this portrait and the date of execution must be fairly approximate to this moment.

In a history of the reliquary written by a certain Schioppalalba.

Fig. 82. Gentile Bellini, portrait of Lorenzo Giustiniani. Private Collection.

in the 18th century we are told that it was Gentile Bellini who painted the cover of this greatly venerated object. Michiel gives quite a minute description of the panel and Sansovino also mentions its existence.

The panel, which was the door of the shrine and on which the cardinal and the two brethren are depicted in adoration before the shrine itself, is now in the August Lederer collection, Vienna, where it was recognized by Professor Planiscig.

In the National Gallery, London (3911), there is an important panel of the Madonna which formerly belonged to the Eastlake and Mond collections (fig. 83).

The Virgin is depicted on an imposing architectural throne to the sides of which pieces of a landscape are visible; she wears a crown and is attired in magnificent robes, while an oriental carpet covers the steps of the throne; the nude Child, Who blesses, stands on her knee. On a strip below we read: *"Opus Gentilis Bellini Veneti Equitis"*. As we know that Gentile was knighted in 1469 this picture must date from after that year ([1]). On the other hand the resemblance it shows to Jacopo's Madonnas is so obvious that we cannot place it very much later in his career. However, the entire panel is restored and it is impossible to form a very precise idea of its original appearance. It is sometimes believed that it formed the centre of the altar-piece mentioned by Ridolfi and Boschini as existing in the Scuola dei Mercanti, near S. Giuliano.

If Gentile painted the portrait of the Doge Niccolo Marcello, also in the National Gallery, London, he must have done so in the years 1473 or 1474, during the short time the doge's reign lasted. I really find no reason to doubt the attribution to Gentile, as so often is done. He seems to have been the portraitist-elect of the doges and several other examples of his work as such are known to us. Compared with his earlier paintings we notice here that the plastic effects are more marked; once more we discern that penetrating comprehension of the sitter's individuality, which was one

---

([1]) *Ffoulkes*, L'Arte, XIV, 1911, p. 168. *Berenson*, Study and Criticism of Italian Art, I, p. 118, has overlooked this and thinks that the word "eques" refers to the title of Bey and consequently that the picture must date from after Gentile's return from Constantinople in 1480. He has since changed his mind. *L. Venturi*, op. cit., p. 332, is of opinion that the whole signature is false; I do not think this is the case although it has certainly been very much retouched.

Fig. 83. Gentile Bellini, Madonna. National Gallery, London.

Photo National Gallery.

of Gentile's great gifts. This picture is of a fine and accurate technique but has little charm.

Considerably more important is the profile portrait of the Doge Andrea Vendramin (1476—1477) which once upon a time was for sale in London but which now forms part of the Frick collection, New York (fig. 84) (¹). We discover in this work a particularly happy development towards a more adequate treatment of plastic values. Whereas the features of Doge Foscari and of St. Lorenzo Giustiniani were obtained chiefly by outlines on a flat surface, here we find a subtly treated, though none the less very evident, opposition of light and shade and a very able treatment of the third dimension. It might be supposed that the influence of his brother Giovanni had a softening effect on Gentile's art because the harshness of his early manner has given place to a certain suavity. As always in Gentile's portraits we are once more struck by the interesting comprehension and rendering of the individuality of the subject.

As Professor Gronau observes (²), a sudden but obvious influence of Antonello da Messina, which, however, was of short duration, leads us to believe that it was about this time, that is to say coinciding with Antonello's activity in Venice, that Gentile executed a bust-length portrait in three-quarters right profile of a man wearing the attire — a black bonnet and a red coat — of a senator. It was formerly for sale in Germany but is now in a private collection in America. Were it not for the elements borrowed from the great Sicilian, we might, on account of the importance given to the linear effects, easily have placed it earlier in Gentile's career.

Gentile's portrait of Mohammed II which formed part of the Layard collection, Venice, but is now in the National Gallery, London (3099) (fig. 85), is — notwithstanding its rather ruined condition — perhaps the finest work we have by the master (³). He must have executed it at the very end of his sojourn in Constantinople because the long inscription which gives the names of the subject and the artist — not omitting his knighthood — ends with the date 25th November 1480. This inscription is not really

---

(¹) *A. Venturi*, op. cit., L'Arte, XXX, p. 1. *Perkins*, op. cit., Apollo, 1927. *Mayer*, op. cit.

(²) *Gronau*, op. cit., Burlington Magazine, 1927.

(³) *A. Venturi*, L'Arte, XV, 1912, p. 451. Rassegna d'Arte, XVII, 1917, p. 198. *Gray*, op. cit. *Loftus-Hare*, op. cit.

Fig. 84. Gentile Bellini, portrait of Doge Andrea Vendramin. Frick Foundation, New York.

in the form of a signature but no doubt the information is correct. The bust of the sultan is depicted within a frame of the Italian Renaissance; its suave beauty is really fascinating and Gentile's great gift for portraiture has not failed to penetrate and render to the full the cold and cruel mysterious nature of the oriental, who certainly looks a somewhat awe-inspiring personality.

Gentile reveals a certain familiarity with Islamic art in a miniature in the Gardner collection, Boston, in which he depicts a Turkish artist drawing on a tablet; it is really a vision of the Thousand and One Nights (fig. 86) ([1]). The richly attired and turbaned oriental colleague of Gentile is quite young and very intent on his activity. Professor Sarre suggests it might be one of those Christian pages, converted to the Islamic religion, who were trained in the arts and sciences. It is executed in gouache and ink on parchment. The little flower in the background may have been added by an oriental, as also the Arabic inscription which tells us that the miniature is the work of *"Ibn Muezzin who was a famous painter among the Franks"*. It has already been explained that this curious name may be due to a misreading of the Greek transcription of that of Gentile. This superb little work, which is pasted in an album containing occidental prints and oriental miniatures, was discovered and acquired by Dr. Martin in Constantinople.

In the Tabbagh collection, Paris, there is a slightly altered version of the same subject by the Persian miniaturist Behzad, who was active in the late 15th century and early 16th ([2]), and as Mr. Hendy remarks, a comparison between the two miniatures proves that Gentile's familiarity with oriental art was decidedly limited; this is manifest chiefly in the rendering of depth or the third dimension, which the Persian artist did not even attempt.

Mr. Berenson mentions other miniatures in the University Library of Constantinople representing the Madonna and Child and a seated Turkish scholar, which he attributes to Gentile Bellini. They are known to me only from some photographs which Mr. Berenson was kind enough to lend me. These miniatures seem to have a rather un-European appearance. Moreover, Gentile had at least one native pupil in Constantinople — Schiblizada Ahmad — and it might have been he who executed these miniatures and that in the Serai Library, Constantinople, which represents Mo-

---

([1]) *Sarre*, op. cit., Jahrb. der K. Preus. Kunstsamml., XXVIII, 1907, p. 51. *Martin*, op. cit. *Ph. Hendy*, Catalogue of the exhibited paintings and drawings, Boston, 1931, p. 30.

([2]) *Martin*, op. cit., Burlington Magazine.

Fig. 85. Gentile Bellini, portrait of Mohammed II. National Gallery, London.   Photo Anderson.

hammed II smelling a flower; this miniature seems to follow Gentile's picture in the National Gallery (¹).

It was no doubt during his stay in Constantinople that Gentile executed a small bust-length portrait on canvas of a young ori-

---

(¹) *Gray*, op. cit.

Fig. 86. Gentile Bellini, a Turkish artist. Gardner Museum, Boston.

ental wearing a turban and turned three-quarters to the right, which I saw some years ago in a private collection in Hungary. It is of very fine quality but more European in technique and spirit.

A marvellous study of two orientals, not without a touch of caricature, is shown in a larger canvas which some time ago was acquired by the Art Institute of Chicago (fig. 87). One of the

Fig. 87. Gentile Bellini, two Orientals. Art Institute, Chicago.

figures is thin and haggard with eyes closed as if in meditation; the other is rather stout, severe, eager and very much awake. The handling of the material is masterly and the treatment somewhat broader than usual; it seems probable that this canvas formed part of a larger composition.

If it can be supposed that Gentile, during his stay among the infidel, made pictures of Christian subjects, and the miniatures in the University Library of Constantinople would entitle us to think he did, then I think we should place in this period an Adoration of the Magi in the National Gallery, London (3098) (fig. 88), in which, apart from the Virgin and St. Joseph, all the figures are oriental; they include Turks and Arabs who are de-

Fig. 88. Gentile Bellini, Adoration of the Magi. National
Gallery, London.   Photo National Gallery.

Fig. 89.   Gentile and Giovanni Bellini, Adoration of
the Magi. Private Collection.

picted in characteristic national costumes. Some horses intermingle with the crowd which fills up the foreground, while in the
distance we see a fine landscape with rocks and trees, on which
birds are perched, and a beautiful cloudy sky. This is the first outdoor scene we have by Gentile and it is really an enchanting one
with much aerial perspective and an excellent effect of distance.
The scene is enveloped in a wonderful warm light which gives the
colouring a very fine transparency. The rocks and more especially
the cavern to the left point again to an inspiration of Mantegna[1].

In a private collection in Rome there exists another picture of
this subject (fig. 89), which is of the same shape and of a somewhat similar composition; the landscape, however, is less elaborate
and the people fewer in number; here too there is only one house
and its position and site are different; there are not so many
orientals and the features are of a more regular beauty; the
colours are brighter and we notice, especially in the two Roman
soldiers, some reminiscenes of Mantegna's art. I think we can
come to the conclusion that this work is due to the combined
labours of Gentile and Giovanni and that in all probability it was
executed some years prior to the painting in the National Gallery.

The drawings of orientals, now in the British Museum, were no
doubt made during Gentile's stay in Turkey. They are not very
characteristic of his manner and their attribution to Gentile has
often been doubted. They should be looked upon as rough
sketches made with the intention of being used at some future
occasion and the painter has even written on them the colours of
certain parts of the woman's dress.

Martin also reproduces two little sketches of animals, — a hind
and a running hare — which were found in Persia ([2]), they look
a little more Pisanellesque than is generally the case for works of
Gentile Bellini, to whom he attributes them.

When Gentile returned to Venice he started at once painting
portraits of the doges, but his principal occupation at this time
was the restoration of the old paintings in the hall of the Gran
Consiglio; these works however are lost.

In the Correr Museum there is a portrait of Giovanni Mocenigo

---

[1] R. *Longhi*, Vita Artistica, II, 1927, p. 134, thinks that this picture
might be a production of the mature years of Giambellino.

[2] *Martin*, op. cit., Burlington Magazine, XVII.

Fig. 90. Gentile Bellini, portrait of Doge Agostino Barbarigo. Harcourt
Collection, Oxfordshire.   Photo Cooper.

who was doge from 1478 till 1485. This painting is in poor condition but seems to have borne considerable resemblance to those
of the Doges Vendramin and Marcello. Recently another portrait
of a doge attributed to Gentile was offered for sale in New York;
it was identified as representing Giovanni Mocenigo ([1]). I know
this work only from a photograph and certainly the attribution

([1]) *Mayer*, op. cit.

seems acceptable but I do not think that the subject is the same as that of the portrait in the Correr Museum. It is possible that it represents Marco Barbarigo, who became doge in 1485 but who died within the year.

The style of the painting does not allow us to suppose that it might be one of the successors of Agostino Barbarigo, who ruled over Venice from 1485 till 1501 and of whom we know the particularly fine portrait by Gentile Bellini in the collection of Viscount Harcourt, Nuneham Court, near Oxford (fig. 90). Here the painter has abandoned the habit of showing the doges in profile and the magnificient head of this venerable ruler is turned three-quarters to the right. In this picture there is something of the peace, of the suave beauty and of the refined technique which we noticed in some of the works executed in Constantinople and which give this panel also a somewhat oriental spirit. On a label below is inscribed the signature: *Gentile Bellini* ([1]). A document of 1493, which I cited before, speaks of a portrait of this doge made by Gentile, which was sent to Francesco Gonzaga, Lord of Mantua, and it seems likely that this is the picture in question.

Of Gentile's last years we have four large canvases dating from 1496, 1500, 1501 and 1504. After his return from Constantinople he undertook several such pictures, no doubt with many figures, for the big council hall. Three of these canvases, which are now in the gallery of Venice (567, 563, 568), originate from the Albergo della Scuola di San Giovanni Evangelista; on the whole they are in poor condition, have suffered restoration and were probably never entirely from the hand of Gentile, although in their present state it is not easy to differentiate the master's share from that of his helper or helpers.

The first of these works depicts the procession of the relic of the cross in the Piazza San Marco and is signed and dated: *"MCCCCLXXXXVI Gentilis Bellini Veneti equitis crucis amore incensus opus"* (figs. 91, 92). The picture represents the square of San Marco with the church as background and other buildings to the sides; the architecture shows great precision and keen obser-

---

([1]) The picture was shown at the exhibition of Italian art held in London in 1930, Dedalo, May 1930, p. 747; for the bibliography and further references v. *Balniel and Clark*, Commemorative Catalogue of the Exhibition of Italian Art etc., Oxford-London, 1931, No. 155.

Fig. 91. Gentile Bellini, Procession in Piazza S. Marco.
Accademia, Venice. Photo Anderson.

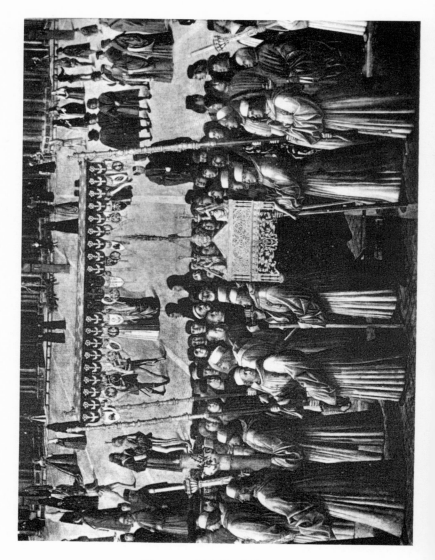

Fig. 92. Detail of fig. 91.   Photo Anderson.

vation on the part of the artist. The procession passes along three
sides of the square, leaving an open space in the centre where a
few noblemen and magistrates are depicted. The relic, which is
carried under a baldaquin and accompanied by a choir of clerics
and musicians, has just reached the centre of the foreground. The
multitude forms a human hedge to either side; the doge himself,

Fig. 93. Gentile Bellini, Miracle of the Cross. Accademia, Venice.

Photo Anderson.

followed by a number of dignitaries, is visible rather far back to
the right. Many of the figures in the foreground are no doubt
portraits. That Gentile actually painted portraits in similar large
compositions is confirmed by Ridolfi who, in some cases, gives the
names of those represented. We know that the old man who, cap

Fig. 94. Detail of fig. 93.

Photo Anders[o...]

Fig. 95. Detail of fig. 93.   Photo Anderson.

in hand, kneels just behind the baldaquin is Jacopo Salis, a
merchant from Brescia, who obtained the grace of the miraculous
cure of his son. On account of a somewhat exaggerated rendering
of perspective the figures in the distance are extremely small but
on close examination we discover that they are very minutely
executed. This is also the case for the mosaics on the façade of
S. Marco, which have since been replaced by more modern ones.
That the more distant figures are from the hand of Mansueti, as
has been supposed, does not seem very probable; only they are
somewhat more restored than the others and have lost much of
their original character. Gentile's extraordinary gift as a realistic
portraitist is revealed in a remarkable manner in the personages
of the principal group.

Gentile has used the picture of the miracle of the cross (figs.
93—95) ([2]) to make a great display of this particular talent. As

([1]) A drawing in the British Museum, of the school of Dürer, represents
the three orientals which in Gentile's picture are reproduced among the
tiny figures in the background, *Pauli*, Vorträge, Bibl., Warburg, 1921-22,
p. 51, pl. 1; *H. Tietze und E. Tietze-Conrat*, Der junge Dürer, Augsburg,
1928, p. 87, pl. 213.

([2]) *Fogolari*, Dedalo, V, pp. 777, 780.

in some of the works of the Florentine painters, such for instance as Benozzo Gozzoli and Ghirlandaio, the event takes a more or less secondary place and the chief scope of the painting seems to be the ostentatious show of portraits, combined perhaps with an outlet for the interest in architecture. The miracle occurred when the relic was being carried to the church of S. Lorenzo; the sacred object fell into the water and all the efforts of the people in gondolas and in the canal to recover it were in vain; the saving of it was reserved to Andrea Vendramin, the Guardiano of the Scuola, who must have felt very gratified over the miracle. Considering the pollution of the Venetian canals, great devotion is, I think, shown by all those who threw themselves into the water.

In the foreground to the right there are five kneeling and four standing figures; the former are all excellent profile portraits. To the left kneels an elderly woman wearing a veil and in front of her a young girl richly attired. Behind the latter figures there is rather a stiff row of noble matrons; the one nearest the spectator wears a crown and is no doubt Caterina Cornaro, Queen of Cyprus. A crowd of noblemen and ladies is seen behind and their features are so individual that undoubtedly they are all portraits. Crowds of people look on from the bridge which crosses the canal. The ungainliness of the composition is compensated by the beauty of the architecture which fills up the background. This canvas, which is considerably restored, shows the signature: *"Gentili Bellini Veneti F. MCCCCC"*; but this has been retouched and is perhaps even entirely new.

The third picture in the gallery of Venice illustrates the miraculous cure of Pietro de Ludovici, brought about by a candle which had been in contact with the holy relic. The event takes place in front of an altar, which in itself looks like a building, in the apse of a handsome late Gothic church, depicted by the painter with great minuteness and care of detail. A priest in his robes, preceded by another cleric, approaches the altar where the healed man, with two figures not entirely visible behind, kneels before a monk. In the body of the church towards the spectator stand several men who all appear to be solemn dignitaries; a plain elderly woman with a candle in her hand begs from the group to the right. This canvas was executed in 1501 and is signed *"Gentilis Bellini Veneti F."*. It has often been thought that some assistant

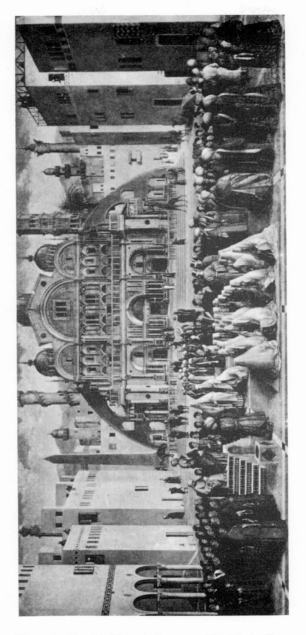

Fig. 96. Gentile Bellini, Sermon of St. Mark. Brera
Gallery, Milan. Photo Anderson.

had a share in the execution but its present restored condition hardly allows us to pronounce an opinion.

The fourth canvas, that of the Sermon of St. Mark in Alexandria, is now in the Brera Gallery, Milan (162) (fig. 96). It was undertaken by Gentile in all probability together with his brother Giovanni, because the conditions he proposes to the Scuola Grande di San Marco, for which institution it is to be executed, stand in both their names.

When Sansovino (p. 102) and Ridolfi (I, p. 79) saw it, it was still in its original site.

I have already said that Gentile in his will expressed the desire that after his death Giovanni should finish this painting and it was only in acquiescing with this condition, which as a matter of fact he did, that he was to receive their father's sketchbook. The subject gives the painter every opportunity of depicting souvenirs of his sojourn in Constantinople. The centre of the background is occupied by an Islamic transformation of S. Marco. According to Ridolfi this building should represent the church of S. Eufemia, but all the other pieces of architecture are of more or less oriental style. We see, besides, minarets, an obelisk and what looks like a mediaeval church tower. Lastly, to the left of the church there is a tall structure with a spiral decoration which apparently is the much discussed column of Theodosius of which Gentile made a drawing; we shall return to this later. St. Mark preaches from a raised platform to a crowd of people, most of whom are Turkish men and women though here and there we find a few Venetians; a large group of the latter stands behind the saint. In depicting a giraffe and a couple of camels, Gentile's intention was evidently to emphasize the oriental character of the scene. This canvas too is in a poor state of preservation and restoration has somewhat changed it, but the free and natural arrangement of the congregation, the brightness of the colours and the fine effect of light make this picture much more pleasing than the others. These qualities may of course be due to Giovanni. The group of Venetians to the left are depicted in rigid rows as were the on-lookers in the miracle of the cross.

Of the same period as these large paintings we have also some portraits. Gentile must have painted one of the Doge Leonardo Loredano, whose rule started in 1501, because there exist several

Fig. 97.   Gentile Bellini, portrait of Catherine Cornaro, Queen of Cyprus.
Gallery, Budapest.   Photo Bard, Berlin.

copies (Bergamo ([1]), Dresden ([2]) and Correr Museum), but none
of them seems to be from the master's own hand. They show the
sitter in right profile, while through a window behind we get a
view of Venice and the lagoon.

([1]) *Ricci*, Le gallerie etc., p. 151.
([2]) (*K. W. Jähnig*), Die Staatliche Gemälde Galerie zu Dresden, I,
Berlin, 1929, No. 53.

Of the other portraits of this last phase of Gentile's activity, the most important is that of Caterina Cornaro, Queen of Cyprus, in the museum of Budapest (fig. 97) (117) (¹). A fairly long inscription on a label in the upper left corner gives the names of the subject and of the painter. Caterina was born in 1454 and we are led to believe that this portrait was executed around the year 1500, perhaps even at the same moment as the canvas of the miracle of the cross in which she appears among the noble matrons. Her attire is the same in both cases and from the portrait we get the impression that she had a quiet but strong and cunning personality. It is the finest work of Gentile's late years and is executed with a rare perfection of technique. This painting is also slightly restored but the retouches here are fairly local.

In the collection of the painter Italo Brass in Venice there is a replica of this work, with only very slight variations, which I think is from Gentile's own hand (²).

A portrait of a Venetian in the Ältere Pinakothek, Munich (1151, old catalogue 1030), which nowadays is generally not included among Gentile's productions, shows so much similarity to some of the figures in the backgrounds of his large canvases that I feel inclined to ascribe it to Gentile himself. Formerly it passed as such but Morelli (³) questioned the attribution and it is now labelled "Venetian, around 1500, from Gentile Bellini's school". The energetic looking youth with a bonnet on his fair hair shows one hand on which he wears a beautiful ring.

In the collection of the Art Academy in Vienna there is a bust-length portrait of a youth — the hands are not visible — with a black bonnet on his bushy hair, and we might imagine that the restoration hides a work by Gentile were it not for the obvious Pintoricchiesque landscape to the left, which makes us rather suspicious.

The attribution to Gentile of a small, bust-length portrait of a

---

(¹) *A. Venturi*, L'Arte, 1900, p. 278.

(²) In the Kunsthalle in Bremen we find a drawing probably of the same lady seen in profile, attributed to Dürer, which is supposed to have been inspired by Gentile's picture. *Tietze und Tietze-Conrat*, op. cit., p. 20, pl. 162.

(³) *G. Morelli*, Italian Painters: the Galleries of Munich and Dresden, London, 1893, p. 11.

Fig. 98.   Gentile Bellini, portrait. Private Collection, Amsterdam.
Photo Eilers.

young Venetian, which not long ago was for sale in London (¹), is
quite acceptable. By him too, but executed during his last phase
when he collaborated with Giovanni, is a small but fine picture
of the bust of a youngish man with a beard shown in three-
quarters left profile and wearing the usual bonnet on his long
hair (fig. 98); a small panel of a clean-shaven, middle-aged man

(¹) *Mayer*, op. cit.

Fig. 99.   Gentile Bellini (?), portrait. National Gallery, London.

Photo National Gallery.

seen in profile, both privately owned, in Amsterdam ([1]) and possibly also the portrait of a stout middle-aged man with an unpleasant expression in the National Gallery (3130) (fig. 99) ([2]).

([1]) Catalogue of the exhibition of ancient Italian art in Dutch possession,
Amsterdam 1934, No. 30.

([2]) *Holmes*, Burlington Magazine, XXXIII, 1918, p. 107, "done under
Gentile's immediate influence".

In the gallery of Padua there are two small portraits, again in bust length, which might be by Gentile, but their condition is such that no attribution can be made with certainty.

One of them (408) is the rather fatigued profile of an old man with a strange face, a long nose, protruding mouth and chin, and no head-dress. The other (42) is that of a richly garbed man with a black beard and a bonnet, he is turned three-quarters to the right and is shown against a landscape background; the painting is over-cleaned and retouched (¹).

There are several drawings which, I think rightly, have been attributed to Gentile (²).

The best known, though at the same time they are not un-animously ascribed to Gentile, are those of two orientals — man and woman (fig. 100) — in the British Museum, which I have al-ready mentioned and which somehow seem to have been known to Pintoricchio, as can be deduced from some figures of orientals in his frescoes in the Borgia Apartment (³).

(¹) Mr. Berenson attributes to Gentile with a point of interrogation still a bust of Petrarch in the Ringling Museum, Sarasota, Florida, proba-bly the same picture published by *Fiocco*, op. cit., as a work of Jacopo Bellini. Apart from the school works which have been erroneously ascribed to the master, I should like to cite as wrong attributions: the profile portrait of an old man in the Campidolio Museum (*A. Venturi*, Arch. Stor. dell' Arte, II, 1889, p. 448, who now gives it to Pisanello); as I said before, I think it is by Jacopo Bellini; the portrait of a mathematician with an instrument in the National Gallery, London (1213), which is ascribed to Gentile in the catalogue and by Mr. Berenson with a question mark; I believe it to be by Giovanni. In the same gallery, No. 808, St. Peter the Martyr (school of Giovanni) and No. 1440, Fra Teodoro da Urbino (by Giovanni) are catalogued as by Gentile, to whom they are also attributed by *von Hadeln*, op. cit., Repert., XXX; sale of the Jackson Higgs coll., New York, Dec. 1933, No. 33, profile portrait of a Byzantine emperor with a peculiar looking hat like that shown in portraits of the Palaeologus (*F. E. Washburn Freund*, Cicerone, 1927, p. 243). *R. Longhi*, Vita Artistica, II, 1927, p. 134, has made the following surprising attributions to Gentile: the polyptych in the Madonna della Misericordia, Asola, with which we shall deal later; the Madonna and saints, generally ascribed to Benaglio, in the gallery of Venice (617); and a St. Sebastian by Bonsignori in the Lanz coll., Amsterdam.

(²) *D. von Hadeln*, Venezianische Zeichnungen des Quattrocento, Berlin, 1925, pls. 4—5.

(³) See vol. XIV, p. 235.

Fig. 100.　Gentile Bellini, Oriental woman, drawing. British Museum, London.　　　　　Photo Anderson·

A particularly fine drawing of an old man in bust-length and three-quarter right profile in the Print Room, Berlin, is supposed to be a self-portrait (fig. 101). In the same collection there is another excellent sketch of a young man turned to the left. A very sketchy drawing of a procession entering a church which is preserved at Chatsworth in the collection of the Duke of Devon-

Fig. 101. Gentile Bellini, portrait of a man, drawing. Print Room,
Berlin.   Official Photo

shire (¹) and, executed in the same manner, another sketch of a
procession, which was acquired recently by the British Museum,
have been attributed to Gentile on account of a similarity in the

---

(¹) *A. Venturi*, L'Arte, 1926, p. 4. *Von Hadeln*, op. cit., pl. 8. *Balniel
and Clark*, Catalogue of the Exhibition of Italian Art, No. 771, as well
as *Popham*, Italian Drawings exhibited at the Royal Academy, 1930,
London, 1931, No. 169.

composition to that of the procession of the relic of the cross. However, of late these sketches are with good reason considered to be by Carpaccio (¹). On the other hand, in the Uffizi there is a particularly finished drawing of a similar subject but very different in composition; it shows an abundance of interesting architecture in the background (fig. 102) (²); it is a typical work of his late years when he created the large canvases illustrating events in the streets of Venice, in which he depicts numerous figures and much architecture.

There exists one medal made by Gentile but it is by no means a fine specimen; it represents the Sultan Mohammed who is shown in profile but with infinitely less personality than in the painting. Three crowns — the emblem of his rule — which were seen also on the panel are found on the verso of the medal along with the signature: *"Gentilis Bellinus Venetus eques auratus comesq. palatinus F."* (³).

∗

Very important works of Gentile Bellini have been lost: in the first place those in the big Council Hall which are fairly minutely described by Sansovino and Ridolfi; then there were the two scenes from the story of Pharaoh and the Jews in the Scuola Grande di San Marco which was destroyed by fire in 1485; nor is anything left of the paintings he made, together with his father and Giovanni, in the Gattamelata chapel in Padua. While in Constantinople Gentile must have executed more than one portrait of the Sultan Mohammed; there was evidently one in profile which seems to have served for the xylograph of the series known as "Elogia virorum illustrium". Ridolfi mentions a portrait of

---

(¹) Apollo, Sept. 1933, p. 211.

(²) In the British Museum there is a drawing on parchment (1891-6-17-23) representing the ceremony of Pope Alexander III handing over a sword to the Doge Zeani which reveals some analogy with the art of Gentile to whom it is hesitatingly ascribed by *G. Gronau*, Künstlerfamilie, p. 34, fig. 20, but it seems to be a copy of considerably later date of one of the paintings that Gentile executed in the big Council Hall v. *von Hadeln*, ed. of Ridolfi, I, p. 59 note 1.

(³) *G. F. Hill*, A Corpus of Italian Medals of the Renaissance, London, 1930, p. 113 and pl. 82, who gives the older literature.

Fig. 102. Gentile Bellini, Procession in a street, drawing. Uffizi, Florence.

Photo Alinari.

Mohammed by Gentile which in his day was in the house of Pietro Zeno, but if this reference is to a painting which was in the Northwick collection it is not by Gentile, nor does it represent the Sultan (¹). In 1780, there existed in the museum of Paolo Giovio a portrait of Mohammed which was attributed to Gentile (²). Mohammed II commanded Gentile to execute paintings of erotic subjects, portraits of courtiers, of a dervish, a self-portrait and a view of Venice. Ridolfi relates the gruesome story of how the sultan, in order to demonstrate that the artist had made a mistake in painting the neck of the beheaded St. John the Baptist, had the head of a slave cut off there and then; this terrified the artist so much that he decided to leave Constantinople at once.

We find reference to two pictures of the Circumcision by Gentile. One of them is mentioned by Ridolfi as in the possession of Signor Barbarigo; perhaps it is the same painting which, at a later date, was in the Leuchtenberg collection, Munich, in which case it is by Catena and not Gentile (³). The other is described in Moschini's Guide (I, p. 207) as in the Palazzo Grimani and signed: "*Opus Gentilis Bellini equitis Veneti*"; further, it is reproduced in Lanzi's history of Italian painting where mention is made also of the picture in the Palazzo Barbarigo which, however, is unfavourably compared with the other example. Ridolfi speaks still of a half-length figure of the Madonna in the midst of saints in the collection of the Dutchman Reinst; it was no doubt one of those oblong panels which recall Giovanni Bellini and his followers more than Gentile. Boschini (p. 147) and Zanetti (p. 59) tell us that in the Scuola de' Mercia at San Giuliano there was a signed altar-piece in six parts, with the Madonna, SS. Daniel and Catherine and above, God the Father and the Annunciation, which was one of Gentile's best works. It has been supposed that the Madonna of the Mond collection, now in the National Gallery, London, might have been the central panel.

In the manuscript catalogue of 1627, illustrated with small

(¹) *von Hadeln*, op. cit., I, p. 58 note 7. *Gray*, op. cit., Burlington Magazine, 1932.

(²) *Thuasne*, op. cit., pp. 32, 59. *The Same*, op. cit., p. 35, mentions still another reproduced in *J. de Hammer*, Storia dell' Impero Osmano, Venice, 1828, but doubts the attribution to Gentile.

(³) *I. N. Muxel*, Gemälde Sammlung in München des Herzogs von Leuchtenberg, Munich, no date, No. 57. *v. Hadeln*, op. cit., p. 62 note 4.

drawings, of the collection of a certain Andrea Vendramin —
there were several of this name — there are two bust-length
portraits of youngish Venetians of the usual type wearing a
bonnet on their long hair and turned three-quarters to the left,
which show the name of Gentile Bellini [1].

The affirmation that Lorenzo de' Medici charged Gentile to
draw the ancient monuments of Constantinople seems to be
somewhat hypothetical [2]; the fact that Gentile must have met
an envoy sent by Lorenzo is the only argument in favour of this
supposition. We know, however, that he actually did draw some
of the ancient monuments because it is a sketch made by Gentile
which reveals to us the appearance of the column of Theodosius
which was almost entirely destroyed in 1695, while among some
drawings by Bellini which were acquired by France in the 17th
century, but have since disappeared, there were sketches of the
reliefs of this column. These were engraved in 1702 on the order
of P. Menestrier. Copies of the drawings made in the 16th or
17th century exist in the Bibliothèque Nationale des Beaux Arts
of Paris and in the Louvre; they have been published several
times on account of their archaeological interest [3]. As I said
before, the column of Theodosius figures in the picture of the
Sermon of St. Mark now in the Brera Gallery.

*_**

The productions of the school of Gentile Bellini are very few in
number. The most important is the picture of the reception in
1512 of the ambassador Trevisano at Cairo which is in the Louvre
(1157); it is a handsome work executed in bright colours but
somewhat hard outlines (fig. 103). Before the event was identified
the painting was generally accepted as a work by Gentile [4]. The

[1] The manuscript is preserved in the British Museum. *T. Borenius*,
The Picture Gallery of Andrea Vendramin, London, 1923, pls. 36 and 52.

[2] *Thuasne*, op. cit., p. 42.

[3] *Thusane*, loc. cit.

[4] The subject was identified by *Ch. Schefer*, Gazette des Beaux Arts
XIV, 1895, p. 201; v. the bibliography given in *Seymour de Ricci*, Descrip-
tion raisonnée des peintures du Louvre, I, Paris, 1913, p. 17. *L. Hautecour*,
La peinture au Musée du Louvre, écoles italiennes, XIII, XIV, XV siècles,
Paris, no. date, p. 89. *Berenson* attributes it to Catena but with a point
of interrogation.

Fig. 103. School of Gentile Bellini, Reception of the Venetian
Ambassador, Domenico Trevisano, in Cairo. Louvre, Paris.

Mus. Photo.

picture was brought to France in 1660 by Raphael du Fresne ([1]) and it belonged to Louis XIV. The attributions to Catena and Mansueti are, in my opinion, not convincing. The scene is shown in a crowded composition, the background of which is formed by the buildings of an oriental city.

Another school work is, I think, the oblong panel of the Adoration of the Magi in the museum of Padua (425) which in general appearance bears a certain resemblance to Gentile's picture of this subject in the National Gallery, but a close comparison reveals that there is really only one detail — the dog in the centre — which corresponds. The greater part of the assembley, some of whom are still approaching on horseback, is composed of turbaned orientals, and only one or two here and there have a more European look. In the landscape of hills and rocks there is also something reminiscent of the work by Gentile to whom, as a matter of fact, the museum authorities ascribe this picture.

In the Liechtenstein Gallery, Vienna (1120), there is a large oblong painting of a combat between oriental and occidental warriors, some of whom are mounted, with a town built on a cliff as background. It reveals a considerable knowledge of Gentile's art although I do not think the painter was actually a pupil of our master.

The author of a panel of the Virgin adoring the Child in the Johnson collection, Philadelphia (163) (fig. 104) shows almost as much connexion with Jacopo Bellini as with Gentile; St. Joseph is depicted in meditation near by, as well as the profile of an adoring doge; in the background we see an open shelter, the Message to the Shepherds and a high hill. The figures are all very wooden and the landscape childish. A comparison with Gentile's portrait of Giovanni Mocenigo in the Correr Museum leaves us in no doubt as to the identity of the person represented in adoration. Mr. Berenson is of opinion that this painting is possibly an early production of Mansueti ([2]).

A picture of St. Jerome in his study and an adorer, in the church of S. Nicola, Bari, has been classified as the work of an

---

([1]) *Boschini*, Carta del navegar, 4th ed., Venice, 1660, p. 31. *Thusane*, op. cit., p. 61.

([2]) *Berenson*, Catalogue of the Italian Pictures of the Johnson coll., p. 99.

Fig. 104. School of Gentile Bellini, Adoration of the Child. Johnson
Collection, Philadelphia.

Courtesy of the John J. Johnson art Collection, Philadelphia.

imitator of Gentile ([1]). A very similar painting exists in the cathedral of Monopoli ([2]).

*
* *

Gentile Bellini's chief merit was without any doubt his gift as a
portraitist. Regarding him as such we get the impression that he
was indeed a great artist. His remarkable rendering of individuality, not only of the features but also of the sitter's psychology,
is equal to that of Antonello da Messina, to whom however he is
inferior in technical accomplishments. Never do we find in his
works that marvellous richness of colour, that transparency and
that certainty of handling which allowed Antonello to deal with
the minutae of detail with such accuracy.

In the works of Gentile we notice quite an interest in non-
religious art which connects him with the masters of the previous
generation; this is evident in the detailed costumes, in the people
swimming in the canal in the scene of the miracle of the relic, in
the figure of the negro whom a Venetian woman seems to prevent
from diving into the water and in the beggar woman in the other
scene of this series. Most of all, however, Gentile was interested in
contemporary architecture; he naturally inherited this interest
from his father but he manifests it in a much more realistic
manner. Nowhere in his paintings do we meet with those fanciful
buildings which constantly appear in Jacopo's works. Architecture is the natural surrounding of his subjects and he obviously
preferred to represent street scenes with bridges and the houses
seen from the outside, rather than interior views.

Gentile's début was not very fortunate; the domination, first
of his father, with whom he collaborated, and then of his far more
gifted brother-in-law Mantegna, possibly obstructed his natural
development. Even at the age of thirty-five we find Gentile as a
poor artist trying to imitate Mantegna (e.g. in the organ doors),
even though he had already made portraits of such strong individuality, but not very fine technique, as that of the Doge Foscari.
Gentile, who must have possessed a subtle adaptability, pro-

([1]) *M. Salmi*, L'Arte, XXII, 1919, p. 170.

([2]) *Frizzoni*, Bollettino d'Arte del Minist. della Pubbl. Istr., VIII, 1914,
p. 39, assigns this picture to the Sienese school.

fitted enormously from his contact with Islamic painting and it was from this school that he acquired the element which had been most missing in his art, namely refinement. In this respect the portrait of Mohammed II and the miniatures in the Gardner Museum leave nothing to desire, while on the other hand his earlier productions were decidedly coarse. In fact, until his departure for Constantinople at the age of fifty he does not seem to have executed anything outstandingly fine, whereas at the court of the sultan and afterwards he produced works of really high standard.

One of his weak points however remained: the arrangement of his groups, which in his large canvases is anything but natural. Worst of all is the long row of kneeling figures in the miracle of the relic. Nor had Gentile any talent for filling up a space with people; this is evident in the deserted body of the church and again in the square of S. Marco in the canvas of the procession of the relic of the cross. In the Sermon of St. Mark there is a considerable improvement in the composition but we know that in this case Giovanni collaborated with his elder brother.

That Gentile acquired the position of the official painter of Venice—because we know that he was the portraitist of the doges, that he was sent by the Signoria to the court of Turkey, that he was in charge of the restoration of the big Council Hall and that he was the illustrator of the great events which occurred in Venice — may have been partly due to his high moral character and the general esteem in which he was held on this account, but what extraordinary deeds, artistic or otherwise, he performed which procured for him in 1469 the imperial knighthood and the title of count, remain something of a mystery.

***

Gentile Bellini had several pupils. Among them should be included Gerolamo da Santacroce whom, however, we know better under a different aspect, for his art really belongs more to the 16th century.

On the other hand Giovanni di Niccolo Mansueti ([1]), who

([1]) *Vasari*, ed. Milanesi, III, p. 648. *Ridolfi*, ed. von Hadeln, I, p. 49. *Thieme-Becker*, Künstlerlexikon, XXIV, p. 36. For the documents v. *Ludwig*, Jahrbuch. d. K. Preus. Kunstsamml., XXXVI, Beiheft, p. 61.

continued his productive existence until 1527, remained at all times a true adherent of the Venetian school of the 15th century although not always faithful to his first teacher Gentile; in fact, in one of his signatures he mentions Giovanni as his master while in another he does not define of which Bellini he is the disciple.

We know very little about Mansueti apart from his works, which are fairly numerous and frequently signed. In 1489 his wife has her will witnessed by Gentile Bellini and, as has already been observed, we can draw the conclusion that Mansueti was in contact with Gentile at this date. His name figures in a testament of 1485; several other documents bearing reference to him (1504, '6, '15,' 24) have been published by Ludwig and we have as well some dated pictures from his hand. His death occurred between September 1526 and March 1527. He is supposed to have been lame and his self-portrait is seen to the left in a large canvas of 1494 of a miracle of the cross in the gallery of Venice (564), in which he has depicted himself holding a label with the signature.

The works of Mansueti can be divided according to their style into three principal groups: first, that in which he is dominated by Gentile Bellini, secondly, that in which he appears to be a pupil of Carpaccio, while the third reveals him as an adherent of Cima da Conegliano. The works of Mansueti are not sufficiently important to describe at length. Consequently, I shall deal in brief with his best paintings and enumerate the others in a note.

Mr. Berenson, as I have already said, thinks it possible that the Nativity in the Johnson collection, Philadelphia, which I included among the productions of the school of Gentile Bellini, might be a work of Mansueti's early years; this attribution is merely hypothetical but certainly we can well imagine that his youthful paintings must have been something similar.

Four large canvases in the gallery of Venice (562, 564, 569, 571) show us Mansueti when the domination of Gentile Bellini was at its culminating point. Besides, these pictures are of the same type as those executed by Bellini himself, not only on account of their size but also because the compositions are very similar. Here too we see crowds of people and an abundance of carefully painted architecture.

The picture of the miracle of the cross (564) originates from the Scuola di S. Giovanni Evangelista, where it was still seen

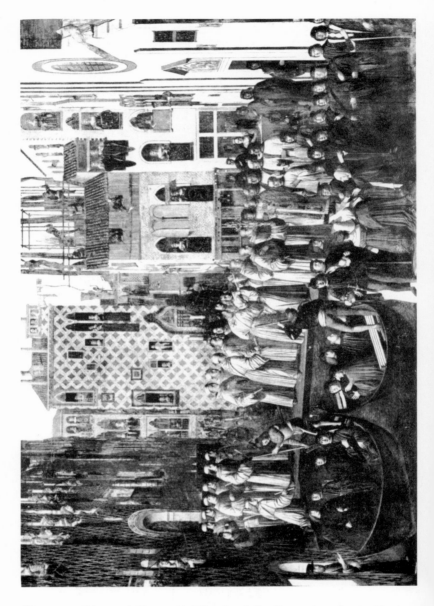

Fig. 105. Giovanni Mansueti, Miracle of the Cross. Accademia, Venice.
Photo Anderson.

by Sansovino, Ridolfi and Zanetti (fig. 105). The cross, while being
carried in a procession, miraculously could not be taken into

Fig. 106. Giovanni Mansueti, Miracle of the Cross. Accademia, Venice.
Photo Anderson.

the church of S. Leo because there was exposed in this building
the corpse of a monk who had refused to accompany the cross on
some other occasion. Mansueti depicts such multitudes of people
that we almost lose sight of the event in their midst. Many on-
lookers appear at the windows of the houses to which the artist
has paid particular attention; some of the people are depicted in
gondolas. Among the figures there are obviously many portraits.
On the façade of the church we see a peacock, while on the roof of

Fig. 107. Giovanni Mansueti, Miracle of St. Mark, 1499. Accademia, Venice.   Photo Alinari.

one of the houses a boy chases a cat; another feature of every day life is the washing which hangs out to dry. This picture, which was executed probably in 1494, is signed: *Joannis De Mansuetis veneti recte sentientium Bellini Discipli*.

One of the other canvases (562) originates from the same Scuola but it is not mentioned by Ridolfi. It illustrates how the daughter of one of the members of the confraternity, a certain Benvenuto da S. Polo, is cured by touching three blessed candles (fig. 106). Again the subject of the painting is almost lost in the details of the sumptuous and very ornate hall in which the incident occurs and in which many elegantly attired people are gathered. The crowd continues as far as the flight of steps which leads to a small square where several dignified Venetians are portrayed; in the canal to the left some gondolas are depicted ar-

Fig. 108. Giovanni Mansueti, St. Mark led out of the Synagogue, 1499.
Liechtenstein Gallery, Vienna.

riving. Some of the figures are dressed in particularly fine clothes;
a seated oriental holds a hunting leopard; in the foreground a
page brings a letter to a fat magistrate.

For the Scuola di San Marco, Mansueti made four paintings of
episodes of the life of St. Mark which are mentioned by the same
ancient authors. Two of these works are in the Accademia (569,
571) (fig. 107), one in the Brera Gallery, Milan, and one, dated
1499, in the Liechtenstein Gallery, Vienna (fig. 108).

As one of the documents published by Ludwig records the fact that Mansueti's heirs had to take legal proceedings about the payment of the paintings executed for the Scuola di San Marco, it has been supposed that these canvases date from the end of the master's activity; the style, however, which reveals his close connexion with Gentile, points to an earlier period. Mansueti, like Gentile, was probably very magnanimous in the contracts he made with these "Scuole" and no doubt allowed them a long credit. Moreover the picture in Vienna is dated.

I shall not describe these four paintings which show the artist under the spell of oriental art. This is not the case, however, for the architecture, which is abundant and heavy and of quite an Italian style, but in each of these scenes the figures for the greater part are oriental and wear large turbans. It is only here and there that he has depicted a group of Venetians, all of whom are obviously portrayed from real life (¹).

Of the other paintings which reveal more connexion with Gentile Bellini than with the two other masters who had such an influence on Mansueti, I shall cite an important panel of the Adoration of the Shepherds with the Virgin and St. Joseph kneeling near by and several angels appearing above, which is preserved in the museum of Berlin (48) and a mystic picture of the Trinity in the National Gallery, London (1478), in which the Virgin, St. John and St. Mary Magdalene are represented around the Crucified as well as four other adorers, one of whom is in oriental costume; two angels in pulpits hold the instruments of the Passion; through the windows of the buildings in the background a landscape is visible.

Mansueti was very much influenced by Gentile when he exe-

(¹) The four pictures are: Venice, Gallery, No. 569, St. Mark curing Anianus which is signed: "*Joannes de Mansuetis fecit*"; No. 571, St. Mark preaching in a large hall; to the left Christ visits St. Mark in prison and to the right we see a session of an oriental judge; a Turkish boy carries the signature: "*Joannes de Mansuetis faciebat*"; Milan, Brera Gallery, No. 153, St. Mark baptizing Ananias, signed: "*Joannes De Mansuetis p.*"; Vienna, Liechtenstein Gallery, No. 857, St. Mark leading away a prisoner, which is shown in the interior of an Italian church but the audience is exclusively oriental; the signature is the same as that on the picture in the Brera but here another label bears the date 1499. Ridolfi does not cite the last mentioned picture.

Fig. 109.   Giovanni Mansueti, portrait. Borghese Gallery, Rome.

Photo Anderson.

cuted the curious bust-length portrait of a man, wearing a high
hat and turned three-quarters to the left, in the Borghese Gallery,
Rome (fig. 109). I know of still two small portraits of this phase
in Mansueti's career. One of them, curiously enough, is of a
bearded man — perhaps an oriental — in Venetian costume,

Fig. 110. Giovanni Mansueti, Baptism. Private Collection,

which many years ago was for sale in Rome. The other depicts a
young Venetian in three-quarter left profile and is at present on
the art market in Paris.

Another production of the same manner is a picture of an in-comprehensible subject — perhaps a baptism — in a private col-lection; it shows several people, among whom some are in oriental dress, standing on the shores of a river or in the water against a background of architecture with a bridge in the distance (fig. 110).

The work most obviously inspired by Carpaccio is an oblong panel of the Virgin and Child between St. Mary Magdalene and a female martyr who protect an adorer and his wife, which a few years ago was for sale in Paris; it shows the signature: *"Joannes De Mansuetis pinxit"* (¹).

Among the more important works of this phase should be in-cluded a large panel in the collection of Signor Italico Brass, Venice, representing St. Mark enthroned in an architectural setting with the emblematic angel and a nun standing close by; below, we see the full-length figures of four saints while three angelic musicians sit on the steps of the throne (fig. 111). The influence of Giovanni Bellini, which was manifest in the foregoing works, seems to be absent in this painting, in the signature of which Mansueti proclaims himself to be a pupil of the great master: *"Opus Joannis De Mansuetis discipuli Domini Joannis Bellinis"* (²). However, the angelic musicians are an innovation of Giovanni, which Carpaccio employed at a much later date. They appear in his famous triptych of 1488 in the Frari church, from which Mansueti may have borrowed also the type of the bearded old saint dressed in black and carrying a pastoral staff, which he depicts in the panel in the Brass collection.

It is quite likely that the different tendencies did not follow one another in a definite chronological order because in the canvas of 1499 in Vienna the influence of Gentile Bellini is obvious, while a picture of 1500 in the gallery of Venice (97) reveals Mansueti very clearly as a pupil of Carpaccio. The latter work originates from the church of S. Francesco, Treviso, where it still hung when

---

(¹) Pantheon, II, 1928, reprod. on p. 613.

(²) *Moschini*, Rivista di Venezia, May 1933. *Milanesi*, in his ed. of Vasari, III, p. 648, note 2, mentions a picture with this signature, cited also by Zanotto, at one time in the church of S. Matteo di Mazorbo and afterwards in the possession of a painter of the name of Sebastiano Santi and of Signori Cornelo in Venice. He does not mention the subject and doubts whether the inscription is right.

Fig. 111. Giovanni Mansueti, St. Mark, Angels and Saints. Brass Collection, Venice.

Fig. 112. Giovanni Mansueti, St. Sebastian and Saints. Accademia, Venice.   Photo Anderson.

Ridolfi saw it, but this writer erroneously describes it as a Madonna and many saints, whereas it depicts St. Sebastian between four saints under a portico (fig. 112). On a little label to the right we read: *"Hoc enim Johanis de Mansuetis opus est 1500"*. Some of the figures, and especially that of St. Francis, lead us to believe that Mansueti had also studied the works of Alvise Vivarini.

Two other panels in the same gallery (877, 878), formerly in that of Padua, illustrate the domination of Carpaccio; one of them shows SS. Lawrence, near whom a small boy holds the gridiron, and Sebastian, the other, SS. Jerome and Francis; each of these works is signed: *"Joanes Mansuetis P."* ([1]). An oblong panel, also in this gallery (75), of the Virgin with the nude Child, Who blesses a donor presented by St. Peter, and two young female saints shows this influence to such an extent that at one

([1]) Rassegna d'Arte, 1923, p. 177.

Fig. 113. Giovanni Mansueti, Coronation of the Virgin. Ex-Crespi Collection, Milan.   Photo Böhler.

time it was attributed to Carpaccio. A panel by Mansueti of
St. Martin on horseback and the beggar, in the Correr Museum,
has obviously been inspired by Carpaccio's representation of this
subject on the polyptych in the cathedral of Zara. To the same
group belong: an elaborate painting of the Assumption in the
museum of Padua (2419); the Madonna is borne by many angels
to heaven where God the Father and saints await her, while

Fig. 114.   Giovanni   Mansueti,   Christ   blessing.   University   Gallery,
Göttingen.

below, against a landscape background, the Apostles and an
adorer kneel around the empty grave; a Pietà composed of five
figures, one of whom is an oriental, in the gallery of Urbino; and
a particularly charming half-length figure of the Madonna with
the nude Child and a view of a landscape to one side (¹), a n d a

<hr />

(¹) International Studio, 1929, p. 93.

panel with two scenes from the legend of St. Augustine, the one in
his study, the other in a courtyard: both not long ago were for
sale in London (¹).

I think that it is in this period that we should classify the
rather small but beautiful canvases representing the Marriage of
the Virgin, the Adoration of the Magi and the Flight into Egypt
which are preserved in the sacristy of S. Martino, Burano.

The works which demonstrate that this artist was subject
also to the influence of Cima da Conegliano are not very great in
number but, none the less, offer us unmistakable proof of the
fact. The most important of these productions is a Coronation of
the Virgin, formerly in the Crespi collection, Milan (¹), and more
recently for sale in Munich (fig. 113); the positions of the central
group seem to point towards a knowledge of Giovanni Bellini's
picture of the same subject at Pesaro. According to the ancient
Venetian iconography, God the Father places His hands on the
shoulders of both the Virgin and the Saviour; eight angels, some
of whom play on musical instruments, surround the broad architectural throne. Very reminiscent of the Saviour in this picture is
a half-length figure of Christ in benediction which belongs to the
museum of Berlin but which for many years has been loaned to
the gallery of Göttingen (107) (fig. 114); it is signed: *"Joannes De
Mansuetis pinsit"*. A charming picture of St. Jerome with his lion
sitting outside a grotto, surrounded by birds and animals, which
was at one time in the Hughes collection, Kew, but has since been
for sale in Berlin, as well as a signed picture of the half-length Madonna with the nude Child between St. Mary Magdalene, St. Ca-
tharine and two adorers, now belonging to Messrs. Wildenstein,
Paris, also reveal the influence of Cima (fig. 115) (²).

A fairly unimportant drawing of St. Sebastian at the column
in the gallery of Venice is attributed to Mansueti; this attribution
is quite possibly correct (³).

(¹) *A. Venturi*, La Galleria Crespi in Milano, Milan, 1900, p. 160. No. 37
of the sale of the Crespi coll., Paris, June 1914.

(²) *R. Fry*, The S. Jerome in the Hughes Collection, Burlington Maga-
zine, XXI, 1912, p. 47. *T. Borenius*, Rassegna d'Arte, XII, 1912, p. 90.
Burlington Fine Arts Club (Exhibition of) Early Venetian Pictures etc.,
London, 1912, No. 21, pl. 19.

(³) *G. Fogolari*, I disegni delle R. Gallerie dell' Accademia (di Venezia),
Milan, 1913, fig. 51.

Fig. 115. Giovanni Mansueti, Madonna and Saints. Wildenstein Collection, Paris.

We are far from the end of the list of works by Mansueti because, though often mediocre, unattractive and boring, he was,
as I said before, a very productive artist ([1]).

([1]) Other works by Mansueti are: **Amsterdam,** Tietje coll., Madonna and
Child with SS. Jerome and John the Baptist, signed, from the Augusteum,
Oldenburg (*T. Borenius,* Burlington Magazine, April 1913, p. 26, Catal.
of the Exhibition of Italian Art in Dutch possession, Amsterdam, 1935,
No. 213). **Bergamo,** Gallery, No. 152, St. Jerome, signed; No. 158, Depos-
ition, signed; No. 166, portrait of a man (*Berenson*); No. 401, Madonna
and Child in benediction (*Berenson*); Marriage of St. Catherine. **Berlin,**
Glogowski coll., bust of a nude woman (*Berenson*). **Châalis,** Jacquemart
André Museum, No. 511, Pietà (*Berenson*). **Cremona,** Gallery, Holy Trinity
with SS. Francis and Bernardine (*Berenson*). **Düsseldorf,** Gallery, No. 42,
Deposition, predella panel; No. 232, Pietà. **Koenigsberg,** on loan from the
museum of Berlin, Madonna, Child and saints. **London,** Annan-Bryce
coll., Virgin and Child (*Crowe and Cavalcaselle,* History of Painting in
North Italy, ed. Borenius, I, p. 226 note 4). **Modena,** Gallery, No. 252,
Madonna, two angels, St. Louis and St. Francis. **Pavia,** Museum, Madonna,
SS. Catherine, John the Baptist and donors. **Richmond,** Cook coll., Madonna crowned by angels, with false signature of Antonello da Messina.
Stuttgart, Gallery, No. 512, Madonna, after Giov. Bellini (*Gronau,* Bellini,
p. 99). **Venice,** S. Giovanni Crisostomo, SS. Jerome, Agatha, Andrew, and
titular saint, panels from the organ (doubtful); Gallery, No. 804, Archangel Gabriel, in store-room, very much damaged; Brass coll., fragment
of an Adoration of the Magi. **Verona,** Gallery, No. 276, Adoration of the
Magi, signed; No. 340, Madonna and St. Jerome, signed. **Vicenza,** Museum,
No. 36, Madonna, SS. Dominic and Jerome, wrongly ascribed to Montagna in the catalogue; *Berenson's* attribution to Mansueti seems to me
somewhat doubtful. **Warsaw,** Gallery, No. 6, Pietà with donors, copy of
Bellini's picture in Toledo (*Berenson*). Among the works wrongly attributed to Mansueti I shall cite: two Madonnas in the gallery of Padua
(409, 413); nor do I agree with Cavalcaselle, Berenson and others that
the Adoration of the Magi in the same collection (425) is by this master;
I have included it among the works of the school of Gentile Bellini.
Works mentioned by ancient authors but now vanished are: **Venice,**
S. Cassiano, various saints among whom is St. Luke; Gesuiti church, Crucifixion, later in the Manfrin Palace; S. Giorgio Maggiore, bust of St. Peter
(*Cicogna,* Iscriz. Venez., IV, pp. 390, 388). A picture of the Virgin adoring
the Child with St. Joseph, the infant St. John and a lamb, which existed
in the San Salvatore Castle at Collalto Susegana, was destroyed during
the great war (*Berenson,* Dedalo, IV, 1923—24, p. 44).

CHAPTER IV

GIOVANNI BELLINI (¹).

The year of Giovanni Bellini's birth is unknown. Nor is it pre-

---

(¹) *B. Berenson*, La sainte Justine de la collection Bagatti-Valsecchi à Milan, Gazette des Beaux Arts, 1913, pp. 461—479, English translation in The Study and Criticism of Italian Art, III, London, 1916, p. 38. *The Same*, Les quatres triptyques bellinesques de l'église de la Carità à Venise, Gazette des Beaux Arts, 1913, pp. 191—202, English translation in Study etc., p. 62. *The Same*, G. B., Venetian Painting in America, London, 1916, pp. 54—95. *The Same*, A Madonna by G. B. recently acquired by Mr. Philip Lehman, Art in America, 1916, p. 3. *M. Logan Berenson*, Le nouveau tableau de B. au Louvre, Gazette des Beaux Arts, LIV, p. IV, VII. *The Same*, B.'s Feast of the Gods, Art in America, IX 1, Dec. 1920. *G. Bernardini*, Per un dipinto nella Gall. Borghese della scuola di B., Rassegna d'Arte, X, 1910, p. 162. *T. Borenius*, The provenance of B.'s Christ in the Louvre, Burlington Magazine, XXVII, 1915, p. 205. *The Same*, An unpublished Pietà by G. B., Pantheon, Dec. 1932, p. 381. *C. (G.)*, Un quadro di Giambellino rubato a Venezia, Rassegna d'Arte, IX, 1909, p. II. *G. Cantalamessa*, La Resurrezione di Cristo, quadro di G. B., Arte e Storia, XXII, 1903, p. 51. *The Same*, La Resurrezione di Cristo, quadro di G. B., Gazetta di Venezia, 25th Jany. 1903. *The Same*, La Madonna di G. B. nella Gall. Borghese, Bollettino d'Arte, 1914, p. 105. *K. Clark*, Mantegna or Bellini, Burlington Magazine, LXI, 1932, p. 232. *P. Courtot*, Sur trois peintres italiens, Revue critique des idées, Paris, July 1920. *L. Cust*, A Portrait by G. B. at Hampton Court Palace, Apollo, June 1928, p. 247. *L. Dussler*, G. B., Frankfort, 1935. *G. Fiocco*, Anconetta primitiva di Giambellino, Rassegna Marchigiana, I, Nov. 1922, p. 43. *G. Fogolari*, La Madonna di Casa Galvani di G. B., L'Arte, 1914, p. 304. *The Same*, Disegni per gioco e incunabuli pittorici del Giambellino, Dedalo, XII, 1932, p. 360. *G. Frizzoni*, Per la reintegrazione della grande pala di G. B. a Pesaro, Emporium, 1913, pp. 227, idem in English, Burlington Magazine, XXII, 1913, p. 250. *R. Fry*, G. B., The Art's Library, London, 1899. *The Same*, The Redeemer by G. B., Louvre, Burlington Magazine, XXI, 1912, p. 10 *The Same*, G. B.'s Madonna and Child, Burlington Magazine, XLVII, 1925, p. 64. *G. Gaginolo*, Intorno a G. B., Rassegna d'Arte, IV, 1904, p. 40. *G. Gerola*, Il Giambellino, no. 77 del Museo di Verona, Rassegna d'Arte, IX, 1909, p. 1. *U. Gnoli*, Una tavola sconosciuta di G. B.,

cisely established that he was the natural son of Jacopo, although

Rassegna d'Arte, XI, 1911, p. 177. *G. Gronau*, Die Künstlerfamilie Bellini, Künstler-Monographien, Bielefeld- Leipzig, 1909. *The Same*, in Thieme-Becker, Künstlerlexikon, III, 1909, p. 259. *The Same*, Lauro Padovano ein Gehilfe des G. B., Collectanea Leoni S. Olschki, Munich, 1921, p. 101. *The Same*, Die Bellini, Das Museum, II, p. 29. *The Same*, Ueber Bildnisse von G. B., Jahrb. der K. Preus. Kunstsamml., XLIII, 1922, p. 97. *The Same*, Ueber eine Madonna-komposition von G. B., Jahrb. der K. Preus. Kunstsamml., XLV, 1924, p. 38. *The Same*, Spätwerke des G. B., Strasbourg, 1928; also in Italian, Pinacoteca, 1928, p. 57. *The Same*, G. B. (Klassiker der Kunst), Stuttgart-Berlin (1931). *J. Guibert*, Note sur une Résurrection du Musée Royal de Berlin, Gazette des Beaux Arts, XXXIV, 1905, p. 380. *V. C. Habicht*, G. B. u. Roger van der Weyden, Belvedere, 1931, p. 54. *D. F. von Hadeln*, Zwei Madonnenkompositionen des G. B., Zeitschr. f. bildende Kunst., XXIII, 1912. p. 12. *The Same*, Ein verschollenes altarbild des G. B., Jahrb. der K. Preus. Kunstsamml., XLV, 1924, p. 206. *The Same*, Two portraits by G. B., Burlington Magazine, LI, 1927, p. 4. *The Same*, B.'s Madonna del Baldachino, Burlington Magazine, LIV, 1928, p. 270. *The Same*, G. B. or Mantegna?, Burlington Magazine, LXI, 1932, p. 229. *B. Haendsch*, Dürers Beziehungen zu Barbari, Pollaiuolo, u Bellini, Jahrb der K. Preus. Kunstsamml., XIX, 1898, p. 162. *Ph. M. von Halm*, Eine Madonnakomposition von G. B., Zeitschr. f. bildende Kunst, N. F., XVI, 1905, p. 238. *G. Hay*, Bellini (Masterpieces in Colour), London, no date. *W. Heil*, Ein Bellini Madonna im Museum zu Detroit, Pantheon, III, 1929, p. 141. *Ph. Hendy*, Two G. B. drawings, Burlington Magazine, LXI, 1932, p. 62. *R. Henniker Heaton*, A Bellini Madonna, Burlington Magazine, LXI, 1932, p. 251. *T. Hetzer*, Recension on Gronau's Bellini, Zeitschr. f. Kunstgesch., I, 1932, p. 65. *R. Longhi*, Piero dei Franceschi e lo sviluppo della pittura veneziana, L'Arte, XVII, 1914, p. 240. *The Same*, Un chiaroscuro e un disegno di G. B., Vita Artistica, July 1927, p. 133. *G. Ludwig*, G. B. sog. Madonna am See in d. Uffizien, eine religiöse Allegorie, Jahrb. d. K. Preus. Kunstsamml., 1902, fasc. III—IV, pp. 163, 186. *The Same u. W. Bode*, Uber das Altar Bild. der Kirche v. S. Michele di Murano und der Auferstehung Bild d. G. B. in d. Berliner Gallerie, Jahrb. d. K. Preus. Kunstsamml., XXIV, pp. 131—146. *F. H. Mather*, G. B.'s Madonna in the Johnson coll. Philadelphia, Burlington Magazine, IX, 1906, p. 351. *A. L. Mayer*, A Portrait of Joerg Fugger ascribed to G. B., Burlington Magazine, LVIII, 1926, p. 219. *E. Meynell*, G. B., London, no date. *P. G. Molmenti*, I pittori B., Nuova Antol., XVI, Serie III, fasc. XIV, 1888. *The Same*, La Resurrezione gia in casa Roncalli a Bergamo, ora nella Galleria di Berlino, Rivista d'Arte, II, 1904, p. 105. *The Same*, La Madonna degli Alberelli di Giambellino, Marzocco, 7th Sept. 1902. *M. Monci*, G. B. teste, Rassegna bibliografica, VII, p. 90. *P. P.*, La Madonna di G. B., rubata a Venezia, Emporium, 1909, p. 319. *A. Pératé*, Le "Sauveur bénissant", peinture de G. B. au Louvre, Les Musées de France, Paris, 1912, No. 2, p. 42. *F. M.*

this is supposed to be the case because he lived apart from the rest of the family and he is not mentioned along with Gentile as the brother of Jacopo's daughter Nicholosa who married Mantegna; neither does he figure with the brother and sister in the will of Jacopo's widow (¹).

According to Vasari, Giovanni was ninety years old when he died, an event which we know for certain occurred in 1516. This would give the date of his birth as 1426 but as Giovanni was younger than Gentile who, as we saw, was born in 1429, Vasari's statement must be incorrect and it has been conjectured that Giovanni was born a few years later, somewhere around 1431.

About his youth and education we know nothing at all except that he and Gentile collaborated with Jacopo — consequently prior to 1470 — in the execution of the altar-piece for the Gatta-melata chapel in Padua. This work, so Michiel tells us, was signed by all three. This would lead us to suppose that Jacopo probably took an active part in the education of his sons but the fact that Giovanni lived in the town of Padua and hence, no doubt, fre-quented the house of his brother-in-law, Mantegna, had a more lasting effect on his art.

Giovanni is mentioned for the first time in a document of 1459, in which he figures as witness; at this time he seems to have been independent and working on his own account. Ridolfi (p. 64) read

---

Perkins, An unpublished Picture by G. B., Burlington Magazine, XV, 1909, p. 126. *A. Pichon*, Le Christ de G. B. récemment acquis par le musée du Louvre, Revue de l'Art ancien et moderne, 1912, pp. 417—424. *W. Rankin*, A Madonna by G. B., Art in America, 1914, p. 317. *A. Ravà*, Antonello da Messina o G. B.?, L'Arte, XXXIII, 1920, p. 279. *C. Ricci*, La Madonna degli Alberetti, Rassegna d'Arte, II, 1902, p. 125. *F. Saccardo*, Le Madonne di G. B., Rassegna bibl. dell'arte italiana, XIV, 1911, No. 1—4, p. 19. *Schefer*, Note sur un tableau du Louvre naguère attribué à G. B., Paris, no date. *W. Suida*, Works by G. B., Burlington Magazine, LI, Oct. 1927, p. 187. *A. Symons*, Notes on G. B., Burlington Magazine, XXXVII, 1920, p. 170. *H. von Tschudi*, Die "Pietà" von G. B. im Berliner Museum, Jahrb. d. K. Preus. Kunstsamml., XII, 1899, p. 219. *A. Venturi*, Disegni inediti di Giambellino e Raffaello nelle pinacoteche civiche di Brescia, L'Arte, XXIV, 1921, p. 7. *The Same*, Giambellino, Nuove ricerche, L'Arte, XXVII, 1924, p. 137. *The Same*, Cristo morto di Giambellino, L'Arte, XXVIII, 1925, p. 217. *The Same*, Tre ignorati quadri di Giam-bellino, L'Arte, 1926, XXIX, p. 68. *E. K. Waterhouse*, A new Bellinesque Picture, Burlington Magazine, LXI, 1932, p. 61.

(¹) *Ridolfi*, ed von Hadeln, I, p. 63 note 1.

the date 1464 on one of the two pictures which he saw in the
Scuola di San Gerolamo and which he praised greatly, as did also
Boschini (p. 462) (¹).

The earliest order recorded dates from 1470 when he undertakes to execute a canvas of the Flood and Noah's Ark for the
Scuola di San Marco. The following year he has a workshop,
together with his brother and in 1473 there is question of his
having to replace Lazzaro Bastiani in the execution of a picture
of the Lord, which in the end Bastiani himself paints. In 1474 he
executed his first dated work, the portrait of Joerg Fugger. When
Gentile left for Constantinople in 1479, Giovanni took his place as
painter of the Palazzo Ducale, where he carried out his most important work which, however, together with many other famous
paintings of the Venetian school, was destroyed by fire in 1577.
Several documents record his activity in this palace and make
special reference to the series of pictures in the big Council Hall.
In 1480 his salary is fixed at 180 ducats a year until he is rewarded with a "Senseria" in the "fondaco dei Tedeschi". In 1483,
always in connexion with the same activity, he is made the recipient of other financial favours, as for instance exemption from
the payment of the tax to the painters' corporation. In 1492 we
find him again at work in the big Council Hall along with several
other painters; during an illness his brother undertakes his share
as well as his own. Payment of this undertaking is recorded as
late as December 1495 (²).

During these years we have other data concerning Giovanni as
member of the different Scuole: San Marco, Sta .Maria, S. Cristoforo de 'Mercanti and della Misericordia.

In 1485 he makes a settlement in favour of his wife Ginevra, and
in her will of 1489 she leaves this sum back to her husband and
after his death to her son Alvise. In 1487 Giovanni witnesses a deed
and it is from this year that the "Madonna degli Alberetti" in the
gallery of Venice dates. During the following year he executes
the important altar-pieces at Murano and in the Frari church.

In 1497 Giovanni Bellini, through the medium of Alberto da

(¹) *Zanetti*, op. cit., p. 66, mentions the miserable remains of these
paintings.

(²) *E. Gaye*, Carteggio inedito d'artisti dei secoli XIV, XV, XVI, II,
Florence, 1840, p. 70.

Bologna, offers his services to the Marchesa Isabella Gonzaga and requests to be allowed to make a picture for her famous "Studiolo" for which Mantegna and Perugino had painted some canvases (¹). Giovanni speaks with such enthusiasm of the princess that it appears obvious that he knew her personally. Isabella sends a canvas to the artist and requests him to paint a view of the town of Paris but Giovanni refuses because he has never seen this city. Between 1501 and 1506 an interminable correspondence takes place between Isabella and her envoys in connexion with a picture which she desired to have from the hand of Giovanni. I shall enter only briefly into these records which have been published several times (²).

The Marchesa chose as the subject an event from ancient history; after some haggling about the price and the time, Bellini received twenty-five ducats down and another seventy-five on the delivery of the picture. Giovanni, however, does not like the subject and he is authorized to change it into something similar. The artist does not start the work; Isabella wants her money back but Bellini proposes to make instead a Nativity for which he is to receive fifty ducats in all. There is further diversity of opinion about a saint and the subject is once more changed and becomes a Madonna and Child with St. John the Baptist. After more furious letters from Isabella, she finally, after four years' delay, gets a picture representing a subject entirely different from what she had requested and . . . . at once orders another painting. Her admiration for the work of art must have been greater than her indignation. Cardinal Bembo, not without difficulty, succeeds in persuading the master to accept the order; he writes "I have waged such a battle that I think the castle will surrender". The painter is to be entirely free in the choice of the subject but the picture is to be executed after some of his own drawings which he had in his workshop. In the inventory of the Gonzaga collection there is mention of a Madonna and Child with St. Sebastian by Giovanni Bellini, and this no doubt is a reference to the second picture which he made for Isabella. We learn from Cardinal Bembo's letters that Giovanni never showed his works

---

(¹) *Luzio*, Arch. Stor. dell' Arte, 1888, p. 277.

(²) *D'Arco*, Delle arti e degli artifici di Mantova, II, pp. 59, 64, 161, 188. *L. Venturi*, Pittori veneziani, p. 345.

before they were finished, while the whole incident proves to what an extent he felt independent of the favours of his all-powerful patrons (¹).

In 1498 Giovanni gives his consent to certain clauses in the will of his son Alvise and discloses considerable generosity on his part, because the settlement he had made on his wife is in this document bequeathed to a Lucrezia who seems to have been a friend of his wife.

It must have been shortly after the death of Alvise Vivarini, which occurred in 1505, that Giovanni painted three canvases for the large Council Hall; Vasari even informs us that he finished one which Alvise had started. The subjects, which are fairly minutely described by Vasari and Sansovino, illustrate the story of Pope Alexander III, the Emperor and the Doge of Venice, and in fact are a continuation of the series on which Gentile also had worked (²). It will be remembered that the latter artist in his will expressed the desire that Giovanni should accomplish this task and, after Gentile's death in 1507, the younger brother finishes the canvas of the Sermon of St. Mark, now in the Brera Gallery and, as arranged in the will, receives their father's sketchbook.

From the years 1505, 1507, 1509, 1510, 1513 and 1515 we have some dated works from Giovanni's hand. One of them, representing the Doge Leonardo Loredano and some patricians of 1507, is of particular importance and has quite an official character. The painter continued working until the very end of his life. In 1514 he receives from Alfonso II of Ferrara eighty-five ducats as the final instalment in the payment of the extant picture of the Feast of Bacchus which Vasari, in his life of Titian, tells us was finished by this artist.

In 1515 the Scuola Grande di San Marco makes a contract with Giovanni, who at this time was well over eighty, for a canvas of the martyrdom of St. Mark in Alexandria. In all probability he died before he completed this work, which was finished by Vittore Belliniano in 1526 and is now in the gallery of Vienna. Judging from its actual appearance one would not say that the master had

---

(¹) *A. Berlotti*, Artisti in relazione coi Gonzaga, Modena, 1885, p. 151. (Estr. degli Atti delle Dep. di Stor. patr. per le prov. Modena e Parma).

(²) *Vasari*, op. cit., p. 156 note 2; p. 159 and note. *Sansovino*, op. cit., pp. 123B, 126A, 128B.

taken a great share in its execution. A picture of the holy Theodore of Urbino in the National Gallery, London, is dated 1515
and there is even mention of a picture by Giovanni showing the
date 1516, which once existed in Padua (¹). On the 29th November
1516 Sanudo writes in his diary that Giovanni Bellini is dead
and was buried near his brother in the vault in the church of
SS. Giovanni e Paolo; he adds that "his fame is known throughout
the world and old as he was he still painted excellently".

Many people have written in praise of Giovanni Bellini and
perhaps not the least important are the words of Albrecht Dürer
who, in a letter of 1506 from Venice, says that though old he is
still the best painter. Ariosto in admiration names him together
with Leonardo and Mantegna:

>   E quei che furo ai nostri di, o son ora
>   Leonardo, Andrea Mantegna e Gian Bellino.

Bembo, the cardinal, who negotiated about the picture for
Isabella Gonzaga, speaks of a portrait of a beloved lady in much
the same manner as Petrarch did about Simone Martini's portrait
of Laura, as indeed has been observed by Vasari, but in other
verses he sings his praises on a somewhat erotic note. The poet
Lorenzini calls him a painter worthy of Alexander. He is
mentioned also by Cillenio. Vittore Camelo, the medallist, who cast
a portrait of Gentile, also made an engraving of Giovanni and this
medal gives us a very clear idea of Giovanni's appearance.

Vasari speaks of the great affection which united the two
brothers and really much of what we know about them seems to
point to this fraternal attachment.

Ridolfi relates that, in order to discover the secret of oil-painting
which Antonello da Messina practised in Venice, Giovanni dressed
up as a nobleman and went to Antonello to have his portrait
painted. But this is a most unlikely anecdote.

*_**

The reconstruction of the early activity of Giovanni Bellini is
one of the very difficult, but at the same time most absorbing

---

(¹) *Moschini*, Guida, II, p. 561; we need not take into consideration the
signed and dated picture of 1527 of the family Delfin al Mal-canton, which
is also mentioned here. Giovanni's widow outlived him by many years
because she made her last testament in 1554. *Cechetti*, Archiv. veneti,
XXXIV, p. 204.

tasks of the historian of Italian painting of the Renaissance. Mr.
Berenson's opinion that Gentile's artistic personality, as well as
that of Giovanni, had no occasion for free development until after
their father's death, because up to this moment they had worked
only as his mere assistants, has been too severely contested, I
think, by several critics. It more or less holds good as far as
Gentile is concerned but it has to be abandoned for Giovanni. An
important contribution to the chronology of Giovanni's early
activity has been made by von Hadeln (¹). The more talented of
the two brothers did not wait until he was forty or over to follow
his own bent, because in 1459, when he must have been about
twenty-eight years old, we find him established as an independent
artist. Moreover, in 1464 he executed the greatly praised pictures
for the Scuola di San Gerolamo "in concorenza d'altri pittori"
(Ridolfi). Further, Michiel's affirmation that when collaborating
with their father in the altar-piece for the Gattamelata altar-
piece, all three artists signed the work, suggests a certain independence on their part even when working together with their
father and there does not seem to have existed that slavish adaptability which was generally expected from the assistants of a
leading artist.

We have no actually dated works before 1474 and they do not
become frequent until 1487, so that for practically all Giovanni's
works from about 1450 till this date, that is to say for close on the
first forty years of his long career, we have to establish a chronology based almost entirely on stylistic considerations.

The few certain facts which we should bear in mind are: first,
the influence of his father, whose pupil he surely was, consequently the works in which this influence is manifest, are certainly of an early phase; secondly, the domination of his brother-in-law
Mantegna, which is obvious in a particular group of works; this
influence was more lasting than that of Jacopo, in fact the real
development of Giovanni's artistic individuality seems to be the
outcome of a Mantegnesque inspiration; and thirdly, the style of
the four important altar-pieces from the Carità church, now in
the gallery of Venice, which, as von Hadeln has demonstrated,
were painted in 1461 or 1462.

Even in these works of the early sixties, there is already some

---

(¹) *D. von Hadeln*, op. cit., Burlington Magazine, 1928.

trace of Mantegna's influence. There are a few, however, in which this feature is absent and in which we can recognize an evolution from Jacopo's art in a direction which was only fully realized after Giovanni had been in close touch with Mantegna. We detect in these paintings the still somewhat hesitating hand of an infinitely gifted but as yet uncertain artist.

The earliest of the first and rather scanty group of paintings is, I think, the small panel of the standing Madonna holding the Child, also standing, on a low wall in front of her, while close by appears the head of St. Jerome; the figures are shown against the background of a landscape and a cloudy sky. This lovely little picture belongs to Mrs. Haas, Detroit (Gronau, 1).

Closely connected with this work is a signed picture in the Johnson collection, Philadelphia ([1]), which however, notwithstanding the correspondence in outline of the half-length figure of the Madonna, reveals a greater freedom of treatment (fig. 116). Although far more pictorial and expressive the composition is really only an evolution of that of Jacopo's Madonna at Lovere and the type of the Child, too, seems to find its source in the father's creations rather than in Mantegna's triptych of 1464 in the Uffizi with which Mr. Berenson compares it; as a result of this comparison he assigns it to too late a date.

I imagine that these two pictures were executed by Giovanni in his twenties, that is to say around the year 1455, and it is just possible that at a slightly later date he painted the sad-looking Madonna in bust length in the collection of the Earl of Harewood, London; she is shown in full-face and holds in her arms the equally mournful-looking Infant Jesus Who grasps a flower; again we see a landscape in the background (Gronau, 39). The same types of Virgin and Child are met with in later works but they might be examples of a return to an earlier manner. In any case this picture is very difficult to date. I do not think it belongs to his Mantegnesque period.

Another rather incomprehensible picture is that in the A. F. Philips collection at Endhoven (Gronau, 16) of the Madonna who looks at the spectator and tenderly clasps the Child, Who stands

([1]) *Mather*, op. cit., Burlington Magazine, IX. *Berenson*, Catalogue of the Italian Pictures of the Johnson coll., No. 165. *The Same*, Venetian Painting in America, p. 65. *L. Venturi*, Pitture italiane in America, pl. 291.

Fig. 116. Giovanni Bellini, Madonna. Johnson Collection, Philadelphia.
Photo Courtesy of the John G. Johnson art Collection.

on a low wall on which an apple is depicted. I do not know the original but judging from the photograph there are certain features, as for instance the reminiscences of Jacopo's manner, the technical details and the absence of the Mantegnesque influence which lead me to believe that if really by Giambellino it must be an early work.

The transition towards the period in which Giovanni Bellini was under the spell of Mantegna is marked by a gradual diminution of Jacopo's influence and I think that certain paintings in which the Mantegnesque elements are not so manifest as in other works might date from the beginning of the domination of the Paduan genius, and not from a later stage in his career when this ascendancy was on the wane.

The four altar-pieces from the Carità church, now in the gallery of Venice (621, 621A, B, and c) were in all probability, as Fogolari has shown us ([1]), painted around the year 1464 and anyhow shortly after 1460—1461, during which period the chapels for which they were destined were constructed. They are mentioned as having been consecrated with the rest of the church in 1471 but there is really no reason to suppose that this is the date of their execution, as has been done ([2]).

These paintings have received many attributions; they include one to the manner of Vivarini, one more or less to Bartolomeo himself ([3]) and one to the school of Giovanni Bellini ([4]). However, at this moment Giambellino had not as yet any pupils who worked in this particular manner because in it we notice elements which only at a later stage became fully developed.

The panels have been considerably restored in places but apart from this we cannot fail to observe an inequality of technique, more especially in the lunettes, from which we can infer that he probably was assisted in the enterprise.

The first of these altar-pieces shows SS. John the Baptist,

([1]) *Fogolari*, Chiesa della Carità, Archiv. Veneto-Trentino, 1923, p. 82. *The Same*, op. cit., Dedalo, 1932.

([2]) *Berenson*, Four Bellinesque triptychs. For the early date v. *Paoletti*, L'architettura e la scultura, I, 1893, note 7. *Paoletti u Ludwig*, Repert. f. Kunstwiss., XXII, 1899, p. 449. *Von Hadeln*, op. cit., Burlington Magazine, 1928. *Gronau*, op. cit., p. 199.

([3]) *Testi*, op. cit., II, p. 490.

([4]) *Berenson*, loc. cit.

Fig. 117. Giovanni Bellini, SS. John the Baptist and Lawrence. Accademia, Venice.   Photo Anderson.

Lawrence (fig. 117) and Antony of Padua. In the sad but regular features, chiefly those of St. Lawrence, and in sentiment this work reminds us of the Madonna in the Harewood collection. The Annunciation in the lunette is of a somewhat clumsy composition; the angel with a vase of lilies to one side is separated from the Virgin, who kneels at her prie-dieu, by a huge figure of God the Father.

Fig. 118. Giovanni Bellini, Nativity. Accademia,
Venice.   Photo Anderson.

Fig. 119.   Giovanni Bellini, Caricatures on the back of the Carità
polyptych. Accademia, Venice.   Photo Fiorentini.

The triptych which adorned the altar of St. Sebastian should
have had this saint as central figure but instead he is depicted
to the side and it is St. Antony Abbot who occupies the centre;
the other lateral figure is St. John the Baptist. The decoration

Fig. 120. Giovanni Bellini, Caricatures on the back of the Carità polyptych. Accademia, Venice. Photo Fiorentini.

of the lunette is incomplete; it shows only a rather medi-ocre half-length figure of the Madonna holding the almost nude Child in her arms; both are of melancholy expression.

The third altar-piece shows, in the centre, the Virgin adoring the Child outside an open shelter with St. Joseph seated in meditation near by and the angelic Message to the Shepherds in the background (fig. 118) ([1]); to the sides are depicted SS. Jerome and Louis of Toulouse. The composition of the lunette is again not very satisfactory and I hardly think this part by Giambellino; God the Father enthroned forms, as it were, the background to the Crucified and is represented between the half-length figures of SS. Augustine and Dominic. On the back of some of the panels of this altar-piece there are very amusing sketches, the more interesting of which are caricatures of human faces (figs. 119, 120) but we see as well an elegantly dressed knight with too large a head-dress, a male figure and a St. Sebastian. Also on the verso of one of the panels of the polyptych of the Madonna there is a sketch of a head, but it is less important ([2]).

On the last of these triptychs we see the Madonna between SS. Francis and Theodore and above, Christ half-arisen from His tomb with a somewhat stiff angel flying to either side (fig. 121).

I hardly think it possible that any one but Giovanni could have painted these important works, or at least the principal parts of them. We notice clearly in them that aesthetic aspiration towards regular and harmonious forms, which he realized only at a much later date and to the development of which the influence of Mantegna was perhaps something of an obstacle. In this respect I think the round, beautiful, though somewhat inanimate heads of St. Lawrence and St. Sebastian are very significant. The hands in many cases are marvellously fine pieces of painting, while the types of both the Madonna and the Child correspond perfectly to those of his subsequent works.

It seems to me obvious that the characteristic incisive line, the broken folds, as if in imitation of a metal low relief, and the somewhat fantastic silhouette of the limbs, as for instance those of SS. John the Baptist, derive directly from Mantegna, although it cannot be said that the influence of this master is as yet very strong. It should not be forgotten that a few years

[1] This composition was followed by Bartolomeo Vivarini in his polyptych of 1475.

[2] *Fogolari*, op. cit., Dedalo, 1932.

Fig. 121. Giovanni Bellini, Madonna and Saints. Accademia, Venice.
Photo Böhm.

prior to this period (1453—1454), Mantegna painted an altar
polyptych with saints on a gold background; the work to which
I refer is that from S. Giustino, Padua, now in the Brera Gallery.
The numerous large arrows which pierce St. Sebastian's body provide us with a point of resemblance between Giovanni's representation of this saint and that shown by Mantegna in his pictures at

Aigueperse and Vienna, both of which probably existed before 1461. On the other hand, God the Father with the crucified Redeemer is a motif which Giambellino might have seen in his father's sketch-book; in fact a drawing in the London album reveals many points in common, even to the absence of the dove, which prevents us from calling them representations of the Holy Trinity, while also in the throne there is some analogy. The rounded oval faces with their beautiful regular features which Giovanni portrays in several cases in these altar-pieces are not rare in his father's sketch-books, more especially in that in the British Museum, and might have been inspired by these examples. Further, in the paintings of SS. Louis, Francis and the dead Christ arising from His tomb, I am of opinion that we can detect a knowledge of the corresponding figures in bronze which Donatello executed between 1447 and 1449 for the basilica of Padua.

At one time Mr. Berenson was inclined to believe that the Madonna from the Davis collection, now in the Metropolitan Museum (fig. 122), was the earliest work we possessed by Giovanni. I do not think this is so although it is certainly a production of that period, soon after 1462, when the Mantegnesque influence begins to show in Giovanni's manner, without however dominating him. Baron von Hadeln's theory that the Davis Madonna is anterior to 1464, because Bartolomeo Vivarini practically copied it in the central panel of his polyptych of this year, does not hold good because Bartolomeo did not copy Giovanni's picture but repeated a motif from the polyptych of 1450 in Bologna, in the execution of which he himself had collaborated with his brother Antonio; besides, on account of the position of the Child, there is a much greater resemblance between the painting at Bologna and that of 1464 than between the latter and the Davis Madonna. In all likelihood the prototype of Bellini's composition is to be found in the polyptych of Bologna or some similar picture and not, as Gronau supposes, in the works of such Muranese painters as Quirizio, whose productions with this particular motif are of uncertain but probably later date.

The picture from the Davis collection, consequently, represents the Madonna in half-length figure adoring the Child Who lies in front of her on a cushion on a low wall; small pieces of a

Fig. 122. Giovanni Bellini, Madonna. Metropolitan Museum, New York.

Fig. 123. Giovanni Bellini, Madonna. Lehman Collection, New York.

landscape with a winding road are visible in the background and the strong linear effect due to Mantegna's influence is particularly pronounced in this part of the picture (fig. 122).

More Mantegnesque and hence possibly of slightly later date is the fine Madonna which formerly belonged to Prince Potenziani,

Rieti, but is now in the Lehman collection, New York (fig. 123) (¹). The Virgin is again shown in half-length figure; standing in front of her she holds the Infant Jesus Who is attired in a dainty little dress and bonnet and bestows a blessing. A landscape with the winding shore of a lake and one or two castles is seen behind, while a garland of flowers and fruit hangs in the sky. This is the only occasion on which Giambellino borrows a detail which is the hall-mark of Mantegna and his school.

There are three other pictures of the Madonna which reveal almost to the same degree the increasing influence of Mantegna. One of them is the signed painting in the Malaspina Museum, Pavia (Gronau, 18), in which the Virgin in bust length holds the Child, again tastefully dressed, standing on a wall on which she rests a book. A curtain, above which a piece of sky is visible, forms the background (²). Restoration has added sweetness to the face of the Virgin. The second work is preserved in the collection of Prince Trivulzio, Milan (Gronau, 41). Here the Child is seated on a cushion on a balustrade and the Virgin offers Him a pear. The rich velvet of her cloak and the Kufic lettering in the nimbi remind us more of Jacopo's pictures than the rest of this strange-looking panel, on which some traces of a signature still remain (³).

The third Madonna, which is preserved in the Kessler collection, Brussels (fig. 124) (⁴), slightly resembles in type the works of Jacopo. With both hands the Virgin covers in a gesture of protection the body of Jesus Who stands on a low wall on which a pear is placed. The Child grasps His Mother's hand and looks up with a rather strained expression. Sea, sky and curiously shaped rocks form the background of this beautiful picture, in which

---

(¹) *Gnoli*, op. cit. *Berenson*, op. cit., Art in America, 1916. *The Same*, Venetian Painting in America, p. 71. *Fogolari*, op. cit., Rassegna d'Arte, 1920, p. 118. *L. Venturi*, Pitt. ital. in America, p. 291. Berenson dates this painting from around the year 1469 which I think is slightly too late. He mentions also a copy in the von Pucher collection, Munich.

(²) *Frizzoni*, op. cit., Nuov. Antol., 1911. *Morelli* ascribed this picture to Bartolomeo Vivarini.

(³) *Frizzoni*, L'Arte, X, 1907, p. 461. *A. Venturi*, Stor. dell' Arte, VII, p. 554, calls it an early imitation of Giovanni Bellini.

(⁴) *Gronau*, op. cit., Jahrb. der K. Preus. Kunstsamml., XLV. Reprod. in Catal. of the Exhibition of Italian art of Dutch property, Amsterdam, 1934, No. 32.

Fig. 124. Giovanni Bellini, Madonna. Kessler Collection, Brussels.

the Mantegnesque linear effect is very marked. An argument for dating these three Madonnas, as well as that in the Lehman collection, prior to 1468 is found in the fact that the painter who executed, apparently about this year, a somewhat provincial looking miraculous image of the Virgin at Tresto, near Este,

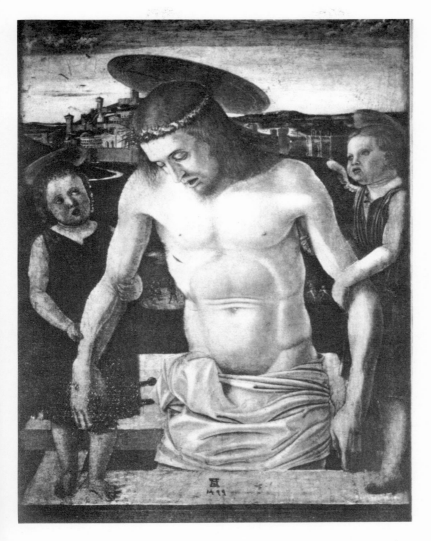

Fig. 125. Giovanni Bellini, dead Christ and Angels. Museo Civico, Venice.
Photo Alinari.

shows a knowledge of the composition and type of these
pictures (¹).

(¹) G. *Fogolari*, La Madonna miracolosa del Tresto, Bollettino d'Arte
del Minist. della Pubbl. Istr., III, 1919, p. 213. Herr Gronau observes
this similarity, more particularly for the Madonna in the Trivulzio collection.

In the museum of Berlin (1177) there is a replica of the Kessler Madonna in which, however, the landscape is entirely different. It is a good studio production (¹).

In the chapel to the right of the choir in the church of S. Trovaso, Venice, there is an almost completely repainted Madonna in half-length figure with the Child on her left arm and a newly gilded background, which in its original state might have been a work of this particular phase in Giovanni Bellini's career.

A strong influence of Mantegna is manifest also in some pictures of other subjects. In the first place I shall mention a Pietà in the Correr Museum, Venice, in which the dead Christ is supported by two angels who stand on the coping of His tomb; a town is depicted in the landscape background (fig. 125). This type of Pietà can be traced back to Donatello's composition in S. Antonio, Padua, but there the angels stand to the sides and do not touch the Saviour. Mantegna in his polyptych in the Brera Gallery represents the dead Saviour alone while Jacopo shows several faithful followers around the body of Our Lord. Consequently, it appears that this particular composition, which Antonello da Messina adopted and developed, and which so many later painters of the Venetian school — up to Paolo Veronese — have represented, is really an invention of Giovanni Bellini.

Of the altar-piece of St. John the Evangelist which Michiel praised in 1530 as one of the fine works of Giambellino, there remain to day but three predella panels; they were formerly in the von Kaufmann collection but are now in that of Prince Ruprecht of Bavaria. Michiel said that he believed them to be by Lauro Padovano, about whom we have some other data; this induced Professor Gronau to build up an artistic personality around this name and he ascribed to him, as well, the predella of the altar-piece in SS. Giovanni e Paolo (²). In the latter pieces the individuality of Giambellino is not so easily recognizable but I feel very certain that he was the author of the three panels from the altar-piece of

---

(¹) *Gronau*, Jahrb. der K. Preus. Kunstsamml., XLV, 1924, p. 38. *The Same*, Bellini, p. 200, is of opinion that the picture in Berlin is also by Giovanni although he admits that it is rougher in execution. In the museum catalogue it is ascribed to the master.

(²) *Gronau*, op. cit., Collectanea Olschki.

St. John the Evangelist. They represent the funeral of Drusiana, her resurrection and the procession of thanksgiving for this miracle. The scenes take place in a profusion of architecture which is more abundant than is usually the case in the master's works; this element is absent in the predella of the Pesaro altar-piece with which we shall deal presently. The very finely designed and beautifully executed figures, full of action and movement, are Mantegnesque, though perhaps not to the same degree as those in the above mentioned pictures and they are less incisive in design. Signor Fogolari is of opinion that this work was executed around 1468.

A strange looking picture, very Mantegnesque in appearance, in the museum of Berlin (1678) is catalogued as a late work of Jacopo Bellini. It depicts the dead Saviour in half-length figure with the Virgin and St. John supporting Him by the arms; certainly in the Paris sketchbook (fol. 78) Jacopo shows us a very similar composition. However, from this master's hand we know nothing which so closely approximates him to the art of his Paduan son-in-law and I think it more likely that it is a work by Giovanni. In fact, in as far as the difference of subject renders it possible, there is a certain similarity between the features of the Saviour and those of the Madonna in the Trivulzio collection. The picture in Berlin is of remarkable quality and not unworthy of Giambellino's brush; however, an attribution of it to the master remains but an hypothesis.

I cannot say the same of another painting of the same subject but slightly different composition — the three figures being closer together — in the gallery of Bergamo (174) (Gronau, 23). There is a Greek inscription above while below on a sort of parapet is written the signature: *Johannes B*. The execution is too rough for us to assign this work to Giovanni's own hand ([1]).

Finally there are three Christological representations in which Giovanni reveals himself, in a very convincing manner, as an adherent of the art of Mantegna. They are the Transfiguration (fig. 126) and the Crucifixion (fig. 127) in the Correr Museum, and the Prayer in the Garden of Olives in the National Gallery,

---

([1]) The attribution is upheld by Herr Gronau. *Morelli*, Gall. Borghese, p.311, did not think it was by Giovanni. *Berenson* is right in judging it to be a studio production.

Fig. 126. Giovanni Bellini, Transfiguration. Correr Museum, Venice.

Photo Anderson.

Fig. 127. Giovanni Bellini, Crucifixion. Correr Museum, Venice. Photo Anderson.

London (726); the latter is probably of a slightly later date than the two other works. A Crucifixion in the museum of Pesaro has also been considered to belong to this group (Fiocco (¹), Gronau, 5, Berenson) but in my opinion this panel does not reach the artistic standard of Giovanni's productions nor is it in any way characteristic of the master.

In the two panels in the Correr Museum Giambellino follows that particular style of Mantegna which is most clearly expressed in the predella panels of the altar-piece in S. Zeno, Verona, executed between 1456 and 1459; here the manner is more grandiose and less attention has been paid to the minute details.

The two rather small pictures by Bellini are of such grandeur and majesty, such breadth of composition and such vastness of horizon that their conception, especially that of the Crucifixion, seems more suitable for a wall painting or a large canvas. In this particular picture we notice also some fantastic features which recall the works of Donatello rather than those of Mantegna, whose examples of incisive outline and design of drapery are, on the other hand, more evident in the Transfiguration. The somewhat elongated proportions which Mantegna affected at this moment are adopted by Bellini in the Crucifixion.

In the Prayer in the Garden of Olives we notice the influence of a slightly later stage of Mantegna's art, of which a typical production is the triptych, probably of 1464, in the Uffizi (fig. 128). Characteristic features here are the neatness of the drapery, which looks as if it were cut in metal, the strong oppositions of bright light and dark shadows and the minute drawing of the hair which again shows a rapid succession of light and shade. In all of these traits,which already proclaim Mantegna's propensity as engraver, Bellini follows him very closely and I imagine that when he executed the panel in London he had seen Mantegna's picture of the same subject which is now also in the National Gallery, although he by no means follows him slavishly. He has reduced the over-crowded landscape of the Paduan master to something infinitely more sober and dignified. Also the accessory elements, such as the trees, the buildings and the angels appearing to the Saviour, play a much less important part in Bellini's picture. His conception thereby has gained greatly in space and in dignity of

---

(¹) G. *Fiocco*, op. cit., Rassegna Marchigiana, 1922.

Fig. 128. Giovanni Bellini, Prayer in the Garden of Olives. National Gallery, London. Photo National Gallery.

Fig. 129. Giovanni Bellini, Pietà. Gallery, Rimini.

composition. Neither the painting by Mantegna nor that by Giambellino shows much connexion with Jacopo's drawings of this subject in the London sketchbook (43a, 448).

This somewhat mannered minuteness characterizes a certain group of works which for this reason can be classified after 1464, when this particular feature appears for the first time in Mantegna's paintings.

The first of these pictures I shall mention is a mystic panel of the Lord standing holding the Cross with blood streaming from His wounds into a cup held by a kneeling angel, which is preserved in the National Gallery, London (1233) ([1]). The landscape is extremely important and pictorial while the grisailles of antique taste which decorate a low wall lead us back to Mantegna. It is more especially in the figure of the angel that we notice those almost too exquisite effects of refinement which characterize this group of productions; at a later date something similar is found in the works of Leonardo and his pupils. They are again very obvious in the Pietà — half-length figure of the Lord

([1]) Rassegna d'Arte, IX, 1909, pl. at p. 55. *Gronau*, 21.

Fig. 130. Giovanni Bellini, Pietà. National Gallery, London.
Photo National Gallery.

between four angels — in the museum of Rimini (fig. 129) (¹).
This work originates from the church of S. Francesco and Vasari
mentions a picture of the same subject in this church and informs

---

(¹) *A. Venturi*, Apollo, April 1930, p. 223.

Fig. 131. Giovanni Bellini, portrait of a youth. National Gallery, London.
Photo National Gallery.

us that it was ordered by Sigismondo Malatesta who died in 1468. Although Vasari speaks of two angels, whereas here there are four, I feel certain that his reference is to this panel and he may have taken this piece of information from some reliable source because it is exactly in this manner that we imagine Giovanni Bellini must have painted towards 1468.

In a picture of the same subject but with only two angels,

Fig. 132.   Giovanni Bellini, portrait of a youth.   Bache Collection,
New York.

which belonged to the Mond collection but is now in the National
Gallery (3912, fig. 130) (¹), the type of the Saviour is very similar.

(¹) *A. Venturi*, L'Arte, XXVII, 1924, p. 202. Burlington Magazine,
XLV, 1924, p. 216. Apollo, VIII, March 1928, p. 101.

Fig. 133. Giovanni Bellini, polyptych. SS. Giovanni e Paolo, Venice.
Photo Anderson.

This painting is often supposed to be an earlier version and this
may very well be the case.

I recognize this manner of Giovanni Bellini in two portraits
which bear a certain resemblance one to the other; both are bust-
length figures of adolescents and are found, one in the National

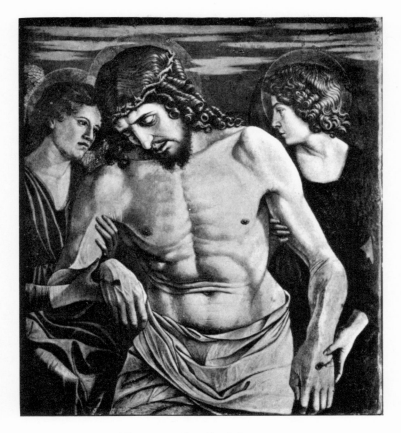

Fig. 134. Detail of fig. 133.   Photo Anderson.

Gallery (2509, fig. 131), the other in the collection of Mr. Jules Bache (fig. 132) (¹). These paintings both figured in the erroneous reconstruction which Mr. Berenson drew up of the personality of Alvise Vinarini; this theory however has since been abandoned by Mr. Berenson who now ascribes both works to Giovanni Bellini.

(¹) Formerly in the Schickler collection, Paris, *L. Venturi*, L'Arte, XI, 1908, p. 449. *Berenson*, Study and Criticism, III, p. 59. *C. Baker*, Burlington Magazine, L, 1927, p. 25. *H. E. Wortham*, Apollo, XI, May 1930, p. 350. *W. Valentiner*, Catalogue of early Paintings exhibited at the Duveen Galleries, New York, privately printed, 1924, No. 42. A Catalogue of the Paintings in the Collection of Jules S. Bache, New York, privately printed, 1929.

In the altar-piece in the church of SS. Giovanni e Paolo (figs. 133, 134) (¹) we notice this taste for detail and minute drawing in the three upper panels, on which are represented the angel and the Virgin of the Annunciation and the dead Saviour supported by two angels; in style all these figures bear a resemblance to the somewhat late manner of the Lombard school. The three standing figures below — SS. Vincent Ferrer, Christopher and Sebastian — on the other hand, are of a larger Mantegnesque technique, showing sharp linear and plastic effects, and this explains why it has been supposed that different hands took part in the execution of this altar-piece. There is certainly a difference between the two rows, though this might perhaps be explained by the fact that a few years separated the execution of the respective parts. The whole work has rather a strange appearance, and this accounts for the great number of opinions which have been expressed about this painting (²). The figure of St. Christopher recalls to a certain extent those of Jacopo's sketchbook.

The most puzzling part is the predella; it is extremely fine and painted with much brio but on the other hand it is more sketchy and different in technique from the rest of the picture. If it is really by Giovanni Bellini, as Professor Fogolari forcibly affirms, Mr. Berenson doubts and Dr. Gronau denies, we have here an instance in which the master worked in three different manners in the execution of one altar-piece. The predella narrates three events from the legend of St. Vincent Ferrer (fig. 135). Professor Gronau attributes it to Lauro Padovano (³) whom, as we saw, Michiel believed to be the author of the predella of the St. John polyptych then in the Carità church. We have some other information concerning this painter and we cannot set aside the possi-

---

(¹) *Fogolari*, op. cit., Dedalo, 1932.

(²) *Sansovino*, op. cit., p. 23B, mentions it as by Giovanni Bellini. *Ridolfi*, op. cit., p. 36, as by Alvise Vivarini. *Boschini*, as by Bartolomeo Vivarini. *Zanotto*, Pinacoteca Veneta, Venice, 1860, p. 91, Carpaccio. *Crowe and Cavalcaselle*, op. cit., III, p. 195, Carpaccio and Bastiani. *Berenson*, in previous editions of his lists of attributions and in his "Lotto" (1901), p. 43, Bonsignori but now thinks it to be by Giovanni Bellini; he is doubtful, however, about the predella. *Longhi*, op. cit., L'Arte, 1914, was the first after Sansovino to proclaim Giov. Bellini the author of this altar-piece v. *Gronau*, Lauro Padovano, *Fogolari*, op. cit., Dedalo, 1932.

(³) *Gronau*, Lauro Padovano.

Fig. 135. Giovanni Bellini (?), scene from the legend of St. Vincent Ferrer. SS. Giovanni e Paolo, Venice.   Photo Böhm.

bility that at some time or other he worked as Bellini's assistant. However, I find the panels of the Carità altar-piece still more convincing in favour of Giambellino's authorship than those of the polyptych in SS. Giovanni e Paolo which, nevertheless, seem to me also too closely connected with Giovanni Bellini to attribute to any other master. As in the predella (all that remains of the destroyed altar-piece of St. John the Evangelist in the Carità church) we notice likewise a liveliness of action and an abundance of architecture in these scenes which otherwise are not very characteristic of Giovanni Bellini; neither is the stiffly outlined sketchiness. On the whole then we are forced to remain somewhat doubtful about this attribution.

On the back of some of the panels of this polyptych there are some rough sketches of caricature-like faces, nudes, architecture, decorative motifs and a composition of antique appearance, which are all very interesting on account of the spontaneity and facility of execution ([1]). These drawings resemble very much those found on the back of some of the panels of the Carità polyptychs and in a way would point towards but a slight interval between the execution of the one and the other, but here I find the style, in fact one might say the three different styles, nevertheless so much more evolved that several years must have elapsed between their execution and that of the S. Vincenzo altar-piece. But I repeat, if we have to attribute the entire work to the master himself he certainly must have painted it at intervals.

In the Brass collection, Venice, there is a small bust-length painting of the dying Saviour, possibly a fragment of the usual composition with two angels, which in every respect markedly resembles the corresponding figure of the foregoing altar-piece and must have been executed by Giovanni Bellini at the same stage.

The principal panels of the polyptych in SS. Giovanni e Paolo mark, I imagine, the transition between the short period of over-refined technique and studied effects and a phase in which there is a considerable broadening-out and relief obtained by fairly large facets, which again coincides with a particular stage in the evolution of Mantegna, that in which he executed the frescoes in the castle of Mantua. For this manner in Giovanni's career we can offer the doubtful date of 1472 which Zanetti (Pit. Venez. p. 49) read on the Pietà in the Palazzo Ducale (fig. 136), but as this date no longer exists and none of the other ancient authors refers to it, I wonder if Zanetti could have made a mistake with the date of 1571 which is very clearly inscribed in the left corner as the year of restoration, when no doubt the background also was entirely repainted. Anyhow, I do not share Herr Gronau's opinion that the date furnished by Zanetti could not possibly be the correct one. I think that the picture is later than that at Rimini and a good many years must separate it from the altar-piece from the Carità church. However, we can still detect a reminiscence of the sketches which the artist's father left of this

([1]) *Fogolari*, op. cit.

DETAIL OF THE PIETA
By Giovanni Bellini, in the Brera Gallery.

Photo Anderson.

Fig. 136. Giovanni Bellini, Pietà. Palace of the Doges, Venice.

Photo Alinari.

subject, though in them he invariably shows more figures around the dead Redeemer.

The restoration of 1571 has considerably changed the panel but the central figures of the Lord emerging from a sarcophagus supported by the Virgin and St. John, as well as the kneeling figure of St. Mark, give us still a fairly exact idea of the original appearance and style, one in which we notice the forms just beginning to evolve from that taste for extreme minuteness which characterized the previous group of paintings.

Perhaps in its original state this picture more closely resembled the Pietà in the Brera (fig. 137 and plate) which is one of the most beautiful pictures of the Quattrocento and with which it has still much in common.

It is difficult to say anything about this master-piece in which the perfection of technique has been so spontaneously used to express the unfathomable depth of tragic feeling. The oppositions of light and shade have been worked with severity into effects of

Fig. 137. Giovanni Bellini, Pietà. Brera Gallery, Milan.

Photo Brogi.

the third dimension, all the gradations of which have been observed. The marvellous play of line in features and anatomy has
never been exceeded. The colouring is strangely sombre and cold
but powerful and dramatic. The monumentality of the figures of
Christ and the Virgin in no way detracts from the realism of their
attitude. In the light facetted volumes there is a souvenir of
Mantegna's manner while in the stiff ringlets — one to the left the
artist himself has painted over — and the minutely painted
features of St. John we notice a connexion with the previous
group. Here, however, the master has passed beyond all that might
be called mannerism.

With regard to the date of execution, I think it must be almost
contemporary with the Pietà in the Palazzo Ducale; hence, for
reasons which I have already stated, I do not agree with Mr. R.
Fry's opinion that it might be "one of the first works done after
1460" but am inclined to place it about a decade later.

Fine, though by no means on the same level as the foregoing

Fig. 138. Giovanni Bellini, Christ in Sarcophagus. Poldi Pezzoli Gallery,
Milan.   Photo Anderson.

work is a picture of the Dead Saviour in the Poldi Pezzoli Museum, Milan (fig. 138) (¹). Here, however, Christ alone is depicted,

---

(¹) According to *Berenson* and *Fry,* it is not from Giovanni Bellini's
own hand. *Gronau* classifies it as a very early production, even prior to
the Carità altar-piece, but to me this seems inadmissible.

His arms folded in front of Him, against a flat landscape with large rocks to either side.

With this work should, I think, be associated the Ecce Homo in the Louvre, in which Christ, attired in white, holds a book and bestows a blessing. This is quite possibly the same picture which Ridolfi describes as existing in the church of S. Stefano ([1]).

There are still some other paintings of the Pietà which bear a certain connexion with the above mentioned examples. The first I shall mention is that in the gallery of Dresden (52a) (fig. 139) in which the Virgin alone supports the arm and head of the Saviour Who is depicted seated on the edge of His coffin, against a landscape background; it is a somewhat coarsely executed painting and is often classified as a studio production; it is quite possibly not entirely by Giambellino's own hand ([2]). A somewhat similar composition, again of only two figures, in which, however, the attitudes resemble more closely those of the picture in the Brera Gallery, is found in the collection of Lord Rothermere, London ([3]). Here the faces express grief in such an intense and realistic manner that the artist has left himself no opportunity of portraying that nobility of feature which we noticed in the panel in Milan.

Finally there is a picture of Christ alone, half arisen from His tomb and with His nimbus adorned by a cross, which I saw not long ago in Holland ([4]). The figure is of a particularly noble design with clear outlines and in technique approaches more closely than the two other examples to the Pietà in the Brera Gallery; however, there is much in this panel which recalls Gentile Bellini and his drawing of the same subject.

([1]) *Fry*, Burlington Magazine, XXI, 1912, p. 10. *M. Logan*, Gazette des Beaux Arts, IV7, 1912, p. 371. *A. Pichon*, Revue de l'art ancien et moderne, XXXIII, 1913, p. 417. *T. Borenius*, Burlington Magazine, XXVII, 1915, p. 205.

([2]) Catalogued as Giovanni Bellini's school. *Berenson* judges it to be a studio production. *A. Venturi*, op. cit., L'Arte, 1925, p. 218 and Studi dal Vero, p. 235, gives it to the master himself, as does also Gronau.

([3]) *T. Borenius*, op. cit., Pantheon, Dec. 1932, p. 381, places this picture between 1465 and 1470, which I find is slightly too early. *P. G. Konody*, Works of Art in the Collection of Viscount Rothermere, privately printed, London, 1932, pl. 28.

([4]) No. 33 of the Catal. of the Exhibition of Italian Art of Dutch property, Amsterdam, 1934.

Fig. 139. Giovanni Bellini, Pietà. Gallery, Dresden.

Photo Alinari.

Somewhat difficult to date, but certainly of a slightly later period, is the picture of the dead Christ supported by two angels in the museum of Berlin (28) (Gronau, 74) which, however, still shows some connexion with this group (¹).

On account of the lack of paintings dated with certainty, any attempt to make a chronological classification of Giovanni Bellini's works prior to 1474 must remain hypothetical; I think, however, that the classification I have proposed above is the only possible one. I do not believe for a moment that the Pietà in the Brera could be an early work, whereas the four Carità altar-pieces are quite acceptable as such, because there is something hesitating and immature in these panels which gives them this character. From this we can infer that Jacopo had been Giovanni's first master, which, as a matter of fact, is more than likely, while the strong influence of Mantegna must have been felt at a later stage, though after some time this domination also waned. If in certain works of Giovanni Bellini this domination of Mantegna clearly points to the latter's manner around the year 1460, I do not see how these works could have been painted very many years after the inspiring examples of the Paduan brother-in-law. Nor can I imagine at what other moment Giambellino could have become to such an extent Mantegnesque, without being confronted by insurmountable difficulties regarding the logical development of his later years. In other words, we can very well imagine that between his most Mantegnesque phase and the dated works of 1487 and 1488, he passed through a stage in which he produced such pictures as the Pietà in the Brera Gallery, but I cannot conceive it possible that an artist who had achieved this master-piece and was finding his way towards the retable in the Frari church should still have to pass through a manner of painting so utterly subjected to the art of another.

In the works of the following group we notice a diminution in the Mantegnesque characteristics, but the same change, as it were, can be followed in Mantegna's own art in which the Paduan in-

---

(¹) *Frizzoni*, Arch. Stor. dell 'Arte, IV, 1891, p. 166. *H. von Tschudi*, op. cit., Jahrb. der K. Preus. Kunstsamml., XII. *Berenson* thinks that it is earlier than the Pietà of Rimini which means probably prior to 1468. *Fry*, about 1465. Catalogue of the museum of Berlin, 1465—1470. *Gronau*, not before 1475.

cisiveness of design diminishes, giving place to broader and more monumental principles, as we see in his frescoes of 1469—1472 in Mantua.

An influence which Mantegna might have exercised on Giambellino in the early seventies is evident in quite a number of pictures, mostly half-length figures of the Madonna with the Child, some of which rank as his finest and most fascinating productions.

Among the early manifestations of this phase should be included the Madonna in the Turner collection, London, the original of which, however, is unknown to me ([1]). Here the Child, completely dressed, is held in the Virgin's arms behind a low wall. A baldaquin of red cut velvet forms most of the background, the rest of which is occupied by a landscape, with a lake and two tall palms, in which three people, two of whom are attired in oriental costume, are seen walking. In the type of the Virgin there is some reminiscence of Jacopo and even of Antonio Vivarini but in the appearance of the Child and in the technique there is nothing which reminds us any more of the previous generation.

In style and type there exists a connexion between the foregoing picture and a Madonna in the collection of Mr. Percy Strauss, New York; the Virgin carrying the Child, Who grasps a small bird, is shown against a landscape with hills and a winding road; the spirit of this work is somewhat more sentimental (fig. 140).

Both of these paintings, however, serve as an introduction to the real type of the Madonnas of this group, which is characterized by a particular composition of triangular shape resting on a broad base. In order to obtain the breadth of the lower part the master depicts the Child lying, sometimes asleep, on His Mother's knee, or as if drawing Himself away from her. The sleeping Child, as we saw before, appears in some of the older examples.

The most typical instance of this tendency is the very fine Madonna in the gallery of Bergamo, in which the Virgin looking down is depicted in full face while the Child, with a somewhat pensive expression on His face, leans over entirely to one side, resting His hand, His bent left knee and His right heel on the low wall (fig. 141). This painting is signed: "*Joannes Bellinus*" and the

([1]) *D. von Hadeln*, op. cit.

Fig. 140. Giovanni Bellini, Madonna. P. Strauss Collection, New York.
Photo Frick Art Reference Library, New York.

second "l" is longer than the first, a detail which should be borne
in mind. The drapery of the Virgin is still of a very marked linear
effect and reminds us of a bronze relief.

Fig. 141. Giovanni Bellini, Madonna. Carrara Museum, Bergamo.
Photo Anderson.

The sleeping Child adored by His Mother appears in a panel in
the museum of Verona; He lies on a low wall, His head supported
by cushions (fig. 142). The Child again asleep on cushions but in
a more upright position with His head supported by the Virgin,
is shown in a picture in the Gardner Museum, Boston, which is

Fig. 142. Giovanni Bellini, Madonna. Museo Civico, Verona.
Photo Anderson.

signed: "*Joannes Bellinus P.*" (fig. 143) ([1]). Closely connected
with the latter work is the Madonna which Gustavo Frizzoni
bequeathed to the Correr Museum, Venice (Gronau, 31) but here the

([1]) *Hendy*, Catalogue of the Gardner Museum, p. 39.

Fig. 143. Giovanni Bellini, Madonna. Gardner Museum, Boston.
Photo Courtesy of Gardner Museum.

Child is seated and not asleep; the Virgin's protecting arm helps to
enlarge the base of the triangle. In a fine picture in the Platt collection, Englewood (Gronau, 46) (¹), the same effect is obtained by

(¹) *Perkins*, op. cit., Burlington Magazine, 1909, p. 126. *The Same*,
op. cit., Rassegna d'Arte, 1911. *Berenson*, Venetian Painting in America,
p. 76. *L. Venturi*, Pitt. ital. in America, p. 293.

Fig. 144.   Giovanni Bellini, Madonna. Sta. Maria dell' Orto, Venice.
Photo Alinari.

the recumbent position of the Infant Jesus. The background in all
these examples is composed of blue sky with little white clouds.
Less triangular in outline and without the sky as background is

Fig. 145. Giovanni Bellini, Madonna. Museum, Berlin.

the very beautiful half-length figure of the Madonna with the Child, whose mouth is open as if He were singing, which is preserved in the church of the Madonna dell' Orto in Venice; it is signed: *Joannes Bellinus*; the background is formed by a curtain, woven with a design of flowers, and Greek monograms (fig. 144). Not any less fine is the somewhat similar Madonna in the museum of Berlin (10A); here, however, the Child is depicted sucking his fingers and the piece of material in the background is plain red (fig. 145). The signature *"Joannes Bellinus P."* shows the long second "l". In all these paintings there is still some trace of the linear element due to the influence of Mantegna; none the less we feel that the artist is gradually acquiring more independence.

Some of the figures of the Child Christ in this group of paintings greatly resemble the five putti represented near an archway in a panel in the gallery of Venice, which was executed in honour of Doge Tron, consequently not earlier than 1471 and very possibly during this year on the occasion of his election to this office. On account of the fine landscape background also I am inclined to believe that this is a work by Giovanni's own hand (¹).

I imagine that it was during this period that Giovanni painted the oblong picture of the Presentation of the Child in the Temple in the Querini-Stampalia Museum, Venice (fig. 146), in which the master reproduces the four principal and central figures of a similar painting by Mantegna, now in the gallery of Berlin; but whereas Mantegna depicts only two other figures apart from the central group, Giovanni Bellini shows us four, one of whom — the woman to the extreme left — is very similar in type to the Madonna in the Pietà in Dresden. However, a detailed comparison between the figures of the two pictures reveals to us that Bellini, even though he was so directly inspired by an example of the Paduan master, now follows aesthetic principles which are entirely his own. There is no longer any trace of that severity and harshness which are still quite evident in Mantegna's panel.

It might have been about this time that Giovanni collaborated with his brother in the execution of an Adoration of the Magi, now in a private collection in Rome, which I mentioned in the previous chapter.

Another painting which reveals a dependence on Mantegna at the same time as conspicuous personal characteristics is a Crucifixion belonging to Count Contini Bonacossi, Florence (Gronau, 25),

---

(¹) *Berenson*, op. cit., Venetian Painting in America, p. 70, believes it to be a studio production.

Fig. 146. Giovanni Bellini, Presentation in the Temple. Querini-Stampalia Gallery, Venice. Photo Alinari.

which was formerly in the Rodolphe Kann collection, Paris ([1]). This picture seems to me in every respect different from that of the same subject in the Correr Museum. Mantegna's influence has become quite external and, technically speaking, it is perhaps the painting which comes nearest to the Pietà in the Brera Gallery; the type of Christ also is very similar. Here too the light effects are excellent and the nude body and the features are well modelled, but the faces express less emotion. The landscape is softer and more pictorial than that in the Correr Crucifixion. The breadth of drapery recalls that of the Madonnas of the foregoing group; the forms of the two lateral figures even tend towards heaviness.

It was possibly about this period that Giambellino painted three rather extraordinary looking half-length figures of the Madonna.

The first I shall cite is in the Fogg Art Museum, Cambridge,

([1]) In 1865, when the panel belonged to Mr. Richard Fisher, it was exhibited at the British Institution as a work of Mantegna: *Crowe and Cavalcaselle*, op. cit., p. 142 note 1.

U.S.A. (Gronau, 44) ([1]); it was formerly in the Crespi collection, Milan ([2]). Mr. Berenson proposed the period of 1475—1478 for this work which, however, is little more than a wreck. The Child standing holds a rose, and we see Greek monograms in the background, but not much more is original than the faces and the Madonna's right hand. Then in Casa Galvani at Cordenons there is a panel in which the Virgin carries the Child Who bestows a blessing (Gronau, 45) which, once upon a time, passed as a very early work ([3]) but, as Gronau observes, seems sooner to be a production of a riper period. The third is a somewhat similar panel in the Mond collection, London (Gronau, 45), in which the Madonna affectionately holds the pathetic-looking Child ([4]).

In the following phase in the evolution of Giovanni Bellini's art, which shows scarcely any Mantegnesque elements, we notice a fairly rapid progress towards his most glorious period, which we might call the period of harmonious beauty; to it his dated altar-pieces of 1488 belong. A painting of the year 1474 gives us some idea of this particular manner. It is the portrait of Joerg Fugger which was discovered a few years ago in the castle actually belonging to the Fugger family (Gronau, 69) ([5]). Although a charming painting it is rather small and can convey to us only a limited impression of Giambellino's art at this period. The youngish man with a garland on his bushy curls is depicted in three-quarters right profile. At first sight one would certainly never call this picture a production of a pupil of Mantegna and even searching for Mantegnesque reminiscences we find hardly any. There are more elements due to the Paduan master in the altar-piece from the church of S. Francesco — Vasari is wrong in

---

([1]) Fogg Art Museum: Collection of Mediaeval and Renaissance Paintings, Cambridge, U.S.A., 1919, No. 45.

([2]) *A. Venturi*, Coll. Crespi, p. 327.

([3]) *G. Fogolari*, Arte Cristiana, II, 1914, p. 129. *The Same*, L'Arte, 1914, p. 304. *The Same*, Rassegna d'Arte, 1920, p. 117.

([4]) *J. P. Richter*, Catalogue of the Mond coll., p. 63. *L. Testi*, op. cit., reproduces it as a work by Jacopo Bellini.

([5]) *Mayer*, op. cit., Burlington Magazine, 1926. As *von Hadeln*, op. cit., Burlington Magazine, 1927, has already observed, Herr Mayer, for chronological reasons, is mistaken in speaking of an influence of Antonello. *Balniel and Clark*, Catalogue of the Exhibition of Italian Art, 1930, No. 167.

Fig. 147. Giovanni Bellini, Coronation of the Virgin. Gallery, Pesaro.

saying S. Domenico — of Pesaro, now in the gallery of this town
(fig. 147) (¹). It represents the Coronation of the Virgin; the Lord
and His Mother are seated on a broad monumental throne the
back of which is decorated with a landscape with a castle which
is supposed to be the Rocca of Gradara. The frame shows a design
in relief work, the upper part of which is composed of minutely
executed figures of antique character after Mantegna's taste but
not executed in his manner. Little groups of cherubim, one en-
circling the dove of the Holy Ghost, are depicted among the

(¹) *Longhi*, L'Arte, XVII, 1914, p. 248.

Fig. 148. Giovanni Bellini, St. George and the Dragon.GalleryPesaro.
Photo Anderson.

clouds of the background. Below, to the sides of the throne stand
the strongly built figures of SS. Paul and Peter, Francis and
Jerome; in the plastic effects of the folds there are still some
reminiscences of the clear cut and somewhat angular drapery
of Mantegna. The signature, *Joannes Bellinus*, is inscribed on
the base of the throne. The Mantegnesque features are also
evident in the small figures of saints which decorate the frame
and in the seven beautiful and very important panels of the
predella representing St. George slaying the dragon (fig. 148), the

Fig. 149. Giovanni Bellini, Vision of St. Francis. Gallery, Pesaro.

Photo Anderson.

Conversion of St. Paul, the Crucifixion of St. Peter, the Virgin
adoring the Child Who lies in front of her with St. Joseph in
meditation seated near by, St. Jerome in penitence, St. Francis
receiving the stigmata (fig. 149) and St. George standing on a
pedestal holding a model of the city.

The draping of the figures in these panels invariably shows
something which reminds us of metal reliefs; the faces are of a
more evolved style and the manner in which the events are
treated reveals on the part of the artist that fine dramatic sense
which we had already observed in the predella panels of his early
altar-pieces. The landscapes are highly important and beautiful,
with good effects of distance, and in one instance — that of the
Adoration of the Child — seem to lead the way to Giorgione's

XVII.   17

paradisiac visions. The bare wintry-looking trees and the winding white roads, as well as the rectangular rocks, are other elements which recall Giambellino's more Mantegnesque years, and because of the presence of these features we might be tempted to classify this altar-piece as prior to the Fugger portrait of 1474, though this painting offers no opportunity of a display of these elements. The treatment of the features, however, is very similar in style so that after all I think the date of around 1475 proposed by others for this altar-piece is practically correct; it is perhaps slightly too late. In the landscapes of the predella panels we notice that Giovanni Bellini shows a particular interest in architecture; in the scene of St. Francis receiving the stigmata, in which the scarcely visible crucifix, which seems to rest on the roof of the church, is an unusual iconographical feature, the artist even goes a step further and depicts with almost technical details the apse of a Gothic church, whereas the architectural elements which surround the statue-like figure of St. George are treated in such a casual manner that we hardly understand what the artist wishes to convey.

The Pietà in the Vatican Gallery (fig. 150) in which Christ seated on the edge of His tomb is shown almost in right profile supported by an old man while St. Mary Magdalene fondles His left hand and a man with a black beard, holding a cup, looks sadly down at the dead Saviour, has apparently been the upper panel of the Pesaro altar-piece [1]. The painting is somewhat different in manner from that of the principal panel. I find that the forms are fuller and the technique smoother. The treatment of the faces and of the hands more especially is of rare beauty. The conception of the Pietà in this case is very different from anything we have seen up till now. The attitudes and expressions convey the impression that the three faithful who surround the Redeemer have not yet realized that He is dead, and such an idea might explain the rather naïve action of the companion holding the cup as if a draught thereof might still be of some relief. This picture has sometimes been attributed to Montagna.

In the principal figures of the altar-piece of Pesaro we notice a broadening out of the forms, which is particularly striking in the

---

[1] *G. Frizzoni*, op. cit., Burlington Magazine, XXII.

Fig. 150. Giovanni Bellini, Pietà. Gallery, Città del Vaticano.
Photo Anderson.

heads and features; the head-dress of the Madonna also becomes
more ample.

A marked resemblance exists between the Madonna at Pesaro
and a half-length figure of the Virgin holding the Child Who
blesses, in the gallery of Bergamo (167) (fig. 151), of which work
there is a replica in the gallery of Berlin (10); here however rays of

Fig. 151. Giovanni Bellini, Madonna. Gallery, Bergamo.
Photo Anderson.

light are traced in the background and the Madonna and Child in
type point to a year or two later in the master's career; also the
sharpness in the drawing of the Child's garment has considerably
diminished. A third version of this Madonna, which is preserved
in the gallery of Treviso, seems to be a workshop production (¹).

(¹) *Coletti*, Bollettino d'Arte, VI, April 1927, p. 472.

Fig. 152. Giovanni Bellini, Madonna. Accademia, Venice.

Photo Anderson.

In the three years which constitute the transition towards Giovanni's best period I place still several pictures.

It was probably at this time that he executed a Madonna enthroned against a cloudy background adoring the Child Who lies sleeping on her knee, which originates from the Magistrato della Milizia di Mare where Moschini still saw it in 1815, but which is now in the gallery of Venice (591) (fig. 152). It is signed *Joannes Bellinus* and has sometimes been considered a studio production, or in part only by the master himself, but I find no reason for these restrictions.

Very much the same type of Virgin is found in a Madonna standing offering two cherries to the Child Who is seated on a wall with the town of Venice and the Lagoon in the background, in the collection of the late Baron Lazzaroni, Rome (fig. 153) ([1]); in a lovely Madonna in half-length figure adoring the Child Who leans on cushions on a low wall against a sky with white clouds, in the National Gallery, London (2901) (fig. 154); in the picture of the Virgin holding the mournful looking Child almost upright in her arms with a curtain and some Greek letters in the background, which originally was in the Palace of the Doges but is now in the Brera Gallery (216) (Gronau, 63); in a very similar picture belonging to Duveen Brothers, New York (Gronau, 62); in the fine painting of the Madonna with the small but more lively Jesus held in the same position against a cloudy sky, in the museum of Verona (110) (fig. 155) ([2]); in the Madonna holding the Child, Who blesses, standing upright against a beautiful landscape background, which is signed *"Joannes Bellinus"*, in the Accademia of Venice (594) (fig. 156) ([3]); in the very fine and somewhat similar composition with the Child in benediction in a private collection in Amsterdam which I have the privilege of publishing here for the first time (fig. 157) ([4]); in two other Madonnas, one in which the Child

([1]) *A. Venturi*, op. cit., L'Arte, XXIX. *The Same*, Studi dal Vero, p. 232, also in Il Messaggero, 11th Dec. 1925.

([2]) *G. Gerola*, op. cit., Rassegna d'Arte, 1909, p. 1. Of this picture a replica existed in the Gualino collection, Turin.

([3]) *Gronau*, op. cit., p. 205 and Rassegna d'Arte, 1917, p. 21, mentions another example of this composition belonging to Count Contini Bonacossi, Florence.

([4]) Reprod in Catal. of the Exhibition of Italian art in Dutch possession, Amsterdam, 1934, No. 32.

Fig. 153. Giovanni Bellini, Madonna. Private Collection, Rome.

Jesus has very curly hair and an open mouth, which is shown against a landscape background and is signed: *Joannes Bellinus p.* in the gallery of Rovigo (Gronau, 61); it is very much retouched; the other in which the Virgin offers a fruit to the nude Infant Who, lying in front of her, looks upwards, painted against a gold

Fig. 154. Giovanni Bellini, Madonna. National Gallery, London.
Photo National Gallery.

background in the Fassini collection, Rome (¹); and lastly, in a
picture in a private collection in Rome, in which the nude Child

(¹) *A. Venturi*, Pitture dal 300 all' 800: Collezione d'Arte del Barone
A. Fassini, I, Rome (1930), pl. 15.

Fig. 155. Giovanni Bellini, Madonna. Museo Civico, Verona.
Photo Anderson.

blessing is depicted on His Mother's knee against the background
of a curtain, which is signed: *"Joannes Bellinus"*.

From these years also date probably the considerably repainted
half-length figure of the Madonna holding the Child, Who blesses
and Whose feet rest on a low wall, in the gallery of Venice (583),

Fig. 156.　Giovanni Bellini, Madonna. Accademia, Venice.
Photo Anderson.

formerly in the Palazzo Camerlenghi (Gronau, 77) ([1]) and a picture
in the gallery of Turin (Gronau, 75) in which Jesus in benediction
is seated on His Mother's knee with a curtain as background,
which shows the signature: "*Joannes Belinus*"; both considerably
restored.

([1]) *Ludwig*, op. cit., Jahrb. d. K. Preus. Kunstsamml., XXIII.

Fig. 157. Giovanni Bellini, Madonna. Private Collection. Amsterdam.
Photo Eilers.

There are some paintings of other subjects which should be
included in this group.

It is to this transitional period from one manner to another,
during which Mantegna's influence loses hold of Giambellino, that
we should attribute two pictures of St. Jerome seated reading
in a rocky landscape with a town in the distance, which in composition are very similar to a picture of a later manner in the
National Gallery, London. One of them is preserved in the
Ashmolean Museum, Oxford; the other, which was previously in
the Palazzo Papafava, Padua, now belongs to Count Contini
Bonacossi, Florence (Gronau, 82).

Fig. 158. Giovanni Bellini, St. Francis in ecstasy. Frick Foundation, New York.

A picture in the Frick Foundation, New York, supposed to represent St. Francis receiving the stigmata (fig. 158) [1], shows a marked connexion in style with the latter work; this is evident not only in the construction of the figure but also in the rocks and the landscape. The conception of this scene is entirely independent of all iconographical traditions. The saint, his mouth open and his arms slightly out-stretched, stands as if in invocation; his hands and feet are already marked with the stigmata. Behind him, under a shelter of branches, we see a simple bench before a desk on which a book and a skull are placed; his wooden sandals and stick are depicted near by. There is no trace of the apparition of the cross or the Crucified. These details lead us to believe that the artist wished to represent an incident which occurred after the miracle of the stigmata; further, the presence of a

[1] Burlington Club, Exhibition of Venetian Painting, 1912, pl. 22.

donkey in a field near by goes to confirm this hypothesis although there were moments in his life prior to the stigmatization when the saint rode on an ass. The painting, which is signed: *"Joannes Bellinus"*, is probably that which Michiel describes as existing in the house of Taddeo Contarini in 1525; a work in which he particularly admires the landscape. His mention of this painting is somewhat strangely phrased (¹) and has been interpreted as meaning that Giovanni only started the painting and that it was finished by another artist. Frimmel, in his edition of Michiel's "Notizia", has translated the passage as if it meant that Giambellino had begun the work for a person (Zuan Michiel) other than the collector in whose house it was in 1525, and no doubt this is the correct interpretation. Mr. Fry (²) judges the work to be almost entirely by Basaiti, and T. Borenius, in his edition of Crowe and Cavalcaselle, agrees with him. But Mr. Berenson (³), who, however, thinks that Gerolamo da Santacroce collaborated in the execution of the trees, confutes this theory and provides us with the very conclusive argument that an attribution to Basaiti would furnish us with much too late a date for this painting which he rightly places around the year 1480. I think if anything it might be even a year or two earlier.

The picture is now almost unanimously accepted as a work by Giambellino and (entirely apart from any interpretation of Michiel's statement) I somewhat reluctantly concur with this attribution; not that I think it a typical production of the master but partly because I can name no other painter who might be held responsible for it.

This was a period when Giovanni Bellini seems to have taken a particular pleasure in painting landscapes with all their outdoor effects of light, and I think it was at this moment that he must have undertaken the Transfiguration in the museum of Naples (fig. 159) (⁴), the Resurrection in the gallery of Berlin (fig. 160)

(¹) La tavola del San Francesco nel deserto a oglio fo opera de Zuan Bellino, cominciata da lui a M. Zuan Michiel et ha un paese propinquo finito e ricercato mirabilmente.

(²) The Nation, X, p. 657.

(³) *Berenson*, op. cit., Venetian Painting in America, pp. 95, 105.

(⁴) *R. Longhi*, L'Arte, XVII, 1914, finds a strong influence of Piero della Francesca in this picture.

Fig. 159. Giovanni Bellini, Transfiguration. Gallery Naples.
Photo Anderson.

and the St. Jerome in the National Gallery (281) (fig. 161). The
last mentioned might be of a somewhat later date, while the
Transfiguration is most reminiscent of the St. Francis in the
Frick collection. These three master-pieces of the Quattrocento
show us the painter in a manner entirely his own, in which there
is not even any trace of Mantegna's influence. The aesthetic

Fig. 160. Giovanni Bellini, Resurrection. Museum, Berlin.

principles are quite different; the regular and noble beauty of the forms is no longer subjected to the linear severity of the Paduan school and still less to its expression of anxious tragedy. These paintings, in which joy and beauty are united with solemnity and dignity, are thoroughly delightful. The colouring is warm and vivid, the forms ample and harmonious and the enchanting landscapes full of light and distance.

In the Transfiguration (1) Mr. Fry has remarked in the

(1) *A. Venturi*, L'Arte, II, 1899, p. 432. *The Same*, IV, 1903, p. 105 and

Fig. 161. Giovanni Bellini, St. Jerome. National Gallery, London.
Photo Nationa. Gallery.

background to the right the presence of the tomb of Theodoric of
Ravenna and the tower of the church of Sant' Appolinare of this

Storia dell' arte ital., VII[4], p. 695, attributes this painting to Bartolomeo
Veneto.

town. This picture once formed part of the Farnese collection. Of the figure of Christ alone I know a very fine replica in a private collection in London.

The Resurrection was originally in the church of S. Michele in Murano where it adorned the altar of Marin Zorzi which seems to have been created between 1475 and 1478 or 1479 ([1]).

The St. Jerome, which in the National Gallery (281) still modestly figures as a work of Basaiti, has recently been restored to its rightful master (Gronau, Berenson). Very significant for our comprehension of the artist's evolution is a comparison in the treatment of the rocks which, prior to this, had been rendered after the manner of engravings but now possess perfect pictorial qualities; moreover the light is soft and even, and there is no longer any trace of spottiness.

To the earlier part of this phase in Giovanni Bellini's career belongs a half-length figure of the Madonna, tenderly holding the Child in her arms against the background of a curtain, in the Huntington Museum, San Marino, California (Gronau, 114); on a label on the parapet the signature: *Joannes Bellinus* is incribed ([2]).

Another panel of the Madonna which is obviously prior to those dated 1487 and 1488 is found in the Grenville L. Winthrop collection, New York (Gronau, 57) ([3]); here the Virgin adores the Child Who lies on cushions on a low wall while the greater part of the background is occupied by a curtain. However, as has already been observed, we can hardly accept this painting as a work entirely from the master's own hand ([4]).

([1]) *Ludwig u. Bode*, Jahrb. K. Preus. Kunstsamml., XXIV, 1903, p. 131; mentioned as a work of Giovanni Bellini by *Ridolfi*, p. 66; of Cima by *Boschini*; of Bartolomeo Veneto by *Venturi*, L'Arte, VI, 1903, p. 105. The picture has been copied in its entirety and in part by different Venetian painters v. *Gronau*, Giovanni Bellini, p. 204.

([2]) Formerly in the Lazzaroni collection, Paris. *Venturi*, op. cit., L'Arte, 1909, p. 319, dates it around the year 1490 or after. *Gronau*, op. cit., pl. 114, places it between 1488 and 1490. *Berenson*, Venetian Painting in America, p. 81, assigns it to soon after 1480; I think it was executed towards 1485.

([3]) *W. Rankin*, Art in America, 1914, p. 317.

([4]) *Berenson*, Venetian Painting in America, p. 78, says "not entirely autograph: probably a replica of a work by Giovanni Bellini of towards 1480".

A picture, however, on which Giovanni has left his signature is the Madonna, formerly in the Eastlake collection, which entered the National Gallery, London (3913), with the Mond bequest (Gronau 129) (¹); the Virgin, offering an apple to the nude Child Who reclines on a low wall, is depicted against a curtain, to the right of which we see a view of a castle on a hill.

I think it was around this date that Giambellino created quite another type of Madonna, which, considering the number of times it has been copied, must have had a great success. The Virgin is depicted facing the spectator against a landscape which for the greater part is hidden by a curtain. The nude Child standing places one hand under His Mother's chin and the other round her neck. Apparently there existed several examples of this composition but the finest and most beautifully designed is no doubt the signed version now in the museum of Chicago (fig. 162). Perhaps it was this picture which figured in 1917 at the Zoubaloff sale. It has been affirmed, however, that this painting originally belonged to a patrician family in Padua.

The composition has been repeated by Licinio as the central feature between SS. Joseph and Mary Magdalene in a signed work in a private collection in England; by Antonello da Saliba in a painting now in the museum of Berlin (v. Vol. XV, fig. 336); more or less by Mazzola in a signed panel in the Stroganoff collection, Rome; by a mediocre anonymous painter in a work in the museum of Vicenza and finally by Giambellino himself in a painting in the Willys collection, Toledo, Ohio, U.S.A., to which we shall return later (²).

A comparison with the altar-piece of 1488 from S. Giobbe has led several critics, including Fry and Berenson, to date the so-called "Madonna del Lago" in the Uffizi from around the same year or even somewhat later, but I agree sooner with Gronau that this painting must have been executed a few years earlier (fig. 163). It is in comparing the corresponding figures in these two works that we notice in the "Madonna del Lago" a more

---

(¹) *Ffoulkes*, L'Arte, XIV, 1911, p. 262.

(²) *Gronau*, Bellini, p. 213. There seems to exist another replica which figured in 1927 in the sale of the Stillmann collection, and there is question of one once upon a time in a private collection in Vienna: perhaps the latter should be identified with one of those mentioned here.

Fig. 162. Giovanni Bellini, Madonna. Art Institute, Chicago.
Museum Photo.

conservative treatment and smoother forms, whereas in the
retable of 1488 there is an impressionistic element. The angular
draping in one or two instances in the former painting reminds us
distinctly of earlier works as, for example, the Transfiguration.

The subject of this composition, which for many years

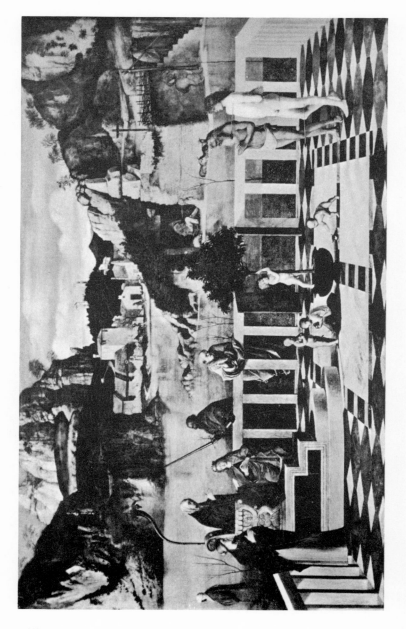

Fig. 163.　Giovanni Bellini, Madonna del Lago. Uffizi, Florence.

Photo Alinari.

Fig. 164. Giovanni Bellini, Allegory of Perseverance(?). Accademia,
Venice. Photo Anderson.

Fig. 165. Giovanni Bellini, Allegory of Prudence. Accademia, Venice.
Photo Anderson.

remained unidentified, was established by Ludwig (¹). It is a representation of the earthly Paradise according to de Deguilleville's "Pèlerinage de l'âme" which dates from the first half of the 14th century. On account of the noble forms, the wonderful design and not least the marvellously luminous and romantic landscape it is one of Bellini's most beautiful creations. The last mentioned feature, compared with the landscape of the two SS. Jerome and that of the St. Francis in the Frick collection, marks a further development in Giovanni's manner.

Slightly more evolved are the five small paintings of allegories in the gallery of Venice (595). They are in all probability the same little panels which Catena, in his will of 1515, mentions as forming the decoration of a piece of furniture. Once again we owe the explanation of the subjects to Ludwig. They are Perseverance (fig. 164), the inconstancy of Fortune, (Gronau 92), the three Virtues Temperance, Courage and Justice united in one (Gronau 93), Prudence (fig. 165) and Shame disclosed (fig. 166) (²). On the whole the master has paid less attention to the landscapes. The colours, it is true, are brilliant and the drawing, especially of the nude figures, particularly interesting; still all the same we are forced to admit, even taking into consideration that these paintings are of a purely decorative nature, that he has executed them in a sketchy, not to say hasty, manner. Consequently they are neither so fine nor so elaborate as the picture in the Uffizi.

The painting known as the "Madonna degli Alberetti" in the gallery of Venice (596) which is signed and dated: "*Joannes Bellinus P. 1487*", has certainly been considerably disfigured by restoration (fig. 167).

After the little Fugger portrait it is the first dated work we have by Giovanni Bellini, who at this time must have been approaching his fiftieth year (³). The problem now arises whether

_____

(¹) G. *Ludwig* op. cit., Jahrb. d. Preus. Kunstsamml., XXII; Burlington Magazine, XLVII, 1925, p. 136; Apollo, Nov. 1925, p. 280.

(²) G. *Ludwig*, Veneziansches Hausrat: Italien Forschungen, I, 1906, p. 187. R. *van Marle*, L'iconographie de l'art profane, II, The Hague, 1932, p. 83.

(³) *Molmenti e Ludwig*, Emporium, XX, 1904, p. 190. The date was doubted by *Morelli*, Gallery of Berlin, p. 79. Regarding the restoration v. *Ricci*, Rassegna d'Arte, 1902, p. 125.

Fig. 166. Giovanni Bellini, Allegory of Shame disclosed(?). Accademia,
Venice. Photo Anderson.

Fig. 167. Giovanni Bellini, Madonna. Accademia, Venice,
Photo Anderson.

the resemblance in type and feeling to certain other pictures,
with which it should at the present moment be grouped, has
always existed or whether it is due to the knowledge and skill of
the restorer.

Quite recently another very fine picture of the Madonna with
the signature "*Joannis Bellinus P.*", which without any doubt is

Fig. 168.   Giovanni Bellini Madonna. Private Collection, Switzerland.

from Giambellino's own hand, has come to light in a private collection (fig. 168). As far as the figures are concerned, the artist has
used the same cartoon, but the clouds and trees to the side of the
curtain which forms the centre of the background, are different.
The slightly more impressionistic handling of the light and shade
effects leads us to believe that this painting might be a few years
later than that of 1487; some doubt, however, has been expressed
as to whether the date on the panel in the Accademia is the

original one. This new discovery is very well preserved and shows the colours in all their original strength and brilliancy.

In both Madonna and Child there is a particular sweetness and softness of expression and form which we find in a strikingly similar manner in a half-length figure of the Madonna, facing the spectator and holding the nude Child, Who seems to listen to some celestial voice, between SS. Peter and Clare, in the Thompson collection, Chicago (fig. 169) (¹).

No doubt a few years prior to these pictures Giovanni Bellini painted the Madonna seen in half-length figure with the nude Child standing to her left, playing with a string to which a little branch is attached (fig. 170). This panel, which until lately formed part of the Barberini Gallery in Rome, was upon a time attributed to Rondinelli, but Herr Gronau has already claimed Giambellino to be its author. He mentions the school replicas and versions which repeat this composition and to which we shall return in the next chapter. Here I only want to state that one of these — the one belonging to Countess Brentani in Bergamo — is dated 1489, but the original by Bellini must have been painted some years before.

Of the year 1488 we have three highly important and authentic altar-pieces. They are that from S. Giobbe, now in the gallery of Venice (38), that in the Frari church and the retable in S. Pietro, Murano. They are the most universally known works of Giambellino and hardly require description.

The important group of six saints and the height of the throne in the S. Giobbe altar-piece (fig. 171) lead us to believe that the composition of Antonello da Messina's panel in S. Cassiano might have had some influence on Giambellino. Possibly also in Antonello's picture there were angels at the foot of the throne. The apse of a church forms at the same time background and frame, and this detail recalls the painting of the Virgin, saints and Duke of Urbino in adoration which Piero della Francesca executed, possibly together with Luca Signorelli and perhaps soon after 1472 (v. Vol. XI, fig. 60). There is, however, little else which connects these two works of art. It is sometimes supposed that this is the first picture which Giambellino painted in oils and certainly

---

(¹) *Valentiner*, Catalogue of the Exhibition of early Italian Paintings in the Duveen Galleries, 1924, privately printed, New York, 1926, No. 43.

Fig. 169. Giovanni Bellini, Madonna and Saints. J. P. Thompson Collection, Chicago. Courtesy Duveen Brothers.

Fig. 170. Giovanni Bellini, Madonna. From the Barberini Gallery, Rome.
Photo Anderson.

the effects, more especially of the blending of colours and fusion
of light and shade, are strangely different. It is signed: *Joannes
Bellinus*.

The retable in the Frari church is in the form of a triptych and
has a particularly ornate frame of later date (fig. 172 and plate).
Again the Virgin is seated on a high throne placed in a niche, and

Fig. 171. Giovanni Bellini, Madonna and Saints, 1488. Accademia, Venice.
Photo Anderson.

holds the Child in much the same manner as in the panel in the
Thompson collection; two angelic musicians are depicted at the
foot of the throne. In each of the lateral panels are two full length

figures of saints, of whom only St. Nicholas to the left and St. Ben-edict to the right can be recognized ([1]). The signature is inscribed in a medallion on the pedestal of the throne.

This panel, which is mentioned by Vasari and Ridolfi, has always been one of Bellini's most celebrated productions and is indeed exceedingly beautiful. It has been conjectured that it may have been begun in 1485 (Fry) and consequently is of slightly earlier date than the S. Giobbe altar-piece; this is not impossible. The general disposition reminds us somewhat of Mantegna's triptych in S. Zeno, Verona.

The large canvas at Murano is not so pleasing (fig. 173) ([2]); the composition is less graceful, the two lateral saints are rather heavy and the four groups of cherubim over-regular. Everything in the composition is either too broad or too distant; if the same elements had been grouped together in less space, the picture might have gained considerably. Also from a technical stand-point it is not on the same level and the Madonna, Child and two saints are less noble in appearance. On the other hand, the kneeling Doge Barbarigo and the two angelic musicians are very fine, although the latter are perhaps somewhat sketchy. The painting was executed for the palace of this doge who, in his will of 1501, bequeathed it to the church of Sta Maria degli Angeli in Murano, where it still was in Ridolfi's day though Moschini describes it in its actual site.

There can be no doubt that in these works Giambellino reveals himself inspired by new aesthetic ideals; he aims at great and harmonious beauty, I should almost say academic and classical, and this he combines with a smoother manner of painting, due quite possibly to the use of oil as medium, which finally obliter-ates all trace of the Mantegnesque linear effects which gave so much grit and character to the master's earlier productions. The temperamental spirit of former years has given way to nobler and more harmoniously beautiful forms, but the change does not leave us without a tinge of regret.

The half-length figures of the Madonna painted in this manner,

---

([1]) In the British Museum there is a drawing of the two saints to the right but it has been made after the picture and at a considerably later date.

([2]) *Ludwig u. Bode*, Jahrb. K. Preus. Kunstsamml., 1903.

Fig. 172. Giovanni Bellini, altar-piece, 1488. Frari church, Venice.
Photo Anderson.

Fig. 173. Giovanni Bellini, Madonna, Saints and Doge Barbarigo, 1488.
S. Pietro Martire, Murano.   Photo Anderson.

consequently between 1485 and 1490 or shortly after, are fairly numerous. They are almost all signed and I shall make only a brief mention of them.

One example, in which the Virgin is turned to the left and the nude Child stands on a low wall, belongs to the Marquis of Northampton, London (Gronau, 107) (¹). The signed Madonna in the gallery of Bergamo was formerly in the Morelli collection; it is supposed to be the same picture which Ridolfi (p. 71) mentions as existing at Alzano, near Bergamo (fig. 174) (²). Here the Virgin is shown against the background of a curtain, to either side of which we see a landscape; the nude Child, Who is seated on her knee, seems to listen to voices which are audible to Him alone. The nude Infant Jesus standing appears again in a panel in the gallery of Stuttgart (431) (Gronau, 109) but the face of the Madonna in this case is not very fine and I do not think that the work is entirely from Giambellino's own hand (³); once more the background is formed by a curtain and a piece of a landscape. Much more beautiful are: the Madonna with the nude Child standing and an important portrait of the donor which belongs to the Earl of Harewood, London (Gronau, 112); the composition against a landscape background and a cloudy sky, in which the Infant lies back in His Mother's arms, in the collection of the late Mr. Ralph H. Booth, Detroit (Gronau, 113) (⁴); the example in which the nude Child in the Virgin's arms harkens to voices, in the Metropolitan Museum, New York (B 41-1) (fig. 175) (⁵); and the Madonna, holding the Child rather high, in the National Gallery, London (280) (Gronau, 124), of which a copy exists in

---

(¹) *R. Fry*, Burlington Magazine, XLVII, 1925, p. 64, was right in attributing this picture, which passed as a work by Rondinelli, to Giovanni Bellini.

(²) *Gronau*, op. cit., p. 208. *Frizzoni*, Le Gallerie dell' Acc. Carrara, p. 64; there exist two copies by Giovanni Battista Moroni.

(³) It was ascribed to Rondinelli but *von Hadeln*, Zeitsch. f. Bild. Kunst, N.F., XXXIII, 1922, p. 112, claimed it for Bellini; it is partly repainted. In the catalogue it is described as a copy after a picture by Rondinelli in the Colonna Gallery, Rome.

(⁴) Bulletin Detroit Museum, 1922, p. 49. *A. Venturi*, Studi dal vero, p. 240. *L. Venturi*, Pitt. ital. in America, pl. 295.

(⁵) *R. Fry*, Bulletin Metrop. Mus., Oct. 1908. *Berenson*, Venetian Painting in America, p. 84. *L. Venturi*, Pitt. ital. in America, pl. 296.

Fig. 174.   Giovanni Bellini, Madonna. Carrara Academy, Bergamo.
Photo Anderson.

the museum of Worcester, U.S.A. (¹). The particularly broad and
dark shadows in this painting remind us of the altar-piece at
Murano. A composition in the museum of Berlin (11) (Gronau,
125) represents the Child, again nude and standing in front of the
Virgin who faces the spectator, but this painting is considerably
retouched (²).

(¹) *Berenson*, Venetian Painting in America, p. 112.
(²) *Borenius*, in his notes on *Crowe and Cavalcaselle*, attributes it to
Rondinelli. *Berenson*, Dedalo, IV, 1923, p. 116.

Fig. 175. Giovanni Bellini, Madonna. Metropolitan Museum, New York.
Museum Photo.

Among the pictures of the half-length figure of the Madonna with the Child which show us the group slightly turned to one side the finest is that in the gallery of Venice (612) (fig. 176), originating from the Scuola Grande della Carità. Here again the Child appears to be listening, but in this case His attention has obviously been attracted by the group of cherubim floating on small clouds above the beautiful landscape. In these pictures Jesus is frequently depicted as a handsome boy with curly hair but He is more charming in this work than in any of the others. In many of the examples of this group most of the background is

Fig. 176. Giovanni Bellini, Madonna and Chorus of Angels. Accademia,
Venice.   Photo Anderson.

occupied by a curtain, as for instance in that from the W. Salo-
mon collection, New York, now belonging to Duveen Brothers
(Gronau, 127) (¹). There exist several replicas of this picture.
One of them is now in the collection of Mr. Nicholaas F. Brady,
New York (Gronau, 128); it was formerly in the Montijo col-

_____

(¹) *Berenson*, op. cit., p. 89.

lection, Madrid, and then in the gallery of Oldenburg. This picture, which is shown against a landscape background, is not known to me but is not always considered to be by Giambellino himself ([1]). Besides a version by Pasqualino Veneziano, with which we shall deal later, there are still two others, one in the museum of Bonn, the other belonging to Count Contini Bonacossi, which, however, show some small changes ([2]).

It must have been at this period that the master executed the replica of the Madonna with the Child upright in the museum of Chicago, belonging to Mr. John N. Willys, formerly at Toledo (Ohio), now in New York, and showing Giovanni's signature (Gronau, 131) ([3]). Comparing it with the Chicago example we notice, as far as the composition is concerned, but slight variations in the landscape but in the technique there is a considerable difference. Here the execution is broader and more pictorial and the pronounced linearity, characteristic of the earlier phase, is less evident. Not only have the artistic principles of the painter changed but also the medium — no doubt oil — which he used for the Willys Madonna is different and has produced quite other effects.

We notice from now onward a tendency on the part of Giovanni Bellini to create pictures more imposing in size and composition. The figure of the Madonna alone becomes the exception rather than the rule, but there are several instances in which she is depicted accompanied by other figures.

The proportions and shape of a panel in the Louvre have not yet changed (fig. 177), but to the right and left of the Madonna, who holds the nude Child standing on a low wall, we see SS. Peter and Sebastian, while in the clouds above are three cherubim. The parapet on which Jesus stands is shown from a corner and it is the first time that we notice this attempt to increase the effect of depth. In style the picture shows a strong resemblance to that at Murano. The old attribution to Rondinelli no longer holds good

([1]) *W. von Bode u. D. von Hadeln*, Zeitschr. f. bild. Kunst, N. F., XXI, 1909, p. 139. *Borenius*, Burlington Magazine, XXIII, 1913, p. 25, is in favour of the attribution to Bellini. *Berenson*, Dedalo, 14, 1923, p. 107.

([2]) *Gronau*, op. cit., p. 212.

([3]) Known to me only from a photograph. *Berenson*, Venetian Painting in America, p. 92. *Fogolari*, Rassegna d'Arte, 1920, p. 120. *Gronau*, op. cit., p. 213.

Fig. 177. Giovanni Bellini, Madonna and Saints. Louvre, Paris.
Photo Alinari.

and the work seems of too high a quality to consider it, as Frizzoni
does, a school production (¹).

(¹) Rassegna d'Arte, I, 1901, p. 113. *Frizzoni*, L'Arte, 1906, p. 413.

Probably the two first pictures to which Giovanni Bellini felt the necessity of giving an oblong shape, on account of the two lateral saints, are the three-quarter length Madonna with the Child on her knee between SS. Catherine and Mary Magdalene in the gallery of Venice (fig. 178) and a similar composition with the same saints but of quite different appearance, in the Prado Gallery, Madrid (50). The latter picture, which belonged to Charles V, is somewhat less beautiful than the painting in Venice, in which we find Giambellino again at his best, and which shows a close connexion with the triptych of 1488 in the Frari church.

Also the compositions of the Pietà executed during these years comprise more figures and the artist definitely abandoned the small but more impressive groups in which only the Virgin and St. John accompany the dead Saviour. There is, however, still one example of this sober composition which on account of the types has to be placed near the dated works of 1488; it is the panel in the museum of Berlin (4) (fig. 179). Again, as in the above mentioned picture in the Louvre, we notice the artist's desire to create an impression of depth, but here it is evident in the re-clining body of the Saviour which is depicted slightly sideways. Hence, this work produces a very different effect from that of the early Pietàs, such as those in the Brera Gallery and in Dresden.

Once more the number of replicas, though not without vari-ations, reveal to us that this picture, which however is not par-ticularly admirable, had a great success. A good early copy is preserved in the gallery of Venice (71); a mediocre one is found in the museum of Padua (423), while another on canvas was for sale in Paris a few years ago. In the museum of Bamberg (358—678) there exists a late and free copy painted in the manner of the Byzantine icons.

Of the Pietàs with many figures, the finest is that executed in grisaille in the Uffizi (943); it was presented by Alvise Moncenigo in 1798 to the Grand Duke of Tuscany (fig. 180). Gronau is of opinion that its actual condition is one of mere preparation but the execution is so elaborate that I hardly think that the artist could ever have had the intention of covering the minute drawing and shading with colour (¹). There are seven figures around the Saviour

(¹) Morelli thought it the latest of these Pietàs. I agree with Gronau that Berenson's "around 1485" seems somewhat early. From a stylistic

Fig. 178. Giovanni Bellini, Madonna and Saints. Accademia, Venice.
Photo Anderson.

Who leans back supported by the Virgin and St. John. It is a masterpiece of draughtsmanship; the composition too is beautiful and dramatic but in opposition with the latter quality we are struck by a certain lack of tragic action and even of expression.

The Pietà in the cathedral of Toledo is of a different composition. Here five figures accompany the Saviour Who, supported by the Virgin, is seated on the far border of His sarcophagus which occupies the foreground and on which we read the artist's signature as well as a later inscription of the master's name in Gothic letters ([1]). Some trees are depicted in the background. Although this picture is generally accepted as an authentic work by Giambellino I think we should all the same limit ourselves to calling it a studio production. The best part is the figure of the Saviour and if we had to decide from it alone we should not hesitate in our judgment, but the other figures are lacking in refinement of execution and in beauty of form. The character of the work points to some years earlier than the marvellous grisaille in the Uffizi.

point of view it should be classified with the Frari altar-piece of 1488.

([1]) From the form of the letters one would say that the inscription had been made in Spain and this would lead us to suppose that the panel, concerning the history of which nothing is known, reached Spain soon after its execution.

Fig. 179. Giovanni Bellini, Pietà. Museum, Berlin.

In the gallery of Padua (26) there exists a replica of the Pietà in Toledo, unless both these works are copies of an original now lost; slight variations are noticeable in the background and in the garments of the man to the extreme left. Crowe and Cavalcaselle mention another version in the Gatschina Castle which is unknown to me; the landscape and the lid of the coffin are both absent.

A signed Pietà in the gallery of Stuttgart has the character of an authentic work of around the year 1488 (¹). Again there are only five figures around the Redeemer, Who lies back in His Mother's arms. The human types, which are of a regular beauty, are very fine. Mansueti has made a copy of this picture with many variations; it is preserved in the gallery of Warsaw.

There is still quite a number of pictures which seem to have been executed in this period when Giovanni Bellini's chief aim was the production of a regular harmonious beauty, conceived

(¹) *C. Loeser*, L'Arte, II, 1899, p. 159.

Fig. 180. Giovanni Bellini, dead Christ in the midst of the Virgin and
Apostles, grisaille. Uffizi, Florence. Photo Anderson.

however, in a still very personal manner, and it was at this moment that he created works which enchant us with all that is best of Quattrocento aesthetics.

Of the paintings of religious subject I shall mention in the first place the St. Justine in the Bagatti Valsecchi collection, Milan.

Mr. Berenson's change of mind about this panel which prompted him to consider Alvise Vivarini, to whom he attributed it, one of the great Venetian masters, is in itself an interesting item in the history of connoisseurship in connexion with the school of Venice. He now claims Giovanni Bellini to be the rightful master ([1]). Even now, however, the picture remains something of a problem. The date of around 1475 proposed by Mr. Berenson is, I think, about ten years too early. Herr Gronau on the contrary finds this date somewhat too late, even though, as he himself remarks, the effect of the clouds in the background is a characteristic rather of the master's later works. The type of face and its harmonious beauty also point to a period not far distant from the altar-piece of 1488. Opposed to this is the incisive and somewhat angular design of the drapery which shows an obvious connexion with the earlier manner, though the hands again are of a shape which appears in the later stage of the artist's career. This intermingling of incoherent elements leaves us rather perplexed. Still, it seems far more likely that an artist at a later moment should show reminiscences of an earlier manner than that at an early phase he should reveal in a prophetic fashion how he is going to paint in the future. I think we must conclude that if the beautiful St. Justine is realy by Giovanni Bellini, he executed it in all probability a year or two prior to 1488.

Painted in the same style and almost equal in beauty to the lateral figures of the Frari triptych is the St. Peter the Martyr against a cloudy background, which was transferred from the church of S. Domenico, Monopoli, to the gallery of Bari ([2]). On

---

([1]) *Berenson*, op. cit., Gazette des Beaux Arts, June 1913. *The Same*, Study and Criticism, III, p. 38. *The Same*, Dedalo, I, 1923—24, p. 15. *Balniel and Clark*, op. cit., No. 164.

([2]) *Frizzoni*, Bollettino d'Arte, VIII, 1914, p. 17. As Herr Gronau observes, the date proposed by Prof. A. Venturi of after the Brera Pietà and before the Pesaro altar-piece is of course far too early. *Salmi*, Rassegna d'Arte, 1920, p. 211.

the back of this panel there is a preparatory sketch of a naked youth near a horse, which seems to be of earlier date.

It was very likely about this time, if not somewhat later, that the master painted a beautiful panel of St. Sebastian, his body pierced with arrows, standing alone in an extensive landscape partly formed by rocks, which in execution recalls to a certain extent that of the St. Jerome in the Contini collection. The human type of the saint, more especially the breadth of his face, however, seems to point to a later date, probably around 1490. The picture is found in the collection of Baron Thyssen-Bornemisza, once at Rohoncz Castle in Hungary, now in Lugano (Gronau, 90) [1].

There are also a few portraits which I think should be classified in this period, the principal productions of which are the dated altar-pieces. The finest of these portraits is no doubt that of a man with a severe autocratic expression and wearing a marvellous cut velvet coat and a bonnet on his head, which belongs to Messrs. Duveen Brothers, New York (fig. 181). It has been wrongly supposed to represent the Condottiere Colleoni, with whom the subject of this painting bears not the slightest resemblance. It has also been identified, I know not for what reason, with the portrait of General Jacomo Marcello which Michiel saw in the Palazzo Marcello in Venice. Previously it was attributed to Gentile Bellini or to Alvise Vivarini but von Hadeln has recently restored it to its true author [2]. In fact, it is a free replica of a portrait of the same person by Gentile which I mentioned when dealing with that artist, but the subject has been considerably flattered. I do not see, however, why it should be dated as "certainly not before 1500". Nor do I find that striking influence of Antonello which persuades Gronau to place it as early as 1480. I think it is very likely a late production of the phase with which we are dealing and which ended soon after 1490.

A fine instance of portraiture of this particular manner is shown in a small panel which entered the museum of Berlin with

---

[1] *R. van Marle*, Dedalo, XI, 1931, p. 1380.

[2] Catal. of the Exhib. of early Venetian Painting, Burlington Club, 1912, pl. 48 (Gentile Bellini (?)). *Fry*, Burlington Magazine, XXI, p. 48 (Gentile). *Berenson*, Study and Criticism, III, p. 58 (Alvise Vivarini). *D. von Hadeln*, op. cit., Burlington Magazine, 1927. *L. Venturi*, Pitt. ital. in America, pl. 288.

Fig. 181. Giovanni Bellini, portrait. Duveen Brothers, New York.

the James Simon collection (fig. 182) (¹). The force of expression

(¹) Previously it was ascribed to the North Italian school of about 1500.
Gronau, Jahrb. K. Preus. Kunstsamml., XLIII, 1922, p. 120, attributes
it to Giovanni Bellini.

Fig. 182. Giovanni Bellini, portrait of a man. Museum, Berlin.

and vigour of technique lead us to associate this work with the foregoing portrait. The same qualities are found in another portrait, once in the de Béarn collection and now belonging to Messrs. Duveen Brothers, New York, in which the sitter is more simply attired in a plain jacket and small bonnet (fig. 183) [1].

An almost equally powerful expression is met with in the small portraits in the Timken and Friedsam collections, New York (Gronau, 134).

[1] *Berenson,* op. cit., formerly assigned it to Alvise Vivarini.

Fig. 183. Giovanni Bellini, portrait. Duveen Brothers, New York.

It was possibly about this time that Giambellino executed one or two other portraits, including the small panel of a rather ugly, coarse-looking man with a bonnet, against a background half of which is a curtain while the other half is a landscape with a cloudy sky, in the National Gallery, London (Gronau, 121) (¹); the

(¹) Previously attributed to Antonello and to Alvise Vivarini. *Collins Baker*, Burlington Magazine, 4, 1927, p. 25, gives it to an unknown

THE DOGE LEONARDO LOREDANO
By Giovanni Bellini, in the National Gallery, London.

portrait of a youth with a bonnet on his fair curls in the museum
of Padua (43) (Gronau, 133); and a picture of a middle-aged man
in three-quarter right profile with a bonnet on his long hair and
a coat trimmed with fur, which was for sale in Paris in 1932.

Then there is a group of portraits which are considerably softer
and smoother in execution and manifest on the part of the artist
a certain desire to create a charming effect. In fact, there are some
in which the aesthetic tendency reveals an obvious similarity
to that of the group of Madonnas of a regular and noble beauty
with which we have already dealt. I think this is particularly
evident if we compare the portrait of a handsome young man
with big eyes in the Mellon collection, Washington (fig. 184) (¹)
with the Madonna adoring the Child in the National Gallery
(2901).

With these portraits we enter the period which separates the
dated works of 1488 from those of the subsequent phase, the
earliest of which date from 1505. Again we have but very few
dates to guide us in the chronological classification of the productions of these seventeen years. We know, however, that the
Baptism at Vicenza was executed between 1500 and 1502, while
we are sure that the portrait of Doge Leonardo Loredano in the
National Gallery (Plate), was painted after 1502, when the rule of
this doge began. As Herr Gronau observes, in all probability it
was made soon after he was elected to this office because there is
another portrait of him of 1507 in which he seems to be considerably older, in fact one would say that he had aged ex-
cessively in this short interval.

Quite a large number of portraits should be associated, on
account of their style, with this marvellous piece of painting in
which, when compared with the previous group, we notice some
slightly impressionistic effects and a less restrained handling,
features which lead the way to Venetian art of the Cinquecento.
The painter's remarkable gift of understanding and rendering his
sitter's psychology reveals to us the penetrating intelligence of

---

follower of Giovanni Bellini. There is a repainted replica in the Correr
Museum.

(¹) *M. Mayer*, Pantheon, V, 1930, p. 25. *L. Venturi*, Pitt. ital. in
America, p. 297.

Fig. 184. Giovanni Bellini, portrait. Mellon Collection, Washington.

Doge Loredano, giving us at the same time an impression of
mysterious reticence.

Unfortunately space limits me to dealing but briefly with those
fine portraits which, stylistically speaking, are closely related with
this masterpiece. This must have been the moment when Giambellino was most active as a portrait painter, at which art he excelled. Vasari tells us that it was chiefly after his brother Gentile's
death in 1507 that he devoted himself to this branch of painting.

On the whole, however, I am inclined to believe that most of the following works were executed in the late nineties or at the latest very soon after 1500.

Although in every respect the latter is less important, there exist strong technical points of contact between the picture of Doge Loredano and a small portrait of a youth dressed in black against a background of a cloudy sky, which was bequeathed to the Louvre (1158) by Count de Vandeuil (fig. 185) ([1]).

I am not entirely convinced of the attribution to Giambellino of a small bust-length portrait of a handsome young man in the Lochis collection in the gallery of Bergamo (Gronau, 135). In the Uffizi there is a signed picture of a youth with broad features against a cloudy sky, but it is not in a perfect state of preservation and no doubt the restorer accounts for much of its actual impressionistic appearance. It must have closely resembled the so-called self-portrait in the Capitol Gallery, Rome (fig. 186) ([2]) as well as the very similar picture formerly in the Carnarvon collection, London (Gronau, 139) ([3]).

Less important and slightly lacking in individuality are a little portrait of a man with a peculiarly shaped hat, in the Royal Institution of Liverpool (Gronau, 136) which, besides, has considerably suffered, and a bust-length painting of a young man, with a sweet but rather expressionless face, against a cloudy skyscape, in the Hage collection, Nivaagaard (Copenhagen) (Gronau, 140) ([4]).

To this group might also belong the bust of a youth against a landscape background in the gallery of Hampton Court (Gronau, 163), but its present condition hardly allows us to come to a very definite conclusion ([5]).

A fine specimen of this phase, and executed in the same manner as the Loredano portrait, is I think the picture of a mathematician

---

([1]) L'Arte, V, 1902, p. 255. *Nicolle*, Revue de l'art ancien et moderne, XVIII, 1905, p. 193.

([2]) *A. Venturi*, Arch. stor. dell' arte, II, 1889, p. 447: school of Giovanni Bellini.

([3]) It figured at the Carnarvon sale held in London in May 1925. Perhaps it was formerly in in the Arundel collection v. *Gronau*, op. cit., p. 213.

([4]) *Frizzoni*, L'Arte, XIII, 1910, p. 402.

([5]) *L. Cust*, Apollo, 1928, p. 247; it is attributed also to Bissolo. *Gronau*, op. cit., p. 216, mentions a poor copy once upon a time on the art market.

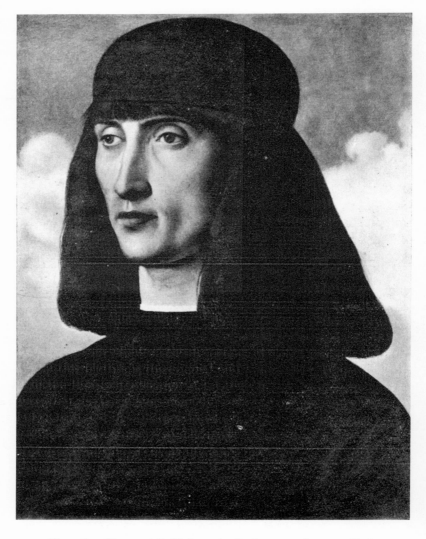

Fig. 185. Giovanni Bellini, portrait of a man. Louvre, Paris.

Photo Alinari.

in the National Gallery (1213) which, however, does not generally
figure among the works of Giovanni Bellini, being more often
attributed to Gentile (¹). It might date from the period when the

(¹) Catalogued as a work by Gentile. Berenson describes it as a late
work of Gentile with a point of interrogation.

Fig. 186. Giovanni Bellini, self-portrait. Capitol Gallery, Rome.
Photo Anderson.

two brothers collaborated, but the refinement and beauty of the
head of the old man show the aesthetic principles of Giovanni
much more than those of Gentile who, besides, never attained this
stage of evolution. The figure is depicted gesticulating with one
hand and holding a compass in the other.

Giambellino seems to have painted but few works of a religious nature at this period but one of them is of great importance; it is the Baptism of Christ in the Corona church of Vicenza (figs. 187, 188) (¹), in which, as has already been observed, Giovanni was obviously inspired by Cima da Conegliano's picture of 1494 in the church of S. Giovanni in Bragora, Venice. It was executed between November 1500 and December 1502. When dealing with Cima, however, we shall see the improvements and important changes which Giambellino made in following the older example of which he really retains only the principal lines of the composition.

This work is a significant document for our knowledge of the changes which again were about to take place in Giovanni's art. In the figures and in the strongly designed and somewhat angular drapery, as well as in the rocks on which the angels and St. John stand, there is still a fairly pronounced Quattrocentesque element; on the other hand in the rest of the landscape, with the softly outlined hills, full of distance and space, we have a creation which, artistically as well as psychologically, belongs to a future phase of evolution. On the other hand, the human forms and faces, which are of a regular and exceeding beauty, are somewhat more reactionary, except for that of God the Father Who, surrounded by angels, appears in the sky and Who, like the landscape, might be called early Titianesque in appearance. These facts might lead us to suppose that Giovanni was assisted in the execution of this important work by a considerably younger and very gifted artist who already belonged to the coming generation; however, this hypothesis becomes less likely when we compare the figure of God the Father here with one in the gallery of Pesaro, which, in fact, is but a free copy (²). The Cinquecento-like softness and impressionistic effects are present also in this painting and I think it was rather out of a mystic inspiration that Giovanni Bellini executed this celestial vision in a hazy and less minute technique, thus placing it, as it were, on a different level from the rest.

Very similar to the head of Christ in the Baptism of Vicenza is

(¹) *D. Bortolan*, S. Corona in Vicenza, Vicenza, 1889, p. 263.

(²) It is very obvious that this panel is in no way connected with the altar-piece of the Coronation of the Virgin in the same gallery.

Fig. 187. Giovanni Bellini, Baptism. Sta. Corona, Vicenza.

Photo Anderson.

Fig. 188. Detail of fig. 187.   Photo Alinari.

that in the S. Fernando Academy, Madrid, which unfortunately has been slightly damaged by fire (Gronau, 101) (¹).

We can perhaps associate another date with an extant picture. In a letter of the 3rd August 1501, Lorenzo da Pavia

(¹) In ancient writings there is mention of several similar heads of Our Lord v. *Gronau*, op. cit., p. 208.

informs Isabella d'Este that Bellini has "at that moment finished a half-length figure of St. Dominic which is very beautiful (assai bella), on a little panel" (¹). In connexion with this piece of information, Gronau quite rightly refers us to the existence of a similar half-length figure of this saint signed: *Joannes Bellinus*, which some time ago was for sale in London (²). The saint, looking down at the open book which he holds in one hand, is a serene and beautiful figure. Also the mountains in the background greatly resemble those in the Baptism at Vicenza.

It was no doubt at this time that Giovanni painted the Transfiguration, mentioned by Zanetti as existing on the high altar of S. Salvatore, Venice, a fragment of which, as Cantalamessa has pointed out, is preserved in the gallery of Venice(87) (³). It represents the Saviour in bust length, His head bent slightly back, His eyes turned heavenward (fig. 189); it is pasted on to another panel, doubtless of the same provenance, which shows a bushy plant, a piece of drapery and the signature: *Joannes Bellinus me pinxit*.

Around the year 1500 or slightly later should, I think, be placed the very pleasing Madonna adoring the Child, Who lies sleeping in her lap, against an enchanting landscape with peasants and cattle in the fields near a fortified castle and a slightly cloudy sky above. This picture, which is found in the National Gallery, London (599) (fig. 190) is rather difficult to classify; it is not always considered to be by Giambellino's own hand and once upon a time was supposed to be by Basaiti (⁴).

A considerable similarity in style exists between the Baptism at Vicenza and a panel of the very aged St. Jerome seated among rocks near a well, in the Clarence Mackay collection, New York

---

(¹) *Luzio*, op. cit., Arch. Stor. dell' Arte, I, 1888, p. 278.

(²) *A. Venturi*, Il Messaggero, 24th Dec. 1925. *The Same,* op. cit., L'Arte, 1926, p. 71. *The Same*, Studi dal Vero, p. 238. *Gronau*, op. cit., pl. 143 and p. 213. *The Same*, Spätwerke, p. 23; Cicerone, 1929, p. 329. *Burlington Magazine*, Dec. 1929, Art market, p. 4.

(³) *G. Cantalamessa*, Le Galerie Nazionali, V, 1902, p. 59. V. also *Gronau*, op. cit., p. 211. In Serra's catalogue it is question-marked and supposed to be "perhaps a school work".

(⁴) *Gronau*, op. cit., p. 214. *The Same*, Spätwerke, p. 12. It is now accepted as a work of Giovanni Bellini by Berenson who previously called it a school production.

Fig. 189. Giovanni Bellini, fragment of a Transfiguration. Accademia, Venice.   Photo Anderson.

Fig. 190. Giovanni Bellini, Madonna. National Gallery, London.

Photo National Gallery.

(Gronau, 159) (¹). A landscape with houses and ruins are visible beyond the grotto, on the threshold of which two rabbits are seen at play while a squirrel on a ledge of rock above seems to look on. In this work, which is signed and dated 1505, we meet with the same soft forms and suave light, although technically it is rather different. It still reveals something of the charm of the Quattro-cento, and in spite of the fact that it is of the same year as the S. Zaccaria altar-piece it is executed in a more conservative manner.

Another late production of this phase and executed about 1505, that is to say very near the beginning of the last period of Giam-

(¹) Formerly in the Benson coll., London. Burlington Club Exhibition of early Venetian Painting, 1912, No. 23. Catalogue of the Italian Pictures collected by R. and E. Benson, London, privately printed, 1914, No. 73. *Balniel and Clark*, op. cit., No. 171. *B. Berenson*, Venetian Painting in America, p. 238, expressed the opinion that we owe this work to the combined efforts of Giambellino and Basaiti and imagined that an X was missing from the date. International Studio, Dec. 1924, p. 34. He now attributes it to Giambellino.

Fig. 191. Giovanni Bellini, Madonna and Saints. Accademia, Venice.
Photo Alinari.

bellino's activity, is the signed oblong picture of the Virgin in
half-length figure holding the Child standing in front of her
between SS. Paul and George, in the gallery of Venice (610) (fig.
191). On account of a certain similarity in type between the
Virgin here and that of the Alberetti of 1487, this work has been
classified around the same year. In my opinion this is far too
early a date, because the full round form of the faces and the
broad proportions, as well as the general spirit of the work, point
to a much later manner. In the Palffy collection, Budapest, there
existed a free copy in which, however, St. George is replaced by
St. Catherine (¹).

I see a particular resemblance in the faces, especially that of
St. George, in the picture in Venice to a very fine portrait of a
patrician wearing a rich red cloak and a bonnet, which was sold
from the gallery of Stuttgart and now belongs to Mr. Ernst
Rosenfeld, New York (fig. 192); a great variety of attributions

---

(¹) *Von Terey*, Kunstchronik, IX, 1915, col. 55.

Fig. 192. Giovanni Bellini, portrait of a man. Rosenfeld Collection, New York.

have been given to this painting ([1]). It is again one of those

---

([1]) *D. von Hadeln*, op. cit., Burlington Magazine, 1927, was the first to restore it to Giambellino.

examples in which we notice the softer technique, so characteristic of Bellini's later manner and so different from the stronger and more linear oppositions of a slightly earlier period. These same characteristics also appear in an important portrait of a man, once in the Glogowski collection in Berlin and now privatedly owned in Holland. (¹)

The same remarks apply to a Madonna, seated against a background formed in part by a curtain and in part by a landscape, holding on her knee the nude, curly-headed Jesus Who fondles her face and grasps a little bird. Almost a hundred years ago this work was attributed to Giovanni Bellini in the catalogue of the Leuchtenberg collection to which it then belonged (²). It was shown to me in 1930 in New York and I understand that it is now in a private collection in that city.

Another painting in private hands shows the same stylistic peculiarities. It is an oblong picture of Christ in benediction between SS. Nicholas, Peter and two female saints without any attributes. It is a beautiful specimen of this manner and one in which the head of the Saviour strongly reminds us of that in the Baptism at Vicenza.

Giovanni Bellini's altar-piece of 1505 in the church of S. Zaccaria, Venice, comprises all the elements which from now onward we expect to find in his art (figs. 193, 194).

The composition is placed in the richly decorated apse of a church and, though we see the beginning of the lateral walls, the apse seems to be detached, at least to the sides we see some trees and a piece of sky. The Madonna is seated on a high throne holding the nude Child standing in benediction on her knee; an angel playing the viola sits on the steps of the throne. To the sides are the full-length figures of SS. Peter, Catherine, Lucy and Jerome, who is depicted reading. When it was taken to Paris in 1815 this beautiful picture was transferred on to linen. Vasari and Ridolfi

---

(¹) Reprod. in Catalogue of the Exhib. of Ancient Italian Art in Dutch possession, Amsterdam 1934, No. 34.

(²) *I. D. Passavant*, Die Gemäldesammlung seiner Kaiserl. Hoheit des Herzogs von Leuchtenberg, gestochen von J. N. Murel, 2nd ed., Frankfort, 1851, No. 5.

Fig. 193. Giovanni Bellini, Madonna and Saints. S. Zaccaria, Venice.
Photo Anderson.

both mention it and the latter tells us that it was considered to be one of the finest and most delicate works of the master.

It is, however, the production of an old and tired, though still always exceedingly gifted artist. It contains much beauty and aesthetic sense but little inspiration. Moreover, the figures are disconnected; SS. Peter and Jerome turn their backs on the others, with whom they are in no way concerned, and although the two female saints face the Virgin, they seem somehow independent of her. The figures are so broad that they tend almost to heaviness, while the forms are hardly visible through the over-abundant

Fig. 194. Detail of fig. 193.   Photo Anderson.

drapery which falls in multiple folds. The faces are of a perfect
though unemotional beauty, the features being painted with
marvellous effects of light. We are filled with admiration for this
really wonderful master-piece, which, however, does not fascinate.
It is an achievement which, technically speaking, not only leads
the way to Giorgione but in this respect is not inferior to the works

of this genius who at this moment had reached the climax of his career. However, we do not find in it any of Giorgione's lyrico-pictorial enchantments. Nor, on the other hand, can we say that it is a picture which leaves us cold and without emotional reaction. In fact, in the venerable old St. Jerome it might be suggested that Giambellino portrays an image of himself; he is peaceful, very old, good and spiritual, as indeed must have been the great Venetian master who, at the time of execution, was close on seventy-five. The niche-shaped background and the arrangement of the figures were obviously intended to give depth to the composition.

We are not surprised that this altar-piece aroused general admiration, which is manifest in the divers copies made of the Madonna, as for instance those by Bissolo and Domenico Mancini [1].

I do not think that any length of time separated the S. Zaccaria altar-piece from that which once existed in SS. Giovanni e Paolo, but which was destroyed by fire in 1867. It is known to us, however, from a print reproduced by Zanotto in his Pinacoteca Veneta (I, pl. 42) (fig. 195) and from the high praise expressed by both Vasari and Ridolfi. It must have been the most imposing creation of this particular type that Giovanni ever produced. The high throne is placed under a vault and to either side of it five saints are depicted; the St. Mary Magdalene bears a certain resemblance to the St. Lucy of the S. Zaccaria retable. Three little angels sing in chorus at the foot of the throne. Cavalcaselle places this work shortly after 1472 and Gronau thinks it "hardly before 1488, leading up to the great altar-pieces" but both these dates are in my opinion much too early. Although the engraver produces a somewhat more conventional drapery, the proportions are so broad and the composition and general effects so monumental that I am inclined to classify it after, rather than before, the S. Zaccaria picture, the only work with which we can compare it. Circumstantial evidence in favour of a late date might perhaps be found in the fact that the curious and by no means usual detail of the lamp hanging from the ceiling is repeated by Basaiti in a picture of 1510 — the Prayer in the Garden of Olives — and it hardly seems likely that he would have taken this detail from a work which, if the early date is to hold good, had been executed thirty years before.

[1] *Gronau*, op. cit., p. 125.

It has been conjectured by von Hadeln that an engraving by Mocetto, a copy of which exists in the Print Room of Dresden, was made after a lost altar-piece of Giovanni Bellini (¹). On a high monumental throne under a vault the Virgin is seated with the Child in benediction on her knee, between SS. John the Evangelist(?) and John the Baptist, with three female saints in the background and three angels at the foot of the throne. The figure of the Baptist certainly corresponds very much to that on one of the Carità altar-pieces, now in the Accademia, and also to that in the picture of the Madonna between four saints and an adorer from the Schlichting collection, now in the Louvre. If von Hadeln's theory is correct, Mocetto's print seems to reproduce a lateish composition of Giovanni Bellini, but I think it possible that in his engraving he may have just collected motifs from different Venetian pictures.

In the Vernon Watney collection at Cornbury there is a signed picture, dated 1505, of the Madonna enthroned with the nude Child on her knee between SS. Peter and Paul; the latter presents a kneeling adorer depicted in profile, a figure which is a very fine example of portraiture (Gronau, 161); a cloudy sky and some hills form the background. Again the artist has paid particular attention to the science of the third dimension; the plasticity of the figures is rendered with an over-elaborate drapery of a Bernini-like Baroque taste. Ridolfi mentions this painting when it still belonged to the Muselli family in Verona; at that time it had two lateral panels on which SS. Francis and Vincent Ferrer were depicted, but these are now lost (²).

It is worthy of our attention that here for the first time we meet with quite a new and different morphological type; it is the small and very rounded oval of the Virgin's head and, as we shall see presently, this was soon to become a usual type in the works of the master (³).

The date 1507 and the signature are inscribed on a large picture

(¹) *Von Hadeln*, Jahrb. d. K. Preus. Kunstsamml., XLV, p. 206.

(²) *G. Gronau*, Repert. f. Kunstwiss., XVIII, 1895, p. 231. Later it belonged to the Counts Sereghi in Verona and to the Ashburnham collection. There is a mediocre copy of this painting in the gallery of Stuttgart (432).

(³) Several of Giambellino's later paintings were ascribed formerly to Pseudo-Basaiti by *Gronau*, Rassegna d'Arte, IX, 1911, p. 95, and to Rocco Marconi by *T. Gerevich*, A Krakói Czartoryski Képtár Olasz Mesterei, Budapest, 1918, p. 160.

Fig. 195. Giovanni Bellini, lost altar-piece from SS. Giovanni
e Paolo, Venice, after a print.

of Doge Loredano presiding at a table, with two patricians seated
to either side (Gronau, 162). This work is mentioned by Ridolfi
(p. 72) as existing in the Loredano palace; he informs us that the
four young men are the two sons of the doge and other "fami-
liari". After changing hands many times (¹), this painting belonged
recently to Mr. J. Spiridon, Paris, and figured at the sale of this
collection (²). At this time the picture was so much repainted that
it was difficult to form a precise judgment. I hear that it has since
been cleaned and that this process has considerably improved its
appearance, but I have not seen it in its actual condition. There is
such a strong resemblance between the figure to the extreme
right in this picture and the subject of a drawing in the Uffizi, in
which he is shown in right profile, that we can very well admit
that they represent the same person.

Of the same year is the signed and dated panel of oblong shape
in the church of S. Francesco della Vigna in Venice (Gronau,
166) (³). It shows the slightly more than half-length figure of the
Virgin with the nude Child, Who bestows a blessing, standing on
her knee between SS. John the Baptist, Francis, Jerome and
Sebastian, against an elaborate landscape with houses. The entire
picture is thoroughly Cinquecentesque in appearance but this in
part may be due to restoration. The figure of the adoring knight
who is presented by St. John the Baptist is, in its actual condition,
of a much later period; in fact it bears considerable resemblance
to Duke Ercole of Ferrara. The Madonna and Child correspond in
position to those of the picture of 1488 at Murano but in type
and appearance they are more like those of the S. Zaccaria altar-

---

(¹) *Gronau*, op. cit., p. 215. *The Same*, Spätwerke, p. 24. *Düssler*,
Pantheon, III, April 1929, p. 161. *R. van Marle*, Cicerone, 1929, p. 187.
Tietze-Conrat, Belvedere, 1929, p. 106. *Berenson*, Venetian Painting in
America, p. 141, calls it a studio production.

(²) No. 4 of the catalogue of the sale which took place in Berlin in May
1929. *R. van Marle*, Cicerone, XXI, 1929, p. 11.

(³) In the will of Jacomo Dolfin of 1506 this work is mentioned as not
yet finished. *Von Hadeln*, Archiv. Beitr. aus der Nachlass Ludwigs, Ital.
Forsch. herausg. vom Kunsthist. Inst. Florenz, IV, 1911, p. 89. *The Same*,
ed. Ridolfi, I, p. 70 note 7. *Fiocco*, L'Arte, 1916, p. 187, is of opinion that
Giambellino was assisted in the execution of this painting. On account of a
misinterpretation of a passage in *Vasari*, ed. Milanesi, III, p. 163, this picture has been attributed to Mocetto by *B. Baron*, Madonna Verona, III,
1909, p. 92.

Fig. 196. Giovanni Bellini, Madonna, 1510. Brera Gallery, Milan.
Photo Anderson.

piece. Again we observe the strangely broken folds in the drapery.

Very similar to the Madonna of this picture is that signed and dated 1509, once upon a time in the Bourbon collection at Castle Frohsdorf (Vienna) and before that in Casa Mocenigo di San Priuli, but now in the gallery of Detroit, U.S.A.; the repaint which disfigured it has recently been removed (Gronau, 167) (¹). The background is occupied in part by a curtain and in part by a hilly landscape. Resembling this work but executed in a more evolved technique is the three-quarter length figure of the Madonna with the nude Child upright on her knee in the Brera Gallery, Milan (fig. 196); a beautiful landscape, the centre of which is concealed by a curtain, forms the background. This picture is signed *Joannes Bellinus* and dated 1510 and we are rather surprised that only one year separates this work from the foregoing example (²).

(¹) *Gronau*, Spätwerke, pp. 14, 24. *The Same*, Pinacotheca, 1928, p. 67. *Heyl*, op. cit., Pantheon, 1929, p. 140. *Valentiner*, Das unbekannte Meisterwerk, No. 17. *L. Venturi*, Pitt. ital. in America, pl. 300.

(²) *Gronau*, Bellini, p. 216, mentions a replica with SS. Peter and Paul to the sides of the Madonna belonging to Count Prinetti, Rome; it is unknown to me.

That this particular type of Madonna was repeated by Giambellino until the end of his career is proved to us by a picture in the gallery of Padua, which is signed and dated 1516 (Gronau, 179). It is the last dated work we have by the master. Cavalcaselle, on account of its deplorable state of preservation, thought it was false, but lately Gronau with good reason has reinstated it as a work by Giovanni Bellini (¹). The Madonna, who is turned to the left, holds the nude Infant seated on her knee; St. John the Baptist stands before them. The landscape, which forms most of the background, must have been very fine.

From between the years 1510 and 1516 date several pictures of the Madonna, which in technique as well as in style are very similar. Whereas in earlier groups the Virgin is depicted almost invariably in half-length figure, she is now represented seated and visible to below the knee. We saw this type already in the panel in the ex-Leuchtenberg collection. It finds its origin probably in the fact that in Giambellino's paintings of this period the Virgin frequently forms the centre of larger compositions in which also other figures are shown.

To this group belongs a signed painting of the Madonna facing the spectator against a background, more than half of which is formed by a curtain and the rest by a wintery landscape, which is owned by Duveen Brothers, New York (fig. 197) (²); the Virgin here bears a particular resemblance to that at Detroit. Slightly rounder forms are found in a Madonna with the nude Child on her knee in the Borghese Gallery, Rome (fig. 198) (³); the background is very similar but the landscape is more spring-like in appearance.

(¹) *Gronau*, op. cit., p. 217; he cites some signed and dated replicas: one in the Querini Stampalia Gallery, one formerly in Crespano which is mentioned also by Crowe and Cavalcaselle and a third at one time for sale in Paris and later sold by auction in Lucerne.

(²) *Gronau*, op. cit., p. 215. Copies exist in the Czernin coll., Vienna, at Ajalà and Crespano. Others by Rocco Marconi are found at Strasbourg and Breslau, while he probably also painted the one in the Giovanelli coll., Venice, which is attributed to Vincenzo da Treviso and to Catena and a painting in the Redentore church, Venice, which is attributed to Bissolo.

(³) *G. Cantalamessa*, Pittura veneta in Sta. Maria in Trastevere, Bollettino d'Arte del Minist. della Pubbl. Istr., 1914, p. 16, ascribes it to the school of Giovanni Bellini. *Bernardini*, Rassegna d'Arte, X, 1910, p. 142, to Catena. L'Arte, XIV, 1911, p. 480. *Gronau*. op. cit., p. 215, to Giambellino.

Fig. 197. Giovanni Bellini, Madonna. Duveen Brothers, New York.

Although the head-dress is slightly larger and more elaborate, there is considerable resemblance between the Madonna of 1510 in the Brera Gallery and another composition of which there exist two examples, one which was damaged by fire, formerly in Sta. Maria in Trastevere, Rome (¹), now in the store-room of the

---

(¹) Attributed to Bissolo by Morelli. *G. Bernardini*, Rassegna d'Arte, 1910, p. 142; 1912, March, p. III, Catena. *A. Venturi*, op. cit., school of

Fig. 198. Giovanni Bellini, Madonna. Borghese Gallery, Rome.

Borghese Gallery (Gronau, 158); it has been restored and at one
time was exhibited in Castel Sant' Angelo; the other was acquired
by Duveen Brothers from the Loeser collection, Florence. The
nude Child with leg outstretched presses his left foot against the
Virgin's hand, while the other leg is bent inwards. The landscape
is very fine as are also the sunlit clouds in the sky.

Giovanni Bellini. It is ascribed to Giambellino by *Cantalamessa*, Bollettino d'Arte, VIII, 1914, p. 105. *G. Gronau*, Spätwerke, pp. 14, 20, 30.

Fig. 199. Giovanni Bellini, Madonna and Saints. Accademia, Venice.

Photo Naya.

Then there is the Madonna in the Bache collection, New York, in which the Virgin turned to one side holds on her knee the curly-headed Child, Who grasps a bird; again the landscape is of great beauty ([1]).

A very similar Madonna, but seen from a different angle with the Child lying on her knee between St. John the Baptist and a female saint — Catherine(?) — against a beautiful landscape with a town on the banks of a river, is met with in a panel which the gallery of Venice acquired from the Giovanelli collection (881) (fig. 199) ([2]). Moschini (II, p. 348) describes it as in the Redentore church. The resemblance which exists between the figure of St. John the Baptist and the corresponding figure in a picture of 1504 by Previtali in the National Gallery, London (1409), has induced Gronau to ascribe the panel to a date prior to this year. The argument is not without significance, more especially as Previtali in the signature on the painting in London calls himself a disciple of Giovanni Bellini; Previtali's picture, however, seems sooner to have been copied from a lost work, attributed to Giambellino, which existed in the sacristy of the church of S. Giobbe; it is mentioned in old guide-books and an engraving of it is reproduced in Zanotto's Pinacoteca Veneta (II, pl. 71). Stylistic peculiarities, especially of the drapery, lead us to believe that the Giovanelli picture, in which the St. John of that formerly in S. Giobbe is an exact reproduction, is not prior to 1510.

Of a quiet and almost academic beauty is a signed altar-piece now also in the Bache collection, but formerly in that of Mr. and Mrs. Benson, London, which I think must have been executed about the same time as the Madonna in the Brera Gallery, that is to say around the year 1510 ([3]). The seated Virgin looks towards

---

([1]) It was previously attributed to Cima and to Basaiti, and was sold in 1882 with the rest of the collection of the Duke of Hamilton. v. A Catalogue of Paintings in the Collection of Jules S. Bache, New York, privately printed, 1929. *Gronau*, op. cit., p. 216; in the Ca d' Oro there is an old copy of this picture.

([2]) *Cantalamessa*, Bollettino d'Arte del Minist. della Pubbl. Istr., 1914, p. 111, ascribed it to an anonymous follower of Giovanni Bellini. Dedalo, VI, 1925, p. 135. Apollo, June 1933, p. 5. Some years ago I saw an old copy of this picture in the L. de Spiridon collection, Paris; it did not figure in the sale of this collection.

([3]) Catalogue of Italian Pictures etc. collected by R. and E. Benson,

Fig. 200. Giovanni Bellini and assistants, Assumption. S. Pietro Martire,
Murano.   Photo Anderson.

the nude Child Whom she holds in her arms; SS. Peter, Catherine, Lucy and John the Baptist are depicted to the sides. The figures are draped in a broad and heavy manner and the features are of a particularly regular beauty.

An important production of this phase in Giambellino's activity is the Assumption in the church of S. Pietro, Murano (fig. 200), formerly in the Angeli church of this town. Ridolfi mentions it as a fine work of Giovanni Bellini and Boschini attributes it to Basaiti. Of the later critics Cavalcaselle ascribes it to Basaiti, von Hadeln to Pseudo-Basaiti, Berenson to Giovanni Bellini in part, Gronau to Bellini and A. Venturi to his school.

There can be no doubt that the Madonna was made from the same cartoon as the paintings in Detroit and in the Brera Gallery, while the figure of St. Louis, who is depicted in the centre of the eight saints below, appears, as we shall see, in the altar-piece of S. Giovanni Crisostomo, Venice, which dates from 1513. If any part of this picture is from the hand of Bellini, it is the Virgin, but even so the drapery seems too heavily elaborate to ascribe it to the master's brush. Also the faces of the over-draped saints are not fine enough in execution to assign them to Giambellino himself. The same applies to the otherwise pleasing but untransparent landscape. In all likelihood the attribution to the studio of Bellini, possibly with some assistance from the master, is the nearest to being correct. The collaboration of Basaiti is not to be excluded.

I see more of Giovanni Bellini's own hand, although here too some assistance has to be admitted, in the Annunciation (fig. 201) and St. Peter — the St. Paul has completely vanished — which formed the decoration of the organ doors in Sta. Maria dei Miracoli, Venice, the pieces of which — the Madonna from Sta. Maria della Vigna, the St. Peter from the Frari Church and the angel Gabriel from the English art market — are now united in the gallery of Venice (734). The attribution to the mediocre Pier Maria Pennacchi which these fine figures carried for many years

---

privately printed, London, 1914, No. 74, with bibliography. Catalogue of Paintings in the Collection of J. S. Bache, with bibliography. Mr. Berenson is of opinion that it is not anterior to 1512. *Gronau*, op. cit., p. 214. *The Same*, Spätwerke, p. 21, is in favour of an earlier date.

Fig. 201. Giovanni Bellini and assistants, Annunciation. Accademia, Venice.

Photo Alinari.

has gradually been given up (¹); but it is equally impossible to believe that these paintings were executed by Giambellino soon after 1489, when the organ is supposed to have been ornamented. If Giovanni Bellini undertook this work, he cannot possibly have

(¹) G. *Fiocco*, Rivista del R. Istituto d'Archeol. e Stor. dell' Arte, I, 1929, p. 111. G. *Fogolari*, La Galleria di Venezia, Milan, no date, pl. 14, "il nome del Bellini non sarebbe di certo profanato, ma non vi sono ancor argomenti sufficienti per pronunciarlo con sicurezza". R. *van Marle*, Dedalo, XIII, 1933 p. 254. *Berenson*, formerly ascribed it to Rondinelli but now thinks that in part it is by Giovanni Bellini.

carried it out much before 1510 and then perhaps he was not alone in the enterprise. The heads are certainly fine enough to be from the master's hand but in the drapery the tendency which can be said to be characteristic of this stage is exaggerated; the folds are too numerous and there are too many oppositions. The architecture in which the figures are set has obviously been inspired by the fine church of Sta. Maria dei Miracoli.

In the collection of pictures in the "Haus Weddels" in Hamburg there is a bust of the Madonna reading, her hands clasped in prayer, which bears a close connexion with the Virgin of the above-mentioned painting (1).

We have two dated works which reveal to us the transformation which Giovanni Bellini's art underwent after Titian began to dominate the school of Venice. In 1513, when the signed and dated altar-piece in the church of S. Giovanni Crisostomo was executed, Titian was thirty-six years old and already at the height of his fame (fig. 202). In fact, the strange composition of the old St. Jerome seated high up in the background with SS. Christopher and Louis in the foreground to the sides, was quite possibly inspired by Titian's picture of St. Mark and four saints in Sta. Maria della Salute which had been painted several years earlier. In the broad proportions and, one might almost say, Michelangelesque forms there is nothing which connects this work with Giambellino's early manner.

That Titian assisted the old master in the execution of this painting can very well be admitted, more especially as we know that the following year he did so for the Feast of Bacchus which Giovanni Bellini undertook to paint for Duke Alfonso I of Ferrara and for which he received the last payment on the 13th November 1514. The picture, which is now in the collection of Mr. Widener, Philadelphia, is signed: "*Joannes Bellinus Venetus p. 1514*" (fig. 203) (2). It was previously the property of the Duke of Northumberland and at the end of the 16th century belonged to Cardinal Aldobrandini. In his life of Titian Vasari tells us with so much detail about this picture, which he calls one of the finest works by Bellini, that I think we can put our faith in his affirmation that

(1) *R. van Marle*, op. cit.

(2) *M. Logan*, op. cit., Art in America, IX, 1920, p. 1. *L. Venturi*, Pitt. ital. in America, pl. 302.

Fig. 202. Giovanni Bellini and Titian(?), SS. Jerome, Christopher
and Augustine. S. Giovanni Crisostomo, Venice.

Photo Anderson.

Fig. 203. Giovanni Bellini and Titian. The Feast of the Gods. Widener,
Collection, Philadelphia.

it was given to Titian to finish ([1]). Several critics have expressed
the opinion that the left part of the background is by the younger
master.

Among the feasting Gods there is not so much nudity as Vasari
leads his readers to believe, in fact there is hardly any at all. We
can easily understand that the artist might have conceived the
scene of a Bacchanal or antique feast of the gods in more naked-
ness than we find here, where the sober divinities of both sexes,
with the exception of Silenus and the little group to the right,
have on the whole the appearance of a rather peaceful gathering.
The figures, however, are of an exceedingly rare beauty and grace,
while the forest, also that part which we imagine to be by Giam-

---

([1]) *Vasari*, ed. Milanesi, VII, p. 433.

bellino, is of a richness and fulness which up till now we had never seen. Consequently the question arises, whether Titian's part in the execution was limited to the one group of trees and it seems hardly likely that the assistance of the younger master would have been solicited only for the execution of a similar detail. If it was on account of Bellini's old age, as Vasari states (²), that Titian's services had to be called upon, it was probably because at the age of about eighty-four the venerable master, whose life-long activity had almost invariably been devoted to the production of sacred paintings, did not care for this task. It should be recalled here that only a few years earlier he had, on his own authority, changed the profane subject of a picture ordered by the Marchesa Isabella Gonzaga into one of a religious nature. Hence I think that considerably more of this marvellously beautiful painting is by Titian than is generally admitted.

That Titian should be held responsible for any part of the composition is not likely. When we compare Bellini's idea of a Bacchanal with that which Titian painted three or four years later, now in the Prado Gallery, we discover such an utter difference of conception, the one so reserved, the other so lascivious, that we understand at once that Titian could never have imagined the Gods feasting in this restrained fashion.

There exists a small sketch for the Bacchanal in the Widener collection; it belongs to the fine collection of the painter, Italo Brass, in Venice. Although the details are unfinished, it is so beautiful that we can easily admit that it is from the hand of

---

(¹) Mr. Berenson formerly affirmed that he could demonstrate that there was not one brush stroke by Bellini in this picture which, he thought, was possibly executed in Bellini's studio but which was a creation of the brain and hand of Basaiti while the landscape background was due to a pupil of Titian. *Frizzoni*, L'Arte I, 1898, p. 78, repeated this opinion with which he agreed Afterwards, Mr. Berenson changed his mind and gave much of the picture to Giambellino and only part of the background to Titian; he has told me that he has come to the conclusion that the canvas was entirely finished by Giambellino but that Titian cut out a piece of the canvas, replacing it with a landscape of his own.

(²) Curiously enough Vasari says as well that in this picture the drapery is sharply cut (tagliente) according to the German taste, a detail which Bellini may have borrowed from the "Fleming" Dürer, a picture by whom had just been brought to Venice. A copy by Poussin of Bellini's Bacchanal exists in the gallery of Edinburgh.

Giovanni Bellini; in fact its character does not allow us to imagine that it is a copy. On the contrary it has the spontaneity of a first inspiration; moreover there are some variations in the background, which, though not very significant, a copyist would not have permitted himself. I think this first sketch is entirely from the hand of Bellini, whereas a considerable part of the execution of the large picture was left to Titian.

On account of their connexion with a small figure in the left corner of the Bacchanal there are two little pictures of Bacchus pouring out liquid from a decanter, which have been attributed to Giambellino. One of them, formerly in the Hertz collection, is now in the National Gallery, Rome [1]; the other was acquired by Duveen Brothers from the Benson collection (Gronau, 174) [2]. Only the landscape backgrounds are different, that in the London picture being wilder and more rocky.

Did Bellini in his extreme old age, just before his death, develop a taste for the female nude? Could this be the case for an artist who, as we know, treated this subject only in those small allegories which once adorned a piece of furniture? It does not seem likely and even his chaste Bacchanal points to the contrary.

This, however, is not the only reason why I abstain from ascribing to him the Orpheus scene also in the Widener collection, Philadelphia; it is a charming picture but it is not of a very high standard, and in every respect extremely different from the Bacchanal(Gronau, 175) [3]. Nor do I think that Bellini is the author of a picture of a nude woman looking into a mirror in the gallery of Vienna (Gronau, 176), which bears the false signature of Giovanni Bellini; Morelli attributed it to Bissolo and many other critics have followed this opinion. Neither is the martyrdom of St. Peter in the National Gallery from Giambellino's own hand; to me it seems to be from the same brush as the Orpheus in the Widener collection.

Quite recently I saw in a private collection what I imagine is the only portrait of a lady we have from the hand of Giambellino;

---

[1] *J. P. Richter*, La Collezione Hertz, Rome, 1928, No. 23.

[2] Catalogue of Pictures collected by R. and E. Benson, No. 174. Burlington Club Exhibition of early Venetian Pictures, 1912, pl. 25.

[3] *A. Venturi*, op. cit., L'Arte, 1924, p. 138, *The Same*, Studi dal Vero, p. 241. *L. Venturi*, Pitt. ital. in America, pl. 301.

it is I think a production of the very last years of the master's activity. The subject is a young woman of handsome and elegant appearance with her hair artfully dressed as if it were a nimbus around her head; she wears a pink on her bodice.

A signed and dated work of 1515, which I suppose to be of about the same period as this lady's portrait, shows us not only the last change in his manner but of what the master was still capable. It is the half-length figure of Fra Teodoro of Urbino represented as St. Dominic, in the National Gallery (1440) (Gronau, 177). The name of the sitter is inscribed below, as well as the words *"Joânis Bellini op. MDXV"* (fig. 204). For a long time this picture was attributed to Gentile Bellini (¹); it has, however, obviously the character of Giovanni's works and for a comparison we should, as Gronau observes, take as starting point the portrait of Doge Loredano. The style here is naturally looser and more evolved but it is not really different, while the psychological penetration makes this canvas — Giambellino's swan-song— a master-piece of portraiture.

***

I have now reached the end of the enumeration of the works which I believe to be from the hand of the great genius, Giovanni Bellini. It is but natural that everyone who studies this painter, who was so versatile and so varied, will come to his own conclusion of what he might have painted and of what is outside the limits of his artistic individuality. I will not therefore follow my usual habit of giving a list of attributions with which I do not agree. Those who wish to establish the opinions I do not share with Messrs Berenson, Fry and Gronau, whose reconstructions of the master's works I have studied with deep attention and great appreciation, can easily work it out for themselves (²). The latest

---

(¹) The catalogue of the National Gallery upholds the attribution to Gentile Bellini which was made by *von Hadeln*, op. cit., Repertorum f. Kunstwiss. XXX, p. 536, who affirms that signature and date are counterfeits. In fact they are retouched as are as well some parts of the drapery. Also Berenson now attributes this picture to Giambellino.

(²) For some other attributions to Giovanni Bellini v. *Fry*, Giovanni Bellini. *A. Venturi*, Storia dell' arte italiana, VII⁴, p. 254. *The Same*, op. cit., L'Arte, 1924, p. 139. *The Same*, op. cit., L'Arte 1926. *The Same*, Studi dal Vero, p. 226. *Ffoulkes*, L'Arte, XIII, 1910, p. 304. *B. Berenson*,

Fig. 204. Giovanni Bellini, Fra Teodoro of Urbino. National Gallery,
London.   Photo National Gallery.

monograph which has appeared on Giovanni Bellini is that of Dr.
Dussler (1935) who claims his work as more scientific than that
of his predecessors. He offers us, however, as others before him

Dedalo, V, 1925, p. 690. *W. Suida*, Burlington Magazine, LI, 1927, p.
187. *R. Longhi*, Vita Artistica, II, 1927, p. 134. *Hendy*, Burlington Magazine, LVI, 1930, p. 198. *R. Henniker-Heaton*, Burlington Magazine, LXI,
1932, p. 251.

have done, but a personal conception — and a very limited one at that -— of the art of Bellini. His elimination of many works from the list of the master's productions seems to me the outcome of the author's incapacity to comprehend the wide range of this genius' possibilities and of his incomplete knowledge of the master's works, rather than the conclusions of a more perspicacious criticism and more scientific methods than those employed by other critics.

The understanding of a master like Giovanni Bellini is still more speculative than is usually the case and the attribution of works to his brush is often even more open to controversy. But although, after spending so much time with the artist's work, one cannot refrain from the conviction that one's opinions are correct, still one is always willing to listen with due respect to the conclusions others have formed. After all everyone has changed his mind some time or other.

For those who prefer the study of the history of art to rejoicing over the dissensions of art critics, I should advise as starting point the very many pictures regarding the attribution of which to Giambellino there is general agreement, instead of the much smaller group of works about which there is still a considerable difference of opinion (¹).

*_*_*

(¹) Of the lost works I shall cite the following, according to the authors who mention them and naturally the attributions are on their authority.

Michiel (the anonimo Morelliano) whose earliest information dates from only a few years after Bellini's death: the above mentioned altar-piece in the Gattamelata chapel, Padua, by Jacopo, Gentile and Giovanni; in the house of the philosopher Leonico Tomeo, the portrait of this Leonico when he was young, etc. now all perished; in Venice, in the house of Antonio Pasqualino, a half-length figure of the Madonna with the Child; in the house of Taddeo Contarini, a life-sized portrait of a woman; in the house of Jeronimo Marcello, a portrait of his ancestor Jacomo (with which the painting of the so called Colleoni belonging to Messrs Duveen has been identified) and a Madonna and Child "painted long ago"; in the house of Giovanantonio Vernier, head of Christ, "delicata e finita quanto e possibile"; in the house of Gabriel Vendramin, profiles of Filippo Vendramin and two young gentlemen; in the Carità church, St. John the Evangelist altar-piece, the extant predella of which I have already described.

Vasari, Vite, ed. Milanesi, III, p. 155, mentions: in the church of S. Giovanni, the altar-piece, Madonna, SS. Dominic, Jerome, Catherine,

Ursula and two other female saints with three angels singing at the foot
of the throne, one of his finest works; cited also by *Ridolfi*, p. 64 and
Moschini, I, p. 132; it was burned in 1867; p. 163, Confraternità di S. Gerolamo, picture of small figures; p. 164, the Meal at Emmaus, dated 1490,
in the possession of G. Cornaro (*Ridolfi*, p. 72); it is known from a print
by P. Monaco (*Gronau*, 184); it seems to have been destroyed by fire in
the Razumowski Palace in Vienna; several free copies exist: one by Catena
in the gallery of Bergamo. a particularly fine one by Diana in the San
Salvatore church, Venice (fig. 205), another in the museum of Berlin (S. 6)
(fig. 206) v. *Geiger*, Jahrb. K. Preus, Kunstsamml., XXXIII, 1912, p. 129.
Berenson, Venetian Painting in America, p. 119. *Gronau*, op. cit., p. 217.
Fiocco, Rivista del R. Ist. d'Archeol. e di Stor. dell' Arte, I, 1929, p. 114,
attributes the one in S. Salvatore to Giambellino.

Sansovino, Venetia Città nobilissima, ed. 1581, p. 100 verso, Albergo
della Scuola di S. Giovanni Evangelista, Miracles of the Cross, part of
these by Diana; p. 101, altar-piece, here also said to be by Giambellino.

In the inventory of a collection Andrea Vendramin which existed in
Venice in 1627 (*T. Borenius*, The Picture Gallery of Andrea Vendramin,
London, 1923), we find attributed to Giovanni Bellini: pl. 1, bust of
Christ; pl. 2, Madonna in half-length figure with the Child in her arms;
pl. 3, half-length portrait of a lady; pl. 10, half-length male portrait; pls.
16 and 17, two bust-length portraits of ladies; pl. 19, bust-length portrait
of a youth which, judging from the drawing, might be by Giovanni Bellini;
pl. 23, idem; pl. 33, idem; pl. 35, man wearing an elegant hat, attributed
to G.B.; pl. 37c, bust of a youth which apparently was signed; pl. 43,
half-length figure of St. Francis, attributed to "Bellino".

Ridolfi, Maraviglie, ed. von Hadeln, p. 64, Magistrato dell' Avogaria in
Palace of the Doges, the already mentioned Pietà, dated 1472; Carità
monastery, Crucifixion and Doctors of the Church in chiaroscuro; Con-
vento dei Miracoli, St. Jerome in the desert (*Boschini*, mentions a triptych
of SS. Jerome, Francis and Clare which *von Hadeln*, p. 66 note 3, supposes
to be the same); p. 71, Murano, Angeli church, Entombment; p. 71, S. Stefano (von Hadeln thinks probably in the monastery), the Lord blessing;
Florence, Signor Quinto, the Saviour and four saints; Antwerp, Signor van
Veerle, Madonna adored by SS. Peter and Jerome; Bergamo, cathedral,
Ridolfi wrongly ascribes to G. B. a Madonna by Cariani; p. 72, Vienna,
Archduke Leopold, Madonna; p. 73, Ridolfi speaks of still other Madonnas
with or without saints which were owned in Venice by Cornaro, Morosini, Lando, Salomone, Zena and Sanuda; in the church of Sta. Maria
Maggiore there were three Madonnas from his hand (*Zanetti*, p. 55,
mentions one with many cherubim) and one in S. Gerolamo (*Boschini*,
p. 62; *Zanetti*, p. 76); p. 72, in the Grimani Palace at Sta. Ermacora he
painted in the Sala two big pictures of "Cosmografia" with the figures of
Ptolemy, Strabon, Pliny and Pompenius Mella, which he signed; he
made many portraits of illustrious people and doges, some in large pictures
with other figures in the Sala del Collegio; he executed portraits of Bartolomeo Liviano, Pietro Bembo, before he became cardinal, and his lady-

Fig. 205. Diana, Contemporary Copy of Giovanni Bellini's Meal at Emmaus.
S. Salvatore, Venice. Photo Anderson.

love. Further, he informs us that Giambellino's paintings were universally admired and that there were many in Rome, Germany, Flanders and England.

Boschini, Le Minere, 1664, apart from those already mentioned, cites still: p. 30, Tribunal in Doges' Palace, Madonna; p. 101, two Madonnas and Our Lord (probably the Child) in the church of S. Geminiano; p. 160, the Virgin and Child with three saints in S. Gioseffo; p. 169, marriage of

A fairly large number of drawings can be attributed to Giovanni Bellini (¹).

I shall deal with them briefly in chronological order according to the different phases in the development of the master's art which we have established from the study of his paintings.

In the Royal Library of Windsor there exists a brush drawing of a bearded old monk (²), which shows such striking similarities with the St. Antony Abbot of one of the triptychs from the Carità church that we should certainly place them near to one another; moreover, the finely designed head is without any doubt a production of Giovanni's early years.

There are several drawings in which the Mantegnesque characteristics predominate and for this reason they can be assigned to

St. Catherine and saints in the Arsenale; Ospedaletto di S. Giobbe, St. Joseph and the Madonna presenting the Infant Jesus to an angel with the child St. John and three other angels and on the other side a Deposition (*Moschini*, II, p. 70).

Zanetti, Della pittura veneziana, 1771, apart from many wrong attributions mentions: p. 48, Scuola di S. Gerolamo, remains of works of 1464, already cited; S. Giovanni alla Giudecca, panel with SS. John the Baptist, Matthew, Romuald, the Presentation above and a predella; p. 51, Murano, S. Cristoforo, SS. John, Jerome, Peter and Paul, dated 1505; p. 54, S. Giobbe sacristy, Virgin with SS. John the Baptist and Catherine (*Moschini*, II, p. 61; reprod. in *Zanotto*, Pinacoteca Veneta, II, Venice, 1860, pl. 71; of this picture there exists a copy signed by Previtali dated 1504, in the National Gallery, No. 1409); p. 55, Palace of the Doges, Hall of the Council of Ten, half-length figure of the Madonna; p. 56, S. Giorgio Maggiore, Saviour "maravigliosamente dipinto".

G. *Moschini*, Guida per la città di Venezia, 1815, I, p. 510, Procuratie Nuove (Royal Palace), Madonna in a landscape; p. 678, Sta. Caterina, Madonna some say by Giambellino; II, p. 349, Redentore sacristy, Madonna with Child in her arms.

See also the list of lost works in *Crowe and Cavalcaselle*, Painting in N. Italy, ed. T. Borenius, I, London, 1912, p. 191 note 2.

(¹) For the greater part they are reproduced in *von Hadeln*, Venezianische Zeichnungen des Quattrocento, pls. 54—72. See also G. *Fogolari*, I disegni della R. Galleria dell' Accademia (Venice), Milan, 1913, pls. 48—50. A. *Venturi*, op. cit., L'Arte, 1926, p. 1. *The Same*, Studi dal Vero, p. 226. K. T. *Parker*, North Italian Drawings of the Quattrocento, London, 1927, pls. 39—42. A. E. *Popham*, Italian Drawings exhibited at the Royal Academy, London, 1930, London, 1931, pls. 139—142. K. *Clark*, op. cit., Burlington Magazine, 1932. *Fogolari*, op. cit., Dedalo, 1932. *Hendy*, op. cit., Burlington Magazine, 1932.

(²) *Parker*, Old Master Drawings, II, 19.

Fig. 205. Ancient copy after Giovanni Bellini's Meal at Emmaus.
Museum, Berlin.   Museum photo.

the period during which Giovanni was subjected to the influence
of his Paduan brother-in-law.

In this category should be classified the sketch of a man seated
holding an unrecognizable object in his hand, which quite recently
was still in the Russell collection, London ([1]). Executed with the

([1]) *Von Hadeln,* op. cit., pl. 66. *Parker,* op. cit. 39. Vasari Society,

Fig. 207. Giovanni Bellini, Saint reading, drawing. British Museum, London.

Photo Vasari Society Reprod.

same ease and virtuosity is the figure of a saint standing reading, in the British Museum (1895-9-15-786) (fig. 207) (¹). More minutely worked but of the same style is a standing figure of St. John the Evangelist holding a book, in the Accademia of Venice (²). The St. Jerome with his lion and part of a landscape in the Uffizi, which Professor A. Venturi attributes to Giambellino, is I think by Mantegna himself.

It was possibly during this phase of his evolution that Giambellino executed two other drawings which until now have not been ascribed to him. One of them is preserved in the Uffizi and represents the Crucifixion with the Virgin and St. John near

2nd series, VII, pl. 3. *T. Borenius*, The Connoisseur, LXVI, 1924, p. 5. International Studio, August 1929, p. 57. It was sold by auction with the rest of the collection in London in July 1929.

(¹) *Von Hadeln*, op. cit., pl. 56. Vasari Society, IV, 6.

(²) *Fogolari*, op.cit., pl.48.

Fig. 208. Giovanni Bellini (?), Crucifixion, drawing. Uffizi, Florence.
Photo Alinari.

the cross, and a rock, a town and some Roman soldiers in the
background (fig. 208) (¹); it corresponds with the picture of the
same subject in the Correr Museum. The other also depicts the
Crucifixion but here it is shown with the three crosses, the

(¹) Photo Alinari drawings 109 (Pollaiuolo).

Fig. 209. Giovanni Bellini (?), Crucifixion, drawing. British Museum,
London.   Photo Anderson.

swooning Virgin, the group of gamblers, mounted soldiers and
several other figures (fig. 209). The artist to whom we owe this
composition certainly knew the predella panel of Mantegna's
altar-piece from S. Zeno, Verona, now in the Louvre, many
features of which are repeated in the drawing; it has even been
supposed that it was Mantegna's study for this picture (¹). However, although the elements borrowed from the Paduan master

---

(¹) *C. Brun*, Zeitschr. f. Bild. Kunst, XVI, p. 119. *Parker*, op. cit.,
pl. 15, attributes it to the school of Mantegna. *Morelli*, Kunstchronik,
III, p. 526, to the school of Foppa.

are very obvious, there are others which point sooner to Giambellino, as for instance the type and shape of the faces, particularly marked in those of the two old men who hold the Saviour's robe; but this is also evident in a general manner in the more regular oval of many of the other faces, while a comparison of the horses here with those in the predella of the Pesaro altar-piece, as well as the hills in the background, offer us striking points of contact.

If this sheet really be by Giovanni Bellini we find him here, though still Mantegnesque, already somewhat more evolved, and of this particular manner I think we possess several drawings. As such I shall cite the fine Entombment in the gallery of Brescia (¹); a leaf with two studies of Christ at the column from the Rayner-Wood collection, Malvern(²);

(¹) *G. Nicodemi*, I disegni della Pinacoteca di Brescia, Milan, 1921, No. 147. *Hadeln*, op. cit., pl. 59. *Venturi*, op. cit., L'Arte, 1921. *Popham*, op. cit., pl. 140, Giovanni Bellini or Mantegna. *Balniel and Clark*, No. 769, idem.

(²) *Popham*, op. cit., pl. 140, G. B. or Mantegna. *Balniel and Clark*, No. 763, idem. *K. Clark*,

Fig. 210. Giovanni Bellini, St. Sebastian, drawing. British Museum, London.

three sketches for a reclining dead figure — probably Our Lord — in the British Museum and on the verso a drawing of two women seated on the ground, no doubt part of a group of the mourning faithful (¹); a sketch of four Apostles in the collection of the Duke of Devonshire at Chatsworth (²), and a reconstructed sheet with two studies of St. John the Baptist and four other saints in the Koenigs collection, Haarlem (³).

That particularly refined manner which contains, as it were, a touch of what was soon to constitute the Lombard school, and of which the large altar-piece in SS. Giovanni e Paolo is the most important example, is manifest in a drawing of St. Sebastian in the British Museum (1895-9-15-800) (fig. 210) (⁴); moreover, there is considerable analogy between this figure and the corresponding saint in the triptych. In the same period we should classify a Pietà in the gallery of Venice (⁵), in which the Saviour's body, falling forward and supported by three women, has much in common — especially in such details as the treatment of the hair — with the corresponding figure of the altar-piece in SS. Giovanni e Paolo (fig. 211). In this manner Giambellino executed a drawing of the Madonna in the Koenigs collection, Haarlem(⁶). A drawing of particular importance and beauty of an antique sacrifice, in the Loeser collection, Florence(⁷), belongs probably also to this period. Resembling in style the Pietà in Lord Rothermere's collection is a drawing of the same subject but of full-length figures, in the museum of Rennes (⁸).

Burlington Magazine, LVI, 1930,p. 181, Mantegna. *Constabile*, Dedalo, XII, 1930, p. 746.

(¹) *Hadeln*, op. cit., pls. 60, 61.

(²) *Venturi*, op. cit.

(³) *Popham*, op. cit., pl. 141, previously in the Boehler collection, Lucerne. *Hadeln*, op. cit., pls. 57, 58. *Parker*, op. cit., pl. 40. *D. von Hadeln*, Meister Zeichnungen der Samml. F. Koenigs, Haarlem; Venez. Meister (Prestel Gesellschaft XV), Frankfort, 1933, pl. 1.

(⁴) *Hadeln*, op. cit., pl. 54.

(⁵) *Loeser*, Rassegna d'Arte, III, 1903, p. 180. *Fogolari*, op. cit., pl. 49. *Hadeln*, Venez. Zeichn., pl. 62. *Popham*, op. cit., pl. 163, G. B. or Mantegna. *Balniel and Clark*, op. cit., No. 764.

(⁶) *W. R. Valentiner*, Burlington Magazine, LXV, 1934, p. 239.

(⁷) *Hadeln*, op. cit., pl. 67. *Meder*, Albertina Zeichnungen, pl. 1077, school of Ferrara.

(⁸) *Parker*, Old Master Drawings, March 1927, p. 50; also reprod. by R. Longhi, Vita Artistica, 1927, p. 138.

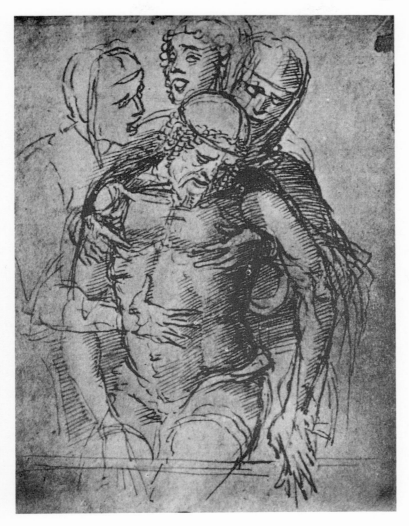

Fig. 211. Giovanni Bellini, Pietà, drawing. Accademia, Venice.

Photo Anderson.

Of the same period as the Pesaro altar-piece are, I think, the
sketch of SS. Peter and Paul in the Bonnat Museum, Bayonne (¹)
and that representing St. Mark curing Anianus in the Print
Room of Berlin; the latter is of particularly high quality and

---

(¹) Catalogue Bonnat coll., II, pl. 10, attributed to Ercole de' Roberti.
Parker, N. Italian Drawings, pl. 41. *Venturi*, Studi dal Vero, pp. 230, 231.

more finished than most of his drawings ([1]). Executed in a somewhat broader manner is a fine drawing of the Pietà in the Louvre,
in which the tragic feeling by no means falls short of that in the
finest painting of this subject which the master has treated so
often ([2]). Another drawing is connected with this composition; it
is preserved in the Uffizi and depicts the turbaned head of an
Oriental (fig. 212) who appears in the Pietà with several figures
in the same gallery, but, because it is in monochrome, it is supposed to be unfinished ([3]).

Of the sketches for small portraits we might take into consideration in the first place that in the gallery of Kassel which, however,
is somewhat lacking in character and expression; moreover, it is
not always accepted as a work by Giambellino ([4]). Nor indeed is
that of a handsome young man almost in full face wearing a
bonnet on one side in the Albertina, Vienna; it is executed in
red chalk but in parts, chiefly in the dress, has been restored ([5]).
Of the many names which have been associated with this drawing,
that of Giovanni Bellini seems the most likely.

Very probably by our master is a drawing of a somewhat older
man turned slightly to the right; he wears a fairly high bonnet
on his curly head and has an energetic expression. I know this
sketch only from a photograph (Giraudon 714) and do not even
know in what collection it is to be found ("collection particu-
lière").

A study in red chalk of the right profile of a youngish man with
an aquiline nose in the Uffizi might be called strongly Belliniesque;
a certain lack of vigour makes me rather doubtful about ascribing
it to the master himself. The sitter is perhaps the same person
who is represented to the extreme right in the picture of 1507 of
Doge Loredano and four young patricians.

I feel uncertain also about the attribution of a beautiful
drawing of the bust of a young man looking up, in the Städelsches

---

([1]) *Hadeln*, op. cit., pl. 68.

([2]) *Morelli*, Gallerie Borghese e Doria, p. 274. *Hadeln*, pl. 69.

([3]) *Gronau*, Künstlerfamilie, p. 102, fig. 74. *Hadeln*, fig. 65.

([4]) *Hadeln*, op. cit., pl. 70 and p. 47, where he mentions the opinions
held by Morelli and Berenson who believe it to be by Jacopo de' Barbari.

([5]) *Hadeln*, op. cit., pl. 71, p. 50; for this drawing the names of Gentile
Bellini, Bonsignori and Lotto (*Venturi*, Studi dal Vero) have been
proposed.

Kunstinstitut, Frankfort, which von Hadeln (pl. 55) claims for Giambellino. In any case, technically speaking I should compare it with the Pietà in the Brera Gallery rather than with the St. Sebastian of the altar-piece in SS. Giovanni e Paolo.

Only just lately two drawings have been attributed to the master and without any doubt correctly. Both depict the Madonna in half-length figure; in one, which is preserved in the British Museum, the nude Child is seated while in the other, which belongs to Dr. Tancred Borenius, London, the naked Jesus stands and affectionately presses His face against that of His Mother ([1]).

***

A résumé of the art of Giovanni Bellini is an exceedingly diffi-cult task, because rarely do we find such talent united to so much versatility, in fact at times it is almost difficult to believe that he had a strong artistic individuality. Let us compare for example

([1]) *Hendy*, op. cit. Other drawings attributed to Giovanni Bellini are: British Museum, O. 09, No. 31, two saints, they have the appearance of a fairly early work of the master; the sheet is supposed to have been restored by Rubens. Several critics see Bellini's hand in a delightful drawing of the bust of a young woman who is shown almost in full face, looking down and who wears a rope of large pearls, in the gallery of Venice: *Loeser*, Rassegna d'Arte, 1903, p. 180. *Hadeln*, op. cit., pl. 64. *Fogolari*, op. cit., pl. 50. I agree with *Popham*, op. cit., p. 45, pl. 137 and *Balniel and Clark*, op. cit., No. 762, that the attribution "must be regarded as extremely doubtful". *A. Venturi*, op. cit., L'Arte, 1926, and Studi dal Vero, is of opinion that it might be by Lotto which seems still more unlikely. A study of drapery around a male figure in the British Museum has been attributed to Giambellino by *Hadeln*, pl. 63 and *the Same*, Jahrb. der Preus. Kunst-samml., XLV, p. 206; *Parker*, op. cit., pl. 44, seems nearer the truth in claiming it for Alvise Vivarini after Bellini. We shall return to this work later. Nor do I think are by Bellini the studies of drapery in the von Lanna coll., Prague, which are reproduced as such by *Meder*, Albertina Zeichnungen, X, pls. 1126, 1127; the broad sketchy pen drawing of Christ and two disciples (the calling of Nathaniel) in the Albertina which *Hadeln*, op. cit., pl. 72, assigns to him with a point of interrogation. *Wickhoff*, Jahrb. der Kunsthist. Samml. des Allerh. Kaiserh., XII[2], No. 1455, pl. 216, proposed the attribution to Basaiti, which I think is the most proba-ble and to which the following writers adhere: *Meder*, Handzeichn. aus der Albertina, pl. 257. *The Same*, Albertina Facsimile, Handzeichn. italien Meister, Vienna, 1923, pl. 32. *A. Stix u. L. Fröhlich-Bum*, Beschreib. Katal. der Handzeichn. in der Albertina, I, Veneziansche Schule, Vienna, 1926, No. 22. On the other hand *Gronau*, Gazette des Beaux Arts, LXXIII, 1894, p. 328, thought that this drawing might be by Campagnola.

Fig. 212. Giovanni Bellini, head of an Oriental, drawing. Uffizi, Florence
Photo Alinari.

the Crucifixion in the Correr Museum and the altar-piece of
S. Giovanni Crisostomo, or again such master-pieces as the
Pietà in the Brera and the picture in S. Zaccaria, and ask ourselves honestly if we should ever have attributed these works to
the same brush if we had not been able to follow the painter's
evolution through the long series of productions which mark so
many phases in his artistic development. There is no need to

go again into all the details of these different phases, but I shall just sum them up briefly.

After a somewhat vaguely delineated early manner, which depended more than anything else on the education received from his father but which was not without reminiscences of the Byzantine style, Giambellino passed through a period of great dependence on his brother-in-law Mantegna, during which we cannot fail to notice a certain influence of Donatello. This period set in after 1464 and lasted for a considerable length of time. Whichever theory we accept for the master's earliest development, we are always faced with the surprising fact that at quite a mature age — around his thirty-fifth year — such a great genius as Giambellino was unquestionably, was so entirely dominated by another painter. A second Mantegnesque phase which marked a more evolved form of the same influence came to an end prior to 1474, when Bellini found his most individual style of painting, one of simple and regular beauty which seems to have lasted until the early nineties.

In the subsequent decade and later we discover a gradual infiltration of Cinquecentesque elements into Giambellino's art, which up till now had been typical of the Quattrocento, and already in 1505 we find him a confirmed adherent of the Cinquecento with tendencies very akin to those of Giorgione and of Titian, his collaborator and no doubt the person who enticed him into this new artistic world.

I do not consider Giovanni to have been an innovator or even an extreme individualist. On the contrary, he seems to have had a most adaptable artistic temperament and to have followed in an almost easy-going manner different tendencies of which others were the chief exponents.

But whatever the manner he chose he seldom failed to reveal a superlative ability, united with the most pronounced gift and taste for noble beauty with which we have ever met in the art of painting. Of pictures like the Brera Pietà or — in quite a different style — the Frari altar-piece there are but few in the world.

Much has been written about the influence of Piero della Francesca (¹), Antonello da Messina and the Flemish school (²)

(¹) *Longhi*, op. cit., L'Arte, 1914.

(²) *Habicht*, op. cit. The observations of Professor Habicht apply

but none of them seems to have had really much importance in the formation of Giovanni Bellini's art. There are some pictures of his second Mantegnesque manner which, as a matter of fact, seem to possess the aerial perspective and atmosphere of Piero's works, but here again the problems of distance and perspective are approached in a very different manner. However, it can be admitted that Bellini, along with many others, profitted from the great technical achievements and progress which Piero had made in Italian painting in general and hence some points of resemblance can be pointed out, though this does not carry with it any argument in favour of a direct dependence.

As for the so-called influence of Antonello, I think the call which has been made on this strange genius to account for the incomprehensible in the art of another not inferior to him, has been in vain. Moreover, Antonello's stay in Venice was apparently of very short duration and while there he created probably only one important work, the altar-piece of San Cassiano. As I have already pointed out, it is not impossible that Giambellino for some of his larger pictures borrowed the tall composition from Antonello and the niche from Piero's examples; even the figures of the triptych in the Frari church, although divided up, form a group which shows much in common with that of Antonello's San Cassiano altar-piece. Nevertheless it was not Antonello's presence in Venice which made Giambellino change his manner. After Giovanni's second Mantegnesque phase, when otherwise we are left so much in the dark regarding his chronology that almost any theory can be upheld, chance would have it that the dated Fugger portrait of 1474 was executed the year before Antonello's arrival in Venice and the transformation, which culminated in the dated works of 1488, had then already definitely set in.

With regard to the Flemish influence I shall be extremely brief because for me it is non-existent. I find everything in Giovanni

---

chiefly to the figure of St. Mary Magdalene at the foot of the cross in the Crucifixion at Pesaro and the connexion existing between it and the corresponding figure in van der Weyden's Deposition in the Uffizi. Even if this figure had anything particularly Flemish in appearance, which I do not think it has, it would not be a convincing argument because, as I said before, I am not of the opinion that this picture is by Bellini.

Bellini's art thoroughly Italian; light, colour, landscapes, types, feeling and above all technique are anything but northern.

Cima da Conegliano did not actually have any influence in the formation of Giambellino's art but he seems all the same to have been the innovator of certain features which the master borrowed from him. In 1494 Cima created the type of Baptism of Our Lord which Giambellino followed a few years later in Vicenza. It was in all probability he too who invented those backgrounds which are formed in part by a curtain and in part by a landscape which Bellini so often employs, but only at a somewhat later date. In fact, as we shall see, it was very likely Cima who, in opposition to the apsidal niches behind Bellini's enthroned Madonnas, invented the open-air background under a vault which Bellini adopted apparently much later in the destroyed altar-piece of SS. Giovanni e Paolo. However, in purely artistic matters Cima was decidedly very dependent on Giambellino's examples.

No one will ever deny that Giovanni Bellini was *par excellence* a religious painter and by far his most favoured subject was the figure of the Madonna. Besides portraits, his activity as painter of profane subjects is limited as far as we know to the little panels of allegories in the gallery of Venice, the Feast of the Gods in the Widener collection, which in part is certainly by Titian, and his intention of executing a profane picture for Isabella Gonzaga which he afterwards changed into a work of a religious subject; after all not really much for an artist by whom we still have a hundred and fifty or more extant paintings. Like other great geniuses — Raphael or Titian — Bellini always varied his subject, because for the really great artist each picture is a source of fresh inspiration. Hence, of his very numerous Madonnas, except of course in cases of absolute repetition or replicas, no two are alike or even similar and the same can be said of his Pietàs which, including paintings and drawings, also exist in considerable number.

Giambellino drew his ever-flowing religious inspiration from a profoundly mystic and lyrical nature. His Madonnas and saints, in fact, seem just as evolved as his portraits. When he painted the Virgin Mary, the Child Jesus or some saint from paradise his image is certainly not lacking in devotion but at the same time neither is it wanting in individuality. The painter had obviously a very clear idea of each figure imprinted on his imagination and these were the images he conveyed to his brush. The little Saviour in many cases seems to listen to some celestial voices, and Mr. Fry has no doubt rightly interpreted the master's idea when he says that Jesus apparently hears a choir of angels who, besides, are sometimes visible.

Bellini's Pietàs are as profoundly tragic as they are mystic, while his conception of St. Francis, as portrayed in the painting in the Frick collection, has a touch of religious fanaticism.

Giambellino was in the true sense of the word an aesthete, rejoicing in beauty and distributing it with generous hands. He must have been as well a sensitive idealist, a mystic, a psychologist and a lover of nature, because not only are his later landscapes of a smiling beauty until then undreamt of, but also he depicts little plants growing out of the rocks, squirrels, sun-lizards and other little animals running around and gaily-coloured birds perched on the trees.

As a portrait painter too Giovanni Bellini shows himself an artist of outstanding merit and second only to Antonello. His human effigies are as varied as they are psychologically penetrating, though in the rendering of the individual features of the sitter these are not unfrequently subjected to the painter's aesthetic principles. His great efforts to obtain the third dimension have produced those marvellous effects of distance and perspective in the backgrounds, even in his earliest works, and it was this also which induced him to depict his groups of the Madonna and saints with the apse of a church as background.

Not many artists have handled the effects of line with such consummate skill as Giambellino during his Mantegnesque period and I think the charm of it is so great that many will agree with me that it was at this stage that he created his most captivating pictures. He was however a greater painter when, probably on account of the change of medium to the use of oils, he achieved those marvellous and impressionistic toned and fused colours which invest his works with volume in that magical manner which makes him an early adherent of the Venetian school of the 16th century.

CHAPTER V

THE WORKSHOP AND PUPILS OF
GIOVANNI BELLINI

Few painters have had an influence which could be compared with that of Giovanni Bellini. With the exception of a group of artists who adhered more closely to the tendency which emanated from Padua through Crivelli and Bartolomeo Vivarini, we might say that Giambellino dominated the entire Venetian school at the end of the 15th century and beginning of the 16th.

Many of the painters, as for example Cima, Catena, Bissolo, Cariani, Rocco Marconi, Diana, Pennacchi, the Santacroce, Rondinelli, Lattanzio da Rimini, Montagna and Previtali evolved more or less rapidly and completely from their first Belliniesque incentive. Marco Basaiti takes a somewhat special place because it was only in later years that he became, artistically speaking, intimate with Giambellino but this intimacy was so close that I think he can be held responsible for certain pictures which are generally supposed to be productions of Bellini's studio. Great masters like Carpaccio, Alvise Vivarini, Giorgione and Titian emancipated themselves very quickly and thoroughly from Bellini's influence; in fact we have to admit that the latter in particular may have helped in the formation of Giambellino's last manner. On the other hand Bellini's inspiration and motifs were kept alive by a group of small painters which includes Duia, Pasqualino Veneziano and Jacopo da Valenza, while even artists who did not actually belong to his school, like Palmezzano and Pietro da Saliba, helped to propagate Bellini's type of Madonna.

Among the very many anonymous works which reveal the domination of Giambellino, we have no doubt to look for the productions of Benedetto Coda da Ferrara, who lived in Rimini and whom Vasari cites as one of his pupils; but regarding this artist we have no further information. To Bellini's own family belonged Vittore Belliniano and the somewhat mysterious Bellino Bellini.

I shall start my survey of the works of his immediate followers and adherents with a description of the studio productions, as it is they which reflect most faithfully the master's own taste and artistic principles; in fact, we can admit that the master generally executed some part of them himself or at least made corrections where anything displeased him. The drawings for these pictures were probably invariably supplied by him. In dealing with this group of works I shall not include the copies of Giambellino's own paintings which I have already mentioned in the previous chapter. Nor shall I cite any arguments against Morelli's strange theory that in the signature of the paintings which are not from the master, the second "l" in the name of Bellini is much longer than the first. It would be a tedious task to review all the paintings which provide proof to the contrary. As a rule it can be said that studio works were often signed by the master, so that the presence of the signature does not always testify to the authenticity of the painting. Nor need it cause surprise that in those workshop productions we recognize the hand of artists who, when independent, never reach the same level because it is only natural that, working under Bellini's supervision and probably often corrected by him, they succeeded in creating works of art far above their normal standard.

I know of no school works of the period when Giambellino was still under his father's influence, nor even of the stage when he was most dominated by Andrea Mantegna. However, there exist some replicas of pictures of this phase, as for example that in the museum of Berlin, which is not from Giambellino's own hand but is a copy of the painting in the Kessler collection, Brussels.

The earliest examples of actual studio productions which are neither by his own hand nor assistants' copies of originals, reflect the master's art when he was already an evolved adherent of Mantegna.

The most significant piece is the half-length figure of the Madonna holding the Child in benediction above the usual wall on which a bird is perched, in the Ca d'Oro, Venice (fig. 213). This panel, which is rather damaged, was formerly in the little church in the Palace of the Doges and before that in the Palazzo dei

Camerlenghi (Gronau, 64) ([1]). The background for the greater part is occupied by a curtain, to the right of which there is a view of some buildings and a palm tree.

By another artist, but executed in this particular late Mantegnesque manner, is a picture of the same subject in the Hurd collection, New York; here however the figure is turned to the other side and is depicted against a hilly landscape.

Another artist who worked in quite a Quattrocentesque manner might possibly be identified with Rondinelli at the period when he was active as an assistant of Giovanni Bellini, which was long before he developed the characteristics from which he can so easily be recognized.

A picture which shows the signature *Joannes Bellinus* is I think unmistakeably by Rondinelli; it is found in the Doria Gallery, Rome (126), and represents the Virgin and St. John the Baptist adoring the Child, Who raises Himself from the cushions on which He has been reclining (Gronau, 115) ([2]).

Rondinelli's own manner however is here clearly recognizable, but there are other Madonnas which manifest a much more direct influence of Giambellino and can only hypothetically be supposed to have been painted by Rondinelli in his master's studio. As such I shall cite three paintings of the Madonna which in as far as the composition is concerned differ only in the

---

([1]) *Ludwig*, Jahrb. der K. Preus Kunstsamml., XXIII, 1902, p. 42. *Ludwig e Molmenti*, Carpaccio, p. 23 attributes it to Lazzaro Bastiani. *L. Venturi*, Orig. pitt. Ven., p. 396, to the workshop of Giambellino at an early period which opinion is much the same as mine. *Berenson*, Venet. Painting in America, p. 82, possibly Bonsignori after Bellini. In the catalogue of the Ca d'Oro it is ascribed to the manner of Giovanni Bellini. *Gronau*, op. cit., p. 204, gives it to Giovanni Bellini.

([2]) This picture has been attributed to Rondinelli by *Morelli*, Gall. Borghese, p. 345 and *Berenson*. *Borenius*, Felix Ravenna, I, 1911, p. 8 and *von Hadeln*. Zeitchn. f. bild. Kunst, N.S., XXIII, 1911[2], p. 289, say it is not by Rondinelli, neither by Giambellino himself. To Bellini it is ascribed by *G. Gronau*, Spätwerke, p. 28 and *The Same*, Giov. Bellini, p. 210. Here he mentions the different copies of this figure of the Madonna with the Child which were made and in some cases signed by Rondinelli and he judges them sufficiently inferior to the picture in question to conclude that the latter is by the master and the others by the pupil Rondinelli.

Fig. 213. Workshop of Giovanni Bellini, Madonna. Ca d'Oro, Venice.
Photo Böhm.

background. The best of them is preserved in the National
Gallery, London (3078) and is catalogued as by Giovanni Bellini
(fig. 214). The Virgin holds the Child seated on her knee and
places one hand on a book which lies on the low wall. There is
still some trace of a signature. Beyond the curtain which occupies

Fig. 214. Rondinelli in the workshop of Giovanni Bellini (?), Madonna.
National Gallery, London.   Photo National Gallery.

the greater part of the background, a wintry landscape is visible.
Less fine is a replica in the Fogg Art Museum, Cambridge, U.S.A.,
in which the entire background is formed by a curtain. This
picture has been ascribed to Rondinelli by Mr. Perkins [1]. A
piece of a summery landscape is depicted in the left corner of the

[1] *Perkins*, Rassegna d'Arte, V, 1905, p. 69.

example with Bellini's signature in the Ellis collection, Worcester, U.S.A., in which the execution of the Madonna, though somewhat hard, is not without merit and very superior to that of the Child. There exist several other copies of this composition, one of which is apparently by Catena (¹). Possibly by the same hand is a picture of the Madonna, facing the spectator, with the nude Child Who blesses on her knee and the hilly landscape intersected by a curtain, which was for sale in Rome many years ago, as well as another Madonna, her hands folded on her breast, looking down on the Child Who lies sleeping with His head on two cushions, which was once in the Paolini collection, Rome (²); here a wild rocky landscape partly concealed by a curtain forms the background, while strange marine monsters adorn the low wall visible below.

A painting of the Madonna with the Child in benediction between St. John the Baptist and an old female saint (Elizabeth?) in the Städelsches Kunstinstitut, Frankfort (853), which shows the signature of Giovanni Bellini (fig. 215), forms a connecting link between the above mentioned works (which quite hypothetically we attribute to Rondinelli) and another almost certain production, again in the Doria Gallery (159), which shows us only the Madonna and Child but in exactly the same attitude (fig. 216). In the picture in Frankfort the central figure is very superior to the others and it can be conjectured that the master took a considerable part in its execution. Another version of this picture exists in the gallery of Urbino (³); it is in a poor state of preservation and seems to be of inferior quality but all the same it might still be from the same hand. The figures of the Madonna and Child of this picture are very probably those which were most frequently repeated by close and distant followers of Giambellino (⁴).

(¹) *Berenson*, Venetian Painting in America, p. 115. *Fogg Art Museum*, Collection of Mediaeval and Renaissance Paintings, Cambridge (U.S.A.), 1919, No. 45, Giovanni Bellini? (Fogg Madonna). *Gronau*, pl. 126 and p. 212 (Ellis coll.). International Studio, Oct. 1928, p. 54 (Ellis coll.).

(²) No. 30 of the catalogue of the Paolini sale which took place in New York in December 1924.

(³) *L. Venturi*, L'Arte, XXVI, 1923, p. 274.

(⁴) *Gronau*, op. cit., p. 211.

Fig. 215. Rondinelli in the workshop of Giovanni Bellini, Madonna and
Saints. Städelsches Kunstinstitut, Frankfort.   Museum Photo.

In seeking for the works which the young Catena might have
executed in Giovanni Bellini's studio we must take into consideration first of all the series of oblong pictures of the Circumcision, of which there exist I believe thirteen examples (¹). I shall
mention only the better versions. On the whole they are all very
similar and as some of them are mentioned in now dispersed collections it is not always easy to discover if there are some cases
in which we are dealing twice with the same picture. The chief
variation is shown in the figure to the extreme left, who is
generally depicted with a beard but is sometimes clean-shaven.
Then the example in the Metropolitan Museum has a landscape
background, whereas the others have a plain dark ground. The
group consists of the old priest Simon, circumcising the Child Who

---

(¹) *Crowe and Cavalcaselle*, ed. Borenius, op. cit., pp. 147, 148 and notes.
Geiger, Jahrb. der K. Preus. Kunstsamml., XXXIII, 1912, p. 10. *Muxel*,
Gemälde Samml. des Herz's v. Leuchtenberg, 57, IIS. L'Arte, VI, p. 339.
Reinach, Repert. de peintures, I, pp. 373, 374. Catalogue of the National
Gallery, under 1455. *Gronau*, op. cit., p. 214.

Fig. 216. Rondinelli in Giovanni Bellini's workshop, Madonna. Doria Gallery, Rome.   Photo Alinari.

is held over a table by the Virgin and Joseph, a young woman with an elaborate head-dress who stands near the Madonna, and a man behind, who holds back Simon's cloak.

The most beautiful version is that in the National Gallery (1455), formerly in the Orleans, the Gramont and the Earl of Carlisle's collections (fig. 217). It bears the signature of Giovanni Bellini

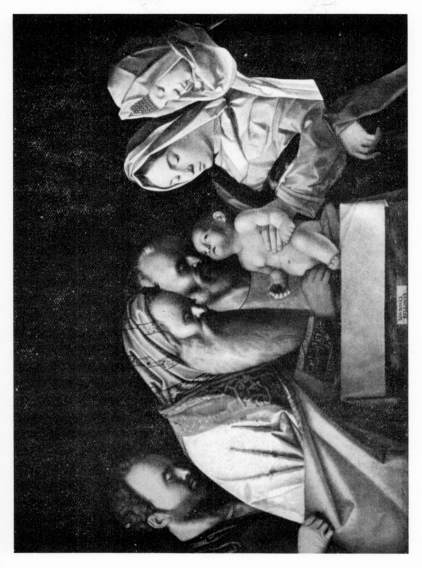

Fig. 217. Catena in Giovanni Bellini's workshop, Circumcision. National
Gallery, London. Photo National Gallery.

and is almost fine enough to be from his own hand to which,
besides, it is still often ascribed ([1]). No doubt Giambellino not

(1) Catalogue National Gallery. *Gronau*, p. 214. *Berenson*, "for the
greater part".

only provided the cartoon for this picture but also closely super-
vised the execution. This however did not prevent a slight
heaviness in the proportions and a lack of skill in the design and
in the drapery, shortcomings which betray the hand of an assistant.

That this assistant was Catena becomes more evident when we
compare the fine painting in the National Gallery with the inferior replicas in the museum of Berlin (1272) and in the Doria
Gallery, Rome (121), which lack those qualities which in the other
example we owe to Bellini himself. Although the picture in the
Doria Gallery has been attributed also to Bissolo, I think the
peculiar technique, with those large lighted facets in opposition to
the darkest of shadows, the sturdy bodies built by these technical
means, and the handsome but rather expressionless faces, are
sufficiently characteristic of Catena to convince us of the attribution to this master. Quite possibly the version in the museum
of Naples (64) was not inferior to these, before time dealt so
roughly with it. Those in the museums of Rovigo, Padua and
Pavia are not of the same quality.

The example in the Metropolitan Museum, New York (Morgan
bequest), in which the background is a landscape and the man
behind Simon is beardless, shows not only the signature of Giovanni Bellini but also the date 1511; in the museum it is classified
as a work by Catena. The date is of considerable interest, not only
because it reveals to us that still at this period Catena was
collaborating with Giovanni Bellini, but also because it proves
that the other copies with which we have dealt are of an earlier
period, since the artistic development which separates the one
from the other must have involved an evolution of more than
ten years, perhaps even twenty.

Another instance in which Catena has greatly profitted from
his proximity to Giambellino is the delightful picture of the
Madonna with the Child Who bends down to caress the infant
St. John, in the National Gallery (3540) (fig. 218). In close collaboration with Giovanni Bellini he certainly had a share in the
execution of the fine altar-piece in the Morgan Library, New York
(Gronau, 151, formerly in the Pourtales collection), in which the
Madonna is depicted almost in profile with the Child in benediction on her knee; she places one hand on the head of the

Fig. 218. Catena, Madonna, Child and St. John. National Gallery,
London. Photo National Gallery.

kneeling adorer (¹). This group appears again in a Belliniesque
picture in the Ca d'Oro, with which I shall deal presently. There
are many other examples of similar representations of the Ma-

(¹) For the many Venetian paintings in which this Belliniesque motif is
repeated, v. *G. Gronau*, Gazette des Beaux Arts, I, 1895, p. 260. *The
Same*, Repert. f. Kunstwiss., XX, 1897. p. 301. *Halm*, op. cit.

donna and Child belonging to this school (¹). Also the four saints of the Morgan picture figure in more or less the same manner in other studio and school productions (²).

The Madonna in the same position, which here is rather meaningless because there is no adorer, is found once more in a picture in the gallery of Stuttgart (428), in which the Virgin rests her out-stretched hand on a book and in which the female saint in adoration, of the Morgan altar-piece, has been copied, and in another painting in the same gallery (429), in which again the Madonna's hand rests on a book though the saint has been replaced by a view of a rocky landscape. They are decidedly by different hands; the former, which is by far the finer of the two, might be by Basaiti helped by Bellini though it is generally attributed to Basaiti; the latter shows the signature: *"Marcho de . . . . ioa. B. P."* which Gronau has interpreted as *"Marcho discipulus Joannis Bellini pictor"*, that is to say Marco Bello.

The same subject — the Virgin holding on her knee the Child Who blesses an adorer — is found once again in a picture which entered the Louvre with the Schlichting collection, but here the Madonna forms the centre of a group and is depicted in full face (Gronau, 116). There are two saints to either side but they are of inferior quality to the central group and the adorer, of which at least the cartoons are from the hand of Bellini, and I do not think this is the case for the lateral figures. I find that the entire picture shows that broad, somewhat superficial and over-clear manner of painting of Catena (³).

The Belliniesque elements have considerably diminished in a hard and severe panel of the Virgin in full face, with the Child in benediction on her knee, between St. Mary Magdalene and another female saint in the gallery of Glasgow (190), and in the very much

---

(¹) *Gronau*, Repert. f. Kunstwiss., XX, 1897, p. 301. *Berenson*, Venetian Painting in America, p. 123.

(²) *Gronau*, Giov. Bellini, p. 214, includes this picture among the authentic works of Giovanni Bellini. *Berenson*, loc. cit., calls it a studio production.

(³) *Baron*, Madonna Verona, IV, 1910, p. 56: Mocetto. *Von Hadeln*, Jahrb. der Preus. Kunstsamml., XLV, 1924, p. 206. *Crowe and Cavalcaselle*, op. cit., p. 183, believe in the collaboration of Bellini with Basaiti. *Gronau*, p. 210, with Pasqualino. As the latter remarks, the Madonna has been repainted by Al. Vivarini and Previtali.

restored Madonna and four saints among whom are SS. John the Baptist and Peter against a skyscape in the Strossmayer Museum, Agram. Both these works show us Catena at his worst but are, all the same, illustrative of what I think might have been the part he took in the execution of some of Giambellino's studio productions.

***

A painter of a particularly sweet disposition co-operated in Bellini's studio in the execution of another group of paintings, and we can easily believe that Bissolo's earliest manner must have been very similar to the style in which these works are painted.

The principal piece of this group is a half-length figure of the Madonna represented against the background of a curtain and behind a low parapet on which we see a label with the signature of Giovanni Bellini; the Child, Who plays with her veil, is attired in a little shirt; behind her shoulder is depicted an adorer, his hands folded in veneration. This painting, which once belonged to Herr von Nemes and recently entered the Metropolitan Museum with the Friedsam collection (Gronau, 117), is generally attributed to Giambellino himself and is in fact a very fine piece of work.

This composition of the Madonna has been frequently repeated, in the first place by the same painter in Bellini's workshop, then by Mazzola (¹) and by Tacconi, who however changed it into an enthroned Madonna which is now in the National Gallery. That this picture is dated 1489 cannot possibly provide us with an argument that the painting in the Friedsam collection is of an earlier period; there must have existed an older and now lost prototype, probably by Giovanni Bellini himself.

By the same hand is no doubt the very much restored Madonna and Child in the same position which is preserved behind the altar in the Scalzi church, Venice (fig. 219). Here, however, a piece of landscape is visible to either side of the curtain which forms the background (²).

(¹) Museum of Padua, No. 411. M. Salmi, Rassegna d'Arte, XVII, 1917. See also Berenson, Venetian Painting in America, p. 113 and von Hadeln, Zeitschr. bild. Kunst, N.F., XXIII, 1911—12, p. 289.

(²) Attributed to Giambellino by Moschini, I, p. 75. Zanotto, Pinac. Venez., I, pl. 5. Hadeln, loc. cit. Ludwig, op. cit., p. 8.

Fig. 219. Workshop of Giovanni Bellini, Madonna. Scalzi church, Venice,
Photo Anderson.

I think it was the same assistant who executed in Giambellino's
studio the half-length figure of the Madonna who seems to offer
a gold coin to the somewhat retouched Child she holds in her
arms, in the Fine Arts Museum, Worcester, Mass. (^{1}), and the

(^{1}) *Berenson*, op. cit., p. 112.

example in which the Child stands to the other side and looks away from His Mother in the gallery of Glasgow (32, old number 89), which in parts, particularly the dress, has been very much restored (Gronau 193) [1]. As Herr Gronau observes, the composition derives from Giambellino's Madonna which was to be seen in the Barberini Gallery.

The composition of the Barberini Madonna is more faithfully repeated in a picture which at one time belonged to Sir B. Samuelson, London, and which, though of inferior quality, might be from the same hand. SS. Bartholomeo and Catherine accompany the Virgin and the background is formed by an extensive landscape. Replicas and copies are very numerous [2]. To some· of them the name of Rondinelli has been assigned but they are certainly not from his hand.

It is just possible that this painter might be held responsible also for a panel of the Madonna in half-length figure adoring the nude Child seated on a low wall in front of her, which bears the signature of Giovanni Bellini, in the Witgenstein collection, Vienna (Gronau, 111). Of this painting also there exist some copies; of those by Pietro da Messina one is preserved in Sta. Maria Formosa, Venice [3].

The sweet prettiness and softness of these paintings is found also in a figure of St. Sebastian against a landscape background, which work is known to me only from reproduction (Gronau, 89).

*_**

Rocco Marconi was not really an adherent of the school of Giovanni Bellini but none the less it is to this environment that we can trace his starting point, because a picture signed by him in the gallery of Strasbourg is but a copy of Bellini's signed Madonna of towards 1510 which belongs to Messrs Duveen; there is only a slight variation in the background, which is more spring-like in appearance. Another copy from his hand exists in the

---

[1] Mr. Berenson is of the opinion that is it for the greater part by Bellini.

[2] They are enumerated by *Gronau*, p. 209; to his list I can add a fairly mediocre example with hills and towns in the background which was for sale in Venice some years ago.

[3] See Vol. XV, p. 570. *Gronau*, op. cit., p. 209.

Fig. 220. Rocco Marconi(?), Madonna and Saints. Redentore Church, Venice.   Photo Anderson.

gallery of Breslau. The Virgin and Child are again repeated but here between SS. Jerome(?) and Francis in an oblong picture in the Redentore church (¹), which is often attributed to Pasqualino (fig. 220), and between SS. John the Baptist and Peter in a painting formerly in the Giovanelli collection, Venice, which was ascribed to Catena. Probably all these are by Rocco Marconi whom we might hold responsible also for the much talked of, but fairly mediocre, oblong picture of the Madonna in half-length figure holding the nude Child in benediction standing in front of her with St. Joseph and a round building in the background,

---

(¹) Attributed to Giambellino by *Ridolfi*, p. 71, who states that here the master took after his pupil Giorgione and that the St. Francis is the portrait of the prior of the monastery. *Moschini*, II, p. 35, repeats Ridolfi's remarks about Giorgione's influence. *Gronau*, op. cit., p. 215, cites, as I mentioned before, other copies of this Madonna by Bellini; he ascribes the painting in the Redentore church to Bissolo and the Giovanelli example to Vincenzo da Treviso.

which is found in the church of S. Fantino ([1]). Lastly, it is just possible that Rocco Marconi, while still in his Belliniesque phase, painted the strange looking Madonna seated on a throne placed high up and holding the nude Child Who blesses standing on her knee, which picture is preserved in the Jacquemart André Museum, Paris (671) ([2]); there is an abundance of drapery which is treated with marked effect and a curtain curiously hung on a rope covers most of the landscape background.

*
* *

Lattanzio da Rimini ([3]) was at one time a faithful pupil of Giovanni Bellini; he collaborated with this master in 1492 in the decoration of the big council hall and was the best-paid artist after Giambellini and Alvise Vivarini ([4]). A Madonna with the Child on her knee in the "Schloss Museum" of Berlin (fig. 221), which is signed "*Alunno Latantio*", is a free copy of one of the master's most popular creations of this period, of which composition there exist many other replicas, all executed in Bellini's workshop ([5]).

In the altar-piece which he painted between 1500 and 1504 for the church of S. Martino at Piazza Brembana, near Bergamo (fig. 222), the artist, as Professor Fiocco has observed, is no longer purely Belliniesque but already shows an influence of Cima, not only in the shape of the polyptych — a large panel showing St. Martin and the beggar with two saints in the lateral panels and two half-length saints to either side above — but also in the types, in the landscape and in the sky. A strong influence of Cima is notice-

---

([1]) *Sansovino*, pp. 46 verso, 47, tells us that the Madonna in this church was miraculous and that it given by the Pisana family. He does not mention Bellini as its author in the text; he does so only in the index. *Boschini*, p. 124. *Moschini*, I, p. 622. *Zanotto*, Pinac. Venez., II, pl. 89, all cite it as a work by Bellini. However, as neither *Sansovino* nor *Boschini* mentions the St. Joseph, one wonders if they really refer to this picture.

([2]) Catalogued as Venetian school towards 1510 with the combined influence of Giovanni Bellini and Giorgione.

([3]) G. *Ludwig*, Jahrb. K. Preus. Kunstsamml., XXIV, 1905, Beiheft, pp. 26, 32. *Berenson*, Venetian Painting in America, p. 227. G. *Fiocco*, L. d. R., Bollettino d'Arte del Minist. dell' Ed. Naz., February 1923, p. 363. *Thieme-Becker*, Künstlerlexikon, XXII, p. 427. R. *Buscaroli*, La pitt. romagnola del Quattrocento, Faenza (1931), p. 442.

([4]) *Gaye*, Carteggio, II, p. 71.

([5]) *Gronau*, op. cit., p. 210.

Fig. 221.　Lattanzio da Rimini, Madonna. Schloss-Museum, Berlin.

Museum photograph.

able also in a signed panel dated 1505 of St. John the Baptist between SS. Peter and John the Evangelist against a landscape background at Mezzoldo (Valle Brembana) and in an important picture of St. John the Baptist between SS. Peter and Paul at Noale, in which the landscape is visible through a loggia. Obviously, several elements in these works have been taken from Cima's altar-piece in the church of the Madonna dell' Orte in

Fig. 222. Lattanzio da Rimini, Triptych. S. Martino, Piazza Brembana.
Photo Ist. di Arti Grafiche.

Venice. A signed painting of the Madonna in half-length figure
with the nude Child on her knee against a landscape background
intersected centrally by a curtain, which at one time was on the
art market (Fiocco, fig. 3), seems to be lacking in style and shows
a certain slackness which tends almost to boorishness.

There are records of a Madonna, formerly in the Guggenheim
collection and afterwards acquired by Prince Liechtenstein, and
again of another Madonna with SS. John the Baptist and Jerome,
signed: "*Lactantius Ariminensis*", which formed part of the
Costabile collection in Ferrara, but we have lost sight of these

works. Both Sansovino and Boschini inform us that Lattanzio, victorious in a competition against Cima, painted in 1499 a "Sermon of St. Mark" for the chapel of the "Annunciata ai Gesuiti", which building was destroyed in 1674.

Evidently this minor artist started his career as a faithful pupil of Bellini; at a later stage he came under the influence of Cima but when he was left to his own devices his artistic standing considerably deteriorated.

Von Hadeln attributes to Lattanzio a drawing of St. Mark preaching, in the library of the Duke of Devonshire at Chatsworth (¹) — possibly the sketch of the painting of 1499 — which drawing, curiously enough, was copied by Rembrandt (²).

There are still several other workshop productions which I do not think can be connected with any particular pupil or collaborator of Giambellino. The most important of them are the large triptych in the gallery of Düsseldorf and the altar-piece of the Madonna enthroned between SS. Peter and Paul, who present three adorers, in the Walters collection, Baltimore (Gronau, 187). The latter is the picture which Ridolfi, who omits to mention the St. Peter, and Zanetti (p. 56) describe as in the "Procuratoria di Ultra" (³). Zanetti affirms that it was signed but the signature, along with the date 1510 which was originally inscribed on it, has since disappeared. However the connection with the dated Madonna of the same year in the Brera is very obvious. It is a fine piece of painting but we cannot fail to remark the very evident Titianesque tendency.

The triptych in Düsseldorf (fig. 223) originates from the Priuli chapel in the church of S. Michele, Murano, the construction of which was commenced in 1495 (⁴), but this date is of little interest

---

(¹) *Hadeln*, Venez. Zeichn. des Quattrocento, pl. 83. *Hofstede de Groot*, Jahrb. K. Preus. Kunstsamml., XV, 1894, p. 177 and *W. Hausenstein*, Carpaccio, Berlin, 1925, p. 154, attribute this drawing to Carpaccio.

(²) *Valentiner*, Rembrandt Handzeichnungen, II (Klassiker der Kunst), pl. 193.

(³) In 1828 it was in the Wendelstadt collection in Frankfort v. *von Hadeln*, ed. Ridolfi, p. 71, note 6 and *Gronau*, Spätwerke, pl. 22. *Berenson*, Venetian Painting in America, p. 136.

(⁴) *E. Ludwig*, Jahrb. der K. Preus. Kuntsamml., XXIV, 1903, p. 142. *Berenson*, Venetian Painting in America, p. 136. *R. Klapheck*, Die Kunstsammlungen der Staatl. Kunst. zu Düsseldorf, Düsseldorf, 1928, p. 26.

Fig. 223. Workshop of Giovanni Bellini, Madonna and Saints. Gallery, Düsseldorf. Photo Söhn.

because the work again shows obvious stylistic connexion with Bellini's Madonnas of 1509 and 1510. Sansovino (p. 86), Vasari probably (p. 163) (¹), Ridolfi (p. 66) and Moschini (II, p. 413) all mention this picture; consequently it was one of the well-known works which passed under the name of Giovanni Bellini, whose signature besides is inscribed on the pedestal of the throne, a corner of which is covered by the rich folds of the Madonna's cloak. In each of the lateral panels we see two full-length figures of saints of whom we can recognize only the St. Peter; at the feet of the two to the right kneels a patrician, hooded and dressed in black. The execution is very soft and pleasing and reminds us to a certain extent of the technique of Basaiti.

The strong influence of Titian which we have already observed in the picture of 1513 in S. Giovanni Crisostomo, Venice, may

---

(¹) It is generally understood that *Vasari*, III, p. 163, in mentioning the picture in S. Michele, Murano, refers to the Madonna of 1488 with the Doge Barbarigo (note 2) but as he speaks of it immediately after the triptych in the Frari church and describes it as "una similmente", it seems more likely that his reference is to a triptych.

Fig. 224. Giovanni Bellini and Vittore Belliniano, Baptism. S. Giovanni
di Malta, Vienna.   Photo Wolfoum.

be due in some cases to the collaboration of Vittore Belliniano.
This observation is confirmed if we look at the picture of the
martyrdom of St. Mark executed for the Scuola di San Marco, for
which Giovanni accepted the order in 1515 but which was executed in 1526 by Vittore, who signed it. For many years it was
in the gallery of Vienna but in 1919 was restored to Venice and
is now in the Accademia ([1]).

I believe that Vittore in all probability assisted Giovanni
Bellini in the execution of the Baptism which likewise was
taken to Austria but is now in its original site in the church of
S. Giovanni di Malta or dei Furlani in Venice, where it was seen

---

([1]) *Suida*, Burlington Magazine, Oct. 1927, p. 182. This painting appears
to be almost unknown. According to Berenson it is for the greater part
by Bellini.

Fig. 225. Workshop of Giovanni Bellini, Circumcision. Museo Civico, Verona. Photo Anderson.

by Ridolfi (fig. 224). The figures of the Saviour and the Baptist are copied from the painting of the same subject in the church of Sta. Corona, Vicenza, and the signature of Giovanni Bellini is inscribed in the same place. Here, however, the angels are different and are only two in number, while a figure of an adorer has been added; he wears the attire of a Knight of Malta but this of course is due to a later alteration. The landscape also is very different and has quite a Cinquecentesque Venetian character.

An interesting workshop production, probably a repetition of a lost original by the master himself — because one can hardly imagine that the numerous extant replicas were all made after this studio work — is the Circumcision with Giovanni Bellini's signature in the museum of Verona (fig. 225). Another good example, in which the features are strongly moulded, exists in the museum of Berlin (36) (fig. 226) (¹), while the finest of them all

(¹) This I believe is the same picture which *Gronau* (189) reproduces as belonging to Messrs Boehler, Munich. For the numerous copies among which are those by Bissolo, Vincenzo da Treviso and Bartolomeo Veneto

Fig. 226. Workshop of Giovanni Bellini, the Circumcision. Museum, Berlin.   Museum Photo.

and the one nearest to the master is that cut into an oval in the

v. *Geiger*, Jahrb. der K. Preus. Kunstsamml., XXXIII, 1912, p. 11. *Gronau*, Spätwerke, p. 16. *The Same*, Pinacoteca, 1928, p. 115. *The Same*, Giovanni Bellini, p. 218. *Von Hadeln*, Cicerone, II, 1910, p. 635.

gallery of Vienna (15), which is attributed to Bissolo and Catena. The example in S. Zaccaria, Venice, which Zanetti (p. 48) and Moschini (I, p. 122) both mention as a work by Bellini, has been claimed with good reason by Mr. Berenson for Francesco da Santacroce. In as far as the figures of the Madonna holding the Child above the table, St. Joseph and the venerable high-priest Simon are concerned all these pictures are the same in composition, but in every case there is some variation in the female figure behind the Virgin. Vincenzo da Treviso, in his very mediocre signed copy in the museum of Padua, depicts here a woman in full face, for which figure he has used as model one of Giovanni Bellini's Madonnas of 1509 or 1510.

A very important and rather perplexing picture is the large altar-piece in the National Gallery (750) representing the Madonna on a niche-shaped throne, with St. Christopher behind and St. John the Baptist presenting the kneeling Doge Giovanni Mocenigo who carries a banner in his hand; the background is formed by a landscape with a lake and a white cloudy sky (fig. 227). This painting is supposed to have been made on the occasion of the plague of 1478, the remedy for which is contained in the vase on the altar. Of the different theories regarding this picture, I think that proposed by Gronau, in agreement with Paoletti, that it might have been begun by Gentile and, after his departure in 1479, finished by Giovanni, seems the most acceptable because, as Prof. A. Venturi has already pointed out, there are elements in this canvas which remind us of both masters [1]. I shall mention very briefly some other studio productions.

In the collection of Sir Herbert Cook, Richmond (Gronau, 195), there is a very handsome Madonna resembling that in the Metropolitan Museum, which is sometimes attributed to Rondinelli, as is also the Madonna in full face with the nude curly-headed Child in benediction, which is found in the Doria Gallery. In the church of S. Trovaso, Venice, there is a picture of the same subject but of a different composition which has been inspired by Bellini's last manner, as is also a Madonna and Child against a landscape

---

[1] *Cavalcaselle*: Carpaccio. *Ludwig*, Repert. fur Kunstwiss., XXIII, 1900, p. 278: Lazzaro Bastiani. *Paoletti*, Arte e Storia, XXVI, 1907, p. 54, *Gronau*, op. cit., p. 204. *L. Venturi*, op. cit., p. 283: Jacopo Belli (?).

Fig. 227. Gentile and Giovanni Bellini(?), Madonna and Saints and
Giovanni Mocenigo. National Gallery, London.

background, with an adorer just visible, in a private collection([1]). Comparing the latter work with the painting signed by Pier Maria Pennacchi in the museum of Bassano ([2]), which however is not the most typical of this master's style, we might very well imagine that it is from the same hand.

Other productions of Giambellino's workshop are the Madonna in the museum of Capodistria ([3]) and that in the museum of Bonn ([4]); the latter shows a connexion with the picture in the Brady collection. A bust of the Saviour in the Maynard collection, London, which seems to be a studio work, is a free copy of the example in Madrid ([5]).

Workshop productions which reflect the master's last manner are: a particularly fine panel of the Madonna holding the sleeping Child bedded on cushions on a low wall, in a private collection (fig. 228), and the weak portrait of a Dominican monk bearing the semblance of St. Peter the Martyr with palm-leaf, sword in breast and knife in his head in the National Gallery, London (808), which work shows the false signature of Giovanni and is ascribed to Gentile by von Hadeln ([6]) and in the old catalogue. Mr. Berenson includes it among the works by Giovanni. In the collection of the seminary of Venice (19) there is an oxidized and scarcely recognizable portrait of a man with a black bonnet which is attributed to Bartolomeo Vivarini but which looks sooner like a fine Belliniesque production. Another beautiful portrait still nearer to Giambellino is the bust of a youth, his head turned to one side, which bears the master's signature but which seems just a little too soft in treatment to be from Bellini's own hand. It formed part of the Holford collection, London ([7]).

A very handsome workshop production which reflects Bellini's art around the year 1509 is an oblong altar-piece recently

[1] I know this work only from the reproduction given by *Gronau*, Spätwerke, pl. 24.

[2] *Fiocco*, Rivista del R. Ist. d'Archeol. e della Storia dell' Arte, I, p. 103, fig. 6.

[3] *F. Semi*, Rivista d'Arte, XVI, 1934, p. 76: Giambellino.

[4] *Berenson*, Venetian Painting in America, p. 91.

[5] Reprod. by *Borenius*, Gall. A. Vendramin, p. 28.

[6] *Von Hadeln*, op. cit., Repert. f. Kunstwiss., XXX.

[7] *R. H. Benson*, The Holford Collection, London, 1924, No. 22. *Gronau*, op. cit., pl. 122 and p. 211. No. 12 of the Holford sale which took place in London in July 1927.

Fig. 228. Workshop of Giovanni Bellini, Madonna. Private Collection.

loaned to the Art Gallery of Birmingham. It represents the seated Madonna, visible to the knees, with the nude Child seated on her hand, between SS. John the Baptist, Sebastian and two other saints (John the Evangelist and Ursula?). It might be one of those works which were executed by Basaiti in Giambellino's studio (¹).

(¹) *Waterhouse*, op. cit. No. 264 of the Exhib. of Art Treasures in the Midlands, Birmingham, 1934.

Executed possibly in Giovanni Bellini's workshop and certainly by a painter who at one time was intimately connected with the master and his art but who since that moment had considerably evolved, is a large and very fine picture in the gallery of Glasgow. Separated from the rich landscape by a curtain the Madonna is seated on a high throne holding on her knee the nude Child Who bestows a blessing, three angels playing on musical instruments are seated on the steps of the throne; the two youthful SS. John as well as SS. Peter and Sebastian are depicted to the sides. This painting is not easily classified; the Belliniesque elements abound but the manner is more evolved and the drapery in particular points to a period slightly later than that in which Giambellino was active [1].

* * *

[1] *J. Paton*, Catalogue of the Pictures in the Glasgow Art Gallery and Museum, Kelvingrove, Glasgow, 1908, p. 17 et seq., mentions the different opinions held about this painting; they range from Giorgione to Montagna. At one time Mr. Berenson ascribed it to Beccaruzzi; *Fiocco*, L'Arte, XIX, 1916, p. 196, to Oliviero.

The following is a list of school works which were not executed in the master's workshop and which are not by any of his identified followers: **Basel,** Bachofen Museum, No. 1133, Madonna with Child in benediction, hilly landscape with buildings in background, greatly restored. **Bergamo,** Gallery, No. 401, Madonna and Child; No. 181, small but handsome bust portrait of a young man. **Bologna,** Davia Bargellini Museum, Madonna. **Boston,** H. Wetzel coll., Madonna with Child standing in benediction, after the same type as Bellini's Madonnas of about 1510 (*Berenson*, Venetian Painting in America, p. 137). **Dijon**, Museum, No. 2, Madonna adoring the sleeping Child. **Dublin,** National Gallery, No. 244, man's portrait, unimportant. **Florence,** Serrestori coll., large picture of Madonna and Child against a landscape background. **Gubbio,** Gallery, Pietà with five figures around the Saviour and an adorer whose appearance points to a later date. **Mombaroccio** (The Marches), Town Hall, Madonna and Child between St. John the Baptist and another saint, unimportant. **New York,** Metropolitan Museum, four polyptych panels, each showing a saint (*Berenson*, Venetian Painting in America, p. 109, fig. 46); Alphonse Kahn sale, January 1927, No. 49, head of Madonna, a fragment; Schneewindt coll., small bust of a beardless man. **Nîmes,** Museum, No. 439, the Madonna adoring the Child Who lies sleeping on a low wall; No. 486, half-length figure of the Madonna with the nude Child between the infant St. John and an adorer. **Padua,** Museum, No. 21, Madonna, slightly turned to the right, wearing a high veil and holding the nude Child, with a curtain and landscape as background; No. 26, the dead Saviour supported in a sitting position by the Virgin and four of the faithful, landscape background, attributed to Montagna; it is by a follower of Bellini; No. 27, Madonna with holy bishop and St. Jerome; No. 28, oblong picture of the Virgin in half-length figure with the Child, one female and two male saints; No. 49, oblong painting of the Madonna seated with the Child on her knee, St. Catherine and St. John the Baptist who presents an adorer; No. 127, Madonna adoring the Child Who lies before her on a low wall against a background of a curtain and a landscape; No. 418, half-length figure of the Madonna with the upright Child Who holds a lamb; No. 423, dead Christ between the Virgin and St. John; No. 2294, half-length figure of the Madonna, turned to the right, adoring the Child Who reclines on a low wall. **Perugia,** Gallery, Adoration of the Magi, a fine picture reflecting Bellini's last manner. **Philadelphia,** Memorial Hall, the Meal at Emmaus, copy with variations of the lost original (*Berenson*, Venetian Painting in America, p. 120, fig. 51). **Pisa,** Schiff coll., half-length figure of the dead Christ. **Rome,** Villa Borghese, profile portrait of Petrarch, shows a vague connexion with Bellini. **Sebenico,** Svetti Lovro, Madonna. **Subiaco,** Sacro Speco, sacristy, two panels, SS. Peter and Paul, vaguely school of Bellini (*Hermanin* in *Egidi, Giovannoni e Hermanin*, Il Sacro-Speco, I, Rome, 1904, p. 531). **Toledo, U. S. A.,** Museum, half-length figure of the blessing Christ. **Venice,** Correr Museum, oblong picture of the Madonna with the nude Child in her arms between SS. John the Baptist and Onophrius, by a follower of Bellini's last manner; oblong painting of the Madonna between SS. Jerome and Catherine, unimportant; Madonna with the Child Who grasps her dress near the neck, landscape and curtain background, approximate to Cima; ex-Recanati-Giustiniani coll., Madonna in full-face holding the nude Child Whose hands are crossed on His breast, landscape with much sky as background (*Fogolari*, Rassegna d'Arte, XX, 1920, copy of lost original. *Gronau*, pl. 197). **Verona,** Museum (Turone room), small bust-length portrait of a man; No. 122, Madonna with the Child on her knee against a background of curtain and landscape. **Würzburg,** ex-von Hirsch coll., half-length figure of the Madonna with the Child, Who grasps a bird and looks round, standing on a low wall, against a landscape background (*Gronau*, 196, thinks that it is possibly by Bellini). **Vienna,** Lanckoronsky coll., head of the Saviour.

The lost Entombment from S. Pietro, Murano, was attributed by Ridolfi to Bellini, by Boschini to his school and by Moschini to Catena. In the "Magistrato delle Legne" in the Palazzo Ducale there was a picture of St. Mark between SS. Jerome, John the Baptist, Nicholas and Bonaventura, which Boschini (p. 99) described as "di maniera a tempi di Bellini".

Of the drawings of the school of Giambellino I shall mention the following: **Paris,** Louvre, 5600, Marriage of the Virgin and her Presentation in the Temple (Vallardi Album 10706—10707); young man on horseback; **Vienna,** Albertina, two saints one of whom reads a book (*Styx und Fröhlich Bum*, op. cit., No. 33). **Washington,** Corcoran Art Gallery, profile of a youngish man with long curly hair and a cap on his head.

There is a miniature painter of the name of Jacometto Veneziano ([1]) who shows, I am of opinion, much more connexion with
Giovanni Bellini than with Antonello da Messino, to whom his
only extant work is generally attributed. I refer to the two
miniature portraits in the Liechtenstein Gallery, Vienna, which,
according to Professor Longhi, provide us with proof of Piero
della Francesca's influence on Antonello.

We owe the information concerning Jacometto to Michiel ([2]),
who mentions in the house of Pietro Bembo in Padua a profile
portrait of this man at the age of eleven; consequently it was
painted in 1481. In the same house there was a small picture of
the life of some person but the name is left open. In 1532 he saw
many drawings by Jacometto in the house of Antonio Pasqualino
in Venice. An hourbook with miniatures by the same artist
belonged in 1512 to Francesco Zio in Venice. Michiel tells us
that the figure of St. Jerome in the famous picture by Antonello,
now in the National Gallery, the author of which had not at that
time been determined, had been "rifatta" by Jacometto. Further,
he speaks of a sketchbook of parchment with pen drawings of
animals and "candelabri" which, in 1530, was in the house of
Gabriel Vendramin in Venice. Michiel mentions as well small
pictures on parchment after Montagna and Raphael, coloured in
the manner of Jacometto by Michele Contarini, in whose house he
saw them in 1543; he also had in his possession small portraits of
Alvise Contarini, of another man, who was already deceased, and
of a nun of San Segondo; he tells us that on the cover of this
picture, which he greatly praises, there is a small carriage (car-
retta) in a landscape but it is more likely, as we shall see, that it
was a "capretta" (goat or hind).

Giovanni Bellini's influence is manifest in several Venetian woodcuts,
as for instance that of the Pietà — the Lord between two angels held
before His tomb — in the Missale Romanum, Venice, 1515 and in "La
Humanità del figliuolo di Dio" by Folengo, Venice, 1533; and that of a
demonstration in anatomy before a dissected body in the "Fasciculus
Medicine" by Ketham, Venice, 1500.

([1]) *Frimmel*, Blätter für Gemälde-Kunde, II, 1915—16, p. 16. G.
Gronau, idem, p. 48. *The Same*, Thieme-Becker, Künstlerlexikon, XVIII,
p. 264. *Lauts*, Jahrb. der Kunsthist. Samml. in Wien, N. F., VII, 1933,
p. 78.

([2]) *Michiel*, ed. Frimmel, pp. 20, 22, 82, 94, 98, 108, 112, 114.

Fig. 229. Jacometto Veneziano, two miniature portraits. Liechtenstein
Gallery, Vienna.

There can be little doubt that these are the portraits which are
now in the Liechtenstein Gallery (fig. 229); certainly the unattractive woman wears the habit of a nun of the order of San
Segondo; the second man is missing but the frame is of more
recent date so that originally there might easily have been three
figures. In an inventory of 1567 of the Vendramin collection
these paintings figure as works by Bellini (¹), and here the hind
which is painted on one of the panels is mentioned. It is probably
to this animal that Michiel refers although inaccurately he states
that it was on the cover. The hind is attached by a chain to a
medallion with the inscription *"AIEI"*, which in dialect means
"always".

The two little portraits are really master-pieces of miniature-
painting, not only on account of the fine technique in which the
figures are executed but also because of the beauty of the distant
landscape and the grandiose style which, in spite of the minute
dimensions, the painter has employed. In all probability practically all of Jacometto's further activity was devoted to miniature

---

(¹) *Rava*, op. cit.

painting and this is the reason why we cannot cite any other pictures from his hand.

We know that in a letter written in September 1497 by Placiola to a councillor of Francesco Gonzaga, Jacometto is mentioned as deceased ([1]).

---

[1] Arch. Stor. dell' Arte, I, 1888, p. 184. Of the two portraits in the Liechtenstein collection there exist copies in Montagna's house. The Connaisseur, XVIII, 1907, p. 141. A lady's portrait in the Guidi-Faenza collection was wrongly attributed to Jacometto: No. 239 and pl. 5 of the catalogue of the sale, Rome, 1902. *Reinach*, Repertoire de peintures, I, p. 251.

CHAPTER VI

CIMA DA CONEGLIANO ([1]).

The documents concerning the charming and very capable but somewhat monotonous artist who was Giovanni Battista Cima da Conegliano were first published by Botteon and Aliprandi; since then they have been repeated by several other historians of art.

As his name appears for the first time in the list of rate-payers of Conegliano in the year 1473 and as the inhabitants of the Veneto were inscribed as such only after they attained their majority — that is to say when they became fourteen years of age — he was born probably in 1459. His family can be traced back to the 14th century and exercised the trade of "cimator" or cloth-shavers, hence the name of Cima.

Although he still figures in the list of tax-payers of Conegliano in 1489, he very likely was already living in Venice, where he

---

([1]) *Berenson*, Venetian Painting in America, p. 186. *W. Bode u. G. Ludwig*, Jahrb. der K. Preus. Kunstsamml., XII, p. 142. *T. Borenius*, St. Jerome by C. da C., Burlington Magazine, XIX, 1911, p. 318. *V. Botteon e A. Aliprandi*, Ricerchi intorno alla vita e alle opere di G. C., Conegliano, 1893. *R. Burckhardt*, C. da C., Leipzig, 1905. *G. Fiocco*, Sebastiano del Piombo e C. da C., L'Arte, XV, 1912, pp. 293—298. *G. Frizzoni*, Il C. da C. di Castiglio alla Pinacoteca di Brera, Bollettino d'Arte, I, 1907, fasc. X. *The Same*, Una piccola tavola di C. da C. nel Museo Poldi Pezzoli, L'Arte, XI, 1908, p. 141. *The Same*, I soggetti mitologici in C. da C. a proposito di un nuovo aquisto del Museo Poldi Pezzoli, Rassegna d'Arte, VIII, 1908, p. 41. *D. von Hadeln*, C. da C. in Thieme-Becker, Künstlerlexikon, VI, 1912, p. 593. *The Same*, An unknown work by C. da C., Burlington Magazine, July 1926, p. 3. *G. Milanese*, Commentario alla vita di Vitt. Scarpaccia, in Vasari, Vite, III, p. 663. *Morelli*, Critical Studies, I, p. 277. *A. Venturi*, Opere poco note di C. da C., L'Arte, XXIX, 1926, p. 182. *The Same*, Quadro inedito di G. C. d. C., L'Arte, XXXVII, 1934, p. 482. *L. V(enturi)*, Recension of Bruckhardt's monograph, in L'Arte, VIII, 1905, p. 308. *M. Wackernagel*, Un altare di C. a Miglionico, L'Arte, X, 1907, p. 372.

is recorded in a document as early as 1492; the following year in the contract for the altar-piece for the cathedral of Conegliano he is mentioned as "pictor eximius Venetiis" and again in 1516 he is spoken of as a painter in Venice. In the last years of his life he returned to Conegliano and there in October 1516 contracted to execute a picture. He was buried in his native town on the 3rd of September of either 1517 or 1518.

As to the question from whom Cima received his education, I should like to state at the outset that I hold the opinion that Cima owes almost all in his work that is not the outcome of his own artistic individuality to Giovanni Bellini. I shall not appeal to the statements made by ancient critics, although I should just like to say that Sansovino calls him Bellini's "allievo", Vasari his "discepolo" and Ridolfi describes him as "tra i primi imitatori di Bellini". As a matter of fact only the modern critics have abandoned this conception of the origin of Cima's art. Burckhardt, in his fine monograph on the master, comes to the conclusion that Bartolomeo Montagna was his real teacher. Mr. Berenson suggests that the fact that we find Cima's earliest activity in Vicenza might have been the cause of this hypothesis; he himself believes that he was probably a pupil of Alvise Vivarini but was formed under the influence of Antonello and Giovanni Bellini ([1]).

The earliest authentic work we know by Cima is the altar-piece from the church of S. Bartolomeo, Vicenza, now in the town gallery (fig. 230). It is signed and dated: "*Joanes Baptista de Conegliano fecit 1489 adi p°. marzo*" and shows a great knowledge of Bellini's art but not a perfect familiarity with the master's latest development; a really intimate collaborator would have painted in a different manner after the creation of the Frari triptych. Cima, however, had certainly seen this master-piece when he painted the picture in Vicenza. The general lines of the composition, with the Madonna on a high pedestal under a vault, the saint to the left in profile and the figure to the right facing the spectator, correspond too closely with the group of the Frari triptych for us to imagine that the resemblance is fortuitous. Further, the way in which the Child stands on His Mother's knee is also similar. However, there is something in the very broken

---

([1]) Previously he thought him to be a pupil of Alvise influenced by Giambellino.

folds of the drapery of St. James which reminds us of several of Montagna's works but as they are all after 1489 it might be conjectured that it was this painter who borrowed the idea from Cima. And when we compare Montagna's Madonna between SS. Sebastian and Roch of 1487 in the gallery of Bergamo — one of his few works prior to 1489 — with Cima's altar-piece at Vicenza we are forced to admit that Cima owes practically nothing to the slightly older artist.

As to the setting of the figures, it might be said that the wall with the tops of trees appearing above it seems to be purely Florentine, in fact this feature can be traced back through Verrocchio and the school of Ghirlandaio to Fra Angelico; and once we are on this road one wonders if the pergola with the vines hanging on it does not betray a knowledge of Benozzo's frescoes of the vintage in Pisa, or of Botticelli's enthroned Madonna between two saints in the gallery of Berlin, or again of Domenico Veneziano's Annunciation, now in the museum of Cambridge. Besides, the form of the framing niche, though not exclusively Florentine, is all the same well known in Florence, particularly in the artistic circle of Verrocchio. The face of the bearded old saint is purely Belliniesque, so too that of St. James who corresponds with Bellini's type of St. John the Baptist.

The Madonna and Child are also closely inspired by Giambellino who, shortly before his Madonna of 1487, seems to have returned to the image of the Virgin with the Infant Jesus standing on her knee. The Madonna herself, with the high draped veil, elongated features and rather severe folds, does not particularly resemble the type employed by Giambellino at this moment, of which that of the Frari triptych is the finest example, but reminds us of that of a slightly earlier period when the reminiscences of Mantegna had not yet entirely disappeared.

As Burckhardt remarks, the fine picture of Vicenza with its finished technique, marvellous colours, monumental composition and perfect rendering of space and perspective looks anything but the work of a beginner and as a matter of fact, for all we know, the artist might have been thirty years old when he executed this important painting.

The question now arises, which works Cima painted prior to this date. Admitting that at an earlier stage he was still more

Fig. 230. Cima da Conegliano, Madonna and Saints, 1489. Museo Civico,
Vicenza.   Photo Alinari.

directly inspired by Bellini, several works enter into consideration.

Burckhardt (¹) has already cited as such the panels on a gold

(¹) *Burckhardt*, op. cit., p. 125.

background of the standing figures of SS. Sebastian, Peter, John
the Baptist and Roch and above, the half-length figures of
SS. Catherine, Jerome, Francis, Mary Magdalene and the Virgin
with the Child. These paintings, which are preserved in the parish
church of Olera, near Bergamo, form part of a retable, the centre
of which is composed of a wooden statue of St. Bartholomew. I
quite agree with Burckhardt's opinion that this work was
painted prior to the altar-piece of 1489 but there are some other
paintings which seem to have been executed at a still earlier
period.

I think the earliest work I know by Cima is a seated Madonna
visible to the knees which I saw some years ago for sale in Amsterdam but of which I have since lost sight. The Madonna faces
three-quarters to the left; the Child in her arms wears a little
shirt, and a curtain and a landscape with a lake form the background. We notice in this work those hesitations and the lack
of finish and perfection which we might expect from a beginner. In the position of the figures there is a certain similarity
with the Madonna in the Cook collection.

There is one consideration which might make us a little doubtful about assigning this picture, along with several others by
Cima, to such an early date; it is that the idea of the landscape
background partly concealed by a curtain does not appear in
Bellini's works until 1487 or 1488 at the very earliest. The
simplest solution, and perhaps the most likely one, would be to
admit that this detail, which after all is not of very great importance, had been introduced by Cima and taken over from him by
Giovanni Bellini, because there are several of Cima's works in
which this background appears which I think are of earlier date
than the paintings in which Bellini first employs this feature.
Moreover, Bellini's Baptism at Vicenza proves to us that he was
not averse to borrowing models from Cima and we come across
still other cases in which he followed Cima's example.

I am rather doubtful about Mr. Berenson's affirmation that
Cima's signed Madonna in the Institute of Arts of Detroit is the
earliest work which has come to our knowledge. The Virgin is
shown in half-length figure, adoring the nude Child Who is seated
in front of her against a background formed by a curtain and a
landscape. It is true that Giovanni Bellini's influence is very

obvious here, but I find that that of Antonello is much less, if at all, visible. The round oval of the face and the ample forms and drapery lead us to believe that we are dealing with a production of a later moment than that in which the above works were created.

On the other hand, something of the Mantegnesque incisiveness in the drawing of the folds, which in Giambellino's works is visible, possibly for the last time, in the Coronation of the Virgin at Pesaro, is evident in a signed Madonna in the Johnson collection, Philadelphia (fig. 231) ([1]); she is depicted in three-quarter left profile holding the nude Child with one hand and supporting His head with the other, a position which seems to be of Cima's own invention. The landscape, which occupies half the background and in which we see a town, is treated with particular care. The type and features of the Madonna, with rather a long face, also correspond more to those of this stage in Giovanni Bellini's career (compare No. 2901 of the National Gallery).

There exist several replicas of this Madonna and I think most of them are from the master's own hand. One of them, which is of slightly later date, is found in the collection of Mr. August Franzen, New York; another, executed in a considerably more evolved style, belongs to a private collection ([2]). Mr. Berenson mentions a signed example, very similar to that in the Johnson collection but of better quality, which at one time was in the possession of the art-dealer Sedelmeyer in Paris; he cites, as well, a copy which he thinks is by Cima's imitator, Antonio Maria da Carpi, in the collection of the late Mr. Davis, Newport.

I agree with the opinion, not generally accepted however, that Cima should be held responsible for the important picture of St. Mark enthroned between St. Andrew with his cross and a young holy bishop reading — St. Louis of Toulouse? — against a background of sea and hills, in the collection of the Art Academy in Vienna (fig. 232). The tiled floor in the foreground, the reliefs which adorn the throne and the birds depicted here and there are of the finest technique. The venerable figure of

---

([1]) No. 176 of Mr. Berenson's catalogue of the Italian pictures in this collection.

([2]) No. 29 of the catalogue of the sale of the Ventura collection, which was held in Milan in April 1932.

Fig. 231. Cima da Conegliano, Madonna. Johnson Collection, Philadelphia.
Courtesy of the John G. Johnson Art Coll., Philadelphia.

St. Andrew shows some connexion with Carpaccio's manner of
painting but the St. Mark and the holy bishop are, I think, quite
typical of Cima at an early period. The picture has been attributed to Busati, Gerolamo da Udine and Bonifacio Pitati.
Apparently the figures of Temperance and Justice, now in the

Fig. 232. Cima da Conegliano, St. Mark and Saints. Art Academy, Vienna.

gallery of Venice (165, 167), formed the lateral parts of this
picture; they seem to be by a close adherent of Cima's early
manner, probably Gerolamo da Udine, with whom we shall deal
later. These paintings originate from the Camera dell' Armamenti
in the Palazzo Ducale where Zanetti saw them ([1]).

Certainly an early work of Cima's is the important but somewhat restored altar-piece in the Brera Gallery, Milan (175); it was
previously in the church of S. Giovanni Battista at Oderzo and
from there was brought to Castiglio (fig. 233) ([2]). Under a vault,
which might be that of the choir of a church, resting on beautifully decorated pillars, the Madonna is seated on a very high
throne accompanied by SS. Sebastian, John the Baptist, Mary
Magdalene and Roch, while two groups of adorers kneel below.
The composition is very different from that of Bellini's triptych
in the Frari church and sooner leads the way to that of the
S. Zaccaria altar-piece. He has introduced the happy novelty of
replacing the apsidal wall by open sky which is visible under the
vault, and this has the effect of increasing the space around the
enthroned Madonna. Again we are confronted with the possibility that this idea originated with Cima and not with Giovanni
Bellini, who also executed a monumental picture of the Madonna
and saints under a vault with a skyscape visible beyond, but it
was destroyed by fire in 1867 in the church of SS. Giovanni e
Paolo and is known to us only from the engraving in Zanotto's
Pinacoteca Veneziana (v. fig. 195). However, we have no certain
date for either the one or the other but, as I said when dealing
with Giambellino's lost altar-piece, if Zanotto's print is a faithful
reproduction the master must have created the work at a moment
not far distant from that in which he executed the S. Zaccaria
retable. This he did in 1505, although Cavalcaselle propounded
the hypothesis that it was painted shortly after 1472, but this
must have been a mere flight of fancy because in his day no
datable work of Bellini's early activity was known. On the other
hand in Cima's picture in the Brera there are some features
so early that both von Hadeln and Berenson were inclined to
place it prior to the painting of 1489, were it not for the fact that,

---

([1]) A copy with variations of the central panel by Busati exists in the
gallery of Venice.

([2]) *Frizzoni*, op. cit., Bollettino d'Arte, 1907.

Fig. 233. Cima da Conegliano, Madonna and Saints. Brera Gallery, Milan.
Photo Alinari.

according to Botteon and Aliprandi, the date 149 . . . was at one time visible on it; nowadays the 9 also has been effaced. Even so, I am of the firm opinion that Cima's altar-piece from Oderzo

XVII.   26

Fig. 234. Cima da Conegliano, Madonna and Saints. Gallery, Troyes.

Photo Bulloz.

was executed before the picture Giambellino made for SS. Giovanni e Paolo.

The graceful type of the Virgin of this retable appears in several other paintings by Cima; two of them are identical. They represent the Madonna, in slightly more than half-length figure, holding in her left arm the nude Child Who bestows a blessing, between SS. John the Baptist and Francis, while six cherubim fly over head; on a little label in the right lower corner we read the signature. The better of the two is preserved in the gallery of Düsseldorf (¹) and the other, which is but slightly inferior, in that of Troyes (fig. 234). The same Madonna and Child but without saints and with a background of sky and a curtain is found on a picture in the Walters collection, Baltimore (²).

Certainly from a period prior to the regular flow of dated works which started with the altar-piece of 1493 in the cathedral of Conegliano are the signed Madonna in the Cook collection,

(¹) *Klapheck*, op. cit., p. 17.
(²) *Berenson*, Venetian Painting in America, p. 195.

Fig. 235. Cima da Conegliano, Madonna. Cook Collection, Richmond.
Photo Anderson.

Richmond, which is strongly Belliniesque (fig. 235), a Crucifixion belonging to Messrs Agnew and a Deposition in the gallery of Venice (604). The Crucifixion (fig. 236) (¹) is one of the finest and

(¹) *Von Hadeln*, op. cit., Burlington Magazine, 1926. *L. Venturi*, Pitt. ital. in America, pl. 311.

Fig. 236. Cima da Conegliano, Crucifixion. Agnew Collection, London.
Photo Cooper.

most inspired pictures I know from the hand of the master. The
draperies of the Virgin and St. John are not without a Mantegnesque touch as transmitted through Bellini, and the plastic effects

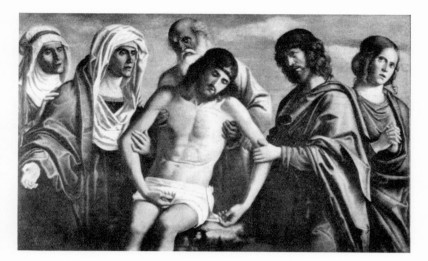

Fig. 237. Cima da Conegliano, Deposition. Accademia, Venice.

Photo Anderson.

are rendered with more subtlety than usual. All the figures, including those in Pilate's palace, to the left, and in the scene of the Prayer in the Garden of Olives, to the right, are enveloped in a beautiful golden light and for once the otherwise rather phlegmatic artist expresses deep emotion in the central group.

Even the signed Deposition in the gallery of Venice, although painted along similar lines, is already not of quite the same quality (fig. 237). The Virgin and St. John who, together with the aged Joseph of Arimathea, hold the body of Christ, are lacking in subtlety when we compare them with those of the Crucifixion. However, this panel also, in which we see as well a middle-aged companion of the Virgin to the left and a handsome young female saint to the right, is still one of Cima's fine creations. Zanetti mentions a picture of this subject in the convent of Sta. Maria del Carmine which might be the same work.

Much finer in quality and probably of the same rather early period is I think the painting of St. Jerome in penitence in a very elaborate landscape with rocks, trees, a lake and hills in the distance, in the National Gallery (1120) (fig. 238). Zanetti speaks of a similar picture in the Scuola dei Mercanti; perhaps it is that now in the National Gallery, the provenance of which is unknown.

Fig. 238. Cima da Conegliano, St. Jerome. National Gallery, London.
Photo National Gallery.

The altar-piece in the cathedral of Conegliano, for which Cima
received the order in January 1493 and which he finished in May,
is of an over-crowded composition (fig. 239); the six saints who
stand to either side of the Madonna's throne are too large for the
available space and compared with the architecture are almost

Fig. 239. Cima da Conegliano, Madonna and Saints, 1493. Cathedral, Conegliano.   Photo Anderson.

gigantic. The picture is mentioned by Ridolfi. In composition it approaches closely to that of Bellini's lost altar-piece in SS. Giovanni e Paolo; here again we see the open vault and the sky as background to the Madonna, but the saints and angels have so greatly increased in number that they occupy all the space around the throne, and comparing the grouping in Bellini's altar-piece with that of Cima's, we are struck all the more by the lack of proportion in the latter work. The individual figures, however, are very fine and reveal a strong influence of Giambellino.

In one of Cima's loveliest pictures, that in the gallery of Berlin (7) (fig. 240), the Madonna and Child show a particular resemblance to those of the Conegliano altar-piece, only here the Virgin is slightly turned to the right and the Child blesses an adorer, of whom only the bust and folded hands are visible. The landscape, which is very extensive, is treated with great detail and can, I think, be considered the finest of Cima's early phase. Cima does not owe the composition to Bellini because it was only much later that similar oblong pictures of the Madonna and an adorer were produced in Bellini's workshop, in which however the Virgin invariably stretches out her hand towards the devotee (Morgan Library, Ca d'Oro, etc.). Giambellino's picture in S. Francesco della Vigna which shows some similarity in composition is dated 1507, consequently it is at least fourteen years later than the panel in Berlin which I am inclined to place prior to the altarpiece of Conegliano, because in the latter the attitude of the Child seems to be a modification of the more logical blessing gesture of the picture in Berlin.

Very similar in style and in type, but all the same not quite of the same quality, is an oblong painting of the Virgin and Child between SS. Jerome and Mary Magdalene with the sky and hills on the horizon in the background, which is preserved in the Ältere Pinakothek, Munich (992). The composition is rendered somewhat unbalanced by the positions of the Virgin and Child Who bend, the former towards St. Jerome, the latter towards the Magdalene. Another picture of this manner and the same oblong shape exists in the gallery of Nivaagaard, near Copenhagen. Here the Virgin and Child are depicted in a more natural position and are accompanied by SS. Ursula(?) and Francis. The figures in

Fig. 240. Cima da Conegliano, Madonna and donor. Museum, Berlin.

this painting, which bears some trace of a signature, are of a particularly pathetic expression (¹).

In the church of S. Giovanni in Bragora, Venice, we find Cima's important picture of the Baptism which dates probably from

(¹) *Frizzoni*, L'Arte, XIII, 1910, p. 403.

1494; anyhow we know that he is given the order for it in December 1492, while he receives the payment in instalments until July
1495 (fig. 241). It was well known and praised by ancient authors,
as for example Ridolfi, Boschini and Moschini. The composition
is the same as that employed by Giambellino in his picture in
Sta Corona, Vicenza, but although in the general lines and composition Bellini was obviously inspired by Cima's example there
is not one figure which is the same either in type or attitude, and
still less the landscape. For Bellini's taste Cima's three somewhat
neo-classical angels formed too regular a group, and he has
changed their attitudes and shows one of them kneeling. All the
figures in Cima's Baptism must have seemed to Bellini over-
monumental and too close to one another and to remedy these
shortcomings he has depicted his figures further away from the
spectator, while in order to produce an effect of space he has placed
St. John the Baptist, to whom he gives a more suave expression,
much higher up. Another change he has made is the suppression
of the prominences in the landscape, which in Cima's picture
disturb the arrangement of the groups and attract the attention
from the principal proceedings. In his panel at Vicenza, Bellini has
reduced the background to a view of a distant landscape, re-
moving the tree from the centre to the extreme left, and where
Cima leaves a vague open space above the central group Bellini
depicts a half-length figure of God the Father, whose outstretched
arms seem to overhang the scene which takes place below.

It is very significant to notice here that Bellini, though he
accepted Cima's suggestions as to the general appearance of the
scene, all the same made numerous changes which clearly prove
his critical sense of the minor artist's capabilities and the conviction of his own incontestable superiority.

Another important altar-piece, dating probably from shortly
after 1495, is that in the gallery of Berlin (2) (fig. 242), which
originates from the church of S. Michele, near Murano, and was
very likely executed in commemoration of the prior Pietro Boldu,
who died that year (1). The picture is mentioned by Ridolfi
Boschini and Zanetti. Ludwig (2) propounded the theory that the

---

(1) See *von Hadeln*, ed. of Ridolfi, I, p. 77 note 2.

(2) *Ludwig*, op. cit., Jahrb. der K. Preus. Kunstsamml., 1903. This
idea is upheld also by *Burckhardt*, op. cit., p. 69.

Fig. 241. Cima da Conegliano, Baptism. S. Giovanni in Bragora,
Venice. Photo Anderson.

Fig. 242. Cima da Conegliano, Madonna and Saints. Museum, Berlin.

picture might have been ordered by Piero di Benedetto Priuli in
1511, but the style of the painting makes this most unlikely.
Again the Madonna's throne is placed under a vault which behind
is open to the sky; to the sides are depicted four bearded saints,
Peter, Romuald, Paul and Bruno, who are very tall in proportion
to the architecture but who are graceful and slender and do
not show the rather clumsy forms we remarked in the altar-piece
of Conegliano. The lower part of the throne is really an altar and
the vault is decorated with mosaics which seem to have been
taken from those illustrating the Old Testament in the peristyle
of the basilica of S. Marco. The proportions of the Madonna are
larger than we have as yet found, and though this breadth does
not become frequent until several years later, the neatness of
line which is not without a slight touch of conventionality makes
a later date than that of the end of the nineties unfeasible. There
is here a new achievement in the masterly diffusion of light and
the strongly opposed shadows; indeed it is a marvellously luminous picture.

The same rather robust type of Virgin appears also with the
nude Child standing — in this case on a low wall — in a very fine
signed panel in the gallery of Bologna (61). The Madonna is
represented in half-length figure against a mountainous landscape,
the types are strongly Belliniesque and the painting seems to be
of earlier date than the altar-piece in Berlin.

If not yet sold there exists in the Hermitage of Petrograd an
Annunciation which is dated 1495 (fig. 243). The Madonna, facing
the spectator, kneels at her prie-dieu in a room, through the large
windows of which we obtain a view of a landscape with a town;
the angel is of the same type as those in the Baptism but is
somewhat more graceful in appearance. The interior is treated
with a minuteness of detail which recalls Antonello's St. Jerome
in London. Burckhardt has attempted to reconstruct a triptych,
the centre of which should be this Annunciation and the lateral
pieces the SS. Mark and Sebastian in the Mond collection, but,
apart from the fact that the latter are too small, they appear to
be executed in a later manner. Sansovino and Ridolfi both
mention an Annunciation by Cima with the figures of SS. Mark
and Sebastian in Sta. Maria de' Crocicchieri. Boschini in his
"Minere" of 1664 refers only to the Annunciation and in his

Fig. 243. Cima da Conegliano, Annunciation. Hermitage, Petrograd.

Photo Hanfstaengl.

"Ricche Minere" of 1674 he speaks of it as having been there. Apparently the picture was transferred to the Scuola della Misericordia. The Annunciation in the Hermitage is the same as that described by Moschini (I, p. 182) as existing in the Scuola del Rosario. However, if these citations all refer to the one picture it might be conjectured that the figures of SS. Mark and Sebastian were joined to it at a later date.

In the same early and neatly designed manner as the altar-piece from S. Michele is another retable in the church of Sta. Maria dell' Orte, which is recorded by both Ridolfi and Zanetti (fig. 244) ([1]). The elongated figures of SS. John the Baptist, Peter, Mark(?), Jerome and Paul are again placed under a vault, but here, however, it is in ruins and the sky which forms the background is also visible above; little plants which grow on the ground are designed in that minute manner which Giovanni Bellini affected at a certain stage in his career. Also the relief and mosaic decorations of the architecture are treated in great detail, and again the fine light and shadow effects recall those in the altar-piece of Berlin.

Not inferior in quality, and another fine production of the same manner but perhaps of a slightly later date ([2]), is the Deposition in the gallery of Modena (187) (fig. 245), in which six of the faithful, St. Francis and St. Bernardine surround the dead Saviour Who is half seated on a stone. The types and still more the landscape, particularly the rocks to the left, are thoroughly Belliniesque. It is one of the rare pictures in which Cima expresses strong emotion; the swooning Virgin forms quite a tragic figure. The composition is original and very harmonious. According to an old tradition cited by Burckhardt, the portrait of the donor, Albertus Pius of Carpi, is to be found in the features of St. John the Baptist.

Of this period is also a not very fine and somewhat damaged oblong picture of the seated Madonna with the nude Child standing on her knee between the adoring St. Jerome and a female saint, in the Ca d'Oro, Venice, in which the figure of the Virgin is reminiscent of that in the painting dated 1496 in the church of Sta. Maria delle Grazie at Gemona. Here the Virgin in half-length figure and the Child are depicted against a landscape background, but the former has been entirely repainted.

The grandiose altar-piece which Cima painted between 1496

([1]) Bollettino d'Arte del Minist. della Pubbl. Istr., II, February 1923, p. 368.

([2]) Burckhardt proposed the date of from shortly after 1504 but this seems to me too late.

Fig. 244. Cima da Conegliano, St. John the Baptist and four Saints.
Madonna dell' Orto, Venice.   Photo Anderson.

Fig. 245. Cima da Conegliano, Deposition. Gallery, Modena.

Photo Anderson.

and 1499 by order of Giorgio Dragan for his chapel in Sta. Maria della Carità, where Ridolfi and Zanetti still saw it, and which is now in the gallery of Venice (36), decidedly marks the beginning of another style in Cima's art (fig. 246). The linear element plays a much less important part, the plastic values are rendered in a more impressionistic manner and there is a greater fusion of light

Fig. 246. Cima da Conegliano, Madonna and Saints. Accademia, Venice.
Photo Anderson.

and shade; at the same time the human proportions become more monumental. The principal lines of the composition are always the same but he has introduced a novelty: the upper part of the vault under which the Madonna's throne is placed is not included in the picture, and the six saints, instead of crowding under the vault, are depicted in front or standing beyond the pillars. Two angels playing on musical instruments are seated on the steps of the throne, while nine cherubim fly above the charming landscape. The new arrangement of the saints, who are no longer grouped within the limits of the vault, reveals on the part of the artist a hitherto unknown and wider conception of the treatment of space.

Then we have some evidence of Cima's activity for Southern Italy, although we have no data to prove that he himself went there. In the Carmine church of Miglionico in the province of Potenza there is an important polyptych signed by him and dated 1499 ([1]). It is of the elaborate shape which was in vogue in Venice. Besides the central group of the enthroned Madonna with the Child, it comprises four full-length and four half-length figures of saints as well as a bust of the dead Saviour above, where Giambellino so frequently places this figure, as for instance in the extant altar-piece in SS. Giovanni e Paolo where, as here, the Lord is depicted between the half-length figures of the Annunciation; the predella is adorned with four half-length figures of saints.

Bellini's inspiration is again very clearly visible in the figures of the bearded old saints against a cloudy sky, who resemble in type those in the Frari triptych, and it was obviously also this picture Cima took as example in his representation of the Madonna and Child as well as in his choice of the shape of the throne.

The same types of Madonna and Child, but shown in a different composition — the Virgin in three-quarter length seated with the nude Child on her knee — °are found in a painting which belongs to Mr. Ernest Rosenfeld, New York.

In a panel of St. Mark curing the hand of Anianus which, like the other works belonging to the same series, certainly dates from 1499, the painter reveals himself as somewhat reactionary and sooner inspired by an earlier manner of Giambellino. This painting, which is now in the gallery of Berlin (15), was formerly in the Annunziata chapel in Sta. Maria de' Crocicchieri where Ridolfi still saw it. The illustration of another episode by Lattanzio da Rimini which is now lost, and the dated one of the same cycle by Mansueti which is preserved in the Liechtenstein Gallery, Vienna, are of the same provenance. In the picture in Berlin the artist has taken a particular pleasure in treating the architecture and its

---

([1]) *M. Wackernagel*, op. cit., L'Arte, X. Bollettino d' Arte, 1914, p. 40. Idem, N.S., X, 1930, p. 173.

Fig. 247. Cima da Conegliano, Presentation of the Virgin in the Temple.
Gallery, Dresden.

decoration with great care and minuteness but the general effect
is somewhat hard and rigid.

To the same period is generally attributed the more pictorial and much finer composition of the Presentation of the Virgin in the Temple, in the gallery of Dresden (63) (fig. 247) (¹). The scene is represented with a marked sense of realistic action which is lacking in the panel of the miracle of Anianus. Certain types, the beautiful, but pale, colours and even the light make us wonder if we should not sooner place it nearer to the fine Crucifixion belonging to Messrs Agnew. Also the landscape is more typical of an earlier phase and again there is a rich display of architecture to the left. The human types, however, induce us to accept the later date.

Dated works of 1502 and 1504 show us very clearly in what direction Cima's art developed. Of the former of these years or of 1501 is the picture of SS. Constantine and Helen standing to the sides of the empty cross in the church of S. Giovanni in Bragora, Venice, which is mentioned by Ridolfi and Zanetti. They are well-painted monumental figures without great interest; the predella is adorned with three scenes from the story of the finding of the Cross.

Between 1502 and 1504 he apparently executed the panel of the Doubting St. Thomas in the National Gallery (816) (fig. 248) which was commissioned in 1497 for the church of S. Francesco at Portogruaro; it is a very fine specimen of Cima's art of this period; the figures are of noble appearance and suave monumental proportions (²).

Of the year 1504 is, in the first place, the altar-piece of St. Peter the Martyr depicted on a high pedestal, at the foot of which sits an angel playing on a musical instrument, between SS. Nicholas and Augustine. This work was ordered in 1504 for the church of the Corpus Domini in Venice, where it is mentioned by Sansovini, Vasari and Zanetti, but it is now in the Brera Gallery (176) (fig. 249). I see no sufficient arguments to admit with Burckhardt that the picture was executed two years later. An imposing architectural vault frames the central figure while the lateral saints, who are far too large in proportion, stand in front of the supporting pillars; a beautiful landscape forms the background. In his creation of the fine heads of the venerable saints Cima's source of inspiration is still always Bellini's triptych in the Frari

(¹) Dedalo, V, p. 618.
(²) *Fiocco*, L'Arte, XV, 1912, p. 296.

Fig. 248. Cima da Conegliano, Doubting Thomas. National Gallery,
London.   Photo National Gallery.

Fig. 249. Cima da Conegliano, St. Peter the Martyr with SS. Augustine
and Nicholas. Brera Gallery, Milan.   Photo Anderson.

Fig. 250. Cima da Conegliano, Madonna and Saints. Accademia, Venice.

Photo Alinari.

church, which was executed sixteen years before, and in this respect we might call Cima reactionary though on the other hand he treats the light and shade effects, especially inside the vault, with a subtle virtuosity which even Bellini himself never surpassed.

Finally, in the church of Sta. Maria della Consolazione at Este we find a signed Madonna dated 1504; the Virgin, visible to the knees, is seated with the lively Child on her knee against a background composed of a curtain and a piece of landscape. This work is an opportune document and enables us to assign with more certainty a few important pictures to their correct chronological place.

Between the altar-pieces of 1499 and the Madonna of 1504 at Este, but nearer to the former, should be classified the signed retable from the convent of Sta. Chiara at Murano (where it is cited by Ridolfi, Zanetti and Moschini) which for many years was in the gallery of Vienna but which after the great war was restored to Italy and is now in the gallery of Venice (815) (figs. 250, 251). It represents the Madonna seated on a rock, which serves also as pedestal, under an orange-tree; sky, trees and a hill on which a little town is perched form the background; some plants among which we see two birds grow on the stony foreground. St. Jerome and the adoring St. Louis stand to either side and again we notice the curious position of the Madonna and Child, each of whom bends towards a saint. Burckhardt has proposed the date of around 1495 but in my opinion this is too early. The picture throughout is of very high quality and most careful execution.

The group of the Virgin and Child has been repeated without any variation by the master in a picture which otherwise is of a totally different appearance; two angels and the ancient St. Joseph(?) stand near them while more to the sides are SS. John the Baptist and Mary Magdalene. This panel is oblong in shape and shows a beautiful and extensive mountainous landscape. A tree, but of a different kind, is again depicted in the centre. The picture, which once belonged to Lord Brownlow, was acquired some years ago by Messrs Colnaghi ([1]).

---

[1] Burlington Club Exhibition of Venetian Painting, 1912, pl. 21. L. *Venturi*, L'Arte, XXVI, 1923, p. 268.

Fig. 251. Detail of fig. 250.

Photo Minist. Ed. Naz.

There is something which recalls the types of the Annunciation of 1495, not only in the Madonna but also in one of the angels. However, it is very obvious that several years must have elapsed between the execution of the slender forms of the painting of 1495 and that of the much more monumental figures of this picture.

I imagine that it was about this time that Cima painted the

Fig. 252. Cima da Conegliano, Madonna and Saints. Gallery, Parma.
Photo, Minist. Ed. Naz.

oblong picture in the von Speck-Sternburg collection which figured at the exhibition of privately owned paintings held in

Berlin in 1925](¹). The Madonna, facing the spectator, is shown in half-length figure, holding on her knee the nude Child Who turns towards St. Jerome, the appearance of whom reminds us of the corresponding figure in the altar-piece restored by Austria and now in the gallery of Venice; St. John the Baptist in adoration forms the pendant. The figures are depicted against a landscape background.

Shortly after this Cima must have executed the fine panel from the church of the Sma. Annunziata, Parma, now in the town gallery (361) (fig. 252). Here the Virgin is seated against the façade of a church in ruins, her feet resting on the steps; the nude Infant is represented sitting on a cornice of the building; St. Andrew, his eyes fixed in meditation on the Child, leans his cross against the side wall while the young and handsome archangel Michael, holding a long spear and the scales, looks away from the central group. A town on the top of a hill occupies the background. Much importance is given to the large piece of ruined architecture which is treated very minutely, as are also the little plants and débris scattered on the ground. The manner of painting is here somewhat broader than in the above mentioned works.

Several pictures of the Madonna show more or less the same type and proportions but they are not all necessarily posterior to 1499. The finest and earliest example is that once in the collection of Mr. Tuck, Paris, and now in the Petit Palais (fig. 253), but I do not think that it could possibly be prior to the Annunciation of 1495, as Mr. Berenson assumes. Of slightly later date and certainly after 1499 are I think that in the Uffizi (902), in which the nude Child grasps His Mother's thumb, and the signed Madonna who, in three-quarter length and turned to the left, holds the foot of her naked Son, which until a few years ago was in the Wantage collection, Lockinge House (²).

(¹) *F. Becker*, Die Gemälde galerie von Speck-Sternburg in Lützschena, Leipzig, 1904, pl. 10, *The Same*, Zeitschr. f. Bild. Kunst., XVI, 1905, p. 263. *A. Venturi*, L'Arte, XXIX, 1926, p. 182.

(²) Burlington Club Exhibition of Venetian Painting, 1912, pl. 20. *A. Venturi*, L'Arte, XXIX, 1926, p. 183. It was afterwards in the possession of Messrs Dowdeswell. *Berenson*, Venetian Painting in America, p. 201, mentions a workshop copy in the Caregiani Palace, Venice, as well as other copies in the National Gallery and in the Gardner collection, Boston, with which works we shall deal later.

Fig. 253. Cima da Conegliano, Madonna. Petit Palais, Paris.
Photo Bulloz.

In the same category should be included the signed Madonna
in which the nude Child standing on His Mother's knee grasps a
little bird, against a landscape full of buildings, which is preserved in the National Gallery (634) (fig. 254) and of which there
exists a signed replica in the museum of Berlin (17), though here
the plastic effects are less marked, the drapery more elaborate and

Fig. 254. Cima da Conegliano, Madonna. National Gallery, London.

Photo Anderson.

the background different. The oblong picture of the Madonna in full face with the Child standing on her knee looking round at St. John the Baptist, while St. Paul stands reading on the other side, in the gallery of Venice (603), which Ridolfi (II, p. 201) describes as in Casa Bortolo Dafino, is also probably of this period, but of the earlier part of it (fig. 255). This work seems to have been executed with the help of an assistant.

Fig. 255. Cima da Conegliano, Madonna and Saints. Accademia, Venice.
Photo Anderson.

A fine production of this particular phase is no doubt the knee-length figure of the Madonna with the nude Jesus Who grasps a bird, against a beautiful landscape background, which belongs to Mrs. Nicholas Brady, New York.

In this group of Madonnas Cima was not specially inspired by Bellini's models; still there are one or two pictures which the latter painted around the nineties, of which the proportions and features might have been in Cima's mind when he created this particular type; this is perhaps most noticeable in the Madonna in the ex-Salomon collection and in that belonging to Mrs Brady, New York.

The disintegrated parts of an important altar-piece which originates from S. Rocco, Mestre ([1]), are, not without reason, generally compared with the picture of 1502 in S. Giovanni in Bragora. The signed central panel, showing St. Catherine on a pedestal between two pillars against a landscape, is found in the Wallace collection, London (fig. 256) ([2]). The lateral parts representing SS. Sebastian and Roch are in the gallery of Strasbourg,

([1]) *Burckhardt*, op. cit., p. 39.
([2]) *Richter*, Zeitschr. f. Bild. Kunst., XVI, 1905, p. 215.

Fig. 256. Cima da Conegliano, St. Catherine of
Alexandria. Wallace Collection, London.

Photo Gray.

while the lunette, adorned with a half-length figure of the Madonna with the Child between SS. Francis and Antony, was formerly in the Taylor collection, London, then in that of Mr. George Blumenthal, New York, who quite recently presented it to the Wallace collection (¹). As Mr. Berenson observes (²), in the last piece there is a heaviness of form which does not seem due to Cima's own hand. The St. Catherine is the finest figure and is very like, and even better than, the saints in the picture in S. Giovanni in Bragora.

Simultaneously with this rather mediocre production, Cima created works which, like his dated altar-pieces of 1504 in the National Gallery and the Brera, show him under his most favourable aspect and inspired by that intrinsic beauty which Bellini displayed in the Frari triptych and other paintings of around 1490. As such I think we have to consider the St. Tobias with the archangel, St. James and St. Nicholas in a landscape, from the Abbey della Misericordia (³), now in the gallery of Venice (592) (fig. 257); the Doubting Thomas with a holy bishop, framed in an arch, from the Scuola dei Muratori a San Samuele, where it is mentioned by Zanetti, now in the same gallery (611) (⁴); and the St. Sebastian in the Berenson collection (fig. 258) (⁵). The last mentioned work, especially when compared with the same saint in the gallery of Strasbourg, seems a master-piece. All these paintings appear to be of more or less the same standard and executed in the same period as the St. Peter the Martyr and two saints of 1504 in the Brera Gallery; that of the Doubting Thomas is perhaps slightly later than the two others.

The signed altar-piece in the gallery of Parma (360) (fig. 259)(⁶), representing the Madonna on a high throne with an angel holding a viol seated on the steps, three saints to the left and St. John the Baptist and two donors to the right, can, with good reason, be considered to have been executed in 1507, because it was painted

---

(¹) *Pantheon*, 1934, p. 96.

(²) *Berenson*, Venetian Painting in America, p. 200.

(³) *Moschini*, II, p. 32; in all probability it should be indentified with the "San Raffaello" by Cima, which *Sansovino*, p. 62 verso, mentions there.

(⁴) *Fiocco*, L'Arte, XV, 1912, p. 295.

(⁵) Reprod. Rassegna d'Arte, XI, 1911, p. 25.

(⁶) *Frizzoni*, Rassegna d'Arte, XII, 1912, p. 119.

Fig. 257. Cima da Conegliano, Tobias and the Archangel. Gallery, Venice.
Photo Anderson.

for the chapel which Bartolomeus Montini, canon of the cathedral,
had ornamented this year and in which he had his tomb prepared ([1]).
Burckhardt is of opinion that not only the two young devotees
in secular attire are relatives of the canon but that the saints
also, with the exception of the old St. John the Evangelist, are,
on account of their individual features, examples of portraiture,
more especially the St. John the Baptist. This is not impossible,
although in other works by Cima we meet with the same fair
type of St. Catherine.

([1]) Documents etc. in *Burckhardt*, op. cit., p. 61 note.

Fig. 258. Cima da Conegliano, St. Sebastian.
Berenson Collection, Settignano.

Fig. 259. Cima da Conegliano, Madonna and Saints. Pinacoteca, Parma.

Photo Minist. Ed. Naz.

MADONNA AND CHILD

By Cima da Gonegliano, in the National Gallery, London.

Photo Anderson.

The setting of the figures here is for Cima a new one and I think it more than likely that, although other painters had created somewhat similar compositions in and around Venice, Cima took the idea directly from Bellini's altar-piece in S. Zaccaria, with which it shows several points in common, as for instance the general appearance of the apse with the mosaic vault, the lateral pillars and the cornice of exactly the same shape and shown in the same way. Cima's tendency to create large figures is very evident here when we compare them with Bellini's; and the throne is higher. The angel at the foot of the throne appears too in Bellini's picture, and the manner in which the bearded old saint is placed near the young fair St. Catherine has no doubt also been taken from this example. The mosaics of Byzantine style in the vault form a strange contrast with the figures which, for the first time in Cima's works, have a decidedly 16th century appearance, chiefly on account of the greater freedom of design and forms, the more impressionistic technique and the more natural attitudes; features which give this panel a less austere and more humanistic character.

Between the Madonnas of 1504 and this new achievement in Cima's art should, I think, be classified several works; they are mostly Madonnas and in five of them the two central figures are practically identical; the Virgin, turned to the left and visible to below the knee, is seated with the nude Child, Who bends slightly backwards, standing on her knee. The finest version is the signed picture in the National Gallery, London (300) (Plate), in which the Madonna is shown against an extensive landscape background. Very like, but with slight variations in the background and the sky, is a painting in the gallery of Venice which is called a copy but, even though of slightly inferior quality, I think it might quite well be from Cima's own hand, as probably also that from the Schlichting collection, now in the Louvre, which is again poorer, and in which half the background is occupied by a curtain. The fourth example, belonging to Prince Kotchoubey, Petrograd, was put up to auction at the sale of art treasures in Russian private collections, which was organized by the Soviet government and held in Berlin in November 1928 (¹). This work is much finer, and the landscape in the background

---

(¹) *Weiner*, L'Arte, XII, 1909, p. 218. Pantheon, II, 1928, p. 528.

is different. Very similar to it is the landscape in the fifth example belonging to the Schuster collection in Amsterdam ([1]), which is a handsome work and shows a variation in the head-gear of the Madonna.

From the years 1504—1507 is, I think, still a Madonna in the National Gallery (2506), in which the Virgin in knee-length figure and turned to the right is depicted with the nude Child seated on her knee against a landscape background. The little Jesus, Who in type is taken from Giambellino's later works, grasps the knot of His Mother's waist-belt, but on the whole the picture is not a very pleasing specimen and we can understand Mr. Berenson's affirmation that it is only for the greater part by Cima. A very fine example of the painter's art at this moment in his career is the knee-length Madonna turned to the left, nursing the nude Child against a landscape background, which formerly was in the Dreyfus collection, Paris ([2]).

The 16th century tendency is still more manifest in the Adoration of the Shepherds in the Carmine church, Venice, which was executed in 1509—1510 (figs. 260, 261) ([3]). The more romantic and softly lit landscape betrays an influence of Giorgione and it might be to the knowledge of this master's art that we owe also the suaver human features. Besides the small group of the Virgin adoring the Child in His cradle and St. Joseph presenting the two shepherds, we see here Tobias and the archangel to the right and SS. Helen and Catherine(?)to the left.

This Giorgionesque charming lyrical style characterizes the few profane representations which originally might have decorated a cassone or some other piece of furniture ([4]). They are the

---

Apollo, Dec. 1928, p. 381. Cicerone, 1928, p. 641.

([1]) No. 79 of the Catalogue of the exhibition of ancient Italian art in Dutch possession, Amsterdam, 1934.

([2]) S. Reinach, Tableaux inédits etc. de colls. franç., pl. 25. A replica which has greatly suffered and in which part of the background is occupied by a curtain, existed until some years ago in the Caffi collection, Marseilles.

([3]) It adorned the altar in front of which the tombstone of Giovanni Calvo bears the date 1509. See Burckhardt, op. cit., p. 66 note. The picture is mentioned by Ridolfi, Zanetti and Moschini, II, p. 456.

([4]) L'Arte, XI, 1908, p. 141. Frizzoni, Rassegna d'Arte, XII, 1912, p. 120. Schubring, Cassoni, Leipzig, 1915, p. 393, pl. 163.

Fig. 260. Cima da Conegliano, Adoration of the Shepherds. Carmine
Church, Venice.   Photo Anderson.

Fig. 261. Detail of fig. 260.   Photo Anderson.

Triumph of Bacchus and Ariadne (fig. 262) in the Poldi Pezzoli
Gallery, Milan; two tondi, one of Endymion and Diana, the other
of Midas judging the musical contest between Pan and Apollo,
in the gallery of Parma (¹); Silenus on his donkey drinking,

(¹) Regarding the correspondence between the latter composition and
a plaquette v. *Burckhardt*, op. cit., p. 86.

Fig. 262. Cima da Conegliano, Triumph of Bacchus and Ariadne. Poldi Pezzoli Gallery, Milan.
Photo Alinari.

accompanied by three fauns (fig. 263), and another representing
a faun who carries a barrel on his shoulder, in the Johnson

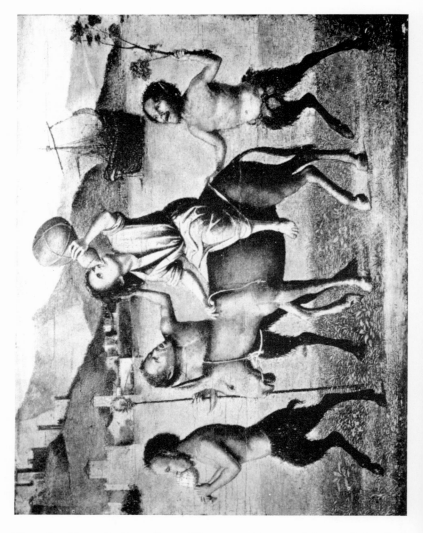

Fig. 263. Cima da Conegliano, Silenus on his ass. Johnson Collection, Philadelphia.   Courtesy of the J. G. Johnson Art Collection.

collection, Philadelphia (¹), formerly in the Thiem collection, San Remo. Another painting of the judgment of Midas exists in the collection of Count Moltke, Copenhagen.

Then, in the Kaiser Friedrich Museum, Berlin (17a), there is a

---

(¹) Nos. 177 and 178 of Berenson's catalogue of the Italian pictures in this collection.

small panel with a Giorgionesque landscape in which we see two miniature figures of knights fighing a duel; this also at one time might have decorated a piece of furniture.

Of the year 1510 is the triptych of the Madonna seated on a high throne between SS. James and George, all against landscape backgrounds with much sky, in the museum of Caen. This work is obviously not entirely from the hand of Cima. The Madonna and the holy warrior suggest a knowledge of Giorgone's panel at Castelfranco.

Between 1510 and the next dated production which is of 1513, Cima must have undertaken, not without help however, the' altar-piece from S. Dionisio at Zermen (Feltre), now in the gallery of Venice (658), in which the Madonna is seated on a throne with a high pedestal between the holy bishop Dionysius and St. Victor, while in the lunette above we see the Saviour between SS. Peter and Paul (¹).

Other productions of this period are: the very fine oblong picture of the Virgin with the Child standing on her knee between SS. John the Baptist and Jerome in the collection of the late Colonel Friedsam, New York; the St. Antony on a pedestal accompanied by SS. Roch and Mary Magdalene in the Metropolitan Museum, New York (fig. 264); and possibly also the somewhat academic, but all the same beautiful, Ecce Homo in the National Gallery (1310) (fig. 265).

A larged signed altar-piece of 1513 in the church of S. Anna at Capodistria (figs. 266, 267), although of flawless execution, is thoroughly lacking in inspiration and there emanates from it an atmosphere of boredom; moreover the accompanying saints — the four standing below and the four in half-length figure above — are rather rigid and lifeless and I imagine that a considerable part of the painting was left to an assistant. Particularly fine in this picture is the Madonna enthroned on a high pedestal, on the foot of which two angelic musicians are seated, Three cherubim are depicted high up but the idea of placing two adoring angels in mid-air to the sides of the Virgin was rather an unhappy one,

(¹) Gall. Naz. Ital., V, p. 22. It is the same picture which *Federici*, Memorie trevigiane, I, p. 223, describes as in the church of San Germano, in the territory of Treviso. *von Hadeln*, p. 78 note 3, calls St. Victor St. Eleuterius.

Fig. 264. Cima da Conegliano, St. Antony with SS. Roch and Catherine.
Metropolitan Museum, New York.

especially as there is hardly sufficient room for them. The terminal is adorned with a half-length figure of the Lord in benediction
between the busts of SS. Peter and Andrew. The latter figures,
and still more that of the Virgin, were obviously influenced by
the great geniuses who worked in Venice in the very first years of
the 16th century: Giorgione and Titian. The Virgin in type recalls
Titian's "Gipsy Madonna" in the gallery of Vienna as well as
Giorgione's master-piece at Castelfranco; the ampleness of form
and drapery however is more reminiscent of the former master.

Less pleasing pictures but equally Cinquecentesque in style
are: a rather damaged Madonna, with the Child at her breast,

Fig. 265. Cima da Conegliano, Ecce Homo. National Gallery, London.
Photo National Gallery.

seated in a landscape in the Rijksmuseum, Amsterdam; a signed
three-quarter length figure of the Madonna, the nude Child in
benediction standing on her knee, seated near an open window
through which a landscape is visible, in the Städelsches Kunstinstitut, Frankfort (852), part of the background is formed by a

Fig. 266. Cima da Conegliano, polyptych. St. Anna, Capodistria.

Photo Alinari.

curtain; and a Madonna, also in three-quarter length, with the nude Child seated on her knee, against a background of part landscape and part curtain, in the Gardner collection, Boston, which is a repetition, but not autograph, of the composition of the picture in the Wantage collection ([1]).

[1] *Berenson*, Venetian Painting in America, p. 202. *Ph. Hendy*, Catalogue of the Paintings etc. of the Gardner Museum, Boston, 1931, p. 93,

Fig. 267. Detail of fig. 266.   Photo Alinari.

considers this picture to be a contemporary copy of the Madonna in the
Wantage collection. *L. Venturi*, Pitt. ital. in America, pl. 312.

Fig. 268. Cima da Conegliano, St. Peter with SS. John and Paul, 1516.
Brera Gallery, Milan.   Photo Anderson.

A further development along the same lines is noticeable in the
signed altar-piece in the Louvre (1259), formerly either in the
cathedral or in the church of S. Domenico in Parma. It represents
the Virgin seated on a throne, the high back of which is adorned
with a rug, in a very beautiful landscape; she seems to play with
the lively Infant Who looks round at the rather effeminate
St. John the Baptist, to whom St. Mary Magdalene forms the
pendant. Here Cima has really achieved something new and
it is not easy to find the link between this enchanting but
thoroughly 16th century panel and his earlier Madonnas.

Cima's last dated work is found in the Brera Gallery, Milan

(174) (fig. 268). This altar-piece, which originates from the Benedictine convent of Sta. Maria Mater Domini in Conegliano where it was seen by Ridolfi, was painted around the year 1516, at least at this date the abbess makes a contract with Cima for the execution of an important picture, and it seems more than likely that the document refers to the painting in question. However, in composition, attitudes and psychology it is slightly more conventional than the retable of three years earlier; it is more purely late Belliniesque in style but without any elements borrowed from Titian. On a throne, the back of which is lengthened by a piece of material, St. Peter, in papal attire and with one hand raised, is seated in a niche; an angel playing the lute sits at the foot of the pedestal while the youthful St. John the Baptist and St. Paul stand to the sides; two pillars and the ceiling frame this over-regular group.

A very similar composition is found in the painting which a few years ago entered the Fitzwilliam Museum, Cambridge, with the Marlay collection (¹). Again a holy bishop — here it is St. Lanfranco of Pavia — is seated on a high throne the back of which is prolonged in the same manner. St. John the Baptist, similar in type but very different in attitude, is depicted to the left while to the right we see St. Benedict with cross and book. The figures are framed in much the same way as in the Brera altar-piece and a landscape forms the background. This panel is executed in Cinquecentesque technique and consequently appears to be of later date than that of 1516, but we have not much time from which to pick and choose because Cima's death occurred soon after this year.

In the same manner he painted an oblong panel in the Morgan collection, New York, of the Madonna in three-quarter length facing the spectator, with the nude Child Who touches the cross of St. John the Baptist, while His Mother holds the ring of the mystic wedding of St. Catherine who stands to the other side (²).

Of all Cima's paintings the most typical of the 16th century manner is a very fine oblong picture in the collection of Mr J. L. Severance, Cleveland, U.S.A. (fig. 269); the Madonna in full face holds on her knee the naked Child Who blesses an adorer whose

---

(¹) *Constable*, Burlington Magazine, XLVII, 1925, pl. 3.

Fig. 269. Cima da Conegliano, Madonna, Saints and Donors. Severance
Collection, Cleveland (Ohio).

bust is visible to the left and who is presented by a bearded old saint, while the Virgin slightly inclines towards a woman in adoration who is recommended by a female saint. Once more we notice the strange position of the Mother and Child. The centre of the landscape background is concealed by a curtain.

This beautiful panel is I think the latest production we have from the hand of Cima.

If the number of works executed in the last years of Cima's activity seem few, it is no doubt because most of the pictures he undertook at this stage were painted in collaboration with assistants; consequently we have quite a number of workshop productions in which the master may have had a share but which, on the whole, reflect his last manner as interpreted by some helper. As such I shall cite the following.

Baltimore, Walters collection, knee-length figure of the Madonna with the scantily attired Child on her lap against a background, formed by a window through which we see a landscape, and a curtain; it is a replica by a pupil of a much finer painting by Cima in the Quincy Shaw collection, Boston, once in the Fabrini collection, Conegliano (¹).

Berlin, Kaiser Friedrich Museum, No. 42, SS. Lucy, Mary Magdalene and Catherine, against a landscape background; it is very near to the master and dates from around 1493 (fig. 270).

Frankfort, Städelsches Kunstinstitut (old catalogue No. 40, not in new one), Madonna in full face and three-quarter length with the Child touching the palm-leaf held by St. Catherine while St. Nicholas is depicted to the other side; again a curtain hides the centre of the landscape.

Göttingen, University collection, No. 33, a similar composition but with SS. John the Baptist and Mary Magdalene; the collaborator here was very probably Antonio da Carpi (fig. 271).

London, National Gallery, No. 3112, ex-Layard collection, a half-length figure of the Madonna with the Child Who touches the cross held by St. Francis while St. Paul is represented as pendant (fig. 272); No. 3113, idem, Madonna in knee-length with nude Child Who takes the golden ball from the·hand of St. Nicholas; this saint is very similar to the corresponding figure at

---

(¹) *Berenson,* Gazette des Beaux Arts, XVI, 1895, p. 208. *The Same,* Venetian Painting in America, p. 202.

Fig. 270. Cima da Conegliano and helper, St. Lucy with SS. Mary Magdalene and Catherine. Museum, Berlin.

Frankfort; the youthful St. John the Baptist is seen on the other
side; the background is formed by a landscape.

Milan, Brera Gallery, No. 195, Madonna, again from the church
of Sta. Maria Mater Domini, Conegliano (¹).

New York, Friedsam collection, Madonna in full face holding
the Infant Jesus Who bends towards St. Nicholas of Tolentino;
St. John the Baptist in adoration is depicted to the other side;
they are shown against an extensive landscape.

(¹) *F. Malaguzzi Valeri*, Rassegna d'Arte, IX, 1909, p. 138.

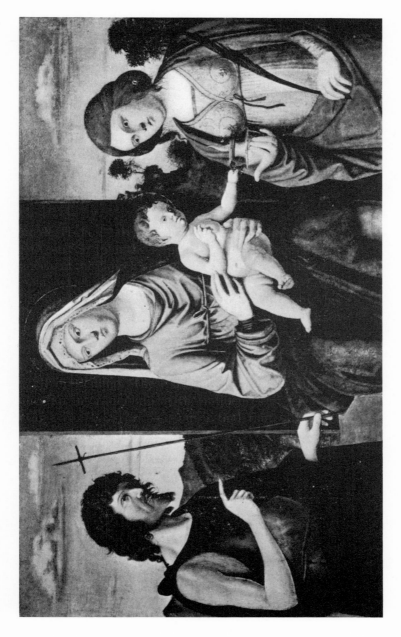

Fig. 271. Cima da Conegliano and Antonio da Carpi, Madonna and Saints. Gallery, Göttingen.

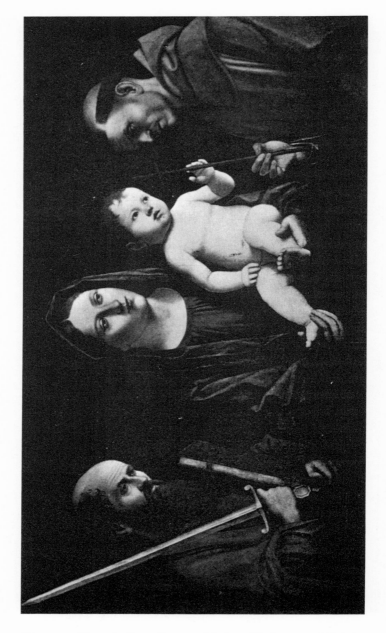

Fig. 272. Cima da Conegliano and helper, Madonna and Saints.
National Gallery, London.   Photo Alinari.

Padua, Museum, Nos. 421, 427, SS. John the Baptist and Jerome, panels of a polyptych.

Rome, once in Palazzo Patrizi(?), Coronation of the Virgin with angelic musicians, cherubim, etc., around a broad throne (known to me only from a photograph); possibly with the help of Gerolamo da Udine.

Venice, SS. Giovanni e Paolo, Coronation of the Virgin with numerous saints and angels to either side of the throne; it was executed quite possibly in collaboration with Gerolamo da Udine (fig. 273).

Gallery, No. 623, St. Christopher, from a polyptych which was painted for the Scuola dei Mercanti.

Vienna, ex-von Auspitz collection, St. John the Baptist standing in an important landscape, from the Weber collection, Hamburg.

There is still quite a number of works which might be ascribed to Cima himself (¹).

_____

(¹) **Agram,** Strossmayer Gallery, SS. Augustine and Benedict, attributed to Giov. Bellini by *Gronau*, Bellini, pl. 81. **Bayonne,** Bonnat Museum, God the Father (*Berenson*). **Bergamo,** Gallery, No. 559, Madonna, restored. **Birmingham,** Art Gallery, dead Saviour (Apollo, April 1930, p. 312). **Bologna,** for sale a few years ago, Madonna on rather a high throne, with landscape background. **Copenhagen,** Gallery, Madonna seated with naked Child on curtain and landscape background, attrib. to Gerolamo da Udine by G. *Richter*, Apollo, March 1934, p. 128. **Dresden,** Gallery, No. 61, beautiful figure of Christ in benediction standing in a landscape, near 1499; No. 62, bust of Christ, late work catalogued as a studio production. **Edinburgh,** National Gallery of Scotland, No. 1190, Madonna in a landscape between SS. Peter and Andrew, unfinished. (*T. Borenius*, Burlington Magazine, XXIX, 1916, p. 164). **Florence,** Berenson coll., two panels illustrating the story of Coriolanus; Cinelli coll., St. Jerome in a landscape; Contini Bonacossi coll., St. Jerome in penitence in a landscape; Serestori coll., St. Jerome in a landscape; for sale a few years ago, head of a bearded old saint against a landscape background, no doubt a fragment, a fine late work. **London,** National Gallery, No. 2505, from Salting coll., David with the head of Goliath and Jonathan walking in a beautiful landscape, early work (*C. Philips*, Burlington Magazine, XVII, 1910, p. 9); H. M. the King's coll., Buckingham Palace, panels of a small polyptych showing the two half-length figures of the Annunciation, SS. George, Vitale, Benedict and Stephen, the two last mentioned in monochrome, a late work; Kennard coll., St. Jerome in the wilderness, with important landscape (*Borenius*, Burlington Magazine, V, 1904, p. 574. Exhib. Old Masters, Grafton Galleries, 1911, No. 24; reprod. A. *Venturi*, Storia dell' arte ital., VII⁴, fig. 313); R. Mond coll., SS. Sebastian and Mark; Welling-

Fig. 273. Cima da Conegliano and Gerolamo da Udine(?),
Coronation of the Virgin. SS. Giovanni e Paolo, Venice.
Photo Alinari.

There are still some drawings which should be included among the authentic works by Cima ([1]).

In the Uffizi we find a sketch of an old bearded saint with a book in his hand which was obviously the study for the figure to the right in the altar-piece of 1489 in Vicenza. A particularly fine and finished drawing executed with great care represents the Saviour with a globe, standing on a cloud supported by four

ton-Salisbury sale, summer 1923, Holy Family. **Milan,** Brera Gallery, No. 217, St. Luke, the Virgin, SS. John the Baptist and Mark standing in a loggia from the S. Giorgio Maggiore convent, Venice, previously attributed to Gerolamo da Santacroce; No. 218, a holy nun, SS. Jerome, Nicholas of Bari and Ursula, same as No. 217; No. 219 St. Jerome in the desert, same provenance as No. 217 (*Boschini* attributed it to a Lamberto which name is written on the back v. *Ludwig*, op. cit., Jahrb. K. Preus. Kunstsamml., p. 52); No. 220, SS. Cornelius. Justine and Cyprian in three separate divisions against a gold background, from the church of Sta. Giustina, Venice; Poldi Pezzoli Museum, No. 623, head of a young woman, fragment (*Frizzoni*, Rassegna d'Arte, XII, 1912, p. 119). **Munich,** Böhler coll., Jason at the court of Aeëtes (No. 274 of the Burlington Club Exhib. of Ital. art, 1930. *Balniel and Clark*, op. cit., pl. 111); ex-von Nemes coll., St. Catherine praying in a landscape. **New York,** sale of the Paolini coll. of Rome, Dec. 1924, No. 50, oblong picture of the three-quarter length figure of the Virgin with the Child adored by a bearded old saint. **Paris,** Musée André, No. 1025, Madonna; Gulbenkean coll., rest during the Flight into Egypt and St. John the Baptist, St. Mary Magdalene and two angels (*Berenson*); for sale 1928, three large figures of saints. **Petrograd,** Hermitage, Entombment, bequeathed by Count Stroganoff (*Berenson*, Venetian Painting in America, p. 209). **Philadelphia,** Johnson coll., No. 1171, head of St. Stephen, **Richmond,** Cook coll., No. 135, dead Saviour supported by two angels; No. 243, Our Lord. **Venice,** Accademia, store-room, St. Jerome and a bearded old bishop(?); Correr Museum, No. 377, Madonna with SS. Lawrence and Peter; Seminary Gallery, No. 72, Madonna and Child.

A Madonna adoring the Child, which in the Rath Museum, Budapest, (No. 147) is attributed to Cima, is by Rondinelli. A Madonna between six saints and a female donor in the G. Ferrario coll., Milan, which has been wrongly attributed to Cima by *A. Venturi*, op. cit., L'Arte, 1934, p. 482, is, I think, by Santacroce. Of the lost works I shall cite: an Adoration of the Shepherds dated 1497 in the church of S. Giorgio d'Alega, one of the few pictures by Cima mentioned by *Sansovino* (p. 86 verso); a Resurrection in the church of S. Martino recorded by *Zanetti* as a work of Cima and by *Boschini* as a school production; and a Madonna with the sleeping Child from the "Anti-secreta del Colleggio", afterwards in the Royal Palace, to which reference is made by *Moschini*, I, p. 510.

([1]) *Popham*, op. cit., Nos. 173, 174, pls. 148, 149. *von Hadeln*, Quattrocento Zeichnungen, pls. 73—78.

Fig. 274. Cima da Conegliano, the Saviour, drawing.
British Museum, London.

Fig. 275. Cima da Conegliano, landscape, drawing. British Museum, London.

cherubim (fig. 274); Mantegna's influence, as transmitted through Bellini, is evident in the incisive drapery; this sketch, which is executed with the brush on blue paper and strengthened in white, is preserved in the British Museum (1895-9-15-803). Another sheet in the same collection (1900-5-15-1) shows rough drafts of landscapes (fig. 275), very similar to the views in the backgrounds of many of his pictures, but they are studied and deepened as in engravings; the spirit of one of them, in which there are many ravines, is somewhat that of Seeghers. Less interesting is the sketch of an old, bald-headed man with a long white beard, in the collection of the late Mr Henry Oppenheimer. In the Uffizi there is a drawing of a mythological subject: Orpheus playing a viol under a tree with some animals listening to him, while in the Koenigs collection, Haarlem, there exists a sketch of the Madonna and Child (¹).

***

Cima's importance was thoroughly understood by his contemporaries; this resulted in the formation of quite a large school but he had, besides, an influence on several important masters, as for instance Mansueti, Sebastiano del Piombo, Marescalco, Boccaccino, Fogolino, to a certain extent even on Giambellino and, as we saw, on the latter's pupil Lattanzio.

Of his more modest followers, some have been identified; they include Antonio Maria da Carpi, Pasqualino Veneziano and others with whom we shall deal presently, but there is quite a number of anonymous school works of which a list will suffice (²).

(¹) *Von Hadeln*, Meister Zeichn. aus der Samml. F. Koenigs, Haarlem; Venez. Meister, pl. 2.

(²) **Bergamo,** Gallery, No. 386, Madonna and Child against a background of a curtain and a landscape. **Cividale,** Museum, three panels, St. John the Baptist, a holy bishop and St. Mary Magdalene, by a late follower. **Conegliano, Near** — S. Fior di Sopra, polyptych, mentioned by Ridolfi (I. p. 78) as a work by Cima. *Crowe and Cavalcaselle*, op. cit., I, p. 251 note 1. **Esztergom** (Hungary), Archiepiscopal coll., No. 135, half-length figure of the Madonna with the sleeping Child and a book, with a background formed by a curtain and a landscape; it is a very poor production of Cima's school, signed *"Giovanni Battista Rositi"* and dated 1507. **Florence,** for sale several years ago, the Virgin, St. Joseph, St. John and St. Catherine adoring the Child in a landscape, a handsome and important picture. **Kassel,** Gallery, No. 487, Madonna in three-quarter length figure with the nude Child standing on her knee against a landscape background; No. 841, Madonna and four cherubim, only a tiny piece of landscape is visible. **London,** National Gallery, No. 3084, Entombment, with resemblances to Cima's painting of the same subject in Modena and still more to the example in the Hermitage (fig. 276); when in the Layard coll. it was at-

On the whole Cima's pictures are incontestably beautiful and he employed incomparable skill in reaching the level which he obviously aimed at. In this respect he might be called academic. Once he had established the artistic canon which pleased him and which greatly depended on Giovanni Bellini's most regularly beautiful manner, as displayed in the Frari altar-piece of 1488, he changed but little. He was not an emotional artist and only few of his pictures show deep feeling. His figures however are anything but lifeless, still their somewhat sedate expression is repeated with such constancy in almost all his pictures that a certain monotony cannot be denied. One of Cima's great achievements is his expression of space and aerial perspective. Of all the painters of the Venetian school of his day, it was he who best understood the artistic value of open air and atmospheric

---

tributed to Sebastiano del Piombo, whose signature it bears, but Cavalcaselle's opinion that the inscription is false has found general agreement (*P. D'Achiardi*, Sebastiano del Piombo, Rome, 1908, p. 23. *Berenson*, Venetian Painting in America, p. 209); Austen sale, March 1921, No. 76, Madonna, Child and saints. **Lucerne,** sale of the Chillingworth coll., Sept, 1922, No. 80, Madonna and Child. **Madrid,** Prado Gallery, Bosch bequest, No. 6, Madonna seated with the nude Child standing on her knee with a landscape background, the centre of which is concealed by a curtain; it bears a false signature. **Milan,** Ambrosiana, Daniel in the lions' den, in grisaille (*Schubring*, Cassoni, No. 775, pl. 161); Brera Gallery, No. 720, Apollo and Daphne (*Schubring*, op. cit., No. 776). **New York,** Grenville Winthrop coll., Madonna and Child Who bestows a blessing on St. James, half-length figures, perhaps by Sebastiano del Piombo (*Berenson*, Venetian Painting in America, p. 208, fig. 86). **Nîmes,** Gallery, No. 444, small picture of the Madonna offering a pomegranate to the Child. **Ravenna,** Gallery, half-length figure of the Madonna with the Infant Jesus, in a landscape (Gall. Naz. ital., III, p. 124); Accademia Belle Arti, St. John the Baptist (*Ricci*, Raccolte artistiche di Ravenna, fig. 74, Venetian school). **Rome,** for sale several years ago, SS. Francis and Antony kneeling in prayer on two panels. **Treviso,** S. Leonardo, triptych, Madonna on a high throne with St. Bartholomew and St. Ambrose(?). **Venice,** Gallery, store-room, Christ crucified with St. Mary Magdalene at the foot of the cross, and other saints, important landscape with architecture; Seminary coll., No. 45, God the Father sending forth the Holy Ghost; ex-Layard coll., Augustine and the sibyl (*A. Venturi*, L'Arte, XV, 1912, p. 449).

A drawing of the school of Cima is found in the collection in Windsor Castle; it represents, in an elaborately designed apse, a holy bishop on a high throne between a king and another bishop, *von Hadeln*, Zeichn. d. Quattrocento, pl. 79.

Fig. 276. School of Cima, Entombment. National Gallery, London.
Museum Photo.

distance. This he shows us not only in his really beautiful and
minutely studied landscapes but also in his obvious aversion to
placing his central figures in apses, niches or with a wall as background. This he almost invariably avoids, and even when the
composition requires a vault, he lets the open air play through it
from all sides. No other Venetian equalled Cima in the painting
of light and he combined with this gift that of being a marvellous colourist.

This painter, who does not seem to have been endowed with
great inventive power, as is obviously seen in the frequency with
which he repeats the same Madonna, strange to say seems all the
same to have launched in Venice some new ideas which were

eagerly taken up by even the most prominent artists. In fact, although there were a few sporadic older examples in Venice, such as those by Antonello da Messina, Bellini and Alvise Vivarini and probably one of Montagna at Vicenza, I think it is Cima who should be held responsible for the wide-spread diffusion of that particular type of Madonna enthroned on a high pedestal — very different from the sort of estrade which had been used before — of which good examples are seen in the school of Ferrara. This tendency towards height was one of Cima's characteristics and we find further evidence of it in his vaults and even in his very tall figures which are sometimes quite out of proportion with the architecture. In the altar-piece of 1493 at Conegliano his figures are too compact but gradually he gives them more space and his groups lose the effect of being over-crowded. In fact, Cima was the painter *par excellence* of the large altar-piece and, compared with his contemporary compatriots, he created an enormous number of this type of picture. Consequently he played an important part in its propagation in Venice, more especially of that particular composition in which the enthroned Madonna forms the central figure, and different artists, including Bonconsiglio and even Lotto in his early years, seem to have adopted Cima's models.

A new feature, the importance of which lies in the number of times it has been repeated by other artists and even by Giovanni Bellini himself, was introduced by Cima. It is that of showing the background of half-length figures of the Madonna divided into two parts: a curtain and a view of a landscape (¹). I think the majority of us would have preferred to see Cima's delightful landscapes occupying all the available space, and the idea might have been used by the painter as a "metodo sbrigativo" because his charming and elaborate landscapes must have taken him much more time to paint than a simple curtain.

Again judging from the material which we have now at our disposal, we must admit that it was from Cima that Giambellino borrowed the principal lines of his composition of the Baptism at

(¹) The picture in the Quincy Shaw collection, Boston, and its replica in the Walters collection, Baltimore, are the only examples in which the background is continued above the curtain and this helps to explain that the idea of the painter was to show the landscape through a window which is partly covered by a curtain.

Vicenza. And this is true in spite of the fact that in Italian painting the disposition of the figures of the Baptism has undergone but little change since the days of Giotto and in spite of the fact also that Bellini, as we said before, altered everything in Cima's picture which was not entirely to his taste. Sebastiano del Piombo, for his Doubting Thomas in the church of S. Tommaso Treviso, also was inspired by Cima's example (¹).

However, the fact that Giambellino took a few ideas from Cima amounts to little when we compare it with all that Cima owes to the Bellini. This influence seems to have manifested itself only after an interval of a few years. Thus in his earliest dated work, that of 1489 at Vicenza, Cima follows the slightly Mantegnesque manner which Bellini had already abandoned for several years, and it was really only towards the middle nineties that we find established in Cima's art those principles of regular and serene beauty which Giambellino displays to the full in his master-piece of 1488 in the Frari church. It was in this style which, besides, best suited the quiet and joyous Cima, that our artist continued to paint until the revolutionary examples created by Giorgione and Titian at the beginning of the 16th century urged him to change his manner, but he did so in order to keep up with the times rather than in imitation of the manner of one of the leading masters.

**

The peculiar appearance of the works of the school of Cima is a strong argument in favour of the affirmation that Cima's art, although considerably influenced by Giovanni Bellini, is far from being a mere subdivision of the school of this great master. On the whole the followers of Cima were fairly modest and somewhat provincial painters but they show characteristics which most decidedly separate them from Giambellino's direct adherents.

In the list of the productions of the school of Cima I have already mentioned the signed picture at Esztergom by the mediocre Rositi.

Decidedly superior is Antonio Maria da Carpi, whose painting in the gallery of Budapest (123) is signed *"Antonius Maria de Charpi"* and dated 1495 (fig. 277) (²). The painter reveals himself

---

(¹) *Fiocco*, op. cit., L'Arte.
(²) *A. Venturi*, L'Arte, III, 1900, p. 232, reads "Maria" as "Mori".

Fig. 277. Antonio da Carpi, Madonna. Gallery, Budapest.

as a very faithful imitator of Cima whose level, however, he does not reach. A replica of this picture with some changes in the background is found in the Pinacoteca of Treviso (¹). Although

G. *von Térey*, Die Gemälde Galerie des Museums f. Bild. Künste in Budapest, Berlin, 1916, p. 94. Formerly it was in the Piccinelli collection, Bergamo. *Berenson*, Venetian Painting in America, p. 199. *W. Suida*, A. M. d. C., Belvedere, IX, 1930, p. 9.

(¹) Bollettino d'Arte del Minist. dell' Ed. Naz., N.S., VI, April 1927, p. 470.

there are considerable variations in the proportions, the composition is but a copy of Cima's painting in the Petit Palais, Paris.

In a picture of the Madonna discovered in the Friulese mountains and now in a private collection in America, of which part of the signature and the date 1497 have been read with difficulty, Antonio da Carpi shows himself less influenced by Cima. Here against a background, occupied half by a landscape and half by a curtain, the Madonna is seen seated with the almost naked Child, Who extends one arm towards Her.

By Antonio da Carpi is, I think, a work in the gallery of Padua (32) (fig. 278), which is a copy of Cima's Madonna, with the Child grasping her thumb, in the Uffizi; also the background of curtain and landscape is repeated. A half-length figure of the Madonna adoring the nude Child Who lies asleep on a wall, against a landscape background, which several years ago was for sale in Rome, should be ascribed to him while, if I remember rightly, also a Madonna in the gallery of Verona might be from his brush. As I said before, Mr Berenson mentions in the Davis collection, Newport, a replica of Cima's Madonna in the Johnson collection, Philadelphia, which he ascribes to this painter, under whose name is classified also an Adoration of the Shepherds in the gallery of Dublin (367).

Naturally Antonio da Carpi was one of the minor artists who assisted Cima in his workshop, and I think he took a considerable part in the execution of the oblong picture of the Virgin between SS. John the Baptist and Mary Magdalene in the gallery of Göttingen, which I have already mentioned among the studio productions.

A less faithful follower of Cima was Pasqualino Veneziano (¹). It is just possible that he was a pupil of Bellini, although his somewhat heavy types sooner show a poor interpretation of those of Cima.

Of the documents published concerning him (²) only those of

(¹) *Crowe and Cavalcaselle*, Painting in N. Italy, ed. Borenius, I, p. 290. *Burckhardt*, op. cit., p. 143. *Berenson*, Venetian Painting in America, p. 210. G. *Gronau*, in Thieme-Becker, Künstlerlexikon, XXVI, p. 18.

(²) *Biscaro*, L'Arte, I, 1898, p. 141. *Nicoletti*, Ateneo veneto Sept.-Oct. 1890. *Paoletti*, Bollettino d'arte e curiosità Veneziane, 1894. *Ludwig*,

Fig. 278. Antonio da Carpi, Madonna. Museo Civico, Padua.

Photo Alinari.

1503 and 1504, in connexion with a Presentation in the Temple, for the Scuola della Carità, for the execution of which he competed and won, but which was afterwards executed by Titian, really refer to Pasqualino, whose death occurred in this year. His signature "*P . . qualinus Venetu*", with the date 1496, is found on a

Jahrb. der K. Preus. Kunstsamml. Beiheft, XXVI, 1905, p. 52. *Testi*, Stor. della pittura venez., I, pp. 131. 135, 136.

picture in the Correr Museum, Venice. Here the Virgin is depicted in half-length figure with the nude Child, Who holds the fingers of her left hand, turned towards St. Mary Magdalene who stands behind (fig. 279). An elaborate landscape forms the background. Pasqualino was obviously trained in a good school but his figures are lacking in life and expression. Other signed works are: the Madonna between four saints and a repainted donor in the Novak collection, Prague (¹), which is much more Belliniesque in character; a Madonna, executed in the same manner, until recently in the Vieweg collection, Brunswick (fig. 280) (²), which is a free replica of Bellini's Madonna from Oldenburg, now in the Brady collection, New York (³); the manner of painting is different and although the attitudes and composition have been altered according to Cima's aesthetic principles, the general lines of the work, which shows the monogram *P. V. P.*, resemble Bellini's example; and the Madonna in more than knee-length figure with the nude Infant standing on her knee, against a background formed by a curtain and a landscape, which once upon a time belonged to Mrs Felton, New York (⁴). In this picture also the elements due to Cima predominate.

On account of a resemblance in style some other paintings have been attributed to Pasqualino. They include: the three-quarter length figure of the Madonna in full face with the Child Jesus in benediction and grasping a little bird, standing on her knee, formerly in the Sartorio collection, now in the gallery of Trieste (fig. 281); here the landscape is seen through a curtained window; that in which the Virgin offers an open book to the nude Child, seated in benediction on her knee, against an extensive landscape, which, in the Pinacoteca of Rovigo, is ascribed to Cima with whom it certainly shows much connexion, whereas the previous work was more Belliniesque; and the rather characterless standing figure of St. Mary Magdalene in the Palazzo Giustiniani, Venice. Classified, but without reason, as works by Pasqua-

---

(¹) Reprod. in *Frimmel*, Handb. der Gemäldekunde, Leipzig, 1894, No. 63.

(²) *Harck*, Archivio Stor. dell' arte, III, 1890, p. 172. No. 30 of the catalogue of the Vieweg sale, Berlin, 1930. Reprod. in Catal. of the Exhib. of ancient Italian art in Dutch possession, Amsterdam, 1934, No. 283.

(³) *Gronau*, Bellini, pl. 128.

(⁴) *Berenson*, op. cit., fig. 87.

Fig. 279. Pasqualino Veneziano, Madonna, 1496. Correr Museum, Venice.

Photo Fiorentini.

lino are two oblong paintings of the Madonna and Child in a landscape background, the one in which we see as well a young female saint and a bearded elderly saint presenting the donor, in the Hermitage, Petrograd (No. 1919 in 1912) [1], the other in which the Madonna is again accompanied by a female saint and

[1] *Liphart*, Starye Gody, July 1908. *L. Venturi*, L'Arte, XV, 1912, p. 134: Diana; more likely by Catena.

Fig. 280. Pasqualino Veneziano, Madonna. Private Collection.

a male saint with a beard — St. Paul? — in the Pálffy collection, Budapest (¹). Gronau rightly attributes to Pasqualino a similar composition with two female saints and the landscape visible through two narrow windows, which is preserved in the Malaspina Museum, Pavia (²).

***

(¹) At one time it was exhibited in the gallery of Budapest.

(²) Illustrated as by Mocetto by *Fiocco* in "Madonna Verona", VIII, 1914, p. 83. *Ludwig*, op. cit., on account of a similarity in the name, wrongly ascribes to Pasqualino a St. Jerome in the Brera Gallery.

Fig. 281. Pasqualino Veneziano, Madonna. Gallery Trieste.

Photo Alinari.

Andrea Busati ([1]) was of Slav origin because he was the son of
Stefano di Demetrio, a curtain painter from Skutari. His two
brothers, Luc' Antonio and Francesco, were also painters. He is
referred to as a Venetian painter in documents of 1503, 1507, 1519
and 1527; in 1528 he made his will but seems to have been active at

([1]) *Crowe and Cavalcaselle*, op. cit., I, p. 291. *Cecchetti*, Arch. venet.,
XXXIII[2], p. 402; XXXIV[1], p. 205. *Ludwig*, op. cit., p. 98. G. *Gronau*, in
Thieme-Becker, Künstlerlexikon, V, p. 277.

least until 1530 because he executed a picture in which the saints
correspond with the Christian names of magistrates who were in
office together around the year 1530 (^{1}). The picture, which was
originally in the room of the "Magistrato delle Rason vecchie" in
the Palazzo Camerlenghi, where it is described by Boschini as by
Andrea Basaiti and by Zanetti as by Marco Basaiti, was restored by
Austria and is now in the gallery of Venice (fig. 282). The work is
executed on canvas and is signed *"Andrea Busati"*. The artist
repeats the composition of Cima's picture in the gallery of the
Academy of Vienna; the SS. Andrew and Mark are identical, as
is also part of the decoration of the throne; only, the holy bishop
reading in Cima's painting has here been replaced by St. Francis
who, however, likewise is shown reading. The background is
different, two imposing trees having been added. Busati's work
is not unpleasant but looks rather mediocre when compared with
Cima's model.

Another signed painting by Busati is a St. Antony in the
gallery of Vicenza (fig. 283); holding a book and a lily against a
poor landscape background, he forms a stiff and ungraceful
figure. The connexion with Cima is here less obvious but he must
have been one of the master's most servile assistants and it is for
this reason that it is difficult to recognize his hand in those
works which are perhaps due to their combined labours. I think
it just possible that he should be held responsible for a half-length
figure of St. James, also in the gallery of Venice (601); it shows
the false signature *"Marci Zotti opus"*. Cima's picture in Vienna,
on account of the similarity in composition with Busati's signed
work, has also been attributed to this master (^{2}). A fruitless
attempt has been made to identify Busati with "Pseudo Basaiti".

* * *

Gerolamo di Bernardino da Udine (^{3}) is revealed to us as a

(^{1}) No importance should be given to the coats-of-arms which, according to Ludwig, are those of the Contarini, Donato and Marcello
families. *Serra*, Catal. delle R. Gal. di Venezia, p. 43, informs us that they
are those of Badoero, Diedo and Gabriel and besides, that they are later
additions.

(^{2}) Arch. Stor. dell' arte, I, p. 313.

(^{3}) *Crowe and Cavalcaselle*, op. cit., III, p. 78. *Joppi e Bampo*, Contrib.
alla stor. dell' arte nel Friuli, IV, 1894, p. 24. *Fiocco*, in Thieme-Becker,
Künstlerlexikon, XIV, p. 183, with bibliography.

Fig. 282. Andrea Busati, St. Mark and Saints. Accademia, Venice.

Fig. 283. Andrea Busati, St. Antony of Padua. Museum,
Vicenza.   Photo Filippi.

Fig. 284. Gerolamo da Udine, Coronation of the Virgin. Museo Comunale,
Udine. Photo Alinari.

skilful pupil of Cima, and thoroughly dominated by him, in the
Coronation of the Virgin, formerly in the church of S. Francesco
dell' Ospedale, Udine, now in the town gallery, a work which is
signed: *"Opus Jeronimi utinensis"* (fig. 284). Under an architectural dais, with a huge curtain which conceals most of the
landscape, the Virgin kneels before God the Father Who places a
crown on her head. The Holy Ghost and the Child Jesus hover above.
On the steps of the throne a little angel plays the lute while the
two SS. John stand one to either side. The types, the proportions
and the somewhat academic spirit of the entire work place it in
the immediate environment of Cima and I see no trace of the
influence of Carpaccio which other critics have found in this
painting. The artist died in 1512 and from documents of 1506,

1508, 1509, 1510 and 1511 we learn that he was living and active in Udine but they offer us no further information about this particular Gerolamo, who has sometimes been confounded with other painters of the same name, including Gerolamo da Santacroce, and because of this mistake his activity has been prolonged for almost thirty years after his death.

A work which I think without sufficient reason has been ascribed to Gerolamo da Udine is the rather problematic picture of St. Mark and two saints in the Academy of Vienna, which I believe to be by Cima (v. p. 397), although I am of opinion that the lateral figures of Justice and Temperance in the Accademia of Venice might be from Gerolamo's hand.

As I said before, he may have assisted Cima in the execution of the Coronation of the Virgin in SS. Giovanni e Paolo as well as in that in the Patrizi Palace, neither of which works are by Cima alone.

I am very much inclined to agree with Fiocco that Gerolamo's hand can be recognized in a lunette of St. Peter the Martyr in the midst of angels, four playing musical instruments and three holding crowns, in the gallery of Udine (fig. 285), but not in the painting of St. Ursula and her companions in the Brera (157), nor in that of the three saints from the Leuchtenberg collection, Vienna, now in the Metropolitan Museum, New York.

*
* *

Bernardino da Murano ([1]) was an artist who was strongly inspired by Cima's later and more monumental manner, if it really was he who executed the picture of St. Helen on a pedestal, holding a large cross, between the holy bishop Avenna and the knight St. Geminianus, which is mentioned by Ridolfi (I, p. 391) and Zanetto (p. 29) as in the church of S. Geminiano, Venice; the former affirms that it is by Bernardino da Murano while the latter tells us that it is signed: *"Bernardin"*. Their description of the author as a more or less retrograde Muranese is not at all appropriate to the master of this already definitely Cinquecentesque panel, which is now preserved in the gallery of the Academy

---

([1]) *Crowe and Cavalcaselle*, op. cit., I, p. 75. *Thieme-Becker*, Künstlerlexikon, III, p. 442. *Ludwig*, Jahrb. Kunsthist. Samml. d. Allerh. Kaiserh., XXII[2], p. 12.

Fig. 285. Gerolamo da Udine, St. Peter the Martyr and Angels. Museo Comunale, Udine.

Photo Alinari.

Fig. 286. Bernardino da Murano, St. Helen. Academy, Vienna.

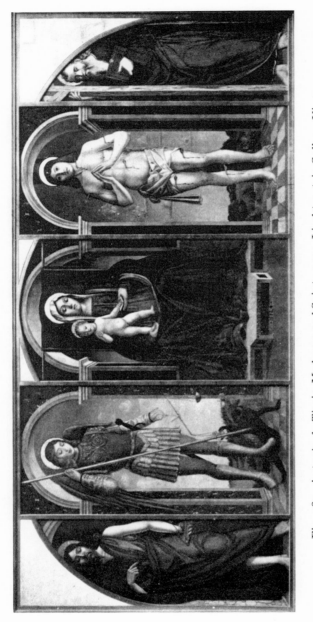

Fig. 287. Antonio de Tisoio, Madonna and Saints, 1512. Liechtenstein Gallery, Vienna.

of Vienna (15) (fig. 286); several critics seem to be in ignorance of the existence of this work (¹).

The attributions to Bernardino of an altar-piece of the Madonna enthroned and four saints in the museum of Vicenzo and and of two large canvases — organ shutters — showing St. Zeno, St. Benedict and the Madonna and angel of the Annunciation, in the museum of Verona (366), are entirely unfounded. I know of no other work which might be by Bernardino da Murano and this artist should not be identified with Bernardino da Verona or da Milano.

* *
*

By Antonio de Tisoio (²) we have a polyptych of the Madonna enthroned between SS. John the Baptist, Michael, Sebastian and Andrew, formerly in the church of Orzes, now in the Liechtenstein Gallery, Vienna, which is signed and dated: "*Antonio de Tisoio pinxit 1512*" (fig. 287). I do not know of any other work by this master, but Crowe and Cavalcaselle, who saw these panels at Orzes when they were in a very damaged condition and arranged in two rows, cite still a signed Madonna in Casa Ragani, three angels belonging to Count Agosti and a fresco of the Madonna in Casa Carlo Miari, all in Belluno. These authors affirm that in the artist's manner an intermingling of the influences of Vivarini, Bellini and Cima can be discerned, but I find that of the last mentioned painter by far the most important. We can put no faith in their hypothesis that Antonio de Tisoio should be identified with Antonio de Cesa.

* *
*

There are several other painters who, at one moment or another of their career, show stylistic connexion with Cima. In the National Gallery there is a Madonna by Tacconi (³) which is dated 1489, but as it is executed in a manner which Cima followed only at a later stage we can but conclude that the similarity is

---

(¹) *Thieme-Becker*, loc. cit. *L. Venturi*, Pitt. venez., p. 252.

(²) *Crowe and Cavalcaselle*, op. cit., III, p. 61.

(³) *Ludwig*, op. cit., Jahrb. K. Preus. Kunstsamml., Beiheft, XXVI, p. 8. *Von Hadeln*, op. cit. Zeitschr. f. Kunstwiss., 1912.

incidental. As I observed before, the composition repeats that of one of the two Madonna's from Giambellino's workshop.

This, however, is not the case for Giovanni Martini da Udine, who at a certain period of his activity was strongly influenced by Cima, as was also the Marchigian painter Pietro Paolo da Sasso-ferrata, called Agapiti, especially at the outset of his career; this is shown in his enthroned Madonna with SS. Peter and Sebastian in the gallery of Padua, which is signed and dated 1497.

CHAPTER VII

MARCO BASAITI (¹).

Marco Basaiti really belongs to the subsequent generation and in dealing with him we enter further into the 16th century than is our habit, but his art at one period is so much linked up with that of Giovanni Bellini that it would be illogical not to include him in a volume in which we treat the school of Giambellino.

Apart from his works we know next to nothing about Marco Basaiti. Ridolfi, who dedicates a paragraph to this artist, informs us that he came from Friuli, while Vasari makes two different persons out of him: one, Marco Basarini, born in Venice of Greek parents, the other Marco Basaiti, about whom he tells us nothing. Very possibly he was of Greek origin; at least in a will of 1526 we learn that his father had the Greek name of Demetrius. Marco was still alive in 1530 when the corporation of painters in Venice started a new register of their members. We have dated works which cover the period of 1496 till 1521 but, apart from one portrait of 1496, we have really no other authentic work by Basaiti before 1510 because in 1503 he only finished the important panel of St. Ambrose with saints and angels in the Frari church, which had been undertaken by Alvise Vivarini, and in which there does not appear to be one of the figures entirely from the brush of Basaiti, so that we are forced to conclude that in finishing this work Basaiti adapted his manner very thoroughly to that of the older master. However, it cannot be said either

---

(¹) *O. Occioni*, M. B., Venice, 1868. *Morelli*, Critical Studies, I, p. 281. *R. Fry*, Portrait of a Knight by M. B., Burlington Magazine, V, p. 574. *G. Gronau*, Ueber ein Madonnenbild des M. B., Repert. f. Kunstwiss., XX, 1897, p. 301. *Anon*, Una Deposizione del B. alla Brera, Rassegna d'Arte, X, 1910, p. 198. *B. Berenson*, Venetian Painting in America, p. 231. *Fogolari*, M. B., in Thieme-Becker, Künstlerlexikon, III, p. 510.

(²) *Ludwig u. Paoletti*, Repert. f. Kunstwiss., XX, 1897, p. 301.

that this painting is very characteristic of Alvise's later style and, when we come to analyse it, we have to admit that it is a somewhat hybrid production. Fogolari is of opinion that Basaiti should be held responsible for the figures of SS. Sebastian and Jerome in the foreground. Basaiti left the following inscription on it: "*Quod Vivarine tua fatali sorte nequisti Marcus Basaitus nobile promsit opus*". However the fact that Basaiti finished a work begun by Alvise by no means implies that the connexion which existed between these two painters was that of master and pupil.

A more than ordinary perspicacity is required to solve the problem — one might almost call it a mystery — which surrounds the art of Basaiti and which has given rise to a great number of widely different hypotheses. Though often wrong, many of these hypotheses are not lacking in arguments. In the first place there is the question of the Pseudo-Basaiti whose creation was contested and whose existence was finally definitely abandoned. Then there is quite a number of pictures which were, or still are, attributed by some to Basaiti and by others to Giambellino, while at the same time we find opposition to the theory that Basaiti ever acted as assistant to Giambellino.

Again we should keep in mind that we know nothing concerning the date of Basaiti's early activity and although he was still alive in 1530 he might easily have been at work prior to the year of his first dated picture, the portrait of 1496. It represents a young man in full face against a landscape background and is found in the von Pannwitz collection, Bennebroek (Holland) (fig. 288) [1]. This delightful piece of work is signed by the master but it is not possible to construct a hypothesis about the origin of Basaiti's art from this painting which, like most Venetian portraits of the end of the 15th century, shows a certain resemblance to those by Giovanni Bellini. Another painting of similar type, signed by Basaiti, exists in the National Gallery, London (2498) (fig. 289) [2].

There is a group of Madonnas, several of which are signed, which leads us to believe that Marco Basaiti was not a pupil of

---

[1] No. 21 of the catalogue of the exhibition of ancient Italian art in Dutch possession, Amsterdam, 1934.

[2] *L. Venturi*, L'Arte, XXVI, 1923, is of the opinion that the signature is spurious and that the painting might be by Mocetto but this theory is without foundation.

Fig. 288. Marco Basaiti, portrait of a man, 1496. Von Pannwitz Collection,
Bennebroek (Holland).   Photo Bruckmann.

Alvise Vivarini but rather started his career with this artist's
uncle, Bartolomeo, whose broad proportions and sturdy forms and
even that touch of Paduan linear mannerism, so characteristic of
his art, he passed on to Basaiti. But there is a small link missing
in the chain because, even though dependent on Bartolomeo
Vivarini, these Madonnas by Basaiti are already somewhat more

Fig. 289. Marco Basaiti, portrait of a man. National Gallery, London.
Photo National Gallery.

evolved than Bartolomeo's examples, and it may well be that we
have to search for the missing link in some of Basaiti's earlier
productions which, however, are unknown to us.

Messrs Frizzoni (¹), Berenson and A. Venturi claim for the

(¹) Arch. stor. dell' arte, N. S., III, 1897, p. 92.

Fig. 290. Marco Basaiti, Madonna. National Gallery, London.
Photo National Gallery.

early years of Basaiti a half-length figure of the Madonna holding
the languid looking nude Child Who stands on a low wall in front
of her, with two angels playing the lute against a very beautiful
landscape background, which is preserved in the museum of
Berlin (40) and is catalogued as a Venetian painting of around the

year 1500. Previously it was ascribed, I think more correctly, to a painter influenced by Alvise and Francesco Bonsignori.

This suggestion is interesting although not very convincing; still it brings us into the artistic circle to which the following works, which are by Basaiti, belong.

The earliest of them might be the composition of the Madonna in half-length figure with the nude Child in benediction standing on a parapet, of which there are two versions, one in the Liechtenstein Gallery, Vienna (846), which is signed and in which the background is all landscape, while a thin veil covers part of the Child's body; the other in the National Gallery, London (2499) in which most of the background is occupied by a curtain and in which the characteristic features are more strongly emphasized (fig. 290). The latter was no doubt the first to be executed. The negroid type of faces of the Virgin and Child, as well as the curious position of the latter, are certainly of Paduan origin.

Somewhat less unusual are: the signed Madonna in the museum of Berlin (1262) and that in the Correr Museum (fig. 291). Both of them show the background of curtain and landscape but are different in composition. In the former the Virgin is depicted in knee-length figure with the nude Child, Who grasps a bird, sitting on her knee; in the latter we see the Virgin standing; she holds upright on a parapet the naked Infant Who bestows a blessing on an adorer, of whom little more than the head is visible.

In three other Madonnas the master reveals a still closer connexion with Bartolomeo Vivarini. One of them, which a short time ago was for sale in Holland, represents, against the background of a wall pierced by a window through which we see a landscape, the Virgin in full face with one hand on her breast while with the other she supports the Child Jesus Who is seated on a wall and Who has a fruit in His hand (fig. 292). Of slightly later date is, I think, a picture in the Vatican Gallery (previously in the store room, 304) (¹), in which the Child Jesus, Who is seated on a cushion on His Mother's knee, blesses the adoring infant St. John. The last of the three is the signed painting in the Harrach collection, Vienna (fig. 293); against a landscape background the Madonna in three-quarter length figure holds on her knee the nude Child Who touches His mouth.

(¹) *De Benedetti*, Apollo, XVIII, Aug. 1933, p. 71.

Fig. 291. Marco Basaiti, Madonna and Donor. Correr Museum, Venice.
Photo Alinari.

Bartolomeo Vivarini's types are found also in a fairly mediocre picture of the Deposition in the gallery of Boston (5) (fig. 294) (¹). As in later versions of the same subject, those for example at Munich and in the Brera, the whole composition is dominated by

(¹) *Berenson*, Gazette des Beaux Arts, XV, 1896, p. 204.

Fig. 292. Marco Basaiti, Madonna. Private Collection, Amsterdam.
Photo Eilers.

the stiff out-stretched leg of the dead Saviour. Vasari mentions
a painting of this subject by Basaiti in the church of S. Francesco
della Vigna. Of much the same quality and similar in style is a
panel, with a spurious signature, of the Lord half-risen from His

Fig. 293. Marco Basaiti, Madonna. Harrach Collection, Vienna.

tomb between two adoring angels, in the Correr Museum ([1]).
That the period in which he was dominated by Bartolomeo

([1]) G. *Fiocco*, Carpaccio, Rome (1933), pl. 9, attributes this panel to
Carpaccio.

Fig. 294. Marco Basaiti, Pietà. Fine Arts Museum, Boston.

Museum Photo.

Vivarini preceded that in which he was subjected to the influence of Bellini seems to me certain.

The latter phase apparently reached its climax between 1509 and 1515, and I think the above mentioned works must have been executed at an earlier date. But again we do not know if these two currents did not overlap in Basaiti's evolution.

The earliest work showing a strong Belliniesque character is, I believe, the signed Pietà, in which the dead Saviour is surrounded by five of the faithful, in the gallery of Berlin (6) (fig. 295); some of the types were obviously borrowed from Giambellino and if we compare this painting with the Pietàs in Toledo, in the museum of Berlin and in Stuttgart, which are productions of Bellini or of his workshop, we discover Basaiti's source of inspiration for the figures of Christ, the Virgin, the curly headed St. John and the bearded old Joseph of Arimathea.

It must have been shortly before the execution of the Call of

Fig. 295. Marco Basaiti, Pietà. Museum, Berlin.   Museum Photo.

the Sons of Zebedee that Basaiti painted his most Belliniesque
picture: the grandiose triptych in the Kaiser Friedrich Museum
(20) (fig. 296), formerly in the church of S. Cristoforo della Pace,

Fig. 296. Marco Basaiti, triptych. Museum, Berlin.

between Venice and Murano. The authorship of this altar-piece
has been a subject of discussion for many generations. Martinioni,
in his edition of Sansovino (1663), thought it was executed in the
manner of Santacroce; Boschini (p. 20) attributed it to Cima;
Waagen, Crowe and Cavalcaselle and at one time also Berenson
were of the opinion that it was by Basaiti; while it was more or
less in honour of this fine triptych that Ludwig and Gronau
created the Pseudo-Basaiti. The latter, however, has since given

up the theory of the existence of this hypothetic painter and now
includes the painting among the works of Giovanni Bellini by
whom, at least for the greater part, Mr Berenson also thinks it
is ([1]). Perhaps the destruction of the Pseudo-Basaiti has been too
radical because I think that a certain artistic output corresponds
to the activity of this imaginary person, an activity which seems
to coincide with the collaboration of Basaiti and Giovanni Bellini.
The popularity which this picture enjoyed is revealed in the
number of replicas which exist of the different figures ([2]).

There are certain features, however, which do not enter the
range of Bellini's art, as for example the soft sweetness of the
figures and faces, the elaborate and artificial drapery, which does
not mould the forms of SS. Jerome and John the Baptist, and the
slight woodenness of the figure of St. Francis, while the landscape,
though very fine, is too minute and almost hard. With regard to
the date of this picture a comparison between the signed painting
of the Madonna in half-length figure with the nude Child between SS. Helen and Veronica in the lunette and that of 1509 by
Bellini in Detroit, excludes the possibility that the triptych in
Berlin could have been executed much earlier than this year.
Hence, if Bellini's collaborator in this case was really Basaiti we
have to admit that the latter worked in Bellini's studio long after
he was independently established.

To the period when Giambellino dominated Basaiti I attribute
still the fine picture of the Madonna, almost in profile, holding the
nude Child on her knee and touching the head of a kneeling donor,
against the background of a curtain and a landscape, in the Ca
d'Oro, Venice (fig. 297) ([3]); probably also the beautiful Pietà in
which the Virgin holds her dead Son lying on her knee in a particularly elaborate landscape with many buildings, in the Dona

---

([1]) E. Ludwig, op. cit., Jahrb. d. K. Preus. Kunstsamml., XXIV, 1903,
p. 114; XXVI, 1905, Beiheft, p. 28. G. Gronau in Die Gemälde Gallerie der
K. Museem zu Berlin, I, Berlin, 1888—1909, Venetian school, p. 39. The
Same, Kunstgesch. Gesellschaft, Sitzungsbericht, VI, 1900. The Same,
Spätwerke, p. 7 et seq. The Same, Bellini, p. 214.

([2]) Gronau, loc. cit.

([3]) Catalogued as school of Bellini. C. Gamba, Bollettino d'arte del
Minist. della Pubbl. Istr., 1916, p. 329: near Catena. R. Longhi, Vita
Artistica, II, 1927, p. 134 and Gronau: late Giovanni Bellini.

Fig. 297. Marco Basaiti, Madonna and Donor. Ca d' Oro, Venice.
Photo Anderson.

delle Rose collection, Venice (Gronau, Bellini, 71) ([1]); the half-length figure of Christ carrying the cross in the museum of Rovigo ([2]); the oblong picture of the Madonna between four saints in Birmingham, which I have already mentioned (p. 386); a Madonna between SS. Augustine and Peter against a landscape background with the signature of Giovanni Bellini and the date 1512, in the Johnson collection, Philadelphia ([3]); and possibly the

---

([1]) *Von Hadeln*, Zeitschr. f. Bild. Kunst, N. F., XXXIII, 1922, p. 112, about 1501—2; he thinks the city represented in the background is Vicenza. *Berenson*, Venetian Painting in America, p. 236: studio version.

([2]) *Hendy*, Burlington Magazine, LVI, 1930, p. 197: Bellini.

([3]) *Perkins*, Rassegna d'Arte, V, 1905, p. 132: Basaiti. *Berenson*, Catal. of the Ital. Pictures of the Johnson coll., No. 184: Gerolamo da Santacroce.

Fig. 298. Marco Basaiti, Madonna and Saint. Gallery, Stuttgart.

St. Jerome in his study in the National Gallery (694) (¹); of the
last mentioned there exists a replica in the Städelsches Kunstinstitut, Frankfort.

The principal figures of the panel in the Ca d'Oro have been
repeated in a picture in the gallery of Stuttgart (428) (fig. 298)

(¹) *Collins Baker*, Burlington Magazine, XLII, 1923, p. 245.

where however, by the absence of the adorer, the attitudes have lost their meaning. The painter has tried to remedy this short-coming by placing the Madonna's outstretched hand on a book. A female saint in adoration stands to the left. In this picture the influence of Giambellino is, if any thing, still more evident.

By the same hand but in an earlier manner and again showing a very close connexion with Bellini is, I believe, the romantic painting of a youth with one shoulder bare in the Martin Le Roy collection, Paris; in spite of the presence of Bellini's signature, this work has been ascribed to Basaiti by other critics [1].

The same applies to the important panel of the death of St. Peter the Martyr in the National Gallery (218), formerly in the Eastlake collection (fig. 299), which is signed: "*Joannes Bellini*" [2]. The event itself, the slaying of St. Peter and Brother Dominic by two soldiers, is really the least important part of this composition in which the landscape, where we see a town and wood-cutters at work in a forest, plays the principal rôle. However, in the execution we notice the same precision, verging on hardness, which charac-terized the triptych in Berlin. The foliage of the trees is painted in a very peculiar manner with strong points of light and is over-minutely designed. A somewhat similar effect is found in the picture of St. Francis in the Frick collection, and it is still more evident in the Orpheus scene in the Widener collection, Phila-delphia, which, as I said before, I believe to be by Basaiti and certainly not by Giambellino.

The replica of the martyrdom of St. Peter which exists in the collection of Viscount Lee of Fareham, Richmond, shows con-siderable variations in style and composition [3]. At one time the

---

[1] *P. Leprieur et A. Pératé*, Catalogue raisonné de la collection Martin Le Roy, Paris, 1909, No. 13. *Reinach*, Repert. des peintures, IV, fig. 689.

[2] Reprod. as a work of Basaiti by *Wölfflin*, Klassische Kunst, 5th ed., Munich, 1912, p. 270.

[3] In the catalogue of the Burlington Club exhibition of Venetian art, 1912, where the latter was exhibited as No. 30, both pictures are attributed to Giambellino with the suggestion that the painting in the National Gallery might have been executed with the assistance of Catena and the one in the Lee collection with that of Basaiti. In *T. Borenius*, Catalogue of the Pictures collected by Viscount and Viscountess Lee of Fareham, I, (1923), privately printed, No. 11, the panel in this collection is assigned

XVII. 32

Fig. 299. Marco Basaiti, Death of St. Peter the Martyr. National Gallery, London.

Photo National Gallery.

THE CALL OF THE SONS OF ZEBEDEE
By Marco Basaiti in the Accademia of Venice.

date 1509 was inscribed on the back and without any doubt it is of a later and more evolved style than the version in the National Gallery and, at the same time, softer and more pleasing in technique and of greater pictorial quality. The two martyrdom scenes are here more central and nearer to one another, while the soldiers are three in number. The forest occupies almost all the background but through a gap in the trees we see a piece of landscape. This painting has certainly more of Basaiti's fascinating sweetness than the example in the National Gallery.

Consequently we are forced to believe that at a certain moment Basaiti worked in Bellini's studio; in several cases, as we have just seen, with the master's help and the use of his cartoons. Moreover, we have to admit a continued intimacy with Bellini's art in order to explain the transformation which Basaiti's art underwent between what I take to be his earliest manner and that in which his pictures of 1510 are executed. Curiously enough, the two large altar-pieces of this year again show a considerable difference. In the Call of the Sons of Zebedee which Vasari, Sansovino, Ridolfi and Zanetti saw in the church of S. Andrea della Certosa but which is now in the gallery of Venice (39), the greater part of the picture is occupied by a very fine landscape, but the importance given to this feature is more after the taste of Cima than of Bellini (Plate). The elements in the landscape itself are apparently borrowed in part from the former and in part from the latter (the rocks to the left). The brightness of the light is more Cimaesque but the older master's refinement is lacking.

The well-proportioned and finely designed figures with noble Belliniesque heads all show that particularly hard and angular drapery which we noticed in the triptych of Berlin, here however it is more pronounced and slightly displeasing but there can be no doubt that it is the outcome of the same artistic mentality.

The vessels moored in the foreground, the seated fisherman and certain details in the background reveal a Carpacciesque taste for the detailed study of human existence. The picture is signed and dated: *"M.D.X. M. Basaiti"*.

More strongly Belliniesque and reflecting the influence of a

to the Venetian school circa 1510. *Gronau*, op. cit., p. 216. *Constable*, International Studio, Feb. 1930, p. 25. *Balniel and Clark*, op. cit., No. 170, ascribe it to Giovanni Bellini.

Fig. 300. Marco Basaiti, Prayer in the Garden of Olives, 1510. Accademia,
Venice.   Photo Anderson.

later manner is the Prayer in the Garden of Olives which Vasari, who makes a mistake about the saints, Ridolfi and Zanetti saw in the Foscari chapel in S. Giobbe but which is now in the gallery of Venice (69) (fig. 300). The inscription: "*1510 Marcus Basitus*", however, leaves us in no doubt as to the date it was executed. The use of an architectural arch as frame is borrowed sooner from Cima but the idea of the lamp suspended from the ceiling he has evidently taken from Bellini's lost altar-piece, once in SS. Giovanni e Paolo. To a certain extent restoration has altered the appearance of this panel but we can be sure that there never existed any trace of that particular type of angular folds which we found in abundance in the other production of the same year. The drapery of the three sleeping Apostles is more severe than that of the lateral saints who, of large build and suave expression, correspond to those we find in Bellini's works of a few years earlier.

Around these two pictures, both Belliniesque but very different in appearance, we can group the following productions. First of all there is the delightful and finely executed figure of St. Catherine in the gallery of Budapest (92) (¹), which I think, should be considered the most charming work we have from the hand of this master (fig. 301). Then we should include in this group: a St. Sebastian attached to the column, with houses on a hill in the background, in the Doria Gallery, Rome (124), of which a replica, with only very slight variations, I believe also by Basaiti, is found in the gallery of Berlin (37); an unimportant painting of St. Jerome in penitence before the crucifix in the gallery of Venice (107), formerly in the church of S. Giorgio Maggiore; and a particularly fine St. Jerome reading in a landscape in the Walters collection, Baltimore (¹). Harder in execution but in style not unlike that of the Call of the Sons of Zebedee is the already mentioned Deposition in the Ältere Pinakothek, Munich (H. G. 48); it is depicted in an important composition with the three crosses and a dramatic and agitated group below; again we see the rigidly outstretched leg of the Saviour (fig. 302).

It is difficult to believe that the artist, who executed the figure

---

(¹) *A. Venturi*, L'Arte, III, 1900, pp. 210, 232.
(²) Reprod. in *Berenson*, Venetian Painting in America, fig. 98.

Fig. 301. Marco Basaiti, St. Catherine. Gallery, Budapest.   Photo Bardt.

of Christ in the Call of the Sons of Zebedee, did not also paint the
picture of the Saviour seated handing the keys to St. Peter in the
Prado Gallery, Madrid (20); however in the same picture there
are three female figures which are painted in a different manner
and to a certain extent they justify Mr Berenson's opinion, in
which he is followed by Professor A. Venturi, that the entire

Fig. 302. Marco Basaiti, Deposition. Ältere Pinakothek, Munich.
Museum Photo.

work is by Catena. In this case we might be tempted to think of the possibility of a collaboration.

Sooner inspired by Bellini's later manner and consequently revealing stylistic analogies with the Prayer in the Garden of

Fig. 303. Marco Basaiti, dead Christ and Angels. Accademia, Venice.

Photo Anderson.

Olives is a fine panel of the beardless Saviour, dead and lying on a stone slab, in the gallery of Venice (108) (fig. 303). He is flanked on either side by an ingenuous playful angel, for which Francesco da Milano is sometimes held responsible, while the background is formed by a rocky landscape. This painting originates from the convent of Sta. Maria dei Miracoli.

In the same group should be classified: the oblong picture of the Madonna and Child with a knight holding a book with a beautiful Persian binding, against the background of a curtain and a landscape above which four cherubim hover in mid-air, in the Johnson collection, Philadelphia (180); and possibly also the signed painting of the Madonna in half-length figure adoring the Child Who lies in front of her, between St. Peter and a holy knight and again three cherubim above, in the gallery of Padua (33) (fig. 304). In the latter work we can discern a knowledge of Giorgione's art. Curiously enough this new element is most clearly manifest in the holy knight, although there is nothing in this figure which particularly recalls Giorgione's representation of a holy warrior in Cinquecento attire, in the Castelfranco altar-piece, which induced other artists to imitate his example.

Compared with the Prayer in the Garden of Olives of 1510, a second picture of the Calling of the Sons of Zebedee — this time of small dimensions — which is signed and dated 1515, seems rather reactionary.

This picture, which in the 17th century was in the collection of the Archduchess of Austria and which Teniers engraved in his "Theatrum pictorium", is now in the gallery of Vienna (fig. 305). It is a very fine piece of painting and although it is composed of the same figures more or less in similar positions, with the exception of the man in the foreground, who in this case is not depicted fishing, it is very different from the painting of 1510 of the same subject. The composition however is shown in the reverse sense and the landscape is quite different. The style of execution is strongly Belliniesque and somewhat more conservative.

Of the last years of Basaiti's activity we have several signed and dated works, which reveal to us the artist's rapid development in accordance with the new principles which appeared in the Venetian school. In the gallery of Bergamo (389) there is a bust of the Saviour in benediction, signed and dated 1517, which is

Fig. 304. Marco Basaiti, Madonna and Saints. Museum, Padua.

Photo Alinari.

decidedly Cinquecentesque in appearance, while a fully signed
and dated picture of 1519 of the Madonna nursing the Child,
which some time ago belonged to Messrs Boehler, Munich, has, as
far as I know, never yet been published (fig. 306). The composition is rather fantastic for a painter who up till now has always
shown himself to be a traditionalist. The Virgin is seated on the
ground and St. Jerome, who is also seated, looks on attentively,

Fig. 305. Marco Basaiti, the Call of the Sons of Zebedee. Gallery, Vienna.
Photo v. J. Löwy.

Fig. 306. Marco Basaiti, Madonna and Saints, 1519. Formerly in the Böhler
Collection, Munich.

while to the other side St. John the Evangelist stands in conversation with another saint. The greater part of the background is
taken up with a distant view of a landscape and quaint clouds.
It is a curious picture and shows practically no stylistic connexion
with that executed four years before; the drapery in particular
is treated with heavy plastic effects of a considerably later style
and one which for the period is fairly advanced. In my opinion
this work is not entirely devoid of Lombard elements. The Christ
Resurrected in the Ambrosiana, Milan, was no doubt executed
about the same time as the picture in Bergamo, as indeed was
probably also the signed Deposition in the Brera Gallery [1].
Here, seven of the faithful are depicted around the body of Our
Lord at the foot of the cross, and once more one of the Saviour's
legs in a rigid horizontal position is a dominating feature in the
lower part of the composition. Again some of the types remind us
of the Lombard school, while stylistically it compares best with
the dated work of 1519.

[1] Rassegna d'Arte, X, 1910, p. 198.

In the gallery of Venice (120) there is still an important picture, signed and dated 1520, of St. George slaying the dragon on the banks of a river (fig. 307). He is mounted on a beautiful white prancing steed and the princess stands close by; a landscape with hills, buildings and a bridge forms the background (¹). This picture, which originates from S. Pietro in Castello, is rather lifeless; both the human types again recall the Lombard school.

In the church from which the St. George was taken there is still an altar-piece of St. Peter enthroned as pope between four full-length figures of saints, one of whom — St. Roch — has one foot on the lowest step of the throne and appears to speak to St. Peter (fig. 308). The wide arch, through which we see an extensive landscape, and the general lines of the composition are obviously inspired by some of Cima's late works, as for instance the enthroned St. Peter of 1516, which might have been finished a few years before this altar-piece was undertaken. It is no doubt contemporary with the St. George of 1520 and from an artistic point of view is even less animated.

There is an interesting, though somewhat restored, portrait dated 1521 from the hand of Basaiti in the gallery of Bergamo (563) (²). It is thoroughly Cinquecentesque in appearance but shows no stylistic connexion with either Titian or Giorgione; it reminds us more of the art of Bartolomeo Veneto.

Very similar and no doubt also from the brush of Basaiti, although somewhat less interesting, is a half-length figure of a man with a beard near a round window in the Johnson collection, Philadelphia (181) (fig. 309). On the other hand we find still attributed to Basaiti particularly striking examples of portraiture in the gallery of Bergamo (394, signed), in the collection of Mrs Stuyvesant in New York (³), in the W.B. Paterson collection, London (⁴), and still another in English private ownership (⁵). There are still several other pictures by Basaiti (⁶).

(¹) Mentioned by Boschini and Zanetti and Moschini: Gallerie Nazionali, II, 1896, p. 27.

(²) *Frizzoni*, Arch. stor. dell' arte, V, 1892, p. 227. *The Same*, Le Gallerie in Bergamo, p. 209. *Chamot*, Apollo, Dec. 1929, p. 319.

(³) Reprod. in *Berenson*, Venetian Painting in America, fig. 100.

(⁴) *R. Fry*, Burlington Magazine, V, 1904, p. 574.

(⁵) *H. Cook*, Burlington Magazine, VIII, 1905, p. 338.

(⁶) **Aix-en-Provence,** Gallery, 461, half-length figure of a seated

Fig. 307. Marco Basaiti, St. George slaying the dragon. Accademia,
Venice.   Photo Anderson.

Only a few drawings can be classified as works by Basaiti. In the first place there are two figures of saints, one with a beard,

Madonna, with the naked Child standing on her knee in a landscape background, attributed to Cima. **Altenburg,** Gallery, No. 158, Madonna. **Bari,** Gallery, No. 97, Pietà; No. 99, St. James and a holy bishop. **Bergamo,** Gallery, No. 940, Madonna nursing the Child (*Berenson*). **Bologna,** Modiano coll., St. Jerome in a landscape (doubtful) (*R. Buscaroli*, La Pittura di paesaggio in Italia, Bologna, 1935, pl. 12). **Budapest,** Gallery, No. 111, portrait of Doge Agostino Barbarigo (catalogued as school of Giovanni Bellini; correctly attributed to Basaiti by Berenson). **Esztergom,** angels(?). **Florence,** Contini Bonacossi coll., signed Madonna, with the nude Child holding a bird, against a landscape background. **Kassel,** Gallery, No. 486, Christ blessing(?). **Milan,** ex-Crespi coll., oblong picture of the Madonna and Christ between SS. Sebastian and Ursula, an important early work (*Venturi*, La Galleria Crespi, p. 121). **Munich,** Ältere Pinakothek, No. 31, Madonna with SS. Sebastian, Jerome and a donor. **New York,** for sale 1921, a signed painting of the Madonna in half-length figure with the nude Child standing against a background of a curtain and a landscape. **Stockholm,** National Gallery, the dead Saviour seated leaning against some stones which are covered with plants; it is attributed to Giovanni Bellini by *O. Sirén*, Italianska tavlor och techningar i National museum etc., Stockholm, 1933, p. 89 and to Rocco Marconi by *G. M. Richter*, Apollo, March 1934, p. 129, but I am sooner of Mr. Berenson's opinion that it is by Basaiti. **Strasbourg,** Gallery, No. 225, St. Jerome seated in a landscape (Arch. stor. dell' arte, N. S., II, 1896, p. 279). **Venice,** Salute church, sacristy, St. Sebastian, late work; Gallery, No. 68, SS. James and Antony Abbot. In his lists and in "Venetian Painting in America" Mr. Berenson attributes to Basaiti still several other pictures which are unknown to me. He no longer holds Basaiti responsible for the portrait (179) in the Johnson collection, Philadelphia. The St. Sebastian and adorer in the gallery of Aix- en -Provence, No. 494, which Mr Berenson gives to Basaiti, seems to me a school production. Of the works wrongly attributed to Basaiti I shall cite the Madonna in the gallery of Stuttgart (429) which is by Marco Bello (*Perkins*, Rassegna d'arte, 1905, p. 132). For other attributions v. Arch. stor. dell' arte, 1888, I, p. 295; idem, N.S., I, p. 76; L'Arte, VIII, p. 285

Paintings mentioned by ancient authors, which are now lost or which cannot be identified, are: a St. Jerome in S. Daniele, Venice, cited by Sansovino and Ridolfi. Ridolfi refers also to a "Death of the Lord" at the "Padri Crociferi" in Padua and a Deposition in the abbey church of Villa di Sesto; the latter is recorded as well by *Lanzi* and by *F. di Maniago*, Storia delle Belle Arti friulane, Venice, 1819, p. 123. Vasari speaks of a "S. Bernardino sopra un sasso e altri santi" in S. Giobbe and Zanetti, who wrongly assigns to this master Bellini's Assumption in Murano, cites besides a picture of St. Peter enthroned between SS. Andrew and Francis in the "Magistrato delle Ragion Vecchie".

Fig. 308. Marco Basaiti, St. Peter and four Saints. S. Pietro in Castello, Venice.   Photo Alinari.

the other clean-shaven, on two separate sheets executed in dark grey and white, in the Louvre. Then in the British Museum (52 II

Fig. 309. Marco Basaiti, portrait of a man. Johnson Collection, Philadelphia.

Photo Courtesy of the John G. Johnson Art Coll., Philadelphia.

vol. II No. 8) a sketch of the Saviour and two figures in a landscape with some other persons in the distance, which is attributed to Montagna, might be included in this category. In the Uffizi we find a drawing of a nude dead body lying on a stone, which perhaps served as the rough sketch for the picture of the dead Christ in the gallery of Venice ([1]), while in the Print

---

([1]) *Fiocco*, Carpaccio, pl. 192, attributes this drawing to Carpaccio.

Room of Berlin, there is a study of a bearded man, with a cap
and a fur coat, who is not unlike the subject of the painting which
belongs to Mrs Stuyvesant (¹).

* *
*

Basaiti at all times has been a greatly appreciated painter. On
two different occasions Sansovino refers to him as "assai celebro
di suo tempo" and "maestro di molto nome". Ridolfi praises his
sweet style and the chasteness which moves souls to devotion.
Zanetti esteems him in a more technical manner and speaks of
his good compositions, the fusion of figures and background, his
bright tasteful colours, his fine drapery and beautiful heads; he
states as well that the master knew how to keep up with the
times.

However, there are few painters who are so difficult to sum up
as Basaiti and the cause of this is his incredible diversity of
manner, a good instance of which we found in the two important
pictures of 1510 which are so dissimilar. His dependence on
Bellini has been exaggerated by some and underrated by others.
I feel certain that at one time, probably towards 1510, Basaiti
either worked in Bellini's studio or in some manner collaborated
with him, and the large triptych in Berlin is one of the fruits of
their joint labours, but in this painting there is more due to
Basaiti than to Bellini. The two different hands which can be
discerned have been the cause of the change in attribution which
this picture has undergone; those who at one time claimed it to
be by Basaiti or Pseudo-Basaiti now ascribe it, at least for the
greater part, to Bellini. But at the same time there are several
other paintings which have been attributed to both these masters.
The St. Francis in the Frick collection, the St. Jerome belonging
to Count Contini, the St. Jerome in the Mackay collection, the
St. Jerome and the martyrdom of St. Peter in the National
Gallery, the martyrdom of St. Peter in the Lee of Fareham
collection, the Feast of Bacchus in the Widener collection have
all at some time or another been assigned to Basaiti and are now
more generaly given to Bellini. Hence I do not think that Mr
Berenson's affirmation that Basaiti and Bellini did not collaborate, holds good. He himself was once upon a time of the

---

(¹) *Von Hadeln*, Venez. Zeichn., pls. 81, 82.

opinion that of the St. Jerome then belonging to Mr Benson, now in the Mackay collection, the figure was by Bellini and the landscape by Basaiti though executed at a later date, but this was but a complicated and unlikely method of surmounting a chronological difficulty. Anyhow this critic now attributes the entire picture to Giovanni Bellini. I sooner agree with his statement that Catena had a lasting influence on Basaiti, although this influence is limited rather to external details. However, the Noli me tangere by Catena in the Brera passed for a long time as a work by Basaiti [1] and, as I said before, the panel in Madrid looks very much like a work painted by these two artists in collaboration.

I do not see much trace of an education received from Alvise Vivarini; besides the opinion about this artist has changed considerably in late years.

Basaiti started his career quite possibly as a pupil of Bartolomeo Vivarini, then, probably towards 1503, he came in contact with Alvise, became the collaborator of Bellini, was subjected to the influence of Cima and of Catena and followed the general change of style which became manifest at the beginning of the 16th century. Then again he seems somehow to have had some connexion with the Lombard school. These I think are the features of the artistic development of Basaiti, who was a clever painter and an enchanting colourist and who, even within one year, produced pictures of very different appearance. Consequently we are not surprised that he did not create a school. To his immediate environment, however, should be assigned a small painting of the Madonna with the Child on her knee against a landscape background on the right wall of the cathedral of Chioggia, and a Madonna in the Platt collection, Englewood, while in the museum of Padua (129) there is a poor picture of the Call of an Apostle which has been more or less inspired by the two examples he painted of a similar subject.

---

[1] *Von Hadeln*, Rassegna d'Arte, 1908, p. 218.

ADDITIONS AND CORRECTIONS
TO VOLUME XVII

p. 11. The predella composed of seven panels on the back of the polyptych of the school of Antonio Vivarini and Giovanni d'Alemagna in S. Zaccaria, Venice (v. fig. 4), is a work by Lorenzo Veneziano and is not repainted. This makes it all the more likely that the Madonna and the two saints nearest to her were, before their thorough restoration, by the same master.

p. 111. Only after this volume had been printed did I notice that I had overlooked a short note by *A. Venturi*, Un opera di Jacopo Bellini, L'Arte, XXXV, 1932, p. 148, in which he makes us acquainted with a very handsome, signed and dated picture of 1443 by Jacopo Bellini, now in the Rasini collection, Milan. It is the earliest dated work we have by this master; it is prior by five years to the small Madonna in the Brera Gallery and slightly more Gothic in style. Considerable space is given to the landscape which shows the curiously shaped spiral rocks we meet with in some of his drawings. A church in the background betrays the interest in architecture which was manifest also in some of the drawings in his sketchbook.

p. 152. Quite recently another portrait of Mohammed II has come to light. It forms part of the A. L. Erlanger collection, New York. Judging from the reproduction given by *W. L. H.*, A new Gentile Bellini, Apollo, XXI, 1935, p. 111, it certainly looks like a fine production of Gentile's own brush. It was executed about the same time as the portrait in the National Gallery but it has even more character and is slightly more oriental in appearance.

p. 200 note 1. I do not agree with Mr Berenson's attribution to Mansueti of the Madonna in the gallery of Bergamo, which I believe to be a production of the school of Giambellino as stated on p. 387 note 1.

p. 334. It has been established that the signature on Bellini's Bacchanal in the Widener collection, Philadelphia reads: *Joannes Bellinus invictus p. 1514* and not "*Venetus*" as was formerly believed (*E. K. Waterhouse*, Burlington Magazine, LXVI, 1935, p. 146. *C. Holmes*, Idem, p. 188). The word "invictus" takes from the inscription the character of a signature, because I cannot imagine an artist signing a picture with the addition of this adjective. Hence, I think that it must have been Bellini's collaborator, Titian, who inscribed these words on the canvas.

p. 339. Possibly by Giovanni Bellini, and in this case a work of his late years, is the bust-length portrait of a friar — according to the inscription the general of the Eremitani order — which belonged to the late Sir George Houston Boswall and which at the beginning of 1935 was exhibited at the Burlington Fine Arts Club. It is, however, considerably restored.

p. 383. A picture of the Circumcision, identical in composition with that in the museum of Berlin, but finer in quality, belongs to Mr. Stewart Borchard, New York, and was published quite recently as a work of Giambellino by *Ph. Hendy*, The Presentation by Giovanni Bellini, Burlington Magazine, LXVI, 1935, p. 122. It bears Bellini's signature and can be traced back to 1783 in the galleries of the Princes of Hessen. Judging from the reproduction, I am more inclined to look upon it as a workshop production, though superior to the other examples we know of the same composition.

INDICES

INDICES TO VOLUME XVII

Compound names divided by di, de, del, etc., will be found under the letter of the first name, all the others under that of the second.

GEOGRAPHICAL INDEX

The ciphers in brackets are those of the museum or sale catalogues. Illustrated descriptions are indicated by bold-faced numbers.

Agram.
  Strossmayer Gallery, *Catena,* Madonna and saints 371; *Cima da Conegliano,* SS. Augustine and Benedict 455[1].
Aigueperse.
  Notre Dame, *Mantegna,* St. Sebastian 218.
Aix en Provence.
  Gallery, *Basaiti, Marco* —, Madonna (461) 509[6];*idem, school of* —, St. Sebastian and adorer 509[6].
Ajalà.
  Bellini, Giovanni —, *copy of* — Madonna belonging to Duveen, Brothers, New York 326[2].
Altenburg.
  Gallery, *Basaiti, Marco* —, Madonna (158) 509[6]; *Vivarini, Antonio* —, Madonna (157) 39[2].
Alzano (near Bergamo).
  Bellini, Giovanni —, Madonna v. Gallery, Bergamo.
America.
  Private coll., *Antonio da Carpi,* Madonna 466; *Bellini, Gentile* —, portrait of a senator, formerly for sale in Germany 150.
Amsterdam.
  Rijksmuseum, *Cima da Conegliano,* Madonna 444.
  Lanz coll., *Bonsignori,* St. Sebastian 173[1].
  Private coll., *Basaiti, Marco* —, Madonna **487;** *Bellini, Gen-*

tile —, bust of young man with a beard **171;** profile of middle-aged clean-shaven man 172; *Bellini, Giovanni* —, Madonna **262.**
  Schuster coll., *Cima da Conegliano,* Madonna 438.
  Tietje coll., *Mansueti, Giovanni* —, Madonna and saints, from the Gallery, Oldenburg 200[1].
  For sale a few years ago, *Cima da Conegliano,* Madonna 396.
Andria.
  Monastery of Frati Minori, *Vivarini, Antonio* —, altar-piece v. Museum, Bari; three half-figures of saints 38, 39.
Antwerp.
  Van Veerle coll. (15th cent.), *Bellini, Giovanni* —, Madonna and saints 341[1].
Apulia.
  Vivarini, Antonio —, active 44.
Arbe. Island of —
  St. Eufemia, *Vivarini, Antonio and Bartolomeo* —, polyptych **34.**
Asola.
  S. Andrea, *Vivarini, Antonio* —, *school of* —, polyptych 43, 44, 44[1].
  Madonna della Misericordia, *Bellini, Gentile* —, *wrongly attrib. to* —, polyptych 173[1].
Baltimore.

Jacobs coll., *Vivarini, Antonio* —, polyptych, St. Michael, Madonna and saints 39[2].
Walters coll., *Basaiti, Marco* —, St. Jerome reading 501; *Bellini, Giovanni* —, *workshop of* —, altar-piece from Procuratoria di Ultra, Venice, later in Wendelstadt coll., Frankfort 378, 378[3]; *Cima da Conegliano*, Madonna 402; *idem, workshop of* —, Madonna 451, 463[1]; *Vivarini, Antonio* —, *attrib to* —, St. Jerome (693) 39[2]; *Vivarini, Antonio* —, *school of* —, three cassone panels (1462—1464) 43, 43[2]; *Venetian school*, Madonna of Humility (537) 39[2].

Bamberg.
Museum, *Bellini, Giovanni* —, *late copy of* —, Pietà 296.

Bari.
S. Nicola, *Bellini, Gentile* —, *school of* —, St. Jerome 181.
Gallery, *Basaiti, Marco* —, Pietà (97) 509[6]; St. James and holy bishop (99) 509[6]; *Bellini, Giovanni* —, St. Peter the Martyr, from S. Domenico, Monopoli 300; *Vivarini, Antonio* —, polyptych panels, from Frati Minori Monastery, Andria 5, 5[1], 38, 39; panel of St. Bernardine, from idem, in storeroom 38, 38[3]; *anonymous*, *15th cent.*, St. Peter, in storeroom 38[3].

Basel.
Bachofen Museum, *Bellini, Giovanni* —, *school of* —, Madonna (1133) 387[2].

Bassano.
Beata Giovanna church, *Giambono*, Madonna 125[4].
Museum, *Bellini, Jacopo* —, *school of* —, scenes of martyrdom of a female saint 129[3]; *Pennacchi, Pier Maria* —, Madonna 385; *Vivarini, Antonio*—, triptych 39[2].

Bayonne.
Bonnat Museum, *Bellini, Giovanni* —, drawing, SS. Peter and Paul 351, 351[1]; *Cima da Conegliano*, God the Father 455[1].

Belluno.
Agosti coll., *Antonio de Tisoio*, three angels, lost 480.
Casa Carlo Miari, *Antonio de Tisoio*, fresco of the Madonna, lost 480.

Casa Ragani, *Antonio de Tisoio*, Madonna, lost 480.

Bennebroek (Holland).
Von Pannwitz coll., *Basaiti, Marco* —, portrait of young man 483, 483[1].

Bergamo.
Cathedral, *Cariani*, Madonna 341[1].
Gallery, *Basaiti, Marco* —, bust of Saviour 505; portrait (563) 509; portrait (394) 509; Madonna (940) 509[6]; *Bellini, Gentile* —, *copy of* —, portrait of Lorenzo Giustiniani 145; *Bellini, Gentile* —, *after* —, portrait of Doge Leonardo Loredano 169; *Bellini, Giovanni* —, Madonna 245; Madonna (167) 259; Madonna, from Alzano 290; *idem, attrib. to* —, portrait of young man 307; *Bellini, Giovanni* —, *school of* —, Saviour with Virgin and St. John (174) 225, 225[1]; Madonna (401), 200[1], 387[2], 516; portrait of a man (181) 387[2]; *Catena*, copy of Giovanni Bellini's lost Meal at Emmaus 342; *Cima da Conegliano*, Madonna (559) 455[1]; *idem, school of* —, Madonna (386) 460[2]; *Francesco de' Franceschi*(?), two scenes of martyrdom 125[4]; *Gentile da Fabriano*, Madonna 125[4]; *Mansueti, Giovanni* —, St. Jerome (152) 200[1]; Deposition (158) 200[1]; portrait of a man (166) 200[1]; *Montagna*, Madonna and saints 394; *Pisanello*, portrait of Leonello d'Este 110; *Vivarini, Bartolomeo* —, St. Jerome and an old saint 40[2].
Brentani coll., *Bellini, Giovanni*—, *school of*—, Madonna 283.
Morelli coll., v. Gallery.
Piccinelli coll., *Antonio da Carpi*, Madonna v. Gallery, Budapest.

Berlin.
Kaiser Friedrich Museum, *Antonello da Saliba*, Madonna 274; *Antonio da Negroponte*(?), St. Michael 54; *Basaiti, Marco* —, Madonna (1262) 487; Pietà (6) 491; triptych, from S. Cristoforo della Pace, between Venice and Murano (20) 492, 494, 497, 499, 514; St. Sebastian (37) 501; *idem, wrongly attrib. to* —, Madonna (40) 486; *Bellini, Gentile* —, Ma-

donna (1180) **136**, 141; *Bellini, Giovanni* —, Pietà (4) **296**, 491; portrait of a man **301**; dead Saviour with two angels (28) 244, 244[1]; Madonna (10A) **252**; Madonna, replica of No. 167 in gallery of Bergamo (10) 259; Resurrection **269—273**; Madonna (11) 291; *idem*(?), dead Saviour with Virgin and St. John (1678) 125[4], 225; *Bellini, Giovanni* —, *workshop of* —, Madonna (1177) 224, 224[1], 360; Circumcision (36) **381**, 517; *Bellini, Giovanni* — *copy of* —, lost Meal at Emmaus (86) **341**[1]; *Botticelli*, Madonna and two saints 394; *Catena in Giovanni Bellini's workshop*, Circumcision (1272) 368; *Cima da Conegliano*, Madonna and donor (7) **408**; Madonna and saints, from S. Michele, nr. Murano (2) **410**, 413, 415; St. Mark curing Anianus, from Sta. Maria de' Crocicchieri, Venice (15) 419, 421; Madonna (17) 429; duel between knights (17a) 443; *idem and helper*, St. Lucy with SS. Mary Magdalene and Catherine (42) 451; *Mansueti, Giovanni* —, Adoration of the Shepherds (48) 190; half-figure of Christ v. Gallery, Göttingen; Madonna and saints v. Gallery, Koenigsberg; *Mantegna, Andrea* —, Madonna (27) 54; Presentation in the Temple 252; *Vivarini, Alvise — and school of Antonio Vivarini*, altar-piece (1143) 44; *Vivarini, Bartolomeo and Antonio* —, *school of* —, twelve panels of saints, in storeroom (1548, 1549, 1549a) 42; *Vivarini, Antonio* —, St. Mary Magdalene borne to heaven, from Sta. Maria delle Verghini, Venice (1154) 38; *idem and Giovanni d'Alemagna*, Adoration of the Magi **30**, 41; *Vivarini, Antonio* —, *workshop of* —, scenes from the lives of the Virgin and Jesus (1058) **42.**

Print Room, *Basaiti, Marco* —, bearded man, drawing 513; *Bellini, Gentile* —, drawings **174**; *Bellini, Giovanni* —, St. Mark curing Anianus, drawing 351.

Schloss Museum, *Lattanzio da Rimini*, Madonna **375.**

Glogowski coll., *Bellini, Giovanni* —, portrait of a man v. Private coll., Holland; *Mansueti, Giovanni* —, bust of nude woman 200[1].

Ex-von Kaufmann coll., *Vivarini, Antonio* —, Madonna 39[2].

Simon coll. v. Museum.

Soviet sale, 1928, *Cima da Conegliano*, Madonna, from Kotchoubey coll., Petrograd 437.

For sale, *Mansueti, Giovanni* —, St. Jerome, from Hughes coll., Kew 198.

Birmingham.

Art Gallery, *Basaiti, Marco* —, in Giovanni Bellini's studio, altarpiece, Madonna and saints 386, 495; *Cima da Conegliano*, dead Saviour 455[1].

Bologna.

Certosa, *Vivarini, Antonio and Bartolomeo* —, polyptych v. Gallery.

Davia Bargellini Museum, *Bellini, Giovanni* —, school of —, Madonna 387[2]; *Vivarini, Bartolomeo* —, Madonna (224) 40[2].

Gallery, *Cima da Conegliano*, Madonna (61) 413; *Vivarini, Antonio and Bartolomeo* —, polyptych, from the Certosa (205) 6, 20, **22**, 218.

University Library, *Bellini, Jacopo* —, wrongly attrib. to —, miniatures 125[4].

Modiano coll., *Basaiti, Marco* —, St. Jerome 509[6].

Zambeccari coll., *Giovanni d'Alemagna*, panel, from S. Mosè triptych, Venice v. National Gallery, London (768).

For sale a few years ago, *Cima da Conegliano*, Madonna 455[1].

Bonn.

Museum, *Bellini, Giovanni* —, workshop of —, Madonna 294, 385.

Bordeaux. Near —

De Savran Ponterci coll., *Bellini, Jacopo* —, album of drawings v. Louvre, Paris.

Boston.

Gallery, *Basaiti, Marco* —, Deposition (5) **488.**

Gardner coll. *Bellini, Gentile* —, miniature of a Turkish artist **152**, 184; *Bellini, Giovanni* —,

Madonna **247**; *Cima da Conegliano, workshop of* —, Madonna 428[2], 446, 446[1].
Quincy Shaw coll., *Cima da Conegliano*, Madonna, from Fabrini coll., Conegliano 451, 463[1].
H. Wetzel coll., *Bellini, Giovanni* —, *school of* —, Madonna 387[2].

Bremen.
Kunsthalle, *Dürer*, drawing 170[2].

Brescia.
S. Alessandro, *Bellini, Jacopo* —(?), Annunciation **101**, 108.
S. Angelo Seminary, *Vivarini, Antonio — and helper*, triptych, St. Ursula and saints 26.
Gallery, *Bellini, Giovanni* —, Entombment, drawing 349.

Breslau.
Ecclesiastical Museum, *Bellini, Gentile* —, *copy of* —, portrait of Lorenzo Giustiniani 145.
Gallery, *Marconi, Rocco* —, Madonna 326[2], 373.

Brooklyn.
Institute of Arts and Sciences, *Bellini, Jacopo* —, St. Jerome, from Healy coll. 103.
Healy coll., *Bellini, Jacopo* —, St. Jerome v. Institute of Arts and Sciences.

Brunswick.
Vieweg coll., *Veneziano, Pasqualino* —, Madonna, formerly there **468**.

Brussels.
Kessler coll., *Bellini, Giovanni* —, Madonna **221**, 224, 360.

Budapest.
Gallery, *Antonio da Carpi*, Madonna, from Piccinelli coll., Bergamo (123) **464**; *Basaiti, Marco* —, St. Catherine (92) **501**; portrait of Doge Agostino Barbarigo (111) 509[6]; *Bellini, Gentile* —, portrait of Caterina Cornaro, Queen of Cyprus (117) **170**; *Giambono*, Madonna (103) 40[2]; *Quirizio da Murano, wrongly attrib. to* —, Madonna (94) 48[1]; *Vivarini, Antonio* —, *school of* — Madonna, from Pálffy coll. 42; *Venetian school, 15th cent.*, two panels of saints (119, 120) 40[2].
Pálffy coll., *Bellini, Giovanni* —, Madonna and saints 316; *Veneziano, Pasqualino* —, wrong-

ly *attrib. to* —, Madonna and saints 469, 469[1], 470; *Vivarini, Antonio* —, Madonna v. Gallery.
Rath coll., *Rondinelli*, Madonna adoring the Child (147)455[1].

Burano.
S. Martino, *Mansueti Giovanni* —, Marriage of Virgin, Adoration of the Magi and Flight into Egypt 198.

Caen.
Museum, *Cima da Conegliano and helper*, Madonna and saints 443.

Cambridge.
Fitzwilliam Museum, *Cima da Conegliano*, holy bishop between saints 449; *Veneziano, Domenico* —, Annunciation 394.

Cambridge, U.S.A.
Fogg Art Museum, *Bellini, Giovanni* —, Madonna, from Crespi coll., Milan 254; *Rondinelli in Giovanni Bellini's workshop*(?), Madonna 363.

Capodistria.
S. Anna, *Cima da Conegliano and helper*, altar-piece 443.
Museum, *Bellini, Giovanni* —, *workshop of* —, Madonna 385.

Casalfiumanese.
Serviti church, *Bellini, Jacopo* —, Madonna v. Brera Gallery, Milan.

Castelfranco.
S. Liberale, *Giorgione*, Madonna and saints 443, 444, 505.

Châalis.
Jacquemart André Museum, *Mansueti, Giovanni* —, Pietà (511) 200[1].

Chartres.
Museum, *Vivarini, Antonio* —, bust of St. Peter (56) 39[2].

Chatsworth.
Devonshire coll., *Bellini, Giovanni* —, four Apostles, drawing 350; *Carpaccio*, procession, drawing 174; *Lattanzio da Rimini*, St. Mark preaching, drawing 378.

Chicago.
Art Institute, *Bellini, Gentile* —, two orientals **154**; *Bellini, Giovanni* —, Madonna **274**, 294.
Thompson coll., *Bellini, Giovanni* —, Madonna **283**.

Chioggia.
Cathedral, *Basaiti, Marco* —, *school of* —, Madonna 515.

Città di Castello.
Gallery, *Vivarini, Antonio* —, Madonna **24**, 26, 28.

Città del Vaticano.
Gallery, *Basaiti, Marco* —, Madonna (previously in store room, 304) 487; *Bellini, Giovanni* —, Pietà **258;** *Vivarini, Antonio* —, triptych, from S. Antonio Abate, Pesaro 6, **36,** 38; St. Peter cutting off ear, in storeroom 39²; dead Christ, in storeroom 39².
Borgia Apartment, *Pintoricchio*, frescoes 173.

Cividale.
Museum, *Cima da Conegliano*, school of —, three panels of saints 460².

Cleveland, U.S.A.
J. L. Severance coll., *Cima da Conegliano*, Madonna, saints and adorer **449.**

Collalto Susegnana.
S. Salvatore Castle, *Mansueti, Giovanni* —, Adoration of the Child, destroyed 200¹.

Conegliano.
Cathedral, *Cima da Conegliano*, altar-piece 393, 402, **406,** 408, 413, 463.
Sta. Maria Mater Domini, *Cima da Conegliano*, altar-piece v. Brera Gallery, Milan (174); *idem, workshop of* —, Madonna v. Brera Gallery, Milan (195).
Fabrini coll., *Cima da Conegliano*, Madonna v. Quincy Shaw coll., Boston.

Conegliano. Near —
S. Fior di Sopra, *Cima da Conegliano*, school of —, polyptych 460².

Constantinople.
Bellini, Gentile —, active for sultan 133, 176, 178, 179.
Serai Library, *Bellini, Gentile* —, *attrib. to* —, miniature, probably by *Schiblizada Ahmad* 152.
University Library, *Bellini, Gentile* —, *attrib. to* —, miniatures 152, 155.

Copenhagen.
Gallery, *Cima da Conegliano*, Madonna enthroned 455¹.

Cordenous.
Casa Galvani, *Bellini, Giovanni* —, Madonna 254.

Cornbury.
Vernon Watney coll., *Bellini*,

Giovanni —, Madonna, saints and adorer, from Muselli family, Verona 322, 322².

Cremona.
Gallery, *Mansueti, Giovanni* —, Holy Trinity and saints 200¹.

Crespano.
Bellini, Giovanni —, replica of Madonna of 1516 in the Gallery, Padua 326¹; *idem, copy of* —, Madonna 326².

Detroit, U.S.A.
Institute of Arts, *Bellini, Giovanni* —, Madonna, from Bourbon coll., nr. Vienna 325, 326, 332, 494; *Cima da Conegliano*, Madonna 396.
R. H. Booth coll., *Bellini, Giovanni* —, Madonna 290.
Haas coll., *Bellini, Giovanni* —, Madonna 209.

Dijon.
Museum, *Bellini, Giovanni* —, school of —, Madonna adoring the Child (2) 387²; *Muranese school*, male saint 55.

Dresden.
Gallery, *Bellini, Gentile* —, *after* —, portrait of Doge Leonardo Loredano 169; *Bellini, Giovanni* —, Pietà (52a) **242,** 252, 253, 296; *Cima da Conegliano*, Presentation of the Virgin in the Temple (63) **421;** Christ in benediction (61) 455¹; bust of Christ (62) 455¹.
Print Room, *Bellini, Giovanni* —, *after* —, engraving of a lost altar-piece 322.

Dublin.
National Gallery of Ireland, *Antonio da Carpi*, Adoration of the Shepherds (367) 466; *Bellini, Giovanni* —, school of —, portrait of a man (244) 387².

Düsseldorf.
Gallery, *Bellini, Giovanni* —, workshop of —, triptych, from S. Michele, Murano **378,** 379¹; *Cima da Conegliano*, Madonna and saints 402; *Mansueti, Giovanni* —, Deposition (42) 200¹; Pietà (232) 200¹.

Edinburgh.
National Gallery of Scotland, *Cima da Conegliano*, Madonna and saints (1190) 455¹; *Poussin*, copy of Giovanni Bellini's Feast

of the Gods in the Widener coll., Philadelphia 337[2].

Edinburgh. Near —
Aberlady, Wemyss coll., *Bellini, Jacopo —, attrib. to —*, Venus and Adonis, perhaps from Elcho coll., London 129, 129[2]; *Quirizio da Murano, attrib. to —*, triptych 48[1].

Endhoven.
A. F. Philips coll., *Bellini, Giovanni —*, Madonna 209.

England.
Private coll., *Licinio*, Madonna 274.
For sale, *Bellini, Giovanni — and helpers*, part of the decoration of the organ doors, from Sta. Maria dei Miracoli, Venice v. Accademia, Venice (734).

Englewood.
Platt coll., *Basaiti, Marco —, school of —*, Madonna 515; *Bellini, Giovanni —*, Madonna 249; *Vivarini, Antonio and Bartolomeo —*, half-figure of the dead Saviour 36.

Este.
Sta. Maria della Consolazione, *Cima da Conegliano*, Madonna 425.

Esztergom.
Archiepiscopal Gallery, *Basaiti, Marco —*, dead Saviour and two angels (160) 509[6]; *Rositi, Giovanni Battista —*, Madonna (135) 460[2], 464.

Ferrara. *f*
Bellini, Jacopo —, active 59. Costabile coll., *Lattanzio da Rimini*, Madonna, lost 377. Ex-Vendeghini coll., *Bellini, Jacopo —, attrib. to —*, Adoration 125.

Florence.
Uffizi, *Basaiti, Marco —*, dead body lying on a slab 513; *Bellini, Gentile —*, procession, drawing 176; *Bellini, Giovanni —*, Madonna del Lago 274, 279; Pietà (943) 296, 297, 352; portrait of a youth 307; portrait of Doge Loredano, drawing 324; head of an oriental, drawing 352; *idem*(?) Crucifixion, drawing 346; sketch for portraits 352; *Bellini, Jacopo —*, Madonna 111, 114, 119, 130; *Cima da Conegliano*, old bearded saint with a book, drawing 457;

mythological subject, drawing 460; Madonna (902) 428, 466; *Gentile da Fabriano*, Adoration of the Magi 99; *Mantegna, Andrea —*, triptych 209, 228; St. Jerome, drawing 346; *van der Weyden*, Deposition 355[2].
Cinelli coll., *Cima da Conegliano*, St. Jerome 455[1].
Contini Bonacossi coll., *Basaiti, Marco —*, Madonna 509[6]; *Bellini, Giovanni —*, Crucifixion, from Rodolphe Kann coll., Paris 252, 253, 253[1]; portrait of Joerg Fugger, from Fugger Castle, nr. Ulm 204, 254, 258, 279, 356; Madonna 262[3]; St. Jerome, from Papafava Palace, Padua 267, 301; Madonna 294; *Cima da Conegliano*, St. Jerome 455[1], 514.
Loeser coll., *Bellini, Giovanni —*, Madonna v. Duveen Brothers, New York; antique sacrifice, drawing 350.
Quinto, belonging to —, *Bellini, Giovanni —*, Saviour and four saints, lost 341[1].
Serestori coll., *Cima da Conegliano*, St. Jerome 455[1].
For sale a few years ago, *Cima da Conegliano*, bearded saint 455[1].
For sale several years ago, *Cima da Conegliano, school of —*, Madonna and saints 460[2].

Frankfort.
Städelsches Kunstinstitut, *Basaiti, Marco —*, St. Jerome 496; *Bellini, Giovanni —*(?), sketch for portrait 352; *Cima da Conegliano*, Madonna (852) 445; *idem, workshop of —*, Madonna and saints (old number 40, not in new catalogue) 451; *Rondinelli in Giovanni Bellini's workshop*, Madonna and saints (853) **364.**
Wendelstadt coll., *Bellini, Giovanni —, workshop of —*, altarpiece, from Procuratoria di Ultra, Venice v. Walters coll., Baltimore.

Gatschina.
Castle, *Bellini, Giovanni — or his workshop*, Pietà 298.

Gemona.
Sta. Maria delle Grazie, *Cima da Conegliano*, Madonna 415.

Germany.
For sale, *Bellini, Gentile —*,

portrait of a senator v. Private coll., America.

Glasgow.
Gallery, *Bellini, Giovanni* —. *workshop of* —, Madonna (32, old no. 89) 373; Madonna and saints 387; *Catena*, Madonna (190) 370.

Göttingen.
University Gallery, *Cima da Conegliano and Antonio da Carpi*, Madonna and saints (33) **451,** 466; *Mansueti, Giovanni* —, half-figure of Christ, from Gallery, Berlin (107) **198.**

Gubbio.
Gallery, *Bellini, Giovanni* —, *school of* —, Pietà 387².

Haarlem.
Koenigs coll., *Bellini, Giovanni* —, St. John the Baptist and four saints, two drawings, from Boehler coll., Lucerne 350, 350³; Madonna, drawing 350; *Cima da Conegliano*, Madonna, drawing 460'

Hamburg.
Haus Weddels, *Bellini, Giovanni* —, Madonna 334.
Weber coll., *Cima da Conegliano, workshop of* —, St. John the Baptist v. ex- von Auspitz coll., Vienna.

Holland.
Private coll., *Bellini, Giovanni* —, dead Saviour 242; portrait of a man, from the Glogowski coll., Berlin 318.

Hungary,
Private coll., *Bellini, Gentile* —, portrait of a young oriental 154.
Thyssen-Bornemisza coll., v. Lugano.

Kassel.
Gallery, *Basaiti, Marco* —, Christ blessing (486) 509⁶; *Bellini, Giovanni* —(?), sketch for a portrait 352, 352⁴; *Cima da Conegliano, school of* —, Madonna (487) 460²; Madonna and cherubim (841) 460².

Kew.
Hughes coll., *Mansueti, Giovanni* —, St. Jerome v. For sale, Berlin.

Koenigsberg.
Gallery, *Mansueti, Giovanni* —, Madonna and saints, on loan from Museum, Berlin 200¹.

Konopischt (Czecho-Slovakia).
Castle, *Vivarini, Antonio* — *and Giovanni d'Alemagna*, Madonna and saints, from S. Francesco, Padua 18.

Lecce.
Museum, *Vivarini, Antonio* —, *workshop of* —, polyptych 41.

Legnago.
Oratorio della Disciplina, *Antonio da Negroponte*(?), Madonna 54.

Legnaro, near Padua.
Bellini, Jacopo —, Madonna v. Accademia, Venice.

Leipzig.
Speck-Sternburg coll., *Cima da Conegliano*, Madonna and saints 427.

Liverpool.
Royal Institution, *Bellini, Giovanni* —, portrait of a man 307.

London.
British Museum, *Basaiti, Marco* —, Saviour, drawing (52 II vol. II, No. 8) 513; *Bellini, Gentile* —, drawings of orientals 158, **173;** *idem, manner of* —, drawing 176²; *Bellini, Giovanni* —, saint reading, drawing (1895-9-15-786) **346;** Crucifixion, drawing 348, 348¹; reclining dead figure and two women, drawings 350; St. Sebastian, drawing (1895-9-15-800) **350;** Madonna, drawing 353; two saints, drawing (0.09-31) 353¹; *idem, after* —, drawing 287¹; *Bellini, Jacopo* —, album of drawings, formerly in the Gabriel Vendramin coll., Venice 61, **62—100,** 116, 118, 119, 121, 125⁴, 127, 131, 218, 230; *idem, wrongly attrib. to* —, drawing of a man 125⁴; *Carpaccio*, drawing of a procession 175; *Cima da Conegliano*, Saviour, drawing (1895-9-15-803) **457;** landscapes, drawings (1900-5-15-1) **459;** *Dürer*, drawing 165¹; *Vivarini, Alvise* —, male figure with drapery, drawing 353¹.
Hampton Court Gallery, *Bellini, Giovanni* —, portrait of a youth 307, 307⁵.
National Gallery, *Antonello da Messina*, St. Jerome 389, 413; *Basaiti, Marco* —, portrait of a young man (2498) **483;** Madonna

(2499) **487;** St. Jerome (694)
496, 514; death of St. Peter the
Martyr, from the Eastlake coll.
(218) **497,** 497², 499, 514; *Bellini,
Gentile* —, Madonna, from the
Eastlake and Mond colls., originally perhaps in the Scuola dei
Mercanti, Venice (3911) **148,**
148¹, 178; portrait of Doge Niccolo Marcello 148, 159; portrait
of Mohammed II, from the Layard coll., Venice (3099) **150,** 184,
516; Adoration of the Magi
(3098) **155—158,** 181; portrait of
a man (3130) **172;** *idem and Bellini, Giovanni* —, altar-piece, Madonna and saints (750) **383;**
Bellini, Giovanni —, portrait of
a mathematician (1213) 173¹,
307; portrait of Fra Teodoro da
Urbino (1440) 173¹, 207, **339;**
Madonna, from Eastlake coll.
(3913) 274; Madonna (280) 290;
portrait of a man 304; portrait of
Doge Leonardo Loredano 206,
305, 307, 339; Madonna (599)
313; Prayer in Garden of Olives
(726) **225—228;** mystic representation of Christ with the cross
(1233) 230; Pietà, from the Mond
coll. (3912) **233;** portrait of a
youth (2509) **235;** Madonna
(2901) **262,** 305, 397; St. Jerome
(281) 267, **270,** 273, 279; *idem,
workshop of* —, Dominican monk
(808) 385; *Bellini, Giovanni* —,
school of —, St. Peter the Martyr
(808) 173¹; *Bissolo, attrib. to* —,
martyrdom of St. Peter 338;
Catena, Madonna and infant St.
John (3540) **368;** *idem in Giovanni Bellini's workshop,* Circumcision (1455) **366;** *Cima da Conegliano,* St. Jerome, perhaps from
the Scuola dei Mercanti (1120)
405; Doubting Thomas, from
S. Francesco, Portogruaro (816)
421, 433; Madonna (634) **429;**
Madonna (300) **437;** David with
the head of Goliath and Jonathan, from the Salting coll.
(2505) 455¹; *idem and helper,* Madonna (2506) **438;** Ecce Homo
(1310) **443;** *Cima da Conegliano,
workshop of* —, Madonna and
saints, from Layard coll., Venice
(3112) **451;** Madonna and saints
(3113) 451; *Cima da Conegliano,
school of* —, Entombment, from

Layard coll., Venice (3084) **460²;**
*Giovanni d'Alemagna and Viva-
rini, Antonio* —, two wings of a
triptych, from S. Mosè, Venice
(768, 1284) **24,** 26; *Mansueti,
Giovanni* —, Trinity (1478) 190;
Mantegna, Andrea —, Prayer in
the Garden of Olives 228; *Previtali,* copy of Giovanni Bellini's
Madonna and saints from the
sacristy of S. Giobbe, Venice
(1409) 330, 341¹; *Rondinelli in
Giovanni Bellini's workshop*(?),
Madonna (3078) **362;** *Tacconi,*
Madonna 371, 480.

H. M. the King's coll., Buckingham Palace, *Cima da Conegliano,* panels of a polyptych
455¹.

Agnew coll., *Cima da Conegliano,* Crucifixion **403,** 421.

Annan-Bryce coll., *Mansueti,
Giovanni* —, Madonna 200¹.

Arundel coll., *Bellini, Giovanni* —, portrait of a youth v.
Carnarvon coll.

Austen sale, 1921, *Cima da
Conegliano, school of* —, Madonna
and saints (76) 460².

Ex-Benson coll., *Bellini, Gio-
vanni* —, St. Jerome v. Clarence
Mackay coll., New York; altar-
piece v. Bache coll., New York;
Bacchus v. Duveen Brothers,
New York.

Borenius coll., *Bellini, Giovanni* —, Madonna, drawing 353.

Boswall coll., *Bellini, Giovanni* —, portrait of a friar 517.

Brownlow coll., *Cima da Conegliano,* Madonna and saints v.
Colnaghi coll.

Burns coll., *Bellini, Jacopo* —,
Madonna 125, 130.

Carnarvon Sale, 1925, *Bellini,
Giovanni* —, portrait of a youth,
perhaps from Arundel coll. 307,
307³.

Colnaghi coll., *Cima da Conegliano,* Madonna and saints, from
Brownlow coll. 425.

Dowdeswell coll., *Cima da
Conegliano,* Madonna, from
Wantage coll. 428, 428², 446,
446¹.

Eastlake coll., *Basaiti, Marco*
—, death of St. Peter the Martyr
v. National Gallery (218); *Bellini, Gentile* —, Madonna v. Na-

tional Gallery (3911); *Bellini, Giovanni* —, Madonna v. National Gallery (3913); *Giovanni d'Alemagna*, panel from S. Mosè triptych v. National Gallery (768).

Elcho coll., *Bellini, Jacopo* —, *attrib. to* —, Venus and Adonis, perhaps now in Wemyss coll., nr. Edinburgh 129, 129[2].

Harewood coll., *Bellini, Giovanni* —, Madonna 209, 212; Madonna and donor 290; *Vivarini, Antonio* —, two monks 39[2].

Ex-Holford coll., *Bellini, Giovanni* —, *workshop of* —, portrait of a youth 385.

Kennard coll., *Cima da Conegliano*, St. Jerome 455[1].

Ludlow coll., *Gerolamo di Giovanni*, Annunciation, from Werner coll. 125[4].

Maynard coll., *Bellini, Giovanni* —, *workshop of* —, bust of Saviour 385.

Mond coll., *Bellini, Giovanni* —, Madonna 254, 254[4]; v. National Gallery.

R. Mond coll., *Cima da Conegliano*, SS. Mark and Sebastian 413, 415, 455[1].

Northumberland coll., *Bellini, Giovanni* —, Madonna 290, 290[1]; *idem and Titian*, Feast of Bacchus v. Widener coll., Philadelphia.

Ex-Oppenheimer coll., *Bellini, Jacopo* —, man on horseback, drawing 96; *Cima da Conegliano*, old man with long white beard, drawing 460.

W. B. Paterson coll., *Basaiti, Marco* —, portrait 509.

Private colls., *Bellini, Giovanni* —, figure of Christ 273; *Bellini, Jacopo* —, mythological scene 116, 119.

Richter coll., *Bellini, Jacopo* —(?), Madonna v. Cagnola coll., Milan; *Vivarini, Antonio* —, panel from S. Mosè triptych v. National Gallery (1284).

Rothermere coll., *Bellini, Giovanni* —, Pietà 242, 350.

Ex-Russel coll., *Bellini, Giovanni* —, drawing 345, 345[1].

Salting coll. v. National Gallery.

Samuelson coll., *Bellini, Giovanni* —, *workshop of* —, Ma-

donna and saints, formerly there 373.

Taylor coll., *Cima da Conegliano*, lunette of altar-piece from S. Rocco, Mestre v. Blumenthal coll., New York.

Turner coll., *Bellini, Giovanni* —, Madonna 245.

Wallace coll., *Cima da Conegliano*, St. Catherine, centre of altar-piece from S. Rocco, Mestre **431**; *idem*(?), lunette of altar-piece from S. Rocco, Mestre, from Blumenthal coll., New York 433.

Wantage coll., *Cima da Conegliano*, Madonna v. Dowdeswell coll.

Wellington-Salisbury sale, 1923, *Cima da Conegliano*, Holy Family 455[1].

Ex-Wernher coll., *Gerolamo di Giovanni*, Annunciation v. Ludlow coll.

For sale, once upon a time, *Bellini, Gentile* —, portrait of Doge Andrea Vendramin v. Frick Foundation, New York.

For sale, some time ago, *Bellini, Giovanni* —, half-figure of St. Dominic 313.

For sale, 1926, *Vivarini, Antonio* —, Madonna 39[2].

For sale, not long ago, *Mansueti, Giovanni* —, Madonna 197; two scenes from legend of St. Augustine 198.

For sale, *Bellini, Gentile* —, portrait of a young Venetian 171.

Lovere.

Tadini Gallery, *Bellini, Jacopo* —, Madonna (255) 61. 111, **114,** 119, 209.

Lucerne.

Boehler coll., *Bellini, Giovanni* —, two drawings of saints v. Koenigs coll., Haarlem.

Chillingworth sale, 1922, *Cima da Conegliano, school of* —, Madonna (80) 460[2].

Auction sale, *Bellini, Giovanni* —, replica of Madonna of 1516 in Gallery, Padua, at one time for sale in Paris 326[1].

Lugano.

Thyssen-Bornemisza coll., *Bellini, Gentile* —, Annunciation **141**; *Bellini, Giovanni* —, St. Sebastian 301.

XVII.

34

Madrid.
    S. Fernando Academy, *Bellini,
Giovanni* —, head of Christ 312,
385.
    Prado, *Basaiti, Marco* —, *and
Catena*(?), Saviour giving Keys to
St. Peter and saints 502, 515;
Bellini, Giovanni —, Madonna
and saints (50) 296; *Cima da
Conegliano, school of* —, Madonna
(6) 460²; *Titian*, Feast of Bacchus
337.
    Montijo, coll., *Bellini, Giovanni*
—, Madonna v. Brady coll., New
York.
Malvern.
    Rayner Wood coll., *Bellini,
Giovanni* —, Christ at column,
drawing 349.
Mantua.
    Bellini, Giovanni —, active for
Marchesa Isabella Gonzaga 205.
    Gonzaga coll., *Bellini, Giovan-
ni* —, Madonna with St. Sebas-
tian 205.
    Castle, *Mantegna, Andrea* —,
frescoes 238, 245.
The Marches.
    Vivarini, Antonio —, active
44.
Marseilles.
    Caffi coll., *Cima da Conegliano*,
replica of Madonna in Dreyfus
coll., Paris 438².
Matelica.
    Piersanti Museum, *Bellini,
Jacopo* —, *school of* —, seven
small panels of saints (34) 129³.
Mestre.
    S. Rocco, *Cima da Conegliano*,
altar-piece v. Wallace coll., London, Gallery, Strasbourg and
Blumenthal coll., New York.
Mezzoldo (Valle Brembana).
    Lattanzio da Rimini, St. John
the Baptist between SS. Peter
and John the Evangelist 376.
Miglionico (prov. Potenza).
    Carmine church, *Cima da Co-
negliano*, polyptych, Madonna
and saints 419.
Milan.
    Ambrosiana, *Cima da Cone-
gliano, school of* —, Daniel in
lions' den, grisaille 460².
    Brera Gallery, *Alamanno, Pie-
tro* —, Madonna, from Monterubbiano and Rovellesca (old no.
485) 125⁴; *Basaiti, Marco* —,

Deposition 488, 508; Christ resurrected 508; *Bellini, Gentile
and Giovanni* —, Sermon of St.
Mark, from the Scuola Grande
di S. Marco, Venice (162) 135,
168, 179, 184, 206; *Bellini, Giovanni* —, Pietà **239**, 242, 244,
296, 300², 353, 354, 355; Madonna, from Palace of the Doges,
Venice (216) 262; Madonna, 1510,
325, 327, 332, 378; *Bellini Jacopo* —, Madonna, from Serviti
church, Casalfiumanese 61, 100,
111, 114, 516; *Catena*, Noli me
tangere 515; *Cima da Conegliano*,
altar-piece, from S. Giovanni
Battista, Oderzo (175) **400**; St.
Peter the Martyr between SS. Nicholas and Benedict, from Corpus
Domini church, Venice (176) **421**,
433, 449; altar-piece, from Sta.
Maria Mater Domini, Conegliano
(174) **449**; St. Luke, the Virgin
and saints, from S. Giorgio Maggiore, Venice (217) 455¹; a holy
nun, SS. Jerome, Nicholas of
Bari and Ursula, from S. Giorgio
Maggiore, Venice (218) 455¹; St.
Jerome, from S. Giorgio Maggiore, Venice (219) 455¹; SS. Cornelius, Justine and Cyprian, from
Sta. Giustina, Venice (220) 455¹;
idem, workshop of —, Madonna,
from Sta. Maria Mater Domini,
Conegliano (195) 452; *Gerolamo
da Udine, wrongly attrib. to* —,
St. Ursula and companions (157)
476; *Mansueti, Giovanni* —, story
of St. Mark, from the Scuola
Grande di S. Marco, Venice 189,
190¹; *Mantegna, Andrea* —, polyptych, from S. Giustino, Padua
217, 224; *Piero della Francesca
and Signorelli, Luca* —(?), Madonna and saints and Duke of
Urbino 283; *Veneziano, Pasqualino* —, *wrongly attrib. to* —, St.
Jerome 470²; *Vivarini, Antonio*
—, two scenes from the life of
St. Jerome (226) 39²; *idem and
Giovanni d'Alemagna*, triptych,
from Praglia **28**, 32.
    Municipal Museum, *Vivarini,
Antonio* —, head of the Madonna
39².
    Poldi Pezzoli Museum, *Bellini,
Giovanni* —, dead Saviour **241**;
Bellini, Jacopo —, Madonna **103**;
Cima da Conegliano, Triumph of

Bacchus and Ariadne **440;** head of a woman (623) 455¹; *Vivarini, Antonio* —, Madonna, of the triptych from S. Mosè, Venice (589) **24.**

Bagatti Valsecchi coll., *Bellini, Giovanni* —, St. Justine 300.

Cagnola coll., *Bellini, Jacopo* —(?), Madonna, from Richter coll., London 100, 108; *Vivarini, Antonio and Bartolomeo* —, triptych 34.

Cologna coll., *Vivarini, Antonio* —, Madonna 39².

Ex-Crespi coll., *Basaiti, Marco* —, Madonna and saints 509⁶; *Bellini, Giovanni* —, Madonna v.

Fogg Art Museum, Cambridge, U.S.A.; *Mansueti, Giovanni* —, Coronation of the Virgin v. For sale, Munich.

G. Ferrario coll., *Gerolamo da Santacroce*, Madonna, saints and female donor 455¹.

Molteni coll., *Vivarini, Antonio — and Giovanni d'Alemagna*, triptych, from S. Mosè, Venice v. Poldi Pezzoli Gallery and National Gallery, London.

Rasini coll., *Bellini, Jacopo* —, St. Jerome 516.

Trivulzio coll., *Bellini, Giovanni* —, Madonna 221, 223¹, 225.

Ventura sale, 1932, *Cima da Conegliano*, Madonna (29) 397, 397².

Modena.

Gallery, *Cima da Conegliano*, Deposition (187) **415,** 460²; *Mansueti, Giovanni* —, Madonna, angels and saints (252) 200¹.

Mombaroccio (The Marches).

Town Hall, *Bellini, Giovanni* —, school of —, Madonna and saints 387².

Monopoli.

Cathedral, *Bellini, Gentile* —, school of —, St. Jerome 183.

S. Domenico, *Bellini, Giovanni* —, St. Peter the Martyr v. Gallery, Bari.

Monterubbiano.

Alamanno, Pietro —, Madonna v. Brera Gallery, Milan.

Munich.

Ältere Pinakothek, *Basaiti, Marco* —, Deposition 488, 501; Madonna, saints and donor (31)

509⁶; *Bellini, Gentile* —, portrait of a Venetian (1151, old catalogue 1030) 170; *Cima da Conegliano*, Madonna and saints (992) 408.

Prince Ruprecht of Bavaria's coll., *Bellini, Giovanni* —, three predella panels of altar-piece from Sta. Maria della Carità, Venice, formerly in Kaufmann coll. 224, 225, 236, 237, 238, 241¹, 341¹.

Boehler coll., *Basaiti, Marco* —, Madonna and saints, formerly there **506;** *Cima da Conegliano*, Jason at the court of Aeëtes 455¹.

Ex-Kaufmann coll., *Bellini, Giovanni* —, three panels from Sta. Maria della Carità, Venice v. coll. of Prince Ruprecht of Bavaria.

Leuchtenberg coll., *Bellini, Gentile* —, Circumcision, from Palazzo Barbarigo, Venice 178; *Bellini, Giovanni* —, Madonna v. Private coll., New York.

Ex-von Nemes coll., *Bellini, Giovanni* —, workshop of — (*Bissolo*), Madonna v. Metropolitan Museum, New York; *Cima da Conegliano*, St. Catherine in prayer 455¹; *Muranese school*, Madonna 55.

Von Pucher coll., *Bellini, Giovanni* —, copy of —, Madonna 221¹.

For sale, *Mansueti, Giovanni* —, Coronation of the Virgin, from ex-Crespi coll., Milan **198.**

Murano.

Sta. Chiara convent, *Cima da Conegliano*, altar-piece v. Accademia, Venice (815).

S. Cristoforo, *Bellini, Giovanni* —, saints, lost 341¹.

Sta. Maria degli Angeli, *Bellini, Giovanni* —, Madonna, saints and Doge Barbarigo v. S. Pietro Martire; Entombment, lost 341¹; *idem and helpers*, Assumption v. S. Pietro Martire.

S. Michele, *Bellini, Giovanni* —, Resurrection v. Museum, Berlin; *idem*, workshop of —, altar-piece v. Gallery, Düsseldorf; *Cima da Conegliano*, Madonna and saints v. Museum, Berlin (2).

S. Pietro Martire, *Bellini, Giovanni* —

vanni —, Madonna, saints and
Doge Barbarigo, from Sta. Maria
degli Angeli 204, **287,** 291, 294,
324; *idem and helpers,* Assumption, from Sta. Maria degli Angeli **332,** 509[6]; *Bellini, Giovanni*
—, *school of* —, Entombment,
lost 387[2].
S. Stefano, *Bellini, Giovanni*
—, Christ blessing, lost 341[1].
Naples.
Museum, *Bellini, Giovanni* —,
Transfiguration from Farnese
coll., Parma 269—**273,** 275; *Catena in Giovanni Bellini's workshop,* Circumcision(64) 368; *Mantegna, Andrea* —, small portrait
145.
New York.
Metropolitan Museum, *Bellini,
Giovanni* —, Madonna, from
Davis coll. **218;** Madonna (B
41—1) **290,** 383; *idem, workshop
of* — (*Bissolo*), Madonna from
Friedsam coll. and von Nemes
coll., Munich 371; *idem (Catena)*
Circumcision 365, 368; *Bellini,
Giovanni* —, *school of* —, four
polyptych panels 387[2]; *Cima da
Conegliano,* St. Antony and saints
443; *Gerolamo da Udine, wrongly
attrib. to* —, three saints, from
Leuchtenberg coll., Vienna 476;
Ferrarese school, 15th cent., profile of a young man 125[4].
Altman coll., v. Metropolitan
Museum.
Bache coll., *Bellini, Giovanni*
—, portrait of a youth, from
Schickler coll., Paris **235;** Madonna 330; altar-piece, from
Benson coll., London 330.
F. L. Bacon coll., *Vivarini,
Antonio* —, four polyptych
panels, from ex-Nevin coll., Rome 10.
Blumenthal coll., *Cima da Conegliano,* lunette of altar-piece
from S. Rocco, Mestre, formerly
in Taylor coll., London v. Wallace coll., London.
S. Borchard coll., *Bellini, Giovanni* —, *workshop of* —, Circumcision 517.
Brady coll., *Bellini, Giovanni*
—, Madonna, from Montijo coll.,
Madrid and Gallery, Oldenburg
293, 385, 431, 468; *Cima da Conegliano,* Madonna 431.

Chapman coll., *Bellini, Jacopo*
—, *school of* —, Marriage of the
Virgin and Adoration of the
Magi 154[4].
Davis coll., *Bellini, Giovanni*
—, Madonna v. Metropolitan
Museum.
Duveen Brothers, *Bellini, Giovanni* —, Madonna 262; Madonna,
from Salomon coll. **293,** 431;
portrait of a man **301;** portrait of
a man, from the de Béarn coll.
303; Madonna **326,** 373; Madonna, from Loeser coll., Florence
328; Bacchus, from Benson coll.,
London 338; *Bellini, Jacopo* —,
portrait of a child, from Dreyfus
coll., Paris **121.**
A. L. Erlanger coll., *Bellini,
Gentile* —, portrait of Mohammed II 516.
Felton coll., *Veneziano, Pasqualino* —, Madonna 468.
A. Franzen coll., *Cima da
Conegliano,* Madonna 397.
Frick Foundation, *Bellini, Gentile* —, portrait of Doge Andrea
Vendramin **150,** 158; *Bellini,
Giovanni* —, St. Francis in ecstasy, formerly in the Taddeo Contarini coll., Venice **268,** 270, 279,
358, 497, 514.
Friedsam coll., *Bellini, Giovanni* —, portrait 303; *idem,
workshop of* — (*Bissolo*), Madonna, from von Nemes coll., Munich v. Metropolitan Museum;
Cima da Conegliano, Madonna
and saints 443; *idem, workshop of*
—, Madonna and saints 452.
Goldman coll., *Gentile da Fabriano,* Madonna 101.
Jackson Higgs sale, *Bellini,
Gentile* —, *wrongly attrib. to* —,
profile portrait of a Byzantine
emperor (33) 173[1].
Hurd coll., *Bellini, Giovanni*
—, *workshop of* —, Madonna 361.
Alphonse Kahn sale v. Paris.
Lehman coll., *Bellini, Giovanni*
—, Madonna, from Potenziani
coll., Rieti **221,** 222.
Clarence Mackay coll., *Bellini,
Giovanni* —, St. Jerome, from
Benson coll., London 313, 315[1],
514.
Morgan Library, *Catena in Giovanni Bellini's workshop,* altarpiece 368, 370, 408; *Cima da*

Conegliano, Madonna and saints 449.

Paolini sale, 1924, *Bellini, Jacopo* —, Madonna 103; *Cima da Conegliano,* Madonna and saints (50) 455[1]; *Quirizio da Murano,* Dominican saint exorcizing an evil spirit 49; *Rondinelli in Giovanni Bellini's workshop,* Madonna (30) 364, 364[1].

Private coll., *Bellini, Giovanni* —, Madonna, from Leuchtenberg coll., Munich 318, 326.

Rosenfeld coll., *Bellini, Giovanni* —, portrait of a man, from Gallery, Stuttgart **316;** *Cima da Conegliano,* Madonna 419.

Salomon coll., *Bellini, Giovanni* —, Madonna v. Duveen Brothers.

Schneewindt coll., *Bellini, Giovanni* —, *school of* —, bust of a man 387[2].

J. I. Strauss coll., *Bellini, Jacopo* —, Madonna **106.**

P. Strauss coll., *Bellini, Giovanni* —, Madonna **245;** *Vivarini, Antonio* —, Madonna, from Northesk coll. **21.**

Stuyvesant coll., *Basaiti, Marco* —, portrait 509, 514.

Timken coll., *Bellini, Giovanni* —, portrait 303.

Willys coll., *Bellini, Giovanni* —, Madonna 274, 294.

Grenville L. Winthrop coll., *Bellini, Giovanni* —, Madonna 273; *Cima da Conegliano, school of* —, Madonna and St. James 460[2].

For sale, 1921, *Basaiti, Marco* —, Madonna 509[6].

For sale, 1930, *Bellini, Giovanni* —, Madonna, from Leuchtenberg coll., Munich v. Private coll.

For sale, *Bellini, Gentile* —, portrait of a doge 159.

Newport.

Davis coll., *Antonio Maria da Carpi,* Madonna 397, 466.

Nîmes.

Gallery, *Bellini, Giovanni* —, *school of* —, Adoration of the Child (439) 387[2]; half-figure of the Madonna (486) 387[2]; *Cima da Conegliano, school of* —, Madonna (444) 460[2].

Nivaagaard, near Copenhagen.

Gallery, *Cima da Conegliano,* Madonna and saints 408.

Hage coll., *Bellini, Giovanni* —, portrait of a man 307.

Noale.

Lattanzio da Rimini, St. John the Baptist between SS. Peter and Paul 376.

Oderzo.

S. Giovanni Battista, *Cima da Conegliano,* Madonna and saints v. Brera Gallery, Milan.

Oldenburg.

Gallery, *Bellini, Giovanni* —, Madonna v. Brady coll., New York; *Mansueti, Giovanni* —, Madonna and saints v. Tietje coll., Amsterdam.

Olera, near Bergamo.

Parish church, *Cima da Conegliano,* retable with saints 396.

Orzes.

Church, *Antonio de Tisoio,* polyptych v. Liechtenstein Gallery, Vienna.

Osimo (The Marches).

Sma. Annunziata, *Vivarini, Antonio and Bartolomeo* —, polyptych v. Town Hall.

Town Hall, *Vivarini, Antonio and Bartolomeo* —, polyptych, from Sma. Annunziata 36.

Oxford.

Ashmolean Museum, *Bellini, Giovanni* —, St. Jerome 267, 279.

University Gallery, *Bellini, Jacopo* —, *school of* —, Dominican monk preaching 125[4].

Oxford. Near —

Harcourt coll., *Bellini, Gentile* —, portrait of Doge Agostino Barbarigo **160,** 160[1].

Padua.

Bellini, Giovanni —, lost picture of 1516 207; *Donatello,* Gattamelata 99; *Giovanni d'Alemagna,* active 4.

S. Antonio, *Bellini, Jacopo, Gentile and Giovanni* —, altarpiece for Gattamelata chap., lost 60, 127, 176, 203, 208, 341[1]; *Bellini, Jacopo* —, fresco on pillar, lost 127; *Donatello,* altar 99, 116, 218, 224.

S. Clemente, *Bellini, Jacopo* —, *school of* —, Madonna, fresco 125[4].

Eremitani chapel, *Mantegna, Andrea* —, frescoes 140, 141; *Vivarini, Antonio* — *and Giovanni d'Alemagna*, frescoes 20.

S. Filippo Oratory, *Vivarini, Antonio* — *and perhaps Giovanni d'Alemagna*, Madonna 28.

S. Francesco, *Vivarini, Antonio* — *and Giovanni d'Alemagna*, Madonna and saints v. Castle, Konopischt (Czecho-Slovakia).

S. Giustino, *Mantegna, Andrea* —, polyptych v. Brera Gallery, Milan.

S. Michele, *Bellini, Jacopo* —, St. Michael 58, 59.

Padri Crociferi, *Basaiti, Marco* —, death of Christ, lost 509[6].

Gallery, *Agapiti,* Madonna and saints 481; *Antonio da Carpi,* Madonna (32) **466;** *Basaiti, Marco* —, Madonna and saints (33) **505;** *idem, school of* —, Call of an Apostle (129) 515; *Bellini, Gentile* —(?), two small portraits (408, 42) 173; *Bellini, Gentile* —, *school of* —, two Madonnas (409, 413) 200[1]; Adoration of the Magi (425) 200[1]; Adoration of the Magi (425) 181; *Bellini, Giovanni* —, portrait of a youth (43) 305; Madonna and saints 326; *idem, school of* —, Pietà (26) 298, 387[2]; Madonna (21) 387[2]; Madonna and saints (27) 387[2]; Madonna and saints (28) 387[2]; Madonna, saints and adorer (49) 387[2]; Madonna (127) 387[2]; Madonna (418) 387[2]; Pietà (423) 296, 387[2]; Madonna (2294) 387[2]; *Bellini, Jacopo* —, Christ in Limbo **119—121,** 121; *idem, school of* —, Madonna (1160) 129[2]; *Catena in Giovanni Bellini's workshop,* Circumcision 368; *Cima da Conegliano, workshop of* —, SS. John the Baptist and Jerome (421, 427) 455; *Mansueti, Giovanni* —, two panels, each of two saints v. Accademia Venice (877, 878); Assumption (2419) 196; *Mantegna, Andrea* —, Madonna adoring the Child 54; *Vincenzo da Treviso,* Circumcision 383.

Pietro Bembo, house of —, *Bellini, Jacopo* —, profile portrait of Gentile da Fabriano, lost 127; *Veneziano, Jacometto* —, portrait of Bembo as a boy, lost 389.

Palazzo Papafava, *Bellini, Giovanni* —, St. Jerome v. Contini Bonacossi coll., Florence.

Leonico Tomeo, house of —, *Bellini, Giovanni* —, portrait of Leonico, lost 341[1].

Parenzo.
Cathedral, *Vivarini, Antonio* —, polyptych 6, **10,** 20, 32.

Paris.
Jacquemart André Museum, *Cima da Conegliano,* Madonna (1025) 455[1]; *Marconi, Rocco* —(?) Madonna (671) 375.

Bibliothèque Nationale, *16th and 17th cent.,* copies of drawings made by Gentile Bellini in Constantinople 179.

Louvre, *Basaiti, Marco* —, drawings 512; *Bellini, Gentile* —, *school of* —, reception of the Venetian ambassador at Cairo (1157) 179; *16th and 17 cent.,* copies of drawings made by Gentile Bellini in Constantinople 179; *Bellini, Giovanni* —, Ecce Homo, perhaps from S. Stefano, Venice 242; Madonna and saints **294,** 296; portrait from de Vandeuil coll. (1158) **307;** Madonna, saints and adorer, from Schlichting coll. 322; Pietà, drawing 352; *idem, school of* —, Marriage of the Virgin and Presentation in the Temple, drawing (5600) 387[2]; young man on horseback, drawing 387[2]; *Bellini, Jacopo* —, album of drawings, from de Savran Ponterci coll., near Bordeaux 61, **62—100,** 111, 114, 119, 121, 122, 225; drawings in Vallardi codex 129; three sheets of drawings, from His de la Salle coll. 62; *idem*(?), Madonna and donor (1279) **108,** 110; *Bellini, Jacopo* —, *wrongly attrib. to* —, head of the Madonna, drawing 125[4]; *Catena,* Madonna, from Schlichting coll. 370; *Cima da Conegliano,* Madonna, from Schlichting coll. 437; altar-piece, from either the Cathedral or S. Domenico, Parma (1259) 448; *Gentile da Fabriano,* predella panel, Presentation in the Temple 98; *Mantegna, Andrea* —, altar-piece, from S. Zeno, Verona 348; *Pisa-*

nello, drawings in Vallardi codex 129; *Vivarini, Antonio* —, St. Louis of Toulouse (1640) 39²; *idem, school of* —, *wrongly attrib. to* —, twelve scenes from the life of the Virgin 45, 45¹.

Petit Palais, *Cima da Conegliano*, Madonna, from the Tuck coll. **428,** 466.

Dreyfus coll., *Bellini, Jacopo* —, portrait of a child v. Duveen Brothers, New York; *Cima da Conegliano*, Madonna 438.

Gulbenkean coll., *Cima da Conegliano*, rest during Flight into Egypt 455¹.

His de la Salle coll. v. Louvre.

Alphonse Kahn coll., *Bellini, Giovanni* —, *school of* —, head of Madonna (49 of sale catalogue) 387².

Rodolphe Kann coll. *Bellini, Giovanni* —, Crucifixion v. Contini Bonacossi coll., Florence.

Lazzaroni coll., *Bellini, Giovanni* —, Madonna v. Huntington Museum, San Marino (California); *Bellini, Jacopo* —, portrait of Leonello d'Este 100, **110,** 122.

Mündler coll., *Bellini, Jacopo* —, portrait of a child v. Duveen Brothers, New York.

Private coll., *Vivarini, Antonio* —, St. Antony of Padua and a holy bishop 39².

Martin Le Roy coll., *Basaiti, Marco* —, portrait of a youth 497.

Schickler coll., *Bellini, Giovanni* —, portrait of a youth v. Bache coll., New York.

Schlichting coll. v. Louvre.

Sedelmeyer coll., *Cima da Conegliano*, Madonna, formerly there 397.

Ex-Spiridon coll., *Bellini, Giovanni* —, portrait of Doge Loredano, from Palazzo Loredano, Venice 324, 324²; *idem, copy of* —, Madonna and saints 330².

Tabbach coll., *Behzad*, miniature of a Turkish artist 152.

Tuck coll., *Cima da Conegliano*, Madonna v. Petit Palais.

De Vandeuil coll., *Bellini, Giovanni* —, portrait v. Louvre (1158).

Wildenstein coll., *Mansueti,*

Giovanni —, Madonna and saints **198.**

For sale 1932, *Bellini, Giovanni* —, portrait of a man 305.

For sale, a few years ago, *Bellini, Giovanni* —, *copy of* —, Pietà 296; *Mansueti, Giovanni* —, Madonna and saints 193.

For sale, *Bellini, Giovanni* —, Madonna v. Auction sale, Lucerne.

For sale, 1935, *Mansueti, Giovanni* —, portrait of a young Venetian 192.

Parma.

Sma. Annunziata, *Cima da Conegliano*, Madonna and saints v. Gallery.

Cathedral, *Cima da Conegliano*, altar-piece, perhaps from S. Domenico v. Louvre; altar-piece, 1507 v. Gallery (360).

S. Domenico, *Cima da Conegliano*, altar-piece, perhaps from Cathedral v. Louvre.

Gallery, *Cima da Conegliano*, Madonna and saints, from Sma. Annunziata (361) **428;** altar-piece, from Cathedral (360) **433;** two tondi 440.

Farnese coll., *Bellini, Giovanni* —, Transfiguration v. Museum, Naples.

Pausola (The Marches).

Collegiata of SS. Pietro, Paolo e Donato, *Vivarini, Antonio and Bartolomeo* —, six polyptych panels 34.

Pavia.

Museum, *Bellini, Giovanni* —, Madonna 221; *Catena in Giovanni Bellini's workshop*, Circumcision 368; *Mansueti, Giovanni* —, Madonna and saints 200¹; *Veneziano, Pasqualino* —, Madonna and saints 470, 470².

Perugia.

Gallery, *Bellini, Giovanni* —, *school of* —, Adoration of the Magi 387².

Pesaro.

S. Antonio Abate, *Vivarini, Antonio* —, triptych v. Gallery, Città del Vaticano.

S. Francesco, *Bellini, Giovanni* —, altar-piece v. Gallery.

Gallery, *Bellini, Giovanni* —, altar-piece, Coronation of the Virgin, from S. Francesco 198,

225, **254—258,** 258, 259, 300², 310², 349, 351, 397; God the Father 310; *idem, wrongly attrib. to —,* Crucifixion 228, 355².

Petrograd.

Hermitage, *Cima da Conegliano,* Annunciation, from the Scuola del Rosario, Venice **413,** 426, 428; Entombment 455¹, 460²; *Veneziano, Pasqualino —, wrongly attrib. to —,* Madonna and saints (1919 in 1912) 469.

Kotchoubey coll., *Cima da Conegliano,* Madonna v. Soviet sale, Berlin.

Philadelphia.

Memorial Hall, *Bellini, Giovanni —, school of —,* Meal at Emmaus 387².

Johnson coll., *Basaiti, Marco —,* Madonna and saints 495; Madonna and knight (180) 505; portrait of a man (181) **509;** *idem*(?), portrait of a man (179) 509⁶; *Bellini, Gentile —, school of —,* Adoration of the Child (163) **181,** 185; *Bellini, Gentile —, late copy of —,* portrait of Lorenzo Giustiniani 145; *Bellini, Giovanni —,* Madonna **209;** *Cima da Conegliano,* Madonna (176) **397,** 466; Silenus on his donkey and three fauns and a faun carrying a barrel, from the Thiem coll., San Remo **441;** head of St. Stephen (1171) 455¹; *Vivarini, Antonio —,* St. Bernardine 39².

Widener coll., *Bellini, Giovanni — and Titian,* Feast of Bacchus, from Northumberland coll., London 206, **334—337,** 338, 357, 514, 516; *Bellini, Giovanni —, school of — (Basaiti),* Orpheus 338, 497.

Piazza Brembana, near Bergamo.

S. Martino, *Lattanzio da Rimini,* altar-piece **375.**

Pisa.

Campo Santo, *Gozzoli, Benozzo —,* frescoes 394.

Schiff coll., *Bellini, Giovanni —, school of —,* half-figure of dead Saviour 387².

Portogruaro.

S. Francesco, *Cima da Conegliano,* Doubting Thomas v. National Gallery, London.

Praglia, near Padua.

Abbey, *Vivarini, Antonio — and Giovanni d'Alemagna,* polyp-

tych v. Brera Gallery, Milan.

Prague.

Von Lanna coll., *Bellini, Giovanni —, wrongly attrib. to —,* studies of drapery 353¹.

Novak coll., *Veneziano, Pasqualino —,* Madonna, saints and donor 468.

Ravenna.

Accademia di Belle Arti, *Cima da Conegliano, school of —,* St. John the Baptist 460²; *Vivarini, Antonio —, wrongly attrib. to —,* St. John weeping (183) 40².

Gallery, *Cima da Conegliano, school of —,* Madonna 460².

Rennes.

Museum, *Bellini, Giovanni —,* Pietà, drawing 350.

Rheims.

Museum, *Vivarini, Antonio —,* two saints 39².

Richmond.

Cook coll., *Bellini, Giovanni —, workshop of —,* Madonna 383; *Cima da Conegliano,* Madonna 396, **402;** dead Saviour and two angels (135) 455²; Our Lord (243) 455²; *Mansueti, Giovanni —,* Madonna crowned by angels 200¹.

Lee of Fareham coll., *Basaiti, Marco —,* death of St. Peter 497, 497², 514; *Vivarini, Antonio —,* Nativity 10.

Rieti.

Potenziani coll., *Bellini, Giovanni —,* Madonna v. Lehman coll., New York.

Rimini.

S. Francesco, *Bellini, Giovanni —,* Pietà v. Museum.

Museum, *Bellini, Giovanni —,* Pietà, from S. Francesco **231,** 238, 244.

Rome.

Sta. Maria in Trastevere, *Bellini, Giovanni —,* Madonna v. Borghese Gallery.

Barberini Gallery, *Bellini, Giovanni —,* Madonna, formerly there **283,** 373.

Borghese Gallery, *Bellini, Giovanni —,* Madonna **326;** Madonna, from Sta. Maria in Trastevere 327; *idem, school of —,* profile portrait of Petrarch 378²; *Mansueti, Giovanni —,* portrait of a man **191.**

Capitol Gallery, *Bellini, Gio-*

vanni —, self portrait **307;** *Bellini, Jacopo* —(?), portrait of an old man **108,** 122, 173[1].
Colonna Gallery, *Rondinelli,* Madonna 290[3].
Doria Gallery, *Basaiti, Marco* —, St. Sebastian (124) 501; *Bellini, Giovanni* —, *workshop of —* (*Catena*), Circumcision (121) 368; *idem (Rondinelli)* (159) **364,** 383; Adoration of the Child (126) 361, 361[2].
National Gallery, *Bellini, Giovanni* —, Bacchus, from Hertz coll. 338.
Fassini coll., *Bellini, Giovanni* —, Madonna 264.
Guidi-Faenza sale, *Veneziano, Jacometto* —, *wrongly attrib. to* —, portrait of a lady 391[1].
Hertz coll., *Bellini, Giovanni* —, Bacchus v. National Gallery.
Lazzaroni coll., *Bellini, Giovanni* —, Madonna **262.**
Ex-Nevin coll., *Vivarini, Antonio* —, four polyptych panels v. Bacon coll., New York.
Palazzo Patrizi, *Cima da Conegliano and*(?) *Gerolamo da Udine,* Coronation of the Virgin, formerly there 455, 476.
Prinetti coll., *Bellini, Giovanni* —, *copy of* —, Madonna 325[2].
Private coll., *Bellini, Gentile and Giovanni* —, Adoration of the Magi **158,** 252.
Stroganoff coll., *Mazzola,* Madonna 274.
For sale, many years ago, *Mansueti, Giovanni* —, portrait of a man 192; *Rondinelli in Giovanni Bellini's workshop*(?), Madonna 364.
For sale, several years ago, *Antonio da Carpi,* Madonna 466; *Cima da Conegliano, school of —,* two panels, SS. Francis and Antony 460[2].
Rovellesca.
Alamanno, Pietro —, Madonna, from Monterubbiano v. Brera Gallery, Milan.
Rovigo.
Gallery, *Basaiti, Marco* —, half-figure of Christ carrying the Cross 495; *Bellini, Giovanni* —, Madonna 263; *Catena in Giovanni Bellini's workshop,* Circumcision 368; *Quirizio da Murano,* St.

Lucy and scenes **46,** 49; *Veneziano, Pasqualino* —, Madonna 468.
Rutigliano.
Parish church, *Vivarini, Antonio — and helper,* Madonna and saints 39.
San Marino (California).
Huntington Museum, *Bellini, Giovanni* —, Madonna, from Lazzaroni coll., Paris 273, 273[2].
San Remo.
Thiem coll., *Cima da Conegliano,* Silenus on donkey and three fauns and a faun carrying a barrel v. Johnson coll., Philadelphia.
Sarasota (Florida).
Ringling Museum, *Bellini, Gentile* —, *attrib. to* —, bust of Petrarch 173[1].
Sebenico.
S. Lorenzo, *Vivarini, Antonio* —, *school of* —, Madonna 42.
Svetti Lovro, *Bellini, Giovanni* —, *school of* —, Madonna 387[2].
Settignano.
Berenson coll., *Cima da Conegliano,* St. Sebastian **433;** two panels of the story of Coriolanus 455[1].
Stockholm.
National Gallery, *Basaiti, Marco* —, dead Saviour 509[6].
Strasbourg.
Gallery, *Basaiti, Marco* —, St. Jerome (225) 509[6]; *Cima da Conegliano,* lateral panels of altarpiece, from S. Rocco, Mestre 431, 433; *Marconi, Rocco* —, Madonna 326[2], 373.
Stuttgart.
Gallery, *Basaiti, Marco* —, Madonna and saint (428) 370, **496;** *Bellini, Giovanni* —, Madonna (431) 290; Pietà 298, 491; portrait of a man v. Rosenfeld coll., New York; *idem, copy of* —, Madonna 322[2]; *Bello, Marco* —, Madonna (429) 370, 509[6]; *Mansueti, Giovanni* —, Madonna (512) 200[1].
Switzerland.
Private coll., *Bellini, Giovanni* —, Madonna **282.**
Toledo.
Cathedral, *Bellini, Giovanni* —, *workshop of* —, Pietà 200[1], 297, 297[1], 298, 491.

Toledo (Ohio).
Willys coll. v. New York.
Toulouse.
Gallery, *Vivarini, Antonio —,
school of —*, four panels of saints
(449, 450, 451, 452) 44².
Trau.
Cathedral, *Bellini, Gentile —,*
SS. Jerome and John the Baptist
141, 141¹.
Tresto, near Este.
Local painter, with knowledge
of Giovanni Bellini's Madonnas,
Madonna 222.
Treviso.
Bellini, Jacopo —, lost works
128.
S. Francesco, *Mansueti, Gio-
vanni —,* St. Sebastian and four
saints v. Accademia, Venice (97).
S. Germano, *Cima da Cone-
gliano,* altar-piece from S. Dio-
nisio, Zerman v. Accademia
Venice (658).
S. Leonardo, *Bellini, Jacopo
—, attrib. to —,* altar-piece 128;
Cima da Conegliano, school of —,
triptych 460².
S. Tommaso, *Sebastiano del
Piombo,* Doubting Thomas 464.
Gallery, *Antonio da Carpi,*
Madonna 465; *Bellini, Giovanni
—, workshop of —,* Madonna
260.
Trieste.
Gallery, *Veneziano, Pasqualino
—,* Madonna, from Sartorio coll.
468.
Sartorio coll., *Veneziano, Pas-
qualino —,* Madonna v. Gallery.
Troyes.
Gallery, *Cima da Conegliano,*
Madonna and saints **402.**
Turin.
Gallery, *Bellini, Giovanni —,*
Madonna 266; *Bellini, Jacopo —,
school of —,* Nativity of the
Virgin and Annunciation (158,
159) 125⁴; *Quirizio da Murano,*
Coronation **48,** 49.
Ex-Gualino coll., *Bellini, Gio-
vanni —,* Madonna 262².
Udine.
S. Francesco dell' Ospedale,
Gerolamo da Udine, Coronation
of the Virgin v. Gallery.
Gallery, *Gerolamo da Udine,*
Coronation of the Virgin, from
S. Francesco dell' Ospedale **475;**

St. Peter the Martyr and angels
476.
Ulm. Near —
Fugger Castle, *Bellini, Gio-
vanni —,* portrait of Joerg Fug-
ger v. Contini Bonacossa coll.,
Florence.
Urbino.
Gallery, *Mansueti, Giovanni
—,* Pietà 197; *Rondinelli in Gio-
vanni Bellini's workshop,* Madon-
na 364.
Venice.
Churches, Monasteries,
etc.
S. Andrea della Certosa, *Ba-
saiti, Marco —,* Call of the Sons
of Zebedee v. Accademia.
Annunciata ai Gesuiti chapel,
Lattanzio da Rimini, Sermon of
St. Mark, destroyed 378.
S. Apollinare, *Vivarini, An-
tonio —,* pictures 5.
S. Cassiano, *Antonello da Mes-
sina,* altar-piece v. Gallery, Vien-
na; *Mansueti, Giovanni —,* saints,
lost 200¹.
Sta. Caterina, *Bellini, Giovanni —, attrib. to —,* Madonna,
lost 341¹.
Corpus Domini church, *Cima
da Conegliano,* St. Peter the Martyr between SS. Nicholas and
Benedict v. Brera Gallery, Milan; *Vivarini, Antonio —, school
of —,* Crucifixion and Passion
scenes v. Ca d' Oro.
S. Daniele, *Basaiti, Marco —,*
St. Jerome, lost 509⁶.
S. Fantino, *Marconi, Rocco
—(?),* Madonna and St. Joseph
374.
S. Francesco della Vigna, *Antonio da Negroponte,* Madonna
52; *Basaiti, Marco —,* Deposition, lost 489; *Bellini, Giovanni
—,* Madonna and saints 324, 408;
Vivarini, Antonio —, school of —,
triptych 40.
Frari church, *Bellini, Giovanni
—,* triptych, 1488, 193, 204, 244,
379¹, 393, 394, 400, 419, 421,
433, 461, 464; altar-piece, **285,**
296, 296¹, 300, 355, 356; *idem and
hepers,* part of organ doors, from
Sta. Maria dei Miracoli v. Accademia (734); *Vivarini, Antonio
— and Basaiti, Marco —,* St.
Ambrose and angels 482.

S. Geminiano, *Bellini, Gentile* —, leaves picture of Madonna to — 135; *Bellini, Giovanni* —, two Madonnas and a picture of Christ, lost 341[1]; *Bernardino da Murano*, St. Helen with the cross and two saints v. Gallery of the Academy, Vienna.

S. Gerolamo, *Bellini, Giovanni* —, Madonna, lost 341[1].

Gesuiti church, *Mansueti, Giovanni* —, Crucifixion, later in Manfrin Palace, lost 200[1].

S. Giobbe, *Basaiti, Marco* —, St. Bernardine and other saints, lost 509[6]; Prayer in Garden of Olives, once in Foscari chapel v. Accademia; *Bellini, Giovanni* —, altar-piece v. Accademia; lost work 330; Madonna and saints, lost 341[1]; *Vivarini, Antonio* —, school of —, triptych 28, **40**, 48[1].

S. Giorgio Maggiore, *Basaiti, Marco* —, St. Jerome v. Accademia; *Bellini, Giovanni* —, Saviour, lost 341[1]; *Bellini, Jacopo* —, attrib. to —, Entry into Jerusalem 128; *Cima da Conegliano*, panels of altar-piece v. Brera Gallery, Milan (217, 218, 219); Adoration of the Shepherds, lost 455[1]; *Mansueti, Giovanni* —, bust of St. Peter, lost 200[1].

S. Gioseffo, *Bellini, Giovanni* —, Madonna and saints, lost 341[1].

S. Giovanni in Bragora, *Cima da Conegliano*, Baptism 310, **409**, 413; SS. Constantine and Helen and predella 421, 431, 433.

S. Giovanni Crisostomo, *Bellini, Giovanni* —, altar-piece 354; idem and(?) *Titian*, altar-piece, 1513 332, **334**; *Bellini, Giovanni — and Belliniano, Vittore* —, picture 379; *Mansueti, Giovanni* —(?), panels of saints 200[1].

S. Giovanni de' Furlani v. S. Giovanni di Malta.

S. Giovanni alla Giudecca, *Bellini, Giovanni* —, lost work 341[1].

S. Giovanni di Malta, *Bellini, Giovanni — and Belliniano, Vittore* —, Baptism **380**.

SS. Giovanni e Paolo, *Bellini, Gentile* —, buried 135; *Bellini, Giovanni* —, buried 207; altar-piece, from S. Vincenzo 224, **236**,

237, 238, 341[1], 350, 353, 419; altar-piece, destroyed 321, 357, 400, 402, 408; idem, after —, print of altar-piece **321**, 400, 501, *Bellini, Jacopo* —, attrib. to —; decoration of a chapel 128; *Cima da Conegliano* and(?) *Gerolamo da Udine*, Coronation of the Virgin **455**.

Sta. Giustina, *Cima da Conegliano*, SS. Cornelius, Justine and Cyprian v. Brera Gallery, Milan.

S. Marco, mosaics 2, 413; *Bellini, Gentile* —, organ doors, in museum 136, **136—141**; *Bellini, Jacopo — and Giambono, attrib. to* —, mosaic of Visitation in Mascoli chapel 125[4]; *Bellini, Jacopo* —, wrongly attrib. to —, large composition in chiaroscuro 125[4].

Sta. Maria della Carità, *Bellini, Giovanni* —, Crucifixion and Doctors of the Church, lost 341[1]; four triptychs v. Accademia; altar-piece v. coll. of Prince Ruprecht of Bavaria, Munich; *Cima da Conegliano*, altar-piece v. Accademia (36).

Sta. Maria del Carmine, *Cima da Conegliano*, Adoration of the Shepherds **438**; Deposition v. perhaps Accademia (604).

Sta. Maria de' Crocicchieri, *Cima da Conegliano*, Annunciation and saints v. Scuola della Misericordia; St. Mark curing Anianus v. Museum, Berlin; *Mansueti, Giovanni* —, story of St. Mark, from Scuola Grande di S. Marco v. Accademia.

Sta. Maria Formosa, *Pietro da Messina*, Madonna 373.

Sta. Maria Maggiore, *Bellini, Giovanni* —, three Madonnas, lost 341[1].

Sta. Maria dei Miracoli, *Basaiti, Marco* —, dead Christ and two angels v. Accademia (108); *Bellini, Giovanni* —, St. Jerome, lost 341[1]; idem and helpers, Annunciation, from organ doors v. Accademia (734).

Sta. Maria della Misericordia, *Cima da Conegliano*, St. Tobias with archangel and saints v. Accademia.

Sta. Maria dell' Orto, *Bellini, Gentile* —, portrait of Lorenzo Giustiniani v. Accademia; *Bel-*

lini, Giovanni —, Madonna **251**; Cima da Conegliano, altar-piece 376; **415**.

Sta. Maria della Salute, *Basaiti, Marco* —, St. Sebastian 509[6]; *Titian*, St. Mark and four saints 334; *Giovanni d'Alemagna*, two holy bishops 24.

Sta. Maria delle Verghini, *Vivarini, Antonio* —, St. Mary Magdalene borne to heaven v. Museum, Berlin.

S. Martino, *Cima da Conegliano*, Resurrection, lost 455[1].

S. Matteo di Mazorbo, *Mansueti, Giovanni* —, signed picture v. Santi and Cornelo colls.

S. Mosè, *Vivarini, Antonio* — *and Giovanni d'Alemagna*, triptych v. Poldi Pezzoli Gallery, Milan and National Gallery, London.

S. Pantaleone, *Vivarini, Antonio* — *and Giovanni d'Alemagna*, Coronation of the Virgin **14**, 54.

S. Pietro in Castello, *Basaiti, Marco* —, St. George and the dragon v. Accademia; St. Peter enthroned and four saints **509**; *Bellini Jacopo* —, portrait of Lorenzo Giustiniani, lost 60, **128**; canvas of SS. Peter, Paul and another saint 60.

Redentore church, *Bellini, Giovanni* —, Madonna and saints v. Accademia (881); Madonna, lost 341[1]; *Marconi, Rocco* —(?) Madonna 326[2], **374**, 374[1].

S. Salvatore, *Bellini, Giovanni* —, Transfiguration v. Accademia (87); *Diana*, Meal at Emmaus 341[1].

Scalzi church, *Bellini, Giovanni* —, *workshop of* —, Madonna **371**.

S. Stefano, *Bellini, Giovanni* —, Ecce Homo v. Louvre, Paris; *Giovanni d'Alemagna and Vivarini, Antonio* —, two altar-pieces 4 v. Gallery, Vienna and Accademia, Venice.

S. Tarasio, *Andrea del Castagno and Francesco da Faenza*, painted decoration 125[4].

S. Trovaso, *Bellini, Giovanni* —, repainted Madonna 224; *idem, workshop of* —, Madonna 383; *Giambono*, St. Chrisogonus 125[4], 131.

S. Vincenzo, *Bellini, Giovanni* —, altar-piece v. SS. Giovanni e Paolo.

S. Zaccaria, *Bellini, Giovanni* —, altar-piece 315, **318—321**, 321, 324, 354, 400, 437; *Francesco da Santacroce*, Circumcision 383; *Giovanni d'Alemagna and Vivarini, Antonio* —, altar-piece, Madonna and saints **11—14,** 516; triptych, St. Sabina **14**; altar-piece, three saints 14; *Veneziano, Lorenzo* —, predella 516.

Public Collections.

Accademia, *Basaiti, Marco* —, Call of the Sons of Zebedee, from S. Andrea della Certosa (39) 492, **499,** 502, 505; Prayer in the Garden of Olives, from Foscari chapel, S. Giobbe (69) **501**, 503, 505; St. Jerome, from S. Giorgio Maggiore (107) 501; dead Christ and angels, from Sta. Maria dei Miracoli (108) **505,** 513; St. George and the dragon, from S. Pietro in Castello (120) **509;** *Bellini, Gentile* —, portrait of Lorenzo Giustiniani, from Sta. Maria dell' Orto 136, 142, **143— 144,** 150; *idem and helpers*, three canvases, from the Scuola di S. Giovanni Evangelista (567, 563, 568) **160—168,** 170, 184; *Bellini, Giovanni* —, four triptychs from Sta. Maria della Carità (621, 621A, B and C) 208, **211—218,** 238, 244, 322, 344; panel of five putti 252, 252[1]; Madonna. from Magistrato della Milizia di Mare (591) **262;** Madonna (594) **262;** Madonna, from Palazzo dei Camerlenghi (583) 265; five paintings of allegories (595) **279,** 357; Madonna degli Alberetti (596) 204, **279,** 282, 316; altar-piece, from S. Giobbe **283,** 287; Madonna, from the Scuola Grande della Carità (612) **292;** Madonna and saints, oblong panel **296;** head of Christ, from Transfiguration from S. Salvatore **313;** Madonna and saints (610) **316;** Madonna and saints, from Giovanelli coll., formerly in Redentore church (881) **330;** St. John the Evangelist, drawing 346; Pietà, drawing **350;** *idem and Belliniano, Vittore* —, martyrdom of St. Mark, from Scuola di S. Marco 206, 380; *Bellini, Giovanni* —, *and helpers*, decoration of organ doors, from Sta. Maria dei Miracoli (734) **332;** *Bellini, Giovanni* —, *attrib. to* —, bust of young woman, drawing 353[1]; *Bellini, Giovanni* —, *copy of* —, Pietà (71) 296; *Bellini, Jacopo* —, Madonna, from Palace of the Doges (582) 61 **122—124;** Madonna, from Legnaro **115,** 130; *idem, attrib. to* —, lost picture of Christ 129; *Benaglio,* Madonna and saints (617) 173[1]; *Bissolo, attrib. to* —, nude woman 338; *Busati, Andrea* —, St. Mark and two saints, from Palazzo dei Camerlenghi 400[1], **472;** half-figure of St. James (601) 472; *Cima da Conegliano,* Deposition, perhaps from Sta. Maria del Carmine (604) 403, **405;** altarpiece, Madonna and saints, from Sta. Maria del Carmine (36) **417;** altar-piece, from Sta. Chiara, Murano (815) **425,** 428; Madonna and saints, from Casa Bortolo Dofino (603) **430;** Tobias with archangel and saints, from Sta. Maria della Misericordia (592) **433,** 433[3]; Doubting Thomas, from Scuola dei Muratori a S. Samuele (611) 433; Madonna 437; altar-piece, from S. Dionisio, Zermen (658) 443, 443[1]; St. Jerome and a holy bishop, in storeroom 455[1]; *idem, workshop of* —, St. Christopher, from polyptych painted for the Scuola dei Mercanti (623) 455; *Cima da Conegliano, school of* —, Christ crucified and St. Mary Magdalene, in storeroom 460[2]; *Jacobello del Fiore,* Coronation 16; *Gerolamo da Udine*(?), Temperance and Justice, from Camera dell' Armamenti in Palace of the Doges (165, 167) 400, 476; *Giambono,* copy of the Coronation by Antonio Vivarini and Giovanni d'Alemagna in S. Pantaleone (33) 15, 16, 40[2]; *Giovanni d' Alemagna and Vivarini, Antonio* —, fragment of St. Monica altar-piece, from S. Stefano (50) 9; Madonna, from Scuola Grande della Carità (625) **16—18,** 20, 24, 28; *Mansueti, Giovanni* —, four canvases,

two from Scuola di S. Marco and two from Scuola di S. Giovanni Evangelista (562, 564, 569, 571) 185, **185—190,** 190[1]; St. Sebastian and four saints, from S. Francesco, Treviso (97) **193;** two panels, each of two saints, from Gallery, Padua (877, 878) 195; Madonna and saints, oblong panel (75) 195; archangel Gabriel, in storeroom (804) 200[1]; *idem, attrib. to* —, St. Sebastian, drawing 198; *Mantegna, Andrea* —, St. George 141; *Quirizio da Murano,* Madonna (29) 46, 47; Saviour giving Holy Sacrament to a nun (659) 46, **48;** Christ with instruments of the Passion (30) 48, 49; *Vivarini, Antonio* —, *school of* —, St. Lawrence (20) 40.

Ca d'Oro *Bellini, Giovanni* —, *workshop of* — (*Basaiti*), Madonna and donor 369, 408, **494,** 496; *Bellini, Giovanni* —, *workshop of* —, Madonna, from Palazzo dei Camerlenghi **360,** 361[1]; *Bellini, Giovanni* —, *copy of* —, Madonna 330[1]; *Cima da Conegliano,* Madonna and saints 415; *Vivarini, Antonio* —, *school of* —, Crucifixion and Passion scenes, from Corpus Domini convent 42, 48[1].

Correr Museum, *Basaiti, Marco* —, Madonna and donor **487;** Pietà 489; *Bellini, Gentile* —, portrait of Doge Francesco Foscari 125[4], **136,** 144, 145, 150, 183; portrait of Giovanni Mocenigo 158, 160, 181; *idem, after* —, portrait of Doge Leonardo Loredano 169; *Bellini, Giovanni* —, Pietà **224;** Transfiguration **225—228;** Crucifixion **225—228,** 253, 347, 354; Madonna, from Frizzoni coll. 248; portrait 304[1]; *idem, school of* —, St. Augustine (62) 125[4]; Madonna with SS. John and Onophrius 387[2]; Madonna with SS. Jerome and Catherine 387[2]; Madonna 387[1]; *Bellini, Jacopo* —, *workshop of* —, Crucifixion 121; *Cima da Conegliano,* Madonna and saints (377) 455[1]; *Mansueti, Giovanni* —, St. Martin and the beggar 196; *Quirizio da Murano,* triptych, Madonna and saints **48;** Madonna and Annunciation(?) (5) 49; St. Jerome 49; *Veneziano, Pasqualino,* —

Madonna and St. Mary Magdalene **467—468.**

Paolo Giovio Museum, *Bellini, Gentile* —, *attrib. to* —, portrait of Mohammed II 178.

Querini-Stampalia Gallery, *Bellini, Giovanni* —, Presentation in the Temple **252;** replica of Madonna of 1516 in Gallery, Padua 326[1].

Seminary Gallery, *Bellini, Gentile* —, portrait of Lorenzo Giustiniani **144;** *Bellini, Giovanni* —, *workshop of* —, portrait of a man 385; *Cima da Conegliano*, Madonna (72) 455[1]; *idem, school of* —, God the Father sending forth the Holy Ghost (45) 460[2].

Public Buildings.

Arsenal, *Bellini, Giovanni* —, mystic marriage of St. Catherine, lost 341[1].

Palazzo dei Camerlenghi, *Bellini, Giovanni* —, Madonna v. Accademia (583); *idem, workshop of* —, Madonna v. Ca d'Oro; *Busati, Andrea* —, St. Mark and two saints v. Accademia.

Palace of the Doges, *Basaiti, Marco* —, St. Peter and two saints, lost 509[6]; *Bellini, Gentile* —, paintings, lost 133, 158, 176, 176[2], 184; *Bellini, Giovanni* —, active 204, 206; Pietà **238,** 240, 241[1]; half-figure of the Madonna, lost 341[1]; Madonna, lost 341[1]; portraits and other pictures, lost 341[1]; Madonna v. Accademia (591); Madonna v. Brera Gallery, Milan (216); altar-piece v. Walters coll., Baltimore; *idem and Lattanzio da Rimini*, active 375; *Bellini, Giovanni* —, *school of* —, St. Mark and two saints 287[2]; *Bellini, Jacopo* —, Madonna v. Accademia (582); *Cima da Conegliano*, Madonna, lost v. Royal Palace; *Gerolamo da Udine*, Temperance and Justice v. Accademia (165, 167); *Pisanello and Gentile da Fabriano*, paintings 133[2].

Ospedaletto di S. Giobbe, *Bellini, Giovanni* —, lost picture 341[1].

Royal Palace, *Bellini, Giovanni* —, Madonna, lost 341[1]; *Cima da Conegliano*, Madonna, from Palace of the Doges, lost 455[1].

Scuola Grande della Carità, *Bellini, Gentile* —, cover of reliquary v. Lederer coll., Vienna; *Bellini, Giovanni* —, Madonna v. Accademia (612); *Bellini, Jacopo* —, gonfalon, lost 128; *Titian*, Presentation in Temple, once there 467; *Veneziano, Pasqualino* —, competed for Presentation in the Temple, executed afterwards by Titian 467; *Vivarini, Antonio* — *and Giovanni d'Alemagna*, Madonna v. Accademia.

Scuola di S. Gerolamo, *Bellini, Giovanni* —, two pictures 204, 208, 341[1]; St. Jerome, lost 341[1].

Scuola di S. Giovanni Evangelista, *Bellini, Gentile* — *and helpers*, three canvases v. Accademia; *Bellini, Gentile* —, *attrib. to* — *and helpers*, story of the Cross 128 v. Accademia; *Bellini, Giovanni* —, *attrib. to* —, lost altar-piece 342; *Bellini, Jacopo* —, *attrib. to* —, story of the Cross, lost 127; cycle of Christological scenes 100; *Mansueti, Giovanni* —, two canvases v. Accademia (562, 564).

Scuola Grande di S. Marco, *Bellini, Gentile* —, active for — 134, 135; two canvases 133, 176; leaves mosaic to — 134; *idem and Bellini, Giovanni* —, Sermon of St. Mark v. Brera Gallery, Milan; *idem and Bellini, Jacopo* —, eighteen scenes from lives of Madonna and Jesus 60, 134; *Bellini, Giovanni* —, makes canvas of Flood and Noah's Ark 204; *idem and Belliniano, Vittore* —, martyrdom of St. Mark v. Accademia; *Bellini, Jacopo* —, lost paintings 60, 128; *Mansueti, Giovanni* —, four canvases v. Accademia (568, 571), Brera Gallery, Milan and Liechtenstein Gallery, Vienna; *Risso, Antonio* —, low reliefs 133.

Scuola dei Mercanti, *Bellini, Gentile* —, altar-piece v. perhaps National Gallery, London; *Cima da Conegliano*, St. Jerome v. perhaps National Gallery, London (1120); *idem, workshop of* —, St. Christopher from polyptych v. Accademia (623).

Scuola de' Mercia v. Scuola dei Mercanti.

Scuola della Misericordia, *Cima da Conegliano*, Annunciation and saints, from Sta. Maria de' Crocicchieri 414.

Scuola dei Muratori a S. Samuele, *Cima da Conegliano*, Doubting Thomas v. Accademia (611).

Scuola del Rosario, *Cima da Conegliano*, Annunciation v. Hermitage Gallery, Petrograd.

P r i v a t e C o l l e c t i o n s.
Casa Albrizzi, *Bellini, Jacopo* —, *school of* —, Crucifixion 59[1], 129[3].

Barbarigo Palace, *Bellini, Gentile*—, Circumcision v. Leuchtenberg coll., Munich.

Brass coll., *Bellini, Gentile* —, portrait of Caterina Cornaro, Queen of Cyprus 170; *Bellini, Giovanni* —, bust of Saviour 238; sketch for Feast of the Gods 337; *Bellini, Jacopo* —, Madonna 111; *Mansueti, Giovanni* —, St. Mark, angels and saints **193**; fragment of an Adoration of the Magi 200[1].

Caregiani Palace, *Cima da Conegliano, workshop of* —, Madonna 428[2].

Michele Contarini, belonging to —, *Veneziano, Jacometto* —, small portraits, afterwards in coll. of Gabriel Vendramin v. Liechtenstein Gallery, Vienna.

Michele Contarini, belonging to —, *Veneziano, Jacometto* —, pictures on parchment, lost 389; small portraits v. Liechtenstein Gallery, Vienna.

Taddeo Contarini, belonging to —, *Bellini, Giovanni* —, St. Francis in ecstasy v. Frick Foundation, New York; portrait of a woman, lost 341[1].

G. Cornaro, belonging to —, *Bellini, Giovanni* —, Meal at Emmaus v. Razumowski Palace, Vienna; Madonna, lost 341[1].

Palazzo Cornaro della Regina, *Bellini, Jacopo*, picture of besiegned city, lost 128; *idem, attrib. to* —, Venus and Adonis 129.

Cornelo coll., *Mansueti, Giovanni* —, signed picture, from S. Matteo di Mazorbo 193[2].

Casa Bortolo Dofino, *Cima da*

Conegliano, Madonna and saints v. Accademia (603).

Dona delle Rose coll., *Basaiti, Marco* —, Pietà 495.

Frizzoni coll., *Bellini, Giovanni* —, Madonna v. Correr Museum.

Giovanelli coll., *Bellini, Giovanni* —, Madonna and saints, from Redentore church v. Accademia (881); *Marconi, Rocco*—(?), Madonna 326[2], 374, 374[1].

Giustiniani Palace, *Veneziano, Pasqualino* —, St. Mary Magdalene 468.

Grimani Palace, *Bellini, Gentile* —, Circumcision, 178; *Bellini, Giovanni* —, two large pictures, lost 341[1].

Lando, belonging to —, *Bellini, Giovanni* —, Madonna, lost 341[1].

Ex-Layard coll., *Cima da Conegliano, school of* —, St. Augustine and sibyl 460[2]; v. National Gallery, London.

Loredano Palace, *Bellini, Giovanni* —, portrait of Doge Loredano v. Spiridon coll., Paris.

Manfrin Palace, *Mansueti, Giovanni* —, Crucifixion, from Gesuiti church, lost 200[1].

Marcello Palace, *Bellini, Giovanni* —, portrait of Jacomo Marcello, lost 301, 341[1]; Madonna 341[1].

Casa Morosini, *Bellini, Giovanni* —, Madonna, lost 341[1].

Antonio Pasqualino, belonging to —, *Bellini, Giovanni* —, Madonna, lost 341[1]; *Veneziano, Jacometto* —, drawings, lost 389.

Ex-Recanati Giustiniani coll., *Bellini, Giovanni* —, *school of* —, Madonna 387[1].

Casa Salomone, *Bellini, Giovanni* —, Madonna, lost 341[1].

Santi coll., *Mansueti, Giovanni* —, signed picture, from S. Matteo di Mazorbo 193[2].

Casa Sanuda, *Bellini, Giovanni* —, Madonna, lost 341[1].

Andrea Vendramin coll., *Bellini, Gentile* —, two bust portraits of young Venetians 179; *Bellini, Giovanni* —, *attrib. to* —, bust of Christ (1) 341[1]; Madonna (2) 341[1]; portrait of a lady (3) 341[1]; portrait of a man (10) 341[1]; two bust portraits of ladies (16, 17)

341¹; bust portrait of a youth (19) 341¹; idem (23) 341¹; idem (33) 341¹; bust portrait of a man (35) 341¹; bust portrait of a youth (37c) 341¹; half-figure of St. Francis (43) 341¹.

Gabriel Vendramin coll., *Bellini, Giovanni* —, profile portraits, lost 341¹; *Bellini, Jacopo* —, album of drawings v. British Museum; *Veneziano, Jacometto* —, small portraits, from house of Michele Contarini v. Liechtenstein Gallery, Vienna; sketchbook, lost 389.

House of Giovanantonio Vernier, *Bellini, Giovanni* —, head of Christ, lost 341¹.

Casa Zena, *Bellini, Giovanni* —, Madonna, lost 341¹.

House of Pietro Zeno, *Bellini, Gentile* —, profile portrait of Mohammed, lost 178.

House of Francesco Zio, *Veneziano, Jacometto* —, hour book with miniatures, lost 389.

For sale, some years ago, *Bellini, Giovanni* —, *workshop of* —, *after* —, Madonna 373².

Venice. Near —
S. Cristoforo della Pace, *Basaiti, Marco* —, triptych v. Museum, Berlin.

Verona.
Cathedral, *Bellini, Jacopo* —, fresco of Crucifixion, lost 59, 59¹, 116, 128.

S. Gerolamo monastery, *Vivarini, Antonio* —, St. Christopher 39².

S. Zeno, *Mantegna, Andrea* —, altar-piece, 228, 287; predella v. Louvre, Paris.

Gallery, *Antonio da Carpi*(?), Madonna 466; *Bellini, Giovanni* —, Madonna (110) **262**; Madonna **247**; *idem, workshop of* —, Circumcision **381**; *Bellini, Giovanni* —, *school of* —, portrait of a man 387²; Madonna (122) 387²; *Bellini, Jacopo* —, Christ on Cross, perhaps fragment of fresco from the Cathedral (365) 59, 61, **116**; Pietà (2148) **103**; St. Jerome (306) **116**; *idem, school of* —, Madonna (2139) 129⁸; *Bernardino da Murano, wrongly attrib. to* —, two canvases (366) 480; *Mansueti, Giovanni* —, Adoration of

the Magi (276) 200¹; Madonna and St. Jerome (304) 200¹.

Museli coll., *Bellini, Giovanni* —, Madonna, saints and adorer v. Vernon Watney coll., Cornbury.

Sereghi coll., *Bellini, Giovanni* —, Madonna, saints and adorer, from Museli coll. v. Vernon Watney coll., Cornbury.

Vicenza.
S. Bartolomeo, *Cima da Conegliano*, altar-piece v. Gallery.

Sta. Corona, *Bellini, Giovanni* —, Baptism 305, **310**, 313, 318, 357, 381, 396, 410, 463.

Gallery, *Bernardino da Murano, wrongly attrib. to* —, Madonna and saints 480; *Busati, Andrea* —, St. Antony of Padua **472**; *Cima da Conegliano*, altar-piece, from S. Bartolomeo **393**, 457, 464; *Mansueti, Giovanni* —(?), Madonna and saints (36) 200¹; *Venetian school, 15th cent.*, Madonna 274.

Vienna.
Art Academy, *Bellini, Gentile* —, portrait of a youth 170; *Bernardino da Murano*, St. Helen with the cross and two saints, from S. Geminiano, Venice (15) **476**; *Cima da Conegliano*, St. Mark and two saints **397**, 472, 476.

Albertina, *Basaiti, Marco* —, Christ and two disciples, drawing 353¹; *Bellini, Giovanni* —(?), portrait, drawing 352; *Bellini, Giovanni* —, *school of* —, two saints, drawing 387²; *Bellini, Jacopo* —, St. Christopher, drawing 96.

Estensische Sammlung, *Giovanni d'Alemagna and Vivarini, Antonio* —, altar-piece, from S. Stefano, Venice v. Gallery.

Gallery, *Antonello da Messina*, altar-piece, from S. Cassiano, Venice 283, 356; *Basaiti, Marco* —, Call of the Sons of Zebedee **505**; *Bellini, Giovanni* —, *workshop of* —, Circumcision (15) 383; *Giovanni d'Alemagna and Vivarini, Antonio*—, altar-piece, from S. Stefano, Venice, formerly in the Estensische Sammlung **6**, 10, 11, 26; *Mantegna, Andrea* —, St. Sebastian 218; *Titian*, Gipsy Madonna 444.

Liechtenstein Gallery, *Antonio de Tisoio*, polyptych, from Orzes **480**; *Basaiti, Marco* —, Madonna (846) 487; *Bellini, Gentile* —, *school of* —, combat between oriental and occidental warriors (1126) 181; *Lattanzio da Rimini*, Madonna 377; *Mansueti, Giovanni* —, story of St. Mark, from the Scuola Grande di S. Marco, Venice **189**, 190[1], 193, 419; *Veneziano, Jacometto* —, two small portraits, from Contarini and Gabriel Vendramin colls., Venice **389—391.**

Archduke Leopold's coll., *Bellini, Giovanni* —, Madonna, lost 341[1].

Ex-von Auspitz coll., *Cima da Conegliano, workshop of* —, St. John the Baptist, from Weber coll., Hamburg 455.

Czernin coll., *Bellini, Giovanni* —, *copy of* —, Madonna 326[2].

Harrach coll., *Basaiti, Marco* —, Madonna **487.**

Lanckoronsky coll., *Bellini, Giovanni* —, *school of* —, head of Saviour 287[2].

Lederer coll., *Bellini, Gentile* —, cover of reliquary, from Scuola Grande della Carità, Venice 145—148; *Bellini, Jacopo* —, Madonna 111, **114.**

Leuchtenberg coll., *Gerolamo da Udine, wrongly attrib. to* —, three saints v. Metropolitan Museum, New York.

Private coll., *Bellini, Giovanni* —, Madonna 274[2].

Razumowski Palace, *Bellini, Giovanni* —, Meal at Emmaus, from house of G. Cornaro, Venice, destroyed by fire 341[1].

Wittgenstein coll., *Bellini, Giovanni* —, *workshop of* —, Madonna 373.

Vienna. Near —
Frohsdorf Castle, Bourbon coll., *Bellini, Giovanni* —, Madonna v. Gallery, Detroit.

Villa di Sesto.
Abbey church, *Basaiti, Marco* —, Deposition, lost 509[6].

Warsaw.
Gallery, *Mansueti, Giovanni* —, Pietà (6) 200[1], 298.

Washington.
Corcoran Art Gallery, *Bellini, Giovanni* —, *school of* —, profile of young man, drawing 387 ; *Bellini, Jacopo* —, *wrongly attrib. to* —, man and two orientals, drawing 125[4].

Mellon coll., *Bellini, Giovanni* —, portrait of a man **305.**

Windsor.
Royal Library, *Bellini, Giovanni* —, drawing 344; *Cima da Conegliano, school of* —, holy bishop enthroned between :.ing and a bishop, drawing 4 :.;.

Worcester, U.S.A.
Fine Arts Museum, *Bellini, Giovanni* —, *workshop of* —, Madonna 372; *Bellini, Giovanni* —, *copy of* —, Madonna 291; *Vivarini, Antonio* —, Madonna 38.

Ellis coll., *Rondinelli in Giovanni Bellini's workshop*(?), Madonna 364.

Würzburg.
Ex-von Hirsch coll., *Bellini, Giovanni* —, *school of* —, half-figure of the Madonna 287[2].

Zara.
Cathedral, *Carpaccio*, polyptych 196.

Zermen (Feltre).
S. Dionisio, *Cima da Conegliano*, altar-piece v. Accademia, Venice (658).

INDEX OF ARTISTS

The more important passages are indicated by bold-faced letters.

Agapiti, 481.
Alamanno, Pietro —, 125[4].
Andrea del Castagno, 125[4].
Andrea da Murano, 54.
Angelico, Fra —, 86, 394.
Antonello da Messina, 150, 183, 200[1], 207, 224, 254[5], 283, 301, 304[1], 355, 356, 358, 389, 393, 397, 413, 463.
Antonello da Saliba, 274.
Antonio da Cesa, 480.
Antonio Maria da Carpi, 397, 451, 460, **464—466.**
Antonio da Murano, v. Vivarini, Antonio —.
Antonio da Negroponte, 45, **52—55.**
Antonio de Tisoio, 480.
Basaiti, Marco —, 269, 273, 313, 315[1], 321, 330[1], 332, 337[1], 353[1], 359, 370, 370[3], 379, 386, 472, **482—513.**
Basarini, Marco —, v. Basaiti, Marco —.
Bastiani, Lazzaro —, 204, 236, 361[1], 383[1].
Beccaruzzi, ·387[2].
Behzad, 152.
Bellini, Bellino —, 360.
Bellini, Gentile —, 44[1], 58, 61, 63, 108, 125[4], 128, **132—184,** 184—200, 203, 204, 206, 207, 208, 242, 301, 306, 308, 308[1], 309, 339[1], 341[1], 352[5], **383,** 385, 516.
Bellini, Giovanni —, 48, 58, 92, 108, 114, 116, 125[4], 133, 134, 135, 150, 158, 158[1], 168, 171, 173[1], 178, 184, 193, 198, 200[1], **201—358,** 358—391, 393—481 passim., 482, 483, 491, 494, 494[1], 494[3], 495, 495[2], 497, 497[2], 499, 501, 503, 509[6], 514, 515, 516, 517.
Bellini, Jacopo —, 2, 44, 45, 52, **56—131,** 134, 135, 140, 148, 173[1], 181, 183, 202, 203, 208, 209, 211, 218, 221, 224, 225, 230, 236, 244, 245, 254[4], 341[1], 516.
Belliniano, Vittore —, 206, 360, **380.**
Bello, Marco —, 370, 509[6].
Benaglio, 173[1].
Bernardino da Milano, 480.
Bernardino da Murano, **476—480.**
Bernardino da Verona, 480.
Bissolo, 307[5], 321, 326[2], 327[1], 338, 359, 368, 371, 374, 374[1], 381[1], 383.
Boccaccino, 460.
Bonconsiglio, 463.
Bonsignori, Francesco —, 173[1], 236[2], 352[5], 361[1].
Botticelli, Sandro —, 394.
Brigadin, Donato —, 49.
Brunelleschi, 83.
Busati, Andrea —, 398, 400[1], **471—472.**
Busati, Francesco —, 471.
Busati, Luc'antonio —, 471.
Cagliari, Paolo —, 59[1].
Campagnola, 353[1].
Cariani, 341[1], 359.
Carpaccio, 135, 141[1], 176, 185, 193, 195, 196, 236[2], 359, 398, 475, 490[1], 513[1].
Catena, 179[4], 181, 279, 326[2], 327[1], 342, 359, 364, **465—371,** 374, 383, 387[2], 469[1], 494[3], 497[3], 503, 515.
Cima da Conegliano, Giovanni Battista —, 185, 198, 273[1], 310, 330[1], 357, 359, 375, 376, **392—464,** 464—481, 493, 499, 501, 509, 509[6], 515.
Coda da Ferrara, Benedetto —, 359.
Cossa, 125[4].
Cristofóro da Ferrara, 15.
Diana, 341[1], 359, 469[1].
Donatello, 99, 116, 218, 224, 228, 355.
Duia, 359.

Dürer, Albrecht —, 165[1], 207, 337[2].
Ercole de' Roberti, 351.
Falerio pictore habitatore Negroponti, Antonio —, 52.
Fogolino, 460.
Foppa, 348[1].
Francesco da Faenza, 125[4].
Francesco de' Franceschi, 45, 125[4].
Francesco da Milano, 505.
Francesco da Negroponte, v. Antonio da Negroponte.
Francesco da Santacroce, 383.
Gentile da Fabriano, 2, 6, 45, 57, 58, 63, 92, 98, 99, 100, 101, 102, 103, 104, 107, 108, 111, 116, 122, 125, 125[4], 127, 130, 133[2].
Gerolamo di Bernardino da Udine, 398, 400, 455, 455[1], 472—476.
Gerolamo da Cremona, 44[1], 184.
Gerolamo di Giovanni, 125[4].
Gerolamo da Santacroce, 134, 269, 359, 455[1], 476, 493, 495[3].
Gerolamo da Udine, v. Gerolamo di Bernardino da Udine.
Ghirlandaio, Domenico —, 166, 394.
Giambono, 2, 6, 15, 16, 38, 39[2], 40[2], 42, 45, 58, 92, 101, 116, 125[4], 129[3], 130.
Giorgione, 2, 257, 320, 321, 355, 359, 374[1], 375[2], 387[2], 438, 443, 444, 464, 505, 509.
Giovanni d' Alemagna, 3—20, 24, 28, 30—32, 38, 38[1], 39[2], 40, 40[2], 42, 44, 45, 54, 516.
Giotto, 464.
Gozzoli, Benozzo —, 166, 394.
Guariento, 16.
Jacobello di Bonomo, 129[3].
Jacobello del Fiore, 16, 17, 59, 130.
Jacopo de' Barbari, 352[4].
Jacopo da Valenza, 359.
Jacobus Pieri pictor de Venetis, v. Bellini, Jacopo —.
Johannes theothonicus, v. Giovanni d'Alemagna.
Lamberto, 455[1].
Lattanzio da Rimini, 359, 373—378, 419.
Leonardo di Paolo, 60.
Leonardo da Vinci, 207, 230.
Licinio, 274.
Lodovicus de For . . . ., 11.
Lorenzo di Credi, 121[1].
Lotto, Lorenzo —, 236[2], 352[5], 353[1], 463.
Maestro Paolo, 2.
Magister Antonius pictor di Muriano, 5[1].

Maistro Jacopo, 125[4].
Mancini, Domenico —, 321.
Mansueti, Giovanni di Niccolo —, 134, 165, 181, 184—200, 298, 419, 460.
Mantegna, Andrea —, 44, 54, 60, 140, 141, 145, 158, 183, 203, 205, 207, 208, 209, 211, 216, 217, 220, 221, 224, 225, 228, 230, 238, 240, 244, 245, 252, 253, 253[1], 254, 255, 256, 267, 270, 287, 345, 346, 348, 348[1], 349, 349[2], 350[5], 355, 360, 394, 459.
Marconi, Rocco —, 322[3], 326[2], 359, 373—375, 509[6].
Marescalco, 460.
Martini da Udine, Giovanni —, 481.
Martini, Simone —, 207.
Masolino, 10[1], 38.
Matteo de' Pasti, 133.
Mazzola, 274, 371.
Michelozzo, 83.
Mocetto, 322, 324[3], 470[2], 483[2].
Montagna, Bartolomeo —, 200[1], 359, 387[2], 389, 393, 394, 463, 513.
Moranzone, Gaspare —, 6.
Moroni, Giovanni Battista —, 290[2].
Oliviero, 387[2].
Padovano, Lauro —, 224, 236, 236[2].
Palmezzano, 359.
Pennacchi, Pier Maria —, 332, 359, 385.
Perugino, 205.
Piero della Francesca, 144, 269[4], 283, 355, 356, 389.
Pietro da Messina, 359, 373.
Pietro Paolo da Sassoferrata, v. Agapiti.
Pietro da Saliba, v. Pietro da Messina.
Pintoricchio, 173.
Pisanello, 2, 45, 59, 60, 64, 69, 92, 98, 100, 108, 110, 129, 131, 133[2].
Pitati, Bonifacio —, 398.
Poussin, 337[2].
Previtali, 330, 341[1], 359, 370[3].
Pseudo-Basaiti, 322[3], 332, 472, 483, 493, 494, 514.
Quirizio da Murano, 39[1], 45—52, 54, 218.
Raphael, 357, 389.
Rembrandt, 378.
Risso, Antonio —, 133.
Rondinelli, 283, 290[1], 290[3], 291[2], 294, 333[1], 359, 361—364, 373, 383, 455[1].
Rositi, Giovanni Battista —, 460[2], 464.
Rubens, 353[1].

Schiblizada Ahmad, 152.
Sebastiano del Piombo, 460, 460², 464.
Seeghers, 460.
Signorelli, Luca —, 283.
Stefano di Demetrio, 471.
Tacconi, 371, 480.
Teniers, 505.
Titian, 2, 206, 334, 337, 337¹, 338, 355, 357, 359, 379, 444, 449, 464, 467, 509, 517.
Tura, 125⁴.
Veneto, Bartolomeo —, 271¹, 381¹, 509.
Veneziano, Domenico —, 131, 394.
Veneziano, Jacometto —, 389—391.
Veneziano, Lorenzo —, 2, 11, 516.
Veneziano, Pasqualino —, 294, 359, 370³, 374, 460, 466—470.

Veronese, Paolo —, 224.
Verrocchio, 394.
Vincenzo da Treviso, 326², 374¹, 381¹, 383.
Vivarini, Alvise —, 5, 195, 206, 211, 235, 236², 300, 301, 301², 303¹, 304¹, 353¹, 359, 370³, 375, 393, 393¹, 463, 480, 482, 483, 484, 487, 515.
Vivarini, Antonio —, 2, 3, 4, 4⁵, 4—45, 46, 47, 48, 49, 52, 54, 55, 218, 245, 516.
Vivarini, Bartolomeo —, 4, 5, 6, 20, 28, 32—36, 40², 42, 45, 46, 47, 48, 49, 52, 54, 129², 211, 216¹, 218, 221², 236, 385, 484, 485, 487, 488, 490, 515.
Vivarini, Giovanni —, v. Giovanni d'Alemagna.
Weyden, Roger van der —, 355².